The American Revolution

Its Character and Limits

Edited by
Jack P. Greene

 NEW YORK UNIVERSITY PRESS
New York and London

Copyright © 1987 by New York University
Manufactured in the United States of America
All rights reserved

Library of Congress Cataloging-in-Publication Data

The American Revolution.

   Papers presented at a symposium held at Johns Hopkins
University, Mar. 29–30, 1985; sponsored by the School of
Continuing Studies and the Dept. of History of the
Johns Hopkins University.
   Includes bibliographies and index.
   1. United States—History—Revolution, 1775–1783—
Influence—Congresses.   2. Republicanism—United States—
History—18th century—Congresses.   3. United States—
History—1783–1815—Congresses.   I. Greene, Jack P.
II. Johns Hopkins University. School of Continuing
Studies.   III. Johns Hopkins University.   Dept. of History
E209.A497   1987   973.7   87-13995

ISBN 0-8147-3012-4

Contents

Preface

This volume emerged out of a suggestion by the Maryland Humanities Council that The Johns Hopkins University hold a symposium to commemorate the bicentennial of the conclusion of the American War for Independence with the promulgation of the Treaty of Paris in 1783. Because there had already been a large number of public conferences and programs specifically celebrating both that event and the success of the young American republic in achieving independence from Britain, I proposed instead a conference with a broader focus, one that, building on the recent work of a great many promising young scholars, would consider some of the many problems that had been raised but not resolved by the American Revolution and that remained to confront the new American society after political independence had been achieved.

This proposal resulted in a public symposium sponsored by the School of Continuing Studies and the Department of History of The Johns Hopkins University and held on the Homewood campus of the university on March 29–30, 1985. In addition to the participants whose work appears in this volume, W.W. Abbot of the University of Virginia; William W. Freehling, Jr., J.G.A. Pocock, and Larzer Ziff of The Johns Hopkins University; Edward C. Papenfuse of the Maryland Hall of Records; Benjamin Quarles of Morgan State University; and Thad Tate of the Institute of Early American History and Culture acted as chairpersons of the various conference sessions. In that role, each made useful suggestions for revising the papers for publication.

Both the conference and the book were supported by grants from the Maryland Humanities Council, Inc., and the National Endowment for the Humanities. Mr. Michael C. Alin and his staff at the School of Continuing Studies provided the necessary secretarial and administrative help in organizing the conference; Mrs. Elizabeth Paynter, Mr. Grant Mabie, and Stephen Young of the Department of History provided valuable assistance in preparing the volume for publication. Jacqueline Megan Greene did the index.

August 25, 1986

Jack P. Greene
Cambridge, England

Contributors

Catherine L. Albanese Professor of Religion, University of California, Santa Barbara

Lance Banning Professor of History, University of Kentucky

Patricia U. Bonomi Professor of American History, New York University

Robert M. Calhoon Professor of History, University of North Carolina at Greensboro

E. Wayne Carp Assistant Professor of History, Pacific Lutheran University

Lester H. Cohen Associate Professor of History and American Studies, Purdue University

Elaine F. Crane Associate Professor of History, Fordham University

Jonathan R. Dull Associate Editor of *The Papers of Benjamin Franklin*, Yale University

Jay Fliegelman Associate Professor of English, Stanford University

Sylvia R. Frey Associate Professor of History, Tulane University

Jack P. Greene Andrew W. Mellon Professor in the Humanities, The Johns Hopkins University

Nathan O. Hatch Associate Dean of the College of Arts and Letters, University of Notre Dame

Don Higginbotham Professor of History, University of North Carolina at Chapel Hill

Winthrop D. Jordan Professor of History and Afro-American Studies, University of Mississippi

Drew R. McCoy Associate Professor of History, Harvard University

James H. Merrell Assistant Professor of History, Vassar College

John M. Murrin Professor of History, Princeton University

Peter S. Onuf Professor of History, Southern Methodist University

J. R. Pole Rhodes Professor of American History and Institutions, University of Oxford

Jack N. Rakove Associate Professor of History, Stanford University

John W. Shy Professor of History, University of Michigan at Ann Arbor

Gordon S. Wood Professor of History, Brown University

Melvin Yazawa Associate Professor of History, University of New Mexico

The Limits of the American Revolution

Jack P. Greene

Invariably, revolutions raise as many problems as they resolve. The American Revolution is no exception to this pattern. Initially undertaken to secure for British Americans guarantees of local autonomy and individual rights equivalent to those enjoyed by Englishmen in the home islands, it quickly became in 1775–76 a struggle for political independence. But the transition from dependent colonies to independent states, from monarchy to republic, from membership in an extended empire in which the several members were connected only through the center to participation in a single federal nation, brought a wholly new and unforeseen set of problems that were not resolved by the formal achievement of independence in 1783. To an important degree, these problems and the ways they were—or were not—confronted and resolved defined the character of the American Revolution and expressed the basic underlying predisposition of the new American society that emerged out of the Revolution and the new American nation it helped to create.

Historians of the American Revolution have long been interested in defining the nature of that event. Indeed, why they occur and what they are are the two classic questions upon which studies of all revolutions have traditionally focused. Notwithstanding the efforts earlier in this century of J. Franklin Jameson, Evarts B. Greene, and others to put the Revolution in a larger social framework, however, most of the work on the character of the Revolution has, until relatively recently, focused very largely upon the public sphere, upon such questions as federal–state relations; the movement for a stronger national government; and the effect of competing economic interests, state and sectional rivalries, and prevailing patterns of social relations upon public life at both the state and national levels.[1]

Only beginning during the mid-1960s did students of the Revolution begin to take a broader approach to this subject. The impetus for this approach came from two complementary directions. One was a deepening concern with the perceptual world within which the Revolution occurred. This concern derived directly out of the important studies of Revolutionary political ideology by Bernard Bailyn and Gordon S. Wood. Like most earlier historians, Bailyn and Wood focused almost entirely upon the public realm. But their work stimulated a new and fuller appreciation of the ways in which ideas spilled over from politics to other areas of American life to challenge and, in some cases, even to force a reconception of some of the basic underlying assumptions about the nature of the existing social order in Anglophone North America.[2]

To an important degree, Bailyn and Wood built their analyses upon J.G.A. Pocock's early essays on the character and importance of civic humanism in early modern British political culture. Published in the mid-1970s, Pocock's *The Machiavellian Moment*, which both traced in detail the movement of the civic humanist or classical republican tradition from Renaissance Florence through the political world of early modern England and argued for its centrality to Revolutionary and early national American political and social life, provided still further stimulus to the growing concern with the ideological dimensions of the early American Republic.[3]

By suggesting how the emerging ideology of American republicanism ramified so widely throughout American public life, these works helped to shift the attention of Revolutionary historians to the intellectual and cultural realms. Using the contemporary linguistic and conceptual worlds depicted by Bailyn, Wood, and Pocock as a point of departure, a large number of younger scholars, many of whom are represented in this volume, began, especially in the mid-1970s, not only to reexamine traditional questions but also to look at aspects of the American Revolutionary experience that had not previously been systematically studied. Together, this literature has resulted in what one commentator has referred to as a "republican synthesis" of the American Revolutionary experience.[4]

Although this new republican paradigm has by no means commanded universal acceptance as the appropriate framework for analyzing the Revolution, it has been enormously influential. Indeed, as several critics have pointed out, it has no doubt produced an exaggerated emphasis upon the ideological dimensions of the Revolution. But it has also helped to stimulate several scholars to begin once again to take a new look at the many substantive socio-economic issues, problems, conditions, behaviors, and developments that shaped American public life during the Revolutionary era.

A second significant source for the renewal and expansion of interest in the character of the Revolution has been the powerful movement toward the construction of a more inclusive history. Over the past two decades, a sweeping revolution in historical studies has taken historians out of the halls of government and into the busy and variegated scenes of private activity that have traditionally comprised the essence of American life. This movement has produced a new concern with analyzing the social impact of war; the nature of political dissent; the experiences of non-dominant groups such as Indians, blacks, and women; the character of family and community relations; and the history of religion and other symbolic cultural systems. With specific regard to the Revolution, this movement has generated an intensifying interest in exploring the ways the Revolution affected contemporary conditions in these and other areas of American life.

This volume is designed to provide a relatively compact introduction to some of the more important findings of this new work. Its core consists of fifteen substantive chapters, each of which treats one of the central problems that had been posed for Americans by the Revolution and the adoption of republicanism. Though some of these problems had been raised far more insistently and far more broadly than others, every one of them had been identified as a problem during the Revolution by at least some contemporaries and remained to confront the new American society at the conclusion of the War for Independence. Although it received far less systematic attention than any of the other issues addressed in this volume, this is true even for the question of the role of women.

The authors of these chapters are mostly representative of an emerging younger generation of scholars of the Revolution. All approach their subjects from the vantage point of the Revolution itself rather than from the perspective of later American developments. Each is a recognized expert on her or his subject. Indeed, although some of these chapters are entirely new, several are summaries and extensions of or updated reflections upon an author's earlier, more extensive monographic work.

That several of the problems considered could not be resolved in the immediate aftermath of the Revolution required that the authors not be required to work within the same time span. Some of the authors do deal with relatively short-term issues arising directly out of the conclusion of the war. Thus, E. Wayne Carp analyzes the problems of demobilization and how a society skeptical about standing armies and reluctant to pay for more than a token military force could defend itself, while Robert M. Calhoon examines the delicate question of how the victorious American polities dealt with Loyalists and other disaffected groups who, having thrown in their lot with the losing side and being unwilling to emigrate, had to be reintegrated into their local societies.

Others deal with a series of essentially political problems that did not require immediate attention but were of continuing concern to contemporary leaders: Jack N. Rakove with the classic question of how to achieve a viable federal union; Lance Banning with the difficult problem of how to organize a new republican political world that would not violate traditional and still cherished conceptions of the sociopolitical order; Drew R. McCoy and Jonathan R. Dull, respectively, with the problems of securing economic independence and diplomatic respect for the new republic; Peter S. Onuf with the question of how to organize the process of territorial expansion and then to incorporate the new polities that resulted from that process into the United States; and James H. Merrell with the meaning of American independence for the lives of American Indians.

Still others treat the implications of the Revolution for the new American society it was helping to create. Sylvia R. Frey and Elaine F. Crane consider what republican ideology meant for two dependent groups, respectively, blacks and women. Melvin Yazawa, Lester H. Cohen, Jay Fliegelman, and Catherine L. Albanese each analyze aspects of the quest for a new individual and corporate identity that would be commensurate with the values of the new American republic, Yazawa with the special requirements for the education of a republican citizenry, Cohen with the efforts of contemporary historians to fashion a national past, and Fliegelman and Albanese with some of the more important strains in early belletristic efforts to define and to depict some of the salient features of the emerging American national culture. Finally, Nathan O. Hatch analyzes the ways Revolutionary ideology reshaped American attitudes about church and state and the more general problem of religious freedom.

The remaining seven and much shorter chapters are critical commentaries designed to explore the general implications of two or, in one case, three of the substantive chapters and to put their findings in a broader perspective. They are all written by distinguished senior scholars—John W. Shy, J.R. Pole, Don Higginbotham, John M. Murrin, Winthrop D. Jordan, Gordon S. Wood, and Patricia U. Bonomi.

The problems treated in detail here by no means exhaust the range of possibilities, and this volume makes no claim to being comprehensive. Several important problems have been omitted. These include short-term economic problems such as management of the Revolutionary debt and the creation of adequate banking facilities and a stable currency system; social reform issues involving such questions as capital punishment, penal reform, poor relief, imprisonment for debt, prostitution, indentured servitude, and the care of illness and insanity; and revision and simplification of the legal system. Nor does it cover still other problems that some scholars have tried, thus far with limited success, to link directly to the Revolution. These include the shift in craft industries from an independent artisanal to a wage-labor system, which does seem to have been in its early stages during the last decades of the eighteenth century, and the alleged transition from a more subsistence-oriented to a more commercial-oriented agriculture, which, in all but the most stagnant areas of British North America, seems to have occurred a long time before the Revolution.

Notwithstanding these omissions, the hope of the contributors is that this collection will serve as an introduction to many of the more important problems faced by the Revolutionary generation after independence had been won. In effect, it constitutes a partial progress report for the mid-1980s on the current state of the ongoing effort to answer the traditional question of what the American Revolution was.

Taken together, the essays in this collection strongly suggest that the possibilities for change during and after the American Revolution were drastically circumscribed by the character and orientation of the society in which it occurred. In the years following the war, political leaders enjoyed only limited success in resolving the various problems confronting American society in ways that were compatible with the goals they had articulated before and during the war. By the end of the 1780s, the Loyalists had been largely reintegrated into American society with surprisingly little retribution, Congress had established a Western policy that would permit the orderly expansion of settlement and the extension of republican society and government into new areas, and the Federal Constitution of 1787 had established an ambiguous but, at least in the short run, viable division of authority between the states and the national government.

In most other areas, however, the record was much less impressive. As the War of 1812 would so amply demonstrate, the nation had not by then managed to resolve the problem of how to achieve an effective defense force in a society that was rarely threatened by external attack and, as John Shy remarks in his commentary, therefore regarded money devoted to maintain a permanent military force as a waste of valuable resources. Tensions among exponents of competing ideologies about the nature and goals of the American polity had, by the 1790s, produced deep party divisions and a vigorous competition for power of a kind traditionally regarded as a harbinger of the collapse of popular governments. Commanding very little diplomatic respect from the major European powers, the United States continued in a state of galling economic dependence upon Britain. Efforts of the national government to implement a policy of justice and assimilation toward the Indians were nullified by the behavior of states and individuals. Although a few states had adopted measures leading to the abolition of chattel slavery, that blatant anomaly in republican America was still the condition of the overwhelming majority of black people. The status of women had improved almost not at all.

Nor did the vision of a self-sacrificing, public-spirited society held out by the republican enthusiasts in the immediate wake of independence any longer seem to be attainable. Despite the efforts of historians, belles-lettrists, and other opinion leaders to define and inculcate a sense of republican national self-consciousness among the broader American public, individual Americans showed, in one area after another, that they had neither the will, nor the commitment, nor the interest required to sustain the selfless patriotism and devotion to the public good that so many Revolutionary leaders in 1776 had thought necessary for the successful functioning of a republic. While elite figures continued to celebrate simplicity and public spiritedness, ordinary Americans showed themselves far more interested in accumulating material goods and promoting the immediate welfare of themselves and their families. Nor were they sufficiently concerned with changing their priorities and the predominant patterns of behavior that derived from those priorities to be willing to spend the money necessary to implement the educational schemes for inculcating republican virtue in the young proposed by Benjamin Rush and others. More and more, even, religion appeared to be becoming a source of discord rather than stability, as people seemed to be more intent on following their own personal dispositions rather than regarding the larger interests of the society.

Perhaps the most important general questions raised by these findings are why, at the conclusion of the War for Independence, the American Revolution, especially as its goals had been defined by political and other opinion leaders in 1775–76 and after, remained incomplete and why, several decades later, the new "American" political society spawned by the Revolution had yet failed to meet those goals. These questions are susceptible to a variety of answers on several different levels of analysis. On one level, it is certainly valid to say that the exigencies of war prevented American leaders at both the national and state levels from addressing all but the most pressing problems between 1776 and 1783. On a still more general level, it is equally correct to suggest that all revolutions and other large-scale political movements have failed to achieve all of the aspirations of their proponents and that the American Revolution is no exception in this regard.

If these answers are true, however, they are also truistic. Surely, a more interesting and revealing approach lies in the analysis of the particular pattern of successes and failures exhibited by the Revolution, not simply during the war but in its immediate aftermath over the next quarter century. Such an approach can be used to define the specific limits of the revolutionary impulse—what might be called the social boundaries of potential political action—within the American Revolution. Perhaps no other single subject is more revealing of the nature of a revolution than the identification of its political and social limits.

What the specific pattern of failures and successes in the American Revolution as exhibited by the essays in this volume reveals, I would suggest, is that the new United States was composed of a group of societies without much capacity for—or interest in—collective public action. From the earliest days of settlement of the English-American colonies, the pursuit of individual happiness had been the primary shaping social value. No other imperative was so important in determining the character of early American society or in forming early American culture. As so much of the new social history has revealed, moreover, for the overwhelming majority of Americans, the pursuit of happiness had always resided in the *private*, rather than in the *public*, realm. Except for the orthodox Puritan colonies of Massachusetts Bay and Connecticut, where, at least during the first generation or two of settlement, the corporate impulse was strong and the public sphere relatively large, every society in colonial British America, including New England after about 1700, exhibited a basically private orientation, a powerful underlying predisposition among the members of its free population to preoccupy themselves with the pursuit of personal and family independence and the social improvements that would guarantee and enhance their individual economic and social achievements, enrich their lives, and give them a sense of personal self-worth.

For all but a few Americans, the pursuit of happiness did not involve the pursuit of public office or even the active occupation of a public—that is, a political—space. There was simply too much scope for the pursuit of individual and family goals in the private sphere for most people to be much interested in having a public space. Although the intensity of civic responsibility differed from place to place and time to time during the colonial era, the primary concerns of most independent Americans were private rather than public. Their allegiances were to themselves and their families rather than to the larger social entities to which they belonged. To quote one observer, they were mostly "too engaged in their respective occupations for the enticements" of public life.[5]

They or their ancestors had, in any case, left Britain or Europe not only to escape want and to gain independence but also, as contemporaries were fond of pointing out, to get away from excessive public intrusions into their private lives, intrusions in the form of high taxes, rapacious civil and religious establishments, obligations to military or naval service, and war. The most popular cultural image invoked by early Americans was the biblical image of the industrious husbandman who sat contentedly, safely, and without want under the shade of his own vine and fig tree presiding over—and luxuriating in—the development of his family and estate.

This new emphasis upon the private orientation of early American society has at least implicitly raised the question of how it affected public life, public institutions, and the collective goals of national life as they were defined by leaders before, during, and after the American Revolution. Throughout the colonial period, the private orientation of American society had meant that in most places and at most times the public realm had been small. With only a tiny bureaucracy and no police, a localized judicial system that rarely met more than fifteen to thirty days in any given year, and legislatures that in peacetime were rarely in session for more than a month in any given year, government was small, intermittent, and inexpensive. Except during wartime, taxes were low, and the only public activities that engaged most men were infrequent militia or jury service and somewhat more frequent participation in vital public works such as building and repairing bridges and roads. With little coercive power—and very little presence—government in America was consensual and depended for its energy upon the force of community opinion, which was, in practice, if not yet in theory, little more than the sum of individual opinions.

Goverment in early America was thus most importantly a device, in the traditional sense, for maintaining orderly relations among people and protecting them from their own and others' human frailties. Even more significantly, it was an agency for the protection of one's individual property in land, goods, and person, one's property in person including the right of striving, of pursuing (as well as protecting) one's interests, of seeking to alter one's place on the scale of economic well-being and social status. While they wanted enough government to secure peace and to maintain a just and open civil order, most Americans were usually, to quote one contemporary, in favor of just "so much government as will do justice, protect property, and defend the country."[6]

The critical point about the implicit conception of political society that underlay this pattern of governance is that it assigned to political society no more authority over the individual, and to the individual no more obligation to political society, than was absolutely necessary to make sure that all free individuals had approximately the same scope for private activity. Political society was thus *regulative* as it was in the traditional societies of Europe. But it was also *facilitative* in at least two senses. First, it acted to "enlarge" the scope of opportunity in the private realm by overseeing and stimulating those public improvements that would provide people with an ever larger field for the pursuit of happiness, for the realization of their individual potentials. Second, it encouraged individuals to pursue their own goals without forcing them to be much concerned with the social well-being of the community as a whole.

The American Revolution represented a radical challenge to these enduring and already quite ancient arrangements and to the traditional preference for devoting energy to the pursuit of activities in the private sphere. To be sure, as Gordon Wood and David Ammerman have shown, the challenge presented by the Coercive Acts and the initial stages of their military enforcement in 1774–76 produced a contagion of "self-sacrifice and patriotism" that was surprisingly extensive, if by no means universal.

This contagion seems even to have stimulated, among the very large proportion of the population that was swept up in it, a powerful and remarkably widely shared sense of public spiritedness and willingness to subordinate private interests to public demands.[7]

But this early flush of enthusiastic national patriotism proved impossible to sustain among a population whose most basic drives were individual rather than collective, private rather than public. Wanting most of all to be left alone, they quickly found themselves confronted with many new and burdensome public intrusions into their private lives. The demands of war both raised taxes and significantly increased the range of public demands upon individuals in the form of military service, supply levies, and demands for declarations of allegiance. At the same time, the imperatives of the new republicanism and the absence of a strong controlling central power encouraged the state governments to involve themselves in a variety of new activities. The result was a dramatic growth of government, especially at the state level, an enlargement of the public realm that represented a massive—and thitherto unprecedented—intrusion of the public into the private realm. Never before in the history of British America had the public realm made such heavy demands upon the citizenry.

At the conclusion of the War for Independence, people expected a return to the old order, a restoration of the old system whereby, in the vast majority of areas, the private realm took precedence over the public. Once the demands that had mobilized the polity had been secured, the people's concern with public affairs invariably took a back seat to their pursuit of their own welfares as individuals. As Jack Rakove remarks in his chapter in this volume, "after eight long years of war and economic dislocation, Americans were [simply] too exhausted to do much more than put their own affairs, too long neglected, in order." Like George Washington, they had throughout the war looked forward to their return to those domestic and private pursuits that had traditionally engaged most of their attentions, and the energy with which they threw themselves into those pursuits in the immediate postwar years was evident in the rapid recovery of the United States from many of the effects of the war. "It is wonderful," Washington wrote to a French correspondent less than three years after the war, "to see how soon the ravages of war are repaired. Houses are rebuilt, fields enclosed, stocks of cattle which were destroyed are replaced, and many a desolated territory assumes again the cheerful appearance of cultivation. In many places the vestiges of conflagration and ruin are hardly to be traced. The arts of peace, such as clearing rivers, building bridges, and establishing conveniences for travelling &c. are assiduously promoted."[8]

As Washington's remark suggests, ordinary free white Americans showed by their behavior that they did not necessarily regard the Revolution as incomplete simply because it had failed to realize the expansive aspirations of some of its leaders. Rather, as Gordon Wood notes in his commentary in this volume, "most ordinary people were ebulliently confident of the success of the Revolution and the promise of America." But they defined that promise almost entirely in terms of their ability to pursue their own goals as individuals. The predominant tendencies in a society with such a profoundly private orientation were centrifugal, not centripetal. Without powerful countervailing pressures, public goals simply could not be sustained unless they promised to enhance the capacity of individuals to pursue their own and their families' private welfares.

The extent to which this private orientation of early American society and this lack of interest in enlarging the public sphere both set limits upon the political potentialities of the American Revolution and continued to shape its public life during the post-Revolutionary era is nowhere better revealed than by its pattern of successes and failures in coping with the many problems it faced in the wake of the Revolution. Leaders simply could not implement any goals that were incompatible with the basically private and highly individualistic predisposition of the society over which they presided. Whatever was compatible with or facilitative of that predisposition was handled with reasonable success; whatever was not was neglected. Thus, Americans were too busy cultivating their own private interests to bother with the sustained persecution of Loyalists. They endorsed the national government's Western policy because it offered individual settlers both favorable opportunities to acquire land and a high degree of local political autonomy. They threw their support behind the new Federal government after 1788 because it seemed to promise to diminish the intrusive power assumed by the state governments during the Revolution, to provide more effective assistance against Indians who blocked the path of expansion, and to enable the nation to command more respect abroad so that it might secure the commercial advantages so necessary to the successful pursuit of their own self-interests as individuals.

On the other hand, any problems whose solutions seemed to require large public expenditures and significantly higher taxes without holding out much promise of immediately contributing to the pursuit of profits and happiness by private individuals were either not systematically addressed or not pursued with energy. These included the establishment of a viable defense force, fulfilling promises to Indians, abolishing chattel slavery, elevating the status of women, improving education, or enlarging the public sphere. At the same time, Americans failed to prevent—and ultimately even accepted—the emergence of political parties and endorsed the principle that government should be neutral in matters of individual religious conviction because those developments seemed to be a logical expression of the self-interested and individualistic society in which they lived.

This pattern of dealing with the problems raised by and during the Revolution only serves to underline that American society during the Revolutionary era was one whose members were overwhelmingly preoccupied with the cultivation of their own individual goals in the private realm and had little interest in devoting sustained energy or committing major resources to activities in the public sphere. As several of the following substantive chapters and John Murrin's commentary make clear, American society in the late eighteenth century was still, to a considerable degree, trapped within the conceptual universe of classical republicanism. But the way that society dealt—and did not deal—with public problems also powerfully argues that the imperatives of classical republicanism had relatively little impact on the behavior of many of its members. Rather, in virtually every area, that behavior served to insure that, no less than the colonial societies established by their ancestors in the previous century, Americans of the Revolutionary era would build their republic not on self-denial and the cultivation of civic virtue in the public realm but on the avid pursuit of self and family concerns in the private sphere.

NOTES

1. J. Franklin Jameson, *The American Revolution Considered as a Social Movement* (Princeton, 1926); Evarts B. Greene, *The Revolutionary Generation, 1763–1790* (New York, 1943).
2. Bernard Bailyn, *The Ideological Origins of the American Revolution* (Cambridge, Mass., 1967); Gordon S. Wood, *The Creation of the American Republic, 1776–1787* (Chapel Hill, N.C., 1969).
3. J.G.A. Pocock, *The Machiavellian Moment: Florentine Political Thought and the Atlantic Republican Tradition* (Princeton, 1975). Pocock's early essays, upon which Bailyn and Wood drew, are collected in his *Politics, Language, and Time* (New York, 1971).
4. Much of this new work in the ideological realm is summarized in Robert E. Shalhope,

"Republicanism and Early American Historiography," *William and Mary Quarterly*, 3d ser., XXXIX (1982), 334–56.

5. Duke de la Rochefoucault Liancourt, *Travels through the United States of North America*, 2 vols. (London, 1799), I, 679.

6. Samuel Williams, *The Natural and Civil History of Vermont*, 2 vols. (Walpole, N.H., 1794), II, 358, 424.

7. Wood, *Creation of the American Republic*, 413–25; David Ammerman, *In the Common Cause: American Response to the Coervice Acts of 1774* (Charlottesville, Va., 1974), 89–101.

8. Washington to Chevalier de la Luzerne, Aug. 1, 1786, in John C. Fitzpatrick, ed., *Writings of George Washington* (Washington, D.C., 1931–40), XXVIII, 500–01.

CHAPTER I

The Problem of National Defense in the Early American Republic

E. Wayne Carp

In an age when fewer and fewer people read what professional historians write, American military history occupies an anomalous position. It enjoys a huge following among nonacademics while most professional historians ignore it. The popular interest in military history, spurred by Americans' participation in World War II, Korea, Vietnam; extensive media coverage of the Vietnam conflict; the threat of war in the nuclear age; and what Peter Paret describes as the "demand for colorful gore and for the vicarious experience of crime and punishment," is exemplified by the many book clubs, periodicals, institutions, and regional, state, and local organizations that exist to serve a clientele estimated by one historian to be in excess of one hundred thousand enthusiasts.[1] Professional historians' neglect of military history can be measured in any number of ways: the dearth of scholarly articles and monographs, the small number of military historians employed in major American universities, the paucity of college-level courses offered, the reluctance of faculty advisors to encourage their graduate students to specialize in the field.[2] In short, as Gunther Rothenberg noted in 1972, "the field has as yet to achieve the legitimacy of general acceptance as an academic discipline."[3]

While there are encouraging signs that professional historians' attitudes are beginning to change, their disdain for military history is not entirely unwarranted. American academics' deep suspicion of military history is itself a product of the historical development of the discipline. During the nineteenth century, the foremost historians of the period—Bancroft, Parkman, and Prescott—made military leaders, battles, and campaigns an integral part of their narratives. But by 1900, with the professionalization of historians and the rejection of the amateur patricians' emphasis on nationalism and romanticism, the scientific historians eschewed military history for the analysis of social, economic, and intellectual problems.[4] The result was that, with the exception of a few talented journalists like Shelby Foote and Bruce Catton and a few professional historians like Bell Irvin Wiley and Samuel Eliot Morison, American military history was left to the military until approximately 1945. As a consequence, the reputation of military history as a respectable discipline plummeted, for neither its content nor its purpose met scholarly standards. Army historians, designing American military histories for use by university ROTC students, wrote at a high-school level, producing texts clearly inferior to those in other fields. As late as 1965, John Shy was able to praise a book by noting that it was "not marred by the romantic distortion, the inadequacies of research, and the pompous judgments masquerading as analysis that have brought the traditional form of military history into low esteem among most professional historians." Not surprisingly, few faculty members wanted to be associated with such an intellectually barren field.[5]

If the content of military history offended academics, its narrowly utilitarian purpose also upset them. Most American military history—the government sponsored documentary editions, the memoirs and biographies, the strategic and operational histories—has had two basic functions: "to train professional military men in the exercise of their profession and . . . to educate governments and peoples in the military requirements of today."[6] The policy orientation inherent in most official military history helps account for professional historians' distrust of and hostility toward the subject.[7] Above all, the intellectual shortcomings and pragmatic purposes of military history feed American academicians' long-standing liberal prejudice against war and, by extension, those who study it.[8]

The history of military thought, a distinct sub-branch of this didactic literature that explicitly attempts to shape America's national military policy, has profoundly affected the way historians have interpreted the nation's military past. Throughout most of American history, as Russell Weigley has cogently noted, military thought has been divided between those who favor and those who oppose the proposition that America should maintain a large regular army in peacetime. Writers in this tradition have wrestled most with the problem of how to guarantee maximum security for the United States in a manner consistent with the nation's democratic institutions. The men who contributed to this body of writings during the first century of the Republic—George Washington, John Calhoun, Henry W. Halleck, Dennis Hart Mahan, William T. Sherman, and U.S. Grant—used examples from military history to bolster their cases but did not write narrative histories of American wars and rarely focused on the lessons of the American Revolutionary War. Two later military theorists, Emory Upton and John McAuley Palmer, not only contributed historical analyses to the continuing debate over national military policy, but also left a permanent stamp on the way professional historians interpreted both the American Revolutionary War and the establishment of the nation's military institutions.[9] Upton, a West Point graduate in 1861, fought bravely in many of the Civil War's major battles, was commandant of cadets at West Point (1870–75), and later served as superintendent of theoretical instruction in the Artillery School at Fort Monroe, Virginia. During the nearly two decades before his death by suicide in 1881, Upton wrote several studies, the most important of which, *The Military Policy of the United States,* lay half completed and unpublished until 1904.[10]

Upton's *Military Policy,* the first narrative history of the United States Army, profoundly affected all subsequent military history. It contained a withering attack on "the folly and criminality" of America's military policy and a plea for the creation of a modern professional army.[11] Critics and admirers agree that the key to Upton's work lies in the chapter on the American Revolutionary War. In it, Upton wrapped himself in the mantle of George Washington's towering prestige and piled quotation upon quotation from the commander-in-chief's writings condemning the militia, short enlistments, the bounty system, and the fear of a standing army.[12] In summarizing the lessons of America's military policy during the Revolution, Upton blamed "the total inexperience of our statesmen in regard to military affairs, which led to vital mistakes in army legislation." He declared that the Confederation was "the weakest of all forms of government" for waging war, and pilloried state governments' role in military affairs because "it lessens the military strength of the whole people and correspondingly increases the national expenditures." Upton concluded his survey of the Revolutionary War by advocating that conscription, a regular army, and, especially, a professional officer corps replace volunteers, the militia, and short enlistments.[13]

By the first quarter of the twentieth century many professional soldiers recognized that the United States would never build a large, professional army on the Uptonian model and that a small army was inappropriate to the type of mass warfare that had broken out in 1914. As many military professionals realized that modern war demanded a large army, they also began to re-evaluate the military potential of a citizen soldiery.[14] This reappraisal lauded the efficiency of the Swiss militia system, discovered hidden merits in the American militia, and argued that citizens could be made into good soldiers on short notice.[15] When the raw troops the United States sent into combat in 1917–18 performed courageously, even Uptonians like General John J. Pershing, commander of the American Expeditionary Force, were convinced that a citizen army could be effective. It was left to Lieutenant Colonel John McAuley Palmer, a West Point graduate, operations officer on Pershing's staff in France in 1917, and commander of the 58th Infantry Brigade of the 29th Division, to make the case that a citizen army could form the basis for America's military establishment.[16]

Setting aside his initial enthusiasm for Uptonian solutions to army problems, Palmer in 1918 began a lifelong crusade to refute Uptonian policy prescriptions and to promote the idea of a citizen army. Palmer's military policy, presented in many books and in expert testimony before Congress, was essentially a mirror image of Upton's. Putting his faith in an armed citizenry and civilian control of the military, Palmer saw no contradiction between a strong army and democratic political institutions. He eloquently argued that "a free state cannot continue to be democratic in peace and autocratic in war. . . . An enduring government by the people must include an army of the people among its institutions." To accomplish this goal, he called for a reduction in the number of American regular army soldiers, universal military training for civilians, and promotion to officer status of civilians who demonstrated a capacity for leadership.[17]

In the late 1920s, Palmer discovered Washington's "Sentiments on a Peace Establishment" (1783) which had remained, unread, in the Library of Congress for over a century. Washington's "Sentiments" gave him the ammunition he needed to challenge Upton's denunciation of the militia and support his own position in favor of a citizen army. In two of his books, *Washington, Lincoln, Wilson: Three War Statesmen* (1930) and *America in Arms* (1941), Palmer, like Upton, began his analysis of America's military policy with the American Revolutionary War. Palmer made his case partly by singling out the militia's commendable performances at Concord, Springfield, and King's Mountain. But the quotations from

Washington's "Sentiments" praising the militia as "the palladium of our security" and recommending proposals for a citizen army formed the centerpiece of Palmer's argument. Palmer sidestepped the militia's poor showing during the Revolutionary War by making the distinction between an untrained and a trained militia. The former was the one Upton denounced, while the latter was what Palmer and Washington favored. For Palmer, as his biographer notes, the trained militia would not only fight as effectively as a regular army but would provide "more defense at less cost than an Uptonian army."[18]

Although Palmer provided a healthy corrective to Upton's view of military history, the Uptonian model dominated twentieth-century interpretations of American military history until the success of guerilla warfare in Vietnam and elsewhere caused many military historians to concur with Palmerian views of the value of trained militia. But the battle continues: Uptonians and Palmerians still fight each other with books and articles to decide the relative merits of regular army soldiers and the militia during America's history, even though the nature of warfare has changed qualitatively with the advent of nuclear weapons.[19] So pervasive is this conflict among military historians that even the scholar who has no policy prescriptions in mind finds it almost impossible to write about early American warfare without being assigned to one camp or the other.[20] There are indications, however, that historians have begun to address issues other than Uptonian/Palmerian ones and to lay the basis for a deeper understanding of the nation's early military heritage. This "new" military history investigates the relationship between war and society by examining not only the impact of war on political institutions, economic developments, and social policy, but also the influence of political, social, economic, and intellectual beliefs and practices on waging war. We must now turn to these studies to understand the subsequent course of the Revolutionary War, the rise of the nationalists, and the postwar debate between Federalists and Republicans over the creation of peacetime military institutions.

Through their research over the past two decades, historians such as Bernard Bailyn, Gordon S. Wood, J.G.A. Pocock, Jack P. Greene, J.R. Pole, Joyce Appleby, John M. Murrin, and others have inadvertently demonstrated the pluralistic nature of American political culture and its importance for understanding the origins of the American Revolution. It is now apparent that colonial Americans' political world was not dominated by a single strand of intellectual thought but rather formed a mosaic of traditional practices, competing ideologies, and expressive symbol systems that included a localistic perspective, deferential political attitudes, Real Whig ideology, Lockean liberalism, and seventeenth-century classical republican thought.[21] The recent work of John Shy, Don Higginbotham, Charles Royster, Lawrence Delbert Cress, John Philip Reid, Fred Anderson, and John Todd White has built upon various parts of this framework, making it abundantly clear that the military history of early America cannot be understood apart from political culture.[22]

Two aspects of colonial American political culture, localism and Real Whig ideology, particularly influenced the colonists' military beliefs and practices. Colonial Americans' localistic perspective resulted largely from more than a half century of "salutary neglect" by British officialdom and the emergence in the colonies of a de facto federal system of self-government. As a result of the colonists' virtual autonomy from centralized control, whether imperial or provincial, political power in the colonies fragmented and tended to gravitate downward to the town, county, or parish level. Consequently, the board of selectmen and the justices of the peace, not the Board of Trade or even colonial assemblies, were the most important political authorities in the colonists' lives. Regional, religious, and ethnic differences, the isolation of rural life, the vast distance between seaboard and hinterland, and poor transportation and communication systems reinforced their localist world view. During the imperial crisis of the 1760s and 1770s, Americans viewed Parliament's taxation and its claims of undivided sovereignty as threats not only to their liberty and property, but also to their traditional and localistic way of life.[23]

In 1782, John Adams declared that four local institutions—the towns, congregations, schools, and militia—"produced the American Revolution."[24] To the extent that the militia symbolized and reinforced Americans' attachments to their local communities, Adams was correct. Citizen soldiers trained and organized for home defense, the militia sprang up with the first English colonies. During the seventeenth century, the necessity of inexpensively defending their settlements from foreign threats and actual Indian attacks pushed colonial assemblies, one by one, to invoke "the historic English principle of a universal obligation to military service, in order to create a military force of armed civilians."[25] Even in the seventeenth century, however, the militia was distinguished from British professional troops by its limited scope and purpose. The militia was made up of part-time citizen soldiers, existing primarily for local defense, who rarely ventured beyond their provincial borders or engaged in offensive war. During the eighteenth century, as settlement grew and population increased, the militia's fighting skills atrophied. Colonists ceased to depend on the militia for defense and instead relied on volunteers and draftees commanded by British regulars or Americans. From the 1620s through the Seven Years' War, provincial authorities used volunteer units to fight first the Indians and later the French.[26] Throughout the colonies, however, the militia continued to function as a local police force, in New England as a night watch, and in the South as a slave patrol. It was also used in conjunction with the *posse comitatus* to suppress civil disturbances. Allan R. Millett and Peter Maslowski summarize the militia's conservative functions: "It preserved the domestic peace, protected propertied and privileged colonists from the disadvantaged elements within society, and quelled movements against the established order."[27]

Although the militia had long ceased to be an effective shield against foreign or Indian attack except on the frontier, the colonists continued to believe that it was invincible when defending home and family. By the eighteenth century, moreover, the militia began to resemble a miniature commonwealth, clearly reflecting the community's inclusiveness, its stratified economic and social structure, and its hierarchical political world. Militia officers were often wealthy, prominent officeholders, while the rank and file comprised every able-bodied man from the age of sixteen to sixty. Training days resembled "secular holidays," during which the militia, rather than being isolated from the community, performed its military exercises to the cheers of the onlooking townspeople.[28] The intimate relationship between the militia and the local community is nowhere better illustrated than in the militia's participation in riots. Although the militia acted as a local police force, it is also apparent from the studies of Pauline Maier, John Lax, William Pencak, Christine Leigh Heyrman, and Edward Countryman that, in defense of the local community, the militia participated in extra-institutional popular uprisings such as anti-impressment, anti-inoculation, and land riots. The militia was also responsive to the will of the community when it refused to obey colonial officials' orders that threatened community interests. Thus, when Governor Bernard called out the Boston militia to quell the Stamp Act riots, the men joined the protestors.[29]

As the colonists' localistic world view caused them to link the militia to the preservation of the community, so their Real Whig ideological beliefs led them to associate standing armies with despotism. By now, we are all too familiar with the crucial elements of Real Whig ideology—the struggle between power and liberty, the fear of enslavement, and the belief in the virtues of the British constitution. But for the purposes of this chapter I want to emphasize the way Real Whig ideology shaped the colonists' distrust of professional standing armies and reinforced their adherence to the militia. Real Whig antimilitary sentiment was a legacy of two experiences during the English Civil War and Protectorate. In the first, the New Model Army's refusal to disband in 1647–48 led to the overthrow of the monarchy and the beheading of Charles I. In the second, the major-generals and new militia during Cromwell's Protectorate replaced the civilian government with what amounted to a military dictatorship. During the Restoration, Whig opposition politicians kept Protestant, nationalist Englishmen's anti-army attitudes at a fever pitch by identifying Charles II's military policies with Catholicism, French influence, and arbitrary power. In the aftermath of the Glorious Revolution, the Declaration of Rights and the Mutiny Act of 1689 placed the ultimate authority for the peacetime army in Parliament, acknowledged the right of Protestants to bear arms, and prohibited the billeting of troops on private subjects. Although these measures effectively placed the military under Parliamentary control, Real Whig writers continued to warn that a standing army endangered liberty. In their view, professional soldiers were a source of social oppression because they were riotous, expensive, and morally corrupt. More significantly, Real Whigs interpreted the very existence of a professional army as evidence of a corrupted populace and unbalanced constitution. The acceptance by most Americans of Real Whig thought made the professional army an ideologically unacceptable alternative to the militia.[30]

The importance of Real Whig arguments against standing armies cannot be overemphasized. As we know from Bernard Bailyn and others, Real Whig ideology became deeply embedded in most colonial Americans' world view. Before the imperial crisis colonists did not often voice their fears of standing armies because British regulars were few in number and stationed at frontier posts, but Americans' denunciations of standing armies became commonplace after British regulars arrived in Boston in 1768. By 1774, in the aftermath of the Boston Massacre and several other violent incidents in New York and South Carolina between British regulars and civilians, most Americans would have agreed with the sentiments of the Boston town meeting that "Standing Armies have forever made Shipwreck of Free States and no People Jealous of their liberties ever patiently suffered Mercenary Troops to be quartered and maintained within their Populous Cities." The British ministry's use of regular soldiers confirmed the colonists' growing fears of its intent to enslave them, fears that eventually led to Lexington and Concord.[31]

When Americans turned against the British crown they enthusiastically embraced republicanism, a term whose protean meaning has bedeviled contemporaries and historians ever since. Politically, as Thomas Paine noted, "a *republic*, is not any *particular form* of government," but for most Americans republics signified a polity resting directly upon the authority and will of the people. Yet republicanism was more than an elective system. Just as important, as Gordon S. Wood has observed, Americans' embrace of republicanism "added a moral dimension, a utopian depth, to the political separation from England—a depth that involved the very character of their society."[32] Americans knew from their reading of ancient history and Real Whig writings that the strength and greatness of republics depended on the virtue of the people. Ancient republics not only required personal virtue—industry, honesty, frugality—from their citizenry, but, most importantly, civic virtue, a willingness to sacrifice self-interest to the commonwealth. A republic's strength, however, was also its source of weakness. The combination of limited government and great freedom caused republics to decay internally as corruption sapped citizens' virtue. Citizens' self-absorption and disregard for the commonwealth also made republics prey to outright attack and to manipulation by foreign powers. A republic's security thus rested on its militia, which could alone guarantee the preservation of liberty and constitutional stability from foreign attack. At the same time, a citizen's participation in the militia—defending the commonwealth and ensuring the maintenance of a balanced constitution—signified civic virtue.

These, then, were the Revolution's ideals: to create a republican society characterized by liberty, a decentralized government resting on the will of the people, and virtuous, self-sacrificing individuals enrolled in the militia. But the experience of the war made many revolutionaries readjust these basic components of republicanism and American political culture. Some came to view strong central government and standing armies not as engines of oppression but as the essential means of preserving independence and, in the early republic, of defending the nation. Thus, at stake in the ferocious debates over standing armies and militia effectiveness, first between the Nationalists and their opponents and later between Federalists and Republicans, were differing conceptions of republicanism. As John R. Howe, Jr. has perceptively written, these controversies were part of "a continuing effort by the American people to decide what for them republicanism was to mean."[33]

One of the greatest ironies of the American Revolution was that those aspects of the colonists' political culture most responsible for propelling Americans into revolt—their fear of concentrated power, their tradition of local self-government, and their abhorrence of standing armies—made waging war difficult and often impossible. The resulting conflict between the colonists' political heritage and the exigencies of fighting the world's most powerful imperial nation surfaced repeatedly during the war in two crucial areas: mobilizing men to fight and supplying the army. By 1780, as a result of military defeats, manpower and supply shortages, public apathy, and financial chaos, the Revolution nearly collapsed. The experience of waging war under a weak national government, uncooperative state legislatures, and the imminent prospect of British military victory convinced many revolutionaries to advocate strengthening Congress's taxing and administrative powers. The irony of attempting to centralize the powers of government in order to save a Revolution originally undertaken in the name of decentralized political power was no doubt lost on these Nationalists. The final irony, however, was yet to come. When the Continental army, now composed of seasoned regulars, defeated the British at Yorktown with the aid of the French, most Americans congratulated themselves on their own and the militia's virtuous resistance against tyranny. The debate over America's national military establishment during the early national period was shaped and distorted by the experience of fighting a war shackled by ideological fears of standing armies and strong government.[34]

None of these ironies was apparent in 1775. Then, the *rage militaire,* Charles Royster's apt phrase for the contagious enthusiasm for war, manifested itself in the thousands of Massachusetts militiamen who streamed into the Boston area upon hearing that hostilities had broken out at Lexington and Concord and who fought to such good effect at Bunker Hill. American revolutionaries believed independence would be won quickly and, except for Washington and a few other officers, whose experience with militia during the Seven Years' War had convinced them otherwise, viewed the militia as the nation's instrument of deliverance. In the following year, however, military realities began to erode Americans' ideological predilections. The men in Washington's army demonstrated that they were imbued with an individualistic ethos and that they understood their commitment to the war as a limited contract.[35] These qualities, while reflecting American values that contributed to the outbreak of war, did not help create a stable or committed fighting force. The great majority of men in the Continental Army refused Washington's entreaties to reenlist and instead went home, leaving Washington's army in January 1776 with only 5,582 men fit for duty. The much vaunted militia, reputedly composed of virtuous farmers who fought selflessly for the commonwealth, evaporated in the face of prolonged conflict. The militia's performance in the field also left much to be desired. The Canada debacle in 1775–1776 owed much to Montgomery's and Arnold's precipitous decision to attack Quebec before the citizen soldiers' enlistments ran out. The militia again failed to distinguish itself at the battles of Long Island, Kip's Bay, and White Plains during the summer and fall campaign of 1776, throwing down its weapons and running away in the face of the enemy. These experiences, coupled with the British use of German mercenaries and the realization that the war would be a long one, convinced both the military leadership and Congress that victory required a regular army enlisted by bounty for three years or the duration of the war.[36]

Despite this consensus, Washington and Congress continued to disagree fundamentally on the function and capability of the militia. Socially conservative and imbued with eighteenth-century notions of limited war, Washington and most of his generals[37] feared that reliance on citizen soldiers would unleash a savage guerilla warfare that would seriously threaten the social and political fabric of the nation. Washington also realized the diplomatic value of a conventional army—foreign support or recognition would never materialize for irregulars—as well as its symbolic importance as a rallying point for American unity and nationalism. Consequently, while occasionally praising the militia for its performance, most notably at Bennington, Springfield, and King's Mountain, America's military leaders tended to magnify its defects. But while the militia was unquestionably unreliable, ill-disciplined, poorly trained, wasteful of supplies, and frequently ineffective, it is also true it was indispensable to American independence in ways that Washington and others never fully understood. Indeed, it is only recently that scholars have recognized the militia's contribution to British defeat. Thanks to the illuminating researches of Don Higginbotham, John Shy, and Clyde Ferguson, we now know that the militia's tenacious defense of the local community—attacking British forage parties and intimidating the disaffected—insured patriot control of state political and legal institutions, forced the Loyalists to remain on the defensive throughout the war, and guaranteed that the British always operated in hostile territory.[38] Just as importantly, as Shy notes, the militia "provided on short notice large numbers of armed men for brief periods of emergency service; and it found and persuaded, drafted or bribed, the smaller number of men needed each year to keep the Continental army alive."[39] Nevertheless, as the war dragged on, Washington increased his requests for conscription, larger bounties, longer terms of enlistments, and after the Valley Forge winter of 1777–78, lifetime pensions at half pay for Continental officers, while intensifying his denunciations of the militia.

Although Congress eventually agreed with Washington that the military effort required a regular army, it did so reluctantly because its ideological fear of standing armies was never far from the surface. As early as August 1776, Congress voted to offer cash bounties and to lengthen the period of enlistment of Continental soldiers, but it worried that military service would corrupt young men and that ultimately the army would subvert the republic. Even though the states rarely filled congressional quotas for the Continental army, Congress never lacked revolutionaries like Pennsylvania's Benjamin Rush, who constantly deplored the idea of a regular army and who announced that he would "despair of our cause if our country contained 60,000 men abandoned enough to enlist for 3 years or during the war."[40] Additional fears of the army emerged with Continental officers' demand for half pay for life. In October 1780, Congress gave in to the officers' pension demands, but only over strenuous opposition. Congressmen worried that passage of the resolve would create a privileged class within American society and that half-pay officers would become the placemen of a strong national government. These fears were strong enough to insure that Congress would not abandon the militia and that the militia, regardless of how badly it fought, would remain a source of community pride and a symbol of American virtue.[41]

American revolutionaries' reluctance to concentrate power either in individuals or institutions and their strong allegiance to states and local communities culminated in the creation of a weak central government under the

Articles of Confederation. The national government's weakness repeatedly revealed itself in its growing inability to feed, clothe, or equip the troops.[42] The history of Congress's efforts to supply the army followed a somewhat more checkered course than that of mobilizing men to fight, but the result was the same: ideology eventually gave way to pragmatic military considerations. During the first year of the war, an inexperienced Congress, believing the war would be won quickly, supplied the army on an ad hoc basis, haphazardly employing congressional committees, creating rudimentary staff departments, and calling upon military commanders, state officials, and private citizens to assist in the war effort. The results were inadequate, the army ill-served. In 1777, Congress, acting on the same principles that underlay its political beliefs, systematically decentralized supply operations by relying more heavily on the staff departments and introducing a system of public accountability to check fraud and corruption. These measures also failed. In 1778, in the wake of Valley Forge and the near disbanding of the army, Congress temporarily put aside its fear of power by centralizing the quartermaster and commissary departments, abandoning restraints on department chiefs, and handsomely remunerating staff officers. Under the leadership of Quartermaster General Nathanael Greene and Commissary General of Purchases Jeremiah Wadsworth, these reforms proved effective. But the army's relief was short-lived: by late 1779 the army once again lacked every necessity and was on the verge of disbanding. Congress instinctively reacted to the crisis by reverting to decentralization. It virtually stopped supervising logistical operations and in early 1780 adopted the system of specific supplies, giving state legislatures primary responsibility for provisioning the army. The results were disastrous, and the states' inability to supply the army led to the prospect of its dissolution. By the fall of 1780, the army's possible disbandment, coupled with serious military defeats in the South, Benedict Arnold's treason, and a bankrupt national treasury, cast serious doubts on the survival of American independence.

The nationalist movement of 1780–1783 was a product of these supply failures and military reverses. Rejecting Americans' heritage of decentralized government, it aimed above all to secure independence, a feat its supporters believed could only be accomplished by strengthening the powers of Congress. The chief supporters of the nationalist movement, Continental army officers and popularly elected state legislators, formed a heterogeneous coalition of individuals spanning the entire political spectrum, from the crypto-monarchist Major General James Mitchell Varnum to the future Anti-Federalist, New York's Governor George Clinton. Despite the nationalists' diverse political, social, and economic background, they all recognized the very real possiblity of losing the war. Thus, they all agreed on the need to win for Congress the power to tax the states and to centralize the civil executive departments. Elected to Congress in late 1780 by recently democratized state assemblies that shared their fears, the nationalists instituted their proposals to empower Congress to tax imports and to create new departments headed by strong leaders. The most salient aspect of the nationalists' short period of leadership was its failure. Their tax measure, the impost, failed to secure unanimous support from the states, while the powers and responsibilities of the newly created civil executive departments strongly resembled the ones they were designed to replace. America's victory at Yorktown in October 1781 owed more to Robert Morris's administrative and financial acumen than to the nationalists' political theory or organizational reforms.

For most Americans, Yorktown signaled the end of the war. As the prospect of peace grew stronger, officers' demands for pensions and the threat of a potential coup d'état reignited the nation's antimilitary prejudices. Historians still disagree on the exact details of the Newburgh conspiracy, but the broad outlines are clear.[43] In late 1782, as the approximately 10,000-man Continental army unofficially began to demobilize at its final cantonment at Newburgh, New York, an impoverished and bitter officer corps feared that the army would disband before Congress made good on its promise to fund their half pay for life pensions. In December 1782, a committee of three, representing the disgruntled officers, carried a petition to Congress offering to accept a commutation of half pay for life to some equivalent lump-sum payment and warning that "any further experiments on their patience may have fatal effects."[44] Extreme nationalists such as Alexander Hamilton, Robert Morris, and Gouverneur Morris, their influence in Congress eroding and their plans for a strong central government thwarted, seized the opportunity presented by a potentially mutinous army to attempt to coerce reluctant congressmen into passing another impost. The effort failed, and amid a chorus of denunciation of officers' greed and fears that a half-pay settlement would corrupt America's republican society, Congress rejected a resolve to commute half pay for life to six years of full payment, preferring that state legislatures handle the problem of officers' pensions. When word reached camp of Congress's refusal to agree to their demands, a second group of officers, encouraged

by extreme nationalists and led by General Horatio Gates, issued the in-
flammatory Newburgh Addresses calling upon the army to refuse to disband if their grievances were not redressed. At an officers' meeting on 15
March 1783, Washington's dramatic appeal to the army's tradition of
subordination to civil authority effectively destroyed their enthusiasm for
challenging that authority. A week later, the tension was further diffused
when word arrived that Congress had voted the officers full pay for five
years and enlisted men full pay for four months, although the source of
funding was left to the future. Yet, as Richard H. Kohn has written, "the
Newburgh conspiracy was the closest an American army has ever come to
revolt or coup d'état," and the fears it raised among political leaders lin-
gered long after the event.[45]

During the last months of the army's demobilization, two other events
insured that America's heritage of distrusting standing armies would
emerge from the war as strong as ever. On 13 May 1783, at Baron von
Steuben's headquarters near Newburgh, General Henry Knox and a small
circle of friends organized the Society of the Cincinnati, a fraternal and
charitable organization of Continental army officers, membership in which
would be hereditary. Within six months, intense public denunciation centering on its aristocratic and unrepublican character embarrassed Washington and led to the society's repudiation of its hereditary proviso.[46] Ordinary soldiers also contributed to Americans' apprehension of the military.
By the end of April 1783, Washington recommended that Congress give
three months full pay to the enlisted men who were rioting and insulting
their officers, but a financially bankrupt Congress refused to heed Washington's advice. Instead, in June Congress furloughed the soldiers to their
homes, pending a discharge once the definitive treaty of peace had been
signed, without any provision for settling their accounts or a word of
appreciation. Outraged, eighty new recruits of the Pennsylvania Line
marched from Lancaster to Philadelphia, joined several hundred other
angry soldiers quartered in the city, and barricaded several members of
Congress and the Executive Council of Pennsylvania in the State House
while demanding their pay. Their target, as Kenneth R. Bowling has
demonstrated, was not Congress, which, lacking a quorum, was techni-
cally not even in session, but the Executive Council, singled out because
"Pennsylvania was simply wealthier and more important than the federal
government." The affair quickly petered out, however, when several congressmen walked out of the State House unharmed amid insults shouted

by drunken soldiers. Targeted or not, Congress moved from Philadelphia to Princeton, and revolutionaries everywhere noted the army's threat to civil authority.[47]

For those Americans who remained wedded to localism and anti-army ideology, the demobilization of the Continental army awakened all their old fears. The complicity of some Nationalists in a threatened military coup d'état during the Newburgh conspiracy, the aristocratic character of the Society of the Cincinnati, and the Pennsylvania Line's defiance of local authority confirmed their belief that the states were the safest depositories of their liberties and that a standing army commanded by Nationalists endangered a republican society. The war experience, however, had convinced many other revolutionaries of the very opposite. These Americans blamed a weak central government unable to command its own revenues for the army's dissatisfaction at Newburgh and Philadelphia. For them the lessons of the war were clear: the national government's powers needed to be increased and a strong professional army created to preserve independence and a republican society. The debates over permanent peacetime military institutions in the early national period would reflect and continue the Revolutionary War's divided legacy over the role a standing army should play in a republic. Like American military policy during the War for Independence, changes in the new nation's military establishment would come about in piecemeal fashion and only as a result of perceived military necessity.

The military historiography of the Confederation period and early republic differs from that of the Revolutionary era in two significant ways. First, there is simply less of it. The recent, remarkably rich outpouring of Revolutionary War studies has not been duplicated for the postwar period. Aside from Richard H. Kohn's superb study, *Eagle and Sword: The Beginnings of the Military Establishment in America* (1975), which expertly delineates the political, economic, and ideological factors impinging upon the Federalist creation of America's peace establishment, and Lawrence Delbert Cress's recent intellectual history, *Citizens in Arms: The Army and the Militia in American Society to the War of 1812* (1982), which skillfully describes the repeated clashes between opposing visions of republicanism, the military history of the early national period lacks the critical mass of monographic literature needed to generate a challenging historiography. One reason for the dearth of early republic military studies lies in historians' avoidance, until recently, of what looked like an unimportant transitional era between the Revolution and the Age of Jackson. Another explanation, perhaps, is that Kohn's fine book appeared to have settled our understanding of the early republic's military matters once and for all.

Second, this historiography differs in quality as well as quantity from its Revolutionary counterpart because the period is dominated by descriptive histories cast in Uptonian terms. In *Military Policy*, Upton characterized the Confederation era's military affairs as "weak, inefficient, and chaotic," a state of affairs that predictably led to Shays' Rebellion. For Upton, the Constitution's military clauses provided the period's only bright spot, bestowing upon the national government "every war power that the most despotic ruler could ask." Yet, whether aimed at Indians in the 1790s or the British in 1812, America's military policy was a failure because, according to Upton, government officials ignored "the great lessons of the Revolution" and from "a shortsighted and mistaken economy" continued to rely on the militia for the nation's defense. As we shall see in the following overview of the creation of America's peacetime establishment, Uptonian questions and answers—the efficiency of regulars versus militia and national versus state control of the militia—run like a thread through most of the military histories of the period.[48]

Even before a formal peace treaty was announced, Congress was forced to consider what kind of permanent military establishment the United States should create when New York and Pennsylvania authorities requested military aid for negotiating Indian treaties and garrisoning British-occupied forts. In April 1783, Congress quickly appointed a committee headed by Alexander Hamilton to provide a plan. Hamilton wrote immediately to ask the advice of Washington, who in turn solicited the opinions of his chief subordinates. Two weeks later, Washington sent Congress his "Sentiments on a Peace Establishment," a remarkably pragmatic and balanced document that reflected his understanding of the nation's future military needs and American republicanism. Washington advocated a small permanent army of 2,631 men designed to protect the frontier and to serve as the nucleus for security in a general war. In an effort to diffuse congressmen's antimilitary prejudices, Washington assured them of his familiarity with the danger to liberty posed by "a *large* standing Army in time of Peace," but argued that "a few Troops, under certain circumstances, are not only safe, but indispensably necessary." Washington also proposed the establishment of a war department, a navy, coastal fortresses to protect major seaports, munitions arsenals, and a military academy. But most suprising, in light of his earlier denunciations, Washington praised the militia—"this great Bulwark of our Liberties and independence"—and recommended that a national militia system be established, consisting of a reserve force of all male citizens between eighteen and fifty and a select group of young men eighteen to twenty-five specially trained for military emergencies. Washington's "Sentiments," a product of wartime experience, represented the nationalists' new understanding of republicanism, which now emphasized military preparedness, a select militia, and a peacetime standing army to protect republican institutions from foreign invasion and domestic insurrection. The "Sentiments" also provided, as J.C.A. Stagg has observed, "the basis for all subsequent discussion about the organization of the armed forces in the early Republic."[49]

In the immediate postwar era, Washington's proposals never stood a chance of enactment. During the debate that took place over the next year many congressmen disputed whether the Articles of Confederation permitted the creation of standing armies in time of peace, and many doubted the nationalists' motives, fearing the potential for corruption and military tyranny in a regular army. Besides having constitutional and ideological reservations about creating a standing army, opponents of the plan denounced the excessive cost and questioned its necessity. Instead, they agreed with Massachusetts delegate Elbridge Gerry that, given America's vast distance from Europe, "the Militia, which has ever been the dernier Resort of Liberty," was adequate for the nation's defense.[50] In early June 1784, Congress enacted its beliefs into resolves and ordered Henry Knox to discharge all but eighty Continental soldiers. Nevertheless, recognizing that Indian defense and the British garrisons in the Northwest demanded a larger force, Congress the next day created the first national peacetime military force in American history by "recommending" that Pennsylvania, New Jersey, New York, and Connecticut furnish 700 men from their militias to serve for one year. The First American Regiment, as it was known, was, in Richard H. Kohn's words, "a compromise force: not under state control, and enlisted for service out-of-state, so clearly not militia; not wholly under Confederation authority, not long-service regulars, and furnished obviously at the pleasure of the states, so certainly not a standing army."[51]

Throughout the Confederation era, Congress's inadequacy was manifest everywhere. Its reliance on the states for militia and money proved insufficient to cope with threats of war from either the Mohawk chief Joseph Brant in the Northwest or the mixed-blood Creek leader Alexander McGillivray in the South. It was forced to stand by as Great Britain continued to dominate the fur trade, influence the Indians, and, in violation of the Treaty of Paris, retain forts in the Northwest. And lastly, Congress looked on helplessly as Spain closed the Mississippi to all United States shipping, refused to recognize the 31st parallel as the northern boundary of Western Florida, and stirred up secessionist spirit in the Southwest. Congress's military budget reflected its impotence. In 1784 military expenditures totaled $297,323; yet in 1787, with war threatening in the West, military appropriations dropped to $176,757. Less than a year earlier, the Board of Treasury had ominously warned that only the adoption of the federal impost could save the country "from Bankruptcy, or preserve the Union of the several States from Dissolution."[52]

Historians agree that Congress's final humiliation occurred in September 1786: when a former Revolutionary war officer, Daniel Shays, and 1,100 debt-ridden farmers marched on the Court of Common Pleas in Hampshire County, Massachusetts, to prevent the seizure of their property for the payment of debts and taxes, the 800 militiamen called out to defend the Court refused to act because of sympathy with the rioters. It became clear that the Confederation could neither rely on the militia nor count on the states for money or troops. Consequently, in October, Congress unanimously resolved to requisition $530,000 from the states in order to raise a special force of 1,340 men to crush the rebellion. But except for Virginia, which placed a tax on tobacco, the states ignored Congress, thus preventing it from raising federal troops. Massachusetts authorities even went so far as to refuse to allow Continental troops raised there to take the field lest they interfere with the state's own efforts to suppress the rebellion. More than any other single event during the Confederation period, Shays' Rebellion revealed the inadequacy of Congress's military policy and injected into the debate over the national government's military powers the issue of public order.[53] As the almost uniformly hostile response to the uprising makes clear, Shays' Rebellion provided a turning point in the evolution of American attitudes toward crowd action. No longer accepted as a necessary extra-institutional wing of government, mobs increasingly came to be viewed as an insult and a threat to republican government.[54]

Most importantly, Shays' Rebellion energized the movement to revise the

Articles of Confederation and led directly to the calling of the Constitutional Convention. When the delegates met in Philadelphia in May 1787, the debate over the Constitution's military provisions, inextricably linked as they were with the question of national versus state power, called forth from the opponents of a strong national government the traditional denunciations of standing armies. But they were not alone. As James Madison, one of the leading Nationalists, wrote, "with respect to a standing army, I believe there was not a member in the Federal Convention who did not feel indignation at such an institution."[55] Nevertheless, compared to the Articles of Confederation, the military clauses of the Constitution represented a significant triumph for the Nationalists.[56] For the first time, the proposed Constitution gave Congress the exclusive power to declare war and raise and support both an army and navy. The President was made commander-in-chief of the armed forces and authorized to appoint military officers with the advice and consent of the Senate. The states were forbidden to keep troops, other than militia, in time of peace without the consent of Congress. In its militia provisions, the Constitution also signified an advance over the Articles of Confederation and thus represented a nationalist victory. Congress was authorized to call out the state militia in order to enforce federal law, maintain civil order, and repel invasions, and to exert control over the organization, arming, and disciplining of the state units.[57] Both clauses represented radical departures from the past when colonial and state militias had been virtually independent of British or congressional direction. Historians who argue that the Constitution's military provisions constitute a "bundle of compromises" cite the retention of a dual military system, the two-year limitation on military appropriations, and the division of power between the President and Congress.[58] But the "bundle of compromises" interpretation wrongly assumes that the Nationalists intended to eliminate the state militias and erect a classic standing army. Both Washington's "Sentiments" and the debates during the Federal Convention make clear that both a well-disciplined militia, and a regular army, were integral to the nationalists' peacetime military program.

The debates over the Constitution's ratification reveal the continuing strength of anti-army prejudice and the power of the Revolutionary War's ambiguous legacy. The Anti-Federalists resorted to the familiar principles of localism and Real Whig ideology in denouncing the proposed new frame of government. They contended that the consolidation of power in the central government would obliterate the states, that it would be impossible

to restrain power in a republican government stretching over a large territory containing a diverse and heterogeneous population, and that the preservation of liberty depended upon the preservation of state sovereignty.
Anti-Federalists particularly feared giving the national government the
power of the purse and control of the military. They worried that the new
government would use the army to collect unpopular and unjust taxes, and
questioned whether the country needed a standing army when at peace.
Drawing on their understanding of the "lessons" of the Revolutionary
War, they argued that the militia was sufficient for the nation's defense.
The self-evident nature of their argument is reflected in the questions
asked in a letter to the *Pennsylvania Herald:* "Had we a standing army
when the British invaded our peaceful shores? Was it a standing army that
gained the battles of Lexington and Bunker's Hill, and took the ill-fated
Burgoyne? Is not a well-regulated militia sufficient for every purpose of
internal defense? And which of you, my fellow citizens, is afraid of any
invasion from foreign powers that our brave militia would not be able
immediately to repel?"[59] Consequently, Anti-Federalist leaders such as
Elbridge Gerry, Luther Martin, and Patrick Henry viewed with particular
alarm the Constitution's militia clauses, which they interpreted, in Martin's words, as "the last *coup de grâce* to the State Governments."[60]

The nationalist advocates of the Constitution—now termed Federalists—denied that the Constitution would consolidate the states and instead
emphasized the division of power between the national government and
the states. In defending the Constitution's military provisions the Federalists also turned to the lessons of the Revolutionary War. Alexander
Hamilton's remarks in *Federalist* No. 25 typified Federalist opinion: "The
American Militia in the course of the late war, have by their valour on
numerous occasions, erected eternal monuments to their fame; but the
bravest of them feel and know, that the liberty of their country could not
have been established by their efforts alone." According to Hamilton, had
the United States relied on citizen soldiers alone during the war they
"would have lost us our independence."[61] Although the Federalists cred-
ited the Continental army with America's military victory, they argued in
both the Federal Convention and the press that a national military force,
encompassing both regular and militia soldiers, was essential to the preservation of American independence. Such a force, Federalists explained,
would prevent the proliferation of standing armies within each state and
thus forestall the Confederation's collapse into warring sections. They also

argued that because of America's geographic isolation, the nation required only a small military establishment to protect the frontier, seaports, and federal arsenals. Federalists stressed repeatedly that a national militia would render a large body of regular troops unnecessary and, in Tench Coxe's words, provide a "powerful check" upon their activities. Thus, as Lawrence Cress has amply documented, the Federalists directly confronted Anti-Federalists' fears of centralized military power by arguing that the Constitution's military provisions were "essential for the survival of republican institutions in America."[62]

The years between 1789 and 1803 were exceptionally violent ones in the history of the Western world, as the French Revolution toppled monarchies and devoured its own, the Napoleonic Wars engulfed all of Europe, and slave revolts wracked the West Indies. During the same period, the United States was not exempt from the social instability and endemic upheavals that beset Europe. In fact, it is no exaggeration to say that war, threats of war, and domestic insurrections were the major preoccupations of Americans in the 1790s. In addition to fighting Indians on the Western frontier and putting down two internal revolts—the Whiskey Rebellion in 1794 and Fries' Rebellion in 1799—the United States edged to the brink of war three times, with England and the Algerian pirates in 1793 and again with France in 1798. During each of these episodes, military policy became the target of partisan political attacks within the wider framework of national politics, as both Federalists and Republicans believed the fate of the republic hung in the balance. As a consequence of ideological and pragmatic reactions of these political parties to the events of this period, the United States created, in piecemeal fashion, a permanent peacetime military establishment that would embody the nation's defense policy for the next century.[63]

Although the Constitution's military clauses represented a nationalist triumph, the passage of the Second Amendment, declaring the necessity of a well-regulated militia "to the security of a free state" and granting citizens the right to bear arms, clearly reveals Americans' divided mind on military policy.[64] Consequently, ratification of the Constitution had very little immediate effect on the nation's peacetime establishment. In 1790, the Washington administration, acutely attuned to public opinion, initially chose a military policy of economy and political expediency by relying on militia with a small core of regulars to contain hostilities on the frontier. At the same time, Secretary of War Henry Knox presented Congress with the government's recommendations for translating the Constitution's military provisions into a permanent peacetime establishment. The cornerstone of the administration's plan called for a select militia in which citizens would be classed by age, with the burden of the required federally supervised monthly training falling on young men under the age of twenty-one. Knox defended the plan not only on the ground of military efficiency, but also because of its compatibility with republican principles. As Lawrence Cress has persuasively argued, Knox, Washington, and other Federalists, whose experience in the Revolutionary War and Confederation periods led them to abandon the notion that virtue alone ensured military preparedness, envisioned the select militia camps "inculcating discipline, discouraging idleness and dissipation, and imparting to the nation's youth a clear understanding" of the advantages of republican government.[65] Thus, Federalists advocated a select militia because they believed service in it could provide an apprenticeship in military proficiency, infuse young men with republican civic consciousness, and prevent the vices that usually caused republics to collapse. Knox also proposed increasing the army's authorized strength from 840 to 2,033 officers and enlisted men, but sharing Americans' fear of the military, he recommended regularly rotating these garrison troops back into the body politic, explaining "whatever may be the efficacy of a standing army in war, it cannot in peace be considered as friendly to the rights of human nature."[66]

Neither of the administration's proposals fared well in Congress, in part because the national legislature consistently reflected widespread fears of federal interference in state matters. In the case of the militia bill, Congress also objected to the cost and delayed acting, but because Indian relations in the Northwest were fast deteriorating, it resolved in 1790 to increase the army's strength to 1,216 men.[67] In 1792, Congress, expressing its traditional reliance on citizen soldiers, rejected outright Knox's proposal for federal control of the militia. Instead, Congress enacted the Uniform Militia Act which, contrary to Knox's plan, provided for universal military training and delegated to the states the responsibility of enrolling all free, white, able-bodied male citizens aged eighteen to forty-five for militia duty. In addition, where Knox's plan called for the federal government to arm the militia, the new law made each citizen responsible for providing his own arms, ammunition, and accoutrements. Congress also provided loopholes in the law to allow the states to evade compliance with federal guidelines. Thus, the law mandated that the militia's tactical organization—the breakdown of the militia into divisions, brigades, regiments, battalions, and companies, so essential to national uniformity—be left to state legislatures to implement when "convenient." Similarly, the law failed to provide guidelines for training the militia, to institute a system of inspection, or to impose penalties on either the states or individuals for noncompliance with its provisions.[68] Historians have failed to agree on the merits of the Uniform Militia Act. Scholars of the Uptonian school, such as John K. Mahon, have denounced the law as a "virtual abdication by the federal government of all authority over the state militias."[69] On the other side, Palmerians such as William H. Riker and Russell F. Weigley, while admitting the act was deficient from a military viewpoint, praise it for preserving the tradition of the citizen soldier and defend it because they believe it is unrealistic to expect more from a poor, dispersed, undisciplined agrarian society.[70] For better or worse, the Uniform Militia Act shaped American militia affairs for the next century.

At the same time that Congress was establishing the nation's militia system, the crushing defeats the Northwest Indians administered to the militia-dominated expeditions of Colonel Josiah Harmar and General Arthur St. Clair in 1790 and 1791 transformed America's policy toward the regular army. In the wake of these military defeats, Congress launched its first investigation of the executive branch of government and began rethinking the merits of professional soldiers, while the Washington administration jettisoned its reliance on militia and pressed for a large, regular army. The result was a watershed in the creation of America's permanent military establishment: Congress agreed with the administration's assessment and authorized a regular force of over 5,000 men enlisted for three years. The vote, not surprisingly, divided along sectional lines; what was significant was that both factions reversed their ideological positions. Except for ideologues such as Fisher Ames and Theodore Sedgwick, Federalist New England opposed the Indian wars and an increase in the number of troops, while the nascent Republicans in the Middle States and the South voted unanimously in favor of the measure, despite serious reservations. In August 1794, General Anthony Wayne, at the head of the newly trained and organized army—dubbed the Legion of the United States—destroyed the power of the Indians in the Northwest at the Battle of Fallen Timbers and attested to the prowess of regulars.[71]

Nevertheless, the success of Wayne's Legion removed the rationale for a sizable regular force and triggered congressional motions to reduce the size of the army. Among the traditional opponents of standing armies, including the Republicans, who had coalesced from a legislative faction in 1790 to a political party by 1794, economic arguments began to overshadow ideological ones. Downplaying their fears of standing armies, they railed instead against the cost of Wayne's Legion and angrily pointed out that 40 percent of the government's total expenditures, nearly $2,700,000, went for the War Department's budget. The Federalists countered that regular troops were cheapest and most effective; with relations with Britain worsening, Republicans conceded the debate. On 3 March 1795, Congress authorized a complete Legion for another three years. A year later, however, the entire context within which Federalists and Republicans debated America's military policy altered with the negotiation of the Jay Treaty promising imminent British evacuation of the Western forts, the Treaty of Grenville establishing peace with the Northwest Indians, and improved conditions in the Southwest. With British influence as good as eliminated from the Northwest and peace prevailing all along the Western frontier, the continued existence of the Legion of the United States could not be justified militarily, though Federalists argued the nation's need for preparedness. When Congress met in 1796, the significance of its actions lay less in the debate which, energized by fierce partisan passions, simply reiterated traditional fears of standing armies and denounced their extravagant cost, or in its decision to cut the Legion's authorized size, but rather in the Republicans' acceptance, albeit with much grumbling, of the necessity of a small, peacetime standing army to garrison frontier posts, coastal forts, and federal arsenals. The far-reaching consequences of Congress's action are underscored by Richard Kohn's statement that "in 1796 Congress ratified the basic dimensions of military policy for the next century, not as wartime expedients, but as a permanent foundation for American security in peacetime." Ironically, while the Federalists failed in their immediate goal to maintain the army's size, they succeeded in their long-sought objective, first enunciated in Washington's "Sentiments": the nation's acceptance of a standing army in peacetime.[72]

This is a story of paradoxes, so perhaps it is appropriate that it was the Republicans, with Thomas Jefferson in the presidency, who by design not only maintained the Federalist-established military institutions, but also extended them in 1802 by founding the United States Military Academy at West Point.[73] As a consequence of the recent work of Dumas Malone,

Reginald C. Stuart, and Theodore J. Crackel, it is no longer tenable to view Jefferson as a dogmatic pacifist intransigently wedded to the militia, for as these works demonstrate, Jefferson's views on foreign diplomacy, domestic politics, and military matters were complex, pragmatic, and flexible. Although a consistent advocate of noninvolvement in foreign affairs, strict governmental economy, and reduction of the national debt, Jefferson also firmly believed, as Stuart has perceptively noted, "that the international sphere was predatory, not benign, that weakness invited aggression, and that the country had to be on perpetual guard against encroachments."[74] Consequently, on the crucial questions of a standing army and the militia, Jefferson's military policies were compatible with Federalist conceptions of a peacetime establishment. At the beginning of his administration, Jefferson rejected the opportunity to disband the regular army; instead, he sought to "Republicanize" it by cosmetically reducing and reorganizing it, a goal he achieved when the Republican-controlled Congress passed the Military Peace Establishment Act of 1802. Earlier historians have interpreted this piece of legislation as evidence of Republicans' hostility toward standing armies and their commitment to frugality in government. But in reality, as Crackel has demonstrated, the Act failed to reduce the actual size of the army and saved very little money.[75] What it did do was allow Jefferson to dismantle the apparatus of Federalist control of the army by eliminating eighty-eight Federalist officers and appointing twenty additional Republican faithful. Similar political motives lay behind Jefferson's creation of a military academy at West Point. Jefferson believed that only by preparing Republican sons for the officer corps would the Federalist monopoly on the commissioned ranks be broken.[76]

Jefferson also conceived of the militia in Federalist terms. As President, he never maintained that the militia should bear the brunt of battle, but, like most Federalists, believed that the country's defense rested on "a well-disciplined militia—our best reliance in peace and for the first moments of war, till regulars may relieve them."[77] In pursuit of this goal, Jefferson spoke throughout his first term of the need to reform the militia, and at the beginning of his second administration presented Congress with a militia classification bill that echoed Henry Knox's 1790 proposals. Consistent with its traditional abhorrence of federal intervention into state military matters, the House of Representatives never let the bill get out of committee. Later, during the War of 1812, Jefferson, sounding like George Washington or Emory Upton, blamed Congress for the performance of the citizen soldiers: "I trust it is now seen that the refusal to class the militia, when proposed years ago, is the real source of all our misfortunes in this war."[78]

Uptonian military history—criticizing civilian military decisions and denouncing battlefield performance with an eye toward affecting military policy—will always be with us, and the conclusions drawn from these studies—increased preparedness and larger armies—will always be controversial, because, at bottom, they are inherently political ones, live issues in the Jamesian sense, intensely relevant to our very existence. Palmerian military history—extolling civilian control of the military and insisting that trained citizen-soldiers are sufficient for the nation's defense—will also always be with us, because it reflects the cherished American belief that military institutions must be made compatible with a democratic society. Together, Uptonian and Palmerian scholars have raised important issues and made invaluable contributions by laying out the institutional development of American military policy and practices. But they have been overly concerned with passing judgments on the results of military legislation and battles and too little interested in understanding the complex circumstances which shaped decisions affecting the armed forces. The studies by the new military historians have, in great part, redressed this failing by locating the creation of a peacetime military establishment within the political, economic, social, and ideological context of colonial, Revolutionary, and early national America. They have shown, for example, how various aspects of colonial political culture affected the way Americans recruited the Continental army, supplied their troops, and motivated their men and how war profoundly affected many revolutionaries, broadening their localistic outlook, weakening their distrust of standing armies, and strengthening their appreciation of a strong national government. Of course, not all Americans experienced the Revolution in the same way; consequently, the war left them with a divided legacy that would continue to shape the debate over the creation of permanent peacetime military institutions in the immediate postwar and early national period.

Most importantly, the new military historians have described the complex factors by which, during the 1790s, Federalists and Republicans forged America's first peacetime military establishment out of the crucible of ideological warfare, economic frugality, and military necessity. But, as J.C.A. Stagg has perceptively noted, the important point to emphasize is not the bitterness of foreign policy quarrels in the 1790s, but rather "the fact that there was still a fair degree of consensus over how the military forces of the republic should be organized."[79] By 1802, that consensus resulted in Federalists and Republicans agreeing, albeit in a piecemeal fashion, to the establishment of a small, peacetime standing army stationed on the frontier, coastal forts, federal arsenals, and a military academy at West Point. It is apparent that the new military historians have begun to do for the early national period what others have done for the Revolution: to portray the complex dynamic between war and society. By transcending the Uptonian/Palmerian questions, these studies can only reinforce scholars' increasing recognition that a deep understanding of the American past—the history of a nation founded in blood—must include a thorough knowledge of military history.[80]

NOTES

1. Peter Paret, "The History of War," in Felix Gilbert and Stephen R. Graubard, eds., *Historical Studies Today* (New York, 1972), 377; Allan R. Millett, "The Study of American Military History in the United States," *Military Affairs*, 41 (1977), 59; Michael Howard, "The Demand for Military History," *Times Literary Supplement*, November 13, 1969, 1294.

2. John Bowditch, "War and the Historian," in H. Stuart Hughes, ed., *Teachers of History: Essays in Honor of Laurence Bradford Packard* (Ithaca, 1954), 322–25; Louis Morton, "The Historian and the Study of War," *Mississippi Valley Historical Review*, 48 (1961), 600–601, 607, 608–10; John K. Mahon, "Teaching and Research on Military History in the United States," *The Historian*, 27 (1965), 170–76. An example of the demoralization that can occur while teaching military history in a hostile academic setting is illustrated by Mahon's plaintive comment in introducing the article's bibliography: "On the remote chance that this article may induce even one reader to approach the threshold of military history, a few sound general works in English, constituting a good introduction to the field are listed below" (ibid., 183).

3. Gunther Rothenberg, "Teaching Military History in a State University," in Major David MacIsaac, ed., *The Military and Society*, Proceedings of the Fifth Military History Symposium, United States Air Force Academy (Washington, D.C., 1972), 90. One scholar would extend the period to 1979. See Walter Emil Kaegi, Jr., "The Crisis in Military Historiography," *Armed Forces and Society*, 7 (1981), 300–302.

4. Morton, "Historian and the Study of War," *MVHR*, 48 (1961), 600.

5. Ibid., 604–605; John Shy, review of Howard H. Peckham, *The Colonial Wars, 1689–1762* (Chicago, 1964), in *William and Mary Quarterly*, 3rd ser., 22 (1965), 156. Don Higginbotham traces this theme with particular reference to the Revolutionary era in "American Historians and the Military History of the American Revolution," *American Historical Review*, 70 (1964), 24–27.

6. Walter Millis, *Military History*, American Historical Association, Service Center for Teachers of History, Publication no. 39 (Washington, D.C., 1961), 16. Russell F.

Weigley offers some sobering and insightful observations on military history's usefulness. See his "Introduction" in Weigley, ed., *New Dimensions in Military History: An Anthology* (San Rafael, Ca., 1975), 1–14. For a more detailed statement of the utilitarian value of studying military history, see Thomas E. Griess, "A Perspective on Military History," in John E. Jessup, Jr. and Robert W. Coakley, eds., *A Guide to the Study and Use of Military History* (Washington, D.C., 1979), 31–39. See also Brooks E. Kleber, "History and Military Education: The U.S. Army," *Mil. Aff.*, 42 (1978), 136.

7. Paret, "History of War," in Gilbert and Graubard, eds., *Historical Studies,* 380.

8. On the nature of American liberalism, see Samuel Huntington, *The Soldier and the State: The Theory and Politics of Civil—Military Relations* (Cambridge, Mass., 1957), 143–62; Morton, "Historian and the Study of War," *MVHR*, 48 (1961), 612–13; Rothenberg, "Teaching Military History," in MacIsaac, ed., *Military and Society*, 90. Historians rarely make explicit their distaste for conventional military history. Richard D. Challener offers an unusually frank statement of such attitudes: "Furthermore, when the army teaches military history, it's trying to achieve certain purposes that a civilian, like myself, doesn't want to have anything to do with." Challener, "Military History as Liberal Education," *Princeton Alumni Weekly*, March 7, 1958, 11.

9. For an incisive history of military thought, see Russell F. Weigley, *Towards an American Army: Military Thought from Washington to Marshall* (New York, 1962). I have relied heavily on this work in my discussion of Upton and Palmer.

10. A useful, short biography of Upton is Stephen E. Ambrose, *Upton and the Army* (Baton Rouge, 1964). See also Peter S. Michie, *The Life and Letters of Emory Upton* (New York, 1885), which reproduces much of Upton's correspondence.

11. Emory Upton to Henry A. Du Pont, 30 September 1877, in Michie, *Upton*, 419.

12. Emory Upton, *The Military Policy of the United States* (Washington, D.C., 1904), 15, 11, 41, 38.

13. Ibid., 66–67; quotations on 66. See also Weigley, *Towards an American Army*, 100–126; Ambrose, *Upton*, 112–35.

14. Weigley, *Towards an American Army*, 199.

15. Ibid., 200–217.

16. Ibid., 224–28. For a massive biography of Palmer, see I.B. Holley, Jr., *General John M. Palmer, Citizen Soldiers, and the Army of a Democracy*, Contributions in Military History, no. 28 (Westport, Conn., 1982).

17. Weigley, *Towards an American Army*, 230–41; quotation on 238.

18. John McAuley Palmer, *Washington, Lincoln, and Wilson: Three War Statesmen* (New York, 1930), pt. 1; Palmer, *America in Arms* (New York, 1941), chaps. 1–4; quotation from Holley, Jr., *Palmer*, 560.

19. For examples of the Uptonian interpretation of the early American army, see C. Joseph Bernardo and Eugene H. Bacon, *American Military Policy: Its Development Since 1775* (Harrisburg, Pa., 1955); William A. Ganoe, *History of the United States Army*, rev. ed. (New York, 1942); R. Ernest and Trevor N. Dupuy, *Military Heritage of America* (New York, 1956). Recently, strong defenders of the militia's role during the American Revolutionary War have appeared. See, for example, Robert C. Pugh, "The Revolutionary Militia in the Southern Campaign, 1780–1781," *William and Mary Quarterly*, 3rd ser., 14 (1957), 154–75; Clyde Ferguson, "Functions of the Partisan-Militia in the South During the American Revolution: An Interpretation," in W. Robert Higgins, ed., *The Revolutionary War in the South: Power, Conflict, and Leadership: Essays in Honor of John Richard Alden* (Durham, N.C., 1979), 239–58; Ferguson, "Carolina and Georgia Patriot and Loyalist Militia in Action, 1778–1783," in Jeffrey J. Crow and Larry E. Tise, eds., *The*

Southern Experience in the American Revolution (Chapel Hill, N.C., 1978), 174–202. As a result of these studies and similar ones, a more balanced account of the relative merits of regular troops and militia has begun to appear. See especially Don Higginbotham, "The American Militia: A Traditional Institution with Revolutionary Responsibilities," in Higginbotham, ed., *Reconsiderations on the Revolutionary War: Selected Essays*, Contributions in Military History, no. 14 (Westport, Conn., 1978), 83–103; Russell F. Weigley, *History of the United States Army*, enlarged ed. (New York, 1984); Robert Middlekauff, *The Glorious Cause: The American Revolution, 1763–1789* (New York, 1983); Allan R. Millett and Peter Maslowski, *For the Common Defense: The Military History of the United States of America* (New York, 1984).

20. It is only within this Uptonian/Palmerian context that one can fully understand John Shy's disclaimer: "My motive [in writing] is not to bolster the Pentagon, the House Armed Services Committee, or the *New York Times* in their latest disagreement over the draft or the volunteer army, not even to provide a new key to the reinterpretation of the American Revolution, but only to offer ways of thinking about our early military history, and of more satisfactorily relating that history to the general history of colonial America." Shy, "A New Look at the Colonial Militia," in *People Numerous and Armed* (New York, 1976), 23–24.

21. Robert E. Shalhope provides a complete bibliography and analysis of these historians' work in two articles: "Republicanism and Early American Historiography," *William and Mary Quarterly*, 3rd ser., 39 (1982), 334–56, and "Toward a Republican Synthesis: The Emergence of an Understanding of Republicanism in American Historiography," ibid., 29 (1972), 49–80. For the most important of the numerous works that have appeared since Shalhope's 1982 article, see John M. Murrin, "Political Development," in Jack P. Greene and J.R. Pole, eds., *Colonial British America: Essays in the New History of the Early Modern Era* (Baltimore and London, 1984), 408–56; J.R. Pole, *The Gift of Government: Political Responsibility from the English Restoration to American Independence* (Athens, Ga., 1983); Joyce Appleby, *Capitalism and a New Social Order: The Republican Social Vision of the 1790s* (New York and London, 1984); John P. Diggins, *The Lost Soul of American Politics: Virtue, Self-Interest, and the Foundations of Liberalism* (New York, 1984); Richard L. Bushman, *King and People in Provincial Massachusetts* (Chapel Hill, N.C., 1985); Lance Banning, "Jeffersonian Ideology Revisited: Liberal and Classical Ideas in the New American Republic," *William and Mary Quarterly*, 3rd ser., 43 (1986), 3–19; Joyce Appleby, "Republicanism in Old and New Contexts," ibid., 20–34. For an effort to analyze colonial America's ideological pluralism in the era of the American Revolution, see E. Wayne Carp, "Up From Civic Virtue," review essay, *Pennsylvania Magazine of History and Biography*, 108 (1984), 367–75. Also useful are Linda Kerber, "The Republican Ideology of the Revolutionary Generation," *American Quarterly*, 37 (1985), 474–96; Cathy Matson and Peter Onuf, "Toward a Republican Empire: Interest and Ideology in Revolutionary America," ibid., 496–531; Daniel Walker Howe, "European Sources of Political Ideas in Jeffersonian America," *Reviews in American History*, 10 (1982), 28–44; John Ashworth, "The Jeffersonians: Classical Republicans or Liberal Capitalists?" review essay, *Journal of American Studies*, 18 (1984), 425–35.

22. John Shy, *Toward Lexington: The Role of the British Army in the Coming of the Revolution* (Princeton, 1965); Shy, *People Numerous and Armed*; Don Higginbotham, *The War of American Independence: Military Attitudes, Policies, and Practice, 1763–1789* (New York, 1971); Higginbotham, *George Washington and the American Military Tradition*, Mercer University Lamar Memorial Lectures, no. 27 (Athens, Ga., 1985); Charles Royster, *A Revolutionary People at War: The Continental Army and American Character, 1775–1783*

(Chapel Hill, N.C., 1979); Royster, *Light-Horse Harry Lee and the Legacy of the American Revolution* (New York, 1981); Lawrence Delbert Cress, *Citizens in Arms: The Army and Militia in American Society to the War of 1812* (Chapel Hill, N.C., 1982); John Philip Reid, *In Defiance of the Law: The Standing Army Controversy, the Two Constitutions, and the Coming of the American Revolution* (Chapel Hill, N.C., 1982); Fred Anderson, *A People's Army: Massachusetts Soldiers and Society in the Seven Years' War* (Chapel Hill, N.C., 1984); John Todd White, "Standing Armies in Time of War: Republican Theory and Military Practice During the American Revolution" (Ph.D. diss., George Washington University, 1978). My own contribution to the literature is *To Starve the Army at Pleasure: Continental Army Administration and American Political Culture, 1775–1783* (Chapel Hill, N.C. and London, 1984). A short overview of this scholarship is provided by Reginald C. Stuart, " 'Engines of Tyranny': Recent Historiography of Standing Armies During the Era of the American Revolution," *Canadian Journal of History*, 19 (1984), 183–99. James Kirby Martin and Mark Edward Lender incorporate much of the "new" military history in their solid synthesis of the entire period, *A Respectable Army: The Military Origins of the Republic, 1763–1789* (Arlington Heights, Ill., 1982).

23. For a discussion of early American political culture and localism in particular, see Carp, *To Starve the Army*, 5–12, 219. For several recent excellent discussions of the importance of localism in colonial political, social, and religious life, see Thomas Bender, *Community and Social Change in America* (New Brunswick, N.J., 1978), 61–71; Christine Leigh Heyrman, *Commerce and Culture: The Maritime Communities of Colonial Massachusetts, 1690–1750* (New York, 1984), 86–95, 136–41, 274–75; Gregory H. Nobles, *Divisions throughout the Whole: Politics and Society in Hampshire County, Massachusetts, 1740–1775* (New York, 1983); Thomas P. Slaughter, "The Tax Man Cometh: Ideological Opposition to Internal Taxes, 1760–1790," *William and Mary Quarterly*, 3rd ser., 41 (1984), 566–91. See also Joshua I. Miller's suggestive study, "Local Autonomy in Early American Politics: Decentralist Ideas and Practices, 1630–1789" (Ph.D. diss., Princeton University, 1984).

24. John Adams to Abbé de Mably, 1782, in Charles F. Adams, ed., *The Works of John Adams* (Boston, 1851), 5: 494–96; quotation on 496.

25. Weigley, *United States Army*, 4.

26. Cress, *Citizens in Arms*, 5–6. For an excellent discussion of recruiting practices during the Seven Years' War in Massachusetts, see Anderson, *People's Army*, chap. 2. A 1695 Massachusetts law entitled "An Act to Prevent the Deserting of the Frontiers" epitomizes the militia's failure as a fighting force. See John M. Murrin, "Anglicizing an American Colony: The Transformation of Provincial Massachusetts" (Ph.D. diss., Yale University, 1966), 69. Marcus Cunliffe discusses the tradition of voluntarism in *Soldiers and Civilians: The Martial Spirit in America* (New York, 1968).

27. Millett and Maslowski, *For the Common Defense*, 7. This and the next paragraph are based on the following studies: Douglas Edward Leach, *Arms for Empire: A Military History of the British Colonies in North America, 1607–1763* (New York, 1973), 9–38; John K. Mahon, *History of the Militia and the National Guard* (New York, 1983), chaps. 1–2; Weigley, *United States Army*, chap. 1; Cress, *Citizens in Arms*, pt. 1; Cress, "Radical Whiggery on the Role of the Military: Ideological Roots of the American Revolutionary Militia," *Journal of the History of Ideas*, 40 (1979), 43–60; Ronald L. Boucher, "The Colonial Militia as a Social Institution: Salem, Massachusetts, 1764–1775," *Mil. Aff.*, 37 (1973), 125–29; John Shy, "A New Look at the Colonial Militia," in Shy, *People Numerous and Armed*, 22–33; Murrin, "Anglicizing an American Colony," chap. 3. For a discussion of the colonial militia within the context of anglicization, see E. Wayne Carp,

"Early American Military History: A Review of Recent Work," *Virginia Magazine of History and Biography*, 94 (1986), 268–72. The bibliography in Mahon, *History of the Militia*, 323–56, and his article, "Bibliographic Essay on Research into the History of the Militia and National Guard," *Mil. Aff.*, 48 (1984), 74–77, provide comprehensive guides to the latest scholarship, much of it unpublished, on the militia.

28. Boucher, "Colonial Militia as a Social Institution," *Mil. Aff.*, 37 (1973), 125–29.

29. Pauline Maier, "Popular Uprisings and Civil Authority in Eighteenth-Century America," *William and Mary Quarterly*, 3rd ser., 27 (1970), 13, 19–20; John Lax and William Pencak, "The Knowles Riot and the Crisis of the 1740s in Massachusetts," *Perspectives in American History*, 10 (1976), 167, 190–91; Heyrman, *Commerce and Culture*, 309–11; Edward Countryman, " 'Out of the Bounds of the Law': Northern Land Rioters in the Eighteenth Century," in Alfred F. Young, ed., *The American Revolution: Explorations in the History of American Radicalism* (Dekalb, Ill., 1976), 43. These studies are by no means definitive. We need a systematic study of the militia's relationship to the eighteenth-century crowd.

30. Lois G. Schwoerer, *"No Standing Armies!": The Antiarmy Ideology in Seventeenth-Century England* (Baltimore, 1974); Cress, *Citizens in Arms*, 16–25; Bernard Bailyn, *The Ideological Origins of the American Revolution* (Cambridge, Mass., 1967), chap. 2.

31. Bernard Bailyn, *The Origins of American Politics* (New York, 1967), chap. 1; quotation from *A Report of the Record Commissioners of the City of Boston Containing the Boston Town Records, 1770 through 1777* (Boston, 1887), 133. For extensive evidence of colonial denunciations of standing armies immediately prior to the war's outbreak, see James Gregory Bradsher, "Preserving the Revolution: Civil-Military Relations During the American War for Independence" (Ph.D. diss., University of Massachusetts, 1984), 5–33, 73–74, 183–84.

32. Gordon Wood, *The Creation of the American Republic, 1776–1787* (Chapel Hill, N.C., 1969), 47. Paine quoted in ibid.

33. John R. Howe, "Republican Thought and Political Violence," *American Quarterly*, 19 (1967), 151. See also Wood, *American Republic*, chap. 2; Willi Paul Adams, *The First American Constitutions: Republican Ideology and the Making of the State Constitutions in the Revolutionary Era* (Chapel Hill, N.C., 1980), chap. 4; Cress, *Citizens in Arms*, 16–18; and both Shalhope articles cited in note 21 above.

34. E. Wayne Carp, "The Origins of the Nationalist Movement of 1780–1783: Congressional Administration and the Continental Army," *PMHB*, 107 (1983), 362–92; Royster, *Revolutionary People at War*, 329–30.

35. Royster, *Revolutionary People at War*, 25; Anderson, *People's Army*, chap. 6.

36. White, "Standing Armies," 138–96; Weigley, *United States Army*, 34–35. On the organization of the Continental Army, see Robert K. Wright, Jr., *The Continental Army*, Army Lineage Series (Washington, D.C., 1983). Richard Buel, Jr., believes that the manpower needs of America's agricultural economy was also a factor in Congress's decision to turn to a regular army. Buel, "Samson Shorn: The Impact of the Revolutionary War on Estimates of the Republic's Strength," in Ronald Hoffman and Peter J. Albert, eds., *Arms and Independence: The Military Character of the American Revolution* (Charlottesville, Va., 1984), 145–48.

37. Interestingly, only Horatio Gates and Charles Lee, both former British officers, strongly advocated reliance on militia. See Paul David Nelson, "Citizen Soldiers or Regulars: The Views of General Officers on the Military Establishment, 1775–1781," *Mil. Aff.*, 43 (1979), 127–30. See also John Shy, "Charles Lee: The Soldier as Radical," in George Athan Billias, ed., *George Washington's Generals* (New York, 1964), 22–48; Cress, *Citi-*

zens in Arms, 54–56. On the importance of a limited-war mentality to the Revolutionary generation, see Reginald C. Stuart, *War and American Thought: From the Revolution to the Monroe Doctrine* (Kent, Ohio, 1982), chap. 2, esp. 31–32.

38. Higginbotham, "American Militia," in Higginbotham, ed., *Reconsiderations on the Revolutionary War*, 91; Ferguson, "Functions of the Partisan-Militia," in Higgins, ed., *Revolutionary War in the South*, 239–58; Ferguson, "Carolina and Georgia Patriot and Loyalist Militia," in Crow and Tise, eds., *Southern Experience*, 174–202. Although Congressmen favored using militia, they too never contemplated a popular guerilla war. See Walter Millis, *Arms and Men: American Military History and Military Policy from the Revolution to the Present* (New York, 1956), 25–26. A study of the Loyalist militia is needed. Its inefficiency is insightfully discussed in Franklin and Mary Wickwire, *Cornwallis and the War of Independence* (London, 1970), 184–86, 226–27.

39. John Shy, "Hearts and Minds in the American Revolution: The Case of 'Long Bill' Scott and Peterborough, New Hampshire," in *People Numerous and Armed*, 177; Mahon, *History of the Militia*, 38–44.

40. Wright, *Continental Army*, 91–92; Benjamin Rush to John Adams, 1 October 1777 in L.H. Butterfield, ed., *Letters of Benjamin Rush* (Princeton, 1951), I, 157. The best study of the difficulties affecting state mobilization of Continental troops is Richard Buel, Jr., *Dear Liberty: Connecticut's Mobilization for the Revolutionary War* (Middletown, Conn., 1980).

41. William Henry Glasson, *History of Military Pension Legislation in the United States* (New York, 1900), 17; White, "Standing Armies," 277–78, 195.

42. This and the following paragraph are based on Carp, *To Starve the Army*, chaps. 1, 2, 7, and 8. See also Erna Risch, *Supplying Washington's Army*, Special Studies Series (Washington, D.C., 1983); R. Arthur Bowler, "Logistics and Operations in the American Revolution," in Higginbotham, ed., *Reconsiderations on the Revolutionary War*, 54–71. For differing interpretations of the Nationalists, see E. James Ferguson, *The Power of the Purse: A History of American Public Finance, 1776–1790* (Chapel Hill, N.C., 1961), chap. 6; Jack N. Rakove, *The Beginnings of National Politics: An Interpretive History of the Continental Congress* (New York, 1979), chap. 13.

43. The fullest account of the Newburgh conspiracy is Richard H. Kohn, "The Inside History of the Newburgh Conspiracy: America and the Coup d'Etat," *William and Mary Quarterly*, 3rd ser., 27 (1970), 187–220. Several scholars have challenged Kohn on various points. See Paul David Nelson, "Horatio Gates at Newburgh: A Misunderstood Role," ibid., 29 (1972), 143–51; C. Edward Skeen, "The Newburgh Conspiracy Reconsidered," ibid., 31 (1974), 273–90. Each article is immediately followed by Kohn's rebuttal. A good short summary of the controverted issues can be found in Martin and Lender, *Respectable Army*, 186–94.

44. Quoted in Kohn, "Inside History of the Newburgh Conspiracy," *William and Mary Quarterly*, 3rd ser., 27 (1970), 189.

45. Richard H. Kohn, *Eagle and Sword: The Beginnings of the Military Establishment in America* (New York, 1975), 17; Glasson, *Military Pension Legislation*, 18–19.

46. Minor Myers, Jr., *Liberty Without Anarchy: A History of the Society of Cincinnati* (Charlottesville, Va., 1983), 49–51; Wallace E. Davies, "The Society of the Cincinnati in New England," *William and Mary Quarterly*, 3rd ser., 5 (1948), 3–25.

47. Kenneth R. Bowling, "New Light on the Philadelphia Mutiny of 1783: Federal-State Confrontation at the Close of the War for Independence," *PMHB*, 101 (1977), 431. The study of the Continental army's demobilization and the postwar reintegration of soldiers into their communities remains a neglected topic. Both Louis C. Hatch, *The Administra-*

tion of the American Revolutionary Army (New York, 1904), chaps. 8–9, and Dixon
Wecter, *When Johnny Comes Marching Home* (New York, 1944), pt. 1, barely scratch the
surface. Although we know that some soldiers experienced a change in political perspective, abandoning localistic orientations for more national, cosmopolitan outlooks, we still
need additional research on the social, economic, and psychological consequences of
Revolutionary War service. For studies of soldiers' altered political perspective, see
William Benton, "Pennsylvania Revolutionary Officers and the Federal Constitution,"
Pennsylvania History, 31 (1964), 419–35; Edwin G. Burrows, "Military Experience and
the Origins of Federalism and Antifederalism," in Jacob Judd and Irwin H. Polishook,
eds., *Aspects of Early New York Society and Politics* (Tarrytown, N.Y., 1974), 83–92;
Carp, *To Starve the Army*, chap. 8. An outstanding study of the war's effects on one
individual is Royster, *Light-Horse Harry*. One little-used but potentially valuable collection for investigating the experiences of the Revolutionary veterans, comprising one-
quarter million items, is the *Revolutionary War Pension and Bounty-Land Warrant Application Files, 1800–1900*, National Archives and Records Service, Microfilm Publication
M804 (Washington, D.C., 1972). For examples of the use of these pension records in
social history, see the special issue of *Prologue: Journal of the National Archives*, 16 (Fall
1984). A representative sample of the pension files has been published in John Dann,
ed., *The Revolution Remembered: Eyewitness Accounts of the War for Independence* (Chicago, 1980).

48. Upton, *Military Policy*, chap. 8; quotations on 72, 74, 79, 75.

49. Kohn, *Eagle and Sword*, 41–47; Higginbotham, *War of American Independence*, 441–43;
Weigley, *United States Army*, 79–80; George Washington, "Sentiments on a Peace Establishment," 2 May 1783, in John C. Fitzpatrick, ed., *The Writings of George Washington
from the Original Manuscript Sources, 1745–1799* (Washington, D.C., 1931–44), 26: 374–
98; quotations on 375, 387; J.C.A. Stagg, *Mr. Madison's War: Politics, Diplomacy, and
Warfare in the Early American Republic, 1783–1830* (Princeton, 1983), 121.

50. Higginbotham, *War of American Independence*, 443–44; quotation on 444.

51. Kohn, *Eagle and Sword*, 60. For a detailed history of the First American Regiment, see
William H. Guthman, *March to Massacre: A History of the First Seven Years of the United
States Army, 1784–1791* (New York, 1970).

52. Higginbotham, *War of American Independence*, 445–46; Weigley, *United States Army*, 83;
Guthman, *March to Massacre*, 130–35; Frederick W. Marks, III, *Independence on Trial:
Foreign Affairs and the Making of the Constitution* (Baton Rouge, La., 1973), chap. 1;
Board of Treasury quotation from Edmund Cody Burnett, *The Continental Congress*
(New York, 1941), 659.

53. Higginbotham, *War of American Independence*, 445–46; Weigley, *United States Army*, 83;
Richard Hobbs Fraser, "The Foundations of American Military Policy (1783–1800),"
(Ph.D. diss., University of Oklahoma, 1959), 68–80. David P. Szatmary, *Shays' Rebellion: The Making of an Agrarian Insurrection* (Amherst, Mass., 1980), has a preface and
notes that provide a comprehensive historiographic overview of the topic. Not mentioned in Szatmary's bibliography, but worth consulting, is Neville Meaney, "The Trial
of Popular Sovereignty in Post-Revolutionary America: The Case of Shays' Rebellion,"
in Meaney, ed., *Studies on the American Revolution* (South Melbourne, Australia, 1976),
152–220.

54. Maier, "Popular Uprisings," *William and Mary Quarterly*, 3rd ser., (1970), 33–34. In a
perceptive discussion of recent interpretations of popular disorder in the early republic,
Paul A. Gilje notes that "the eighteenth-century mob was driven largely by a communal
spirit . . . while nineteenth-century riots represented the shattering of that communal

spirit as different segments within society splintered along ethnic, racial, religious, class and even neighborhood lines." Gilje, " 'The mob begin to think and reason': Recent Trends in Studies of American Popular Disorder, 1700–1850," *Maryland Historian*, 12 (1981), 30–32; quotation on 32. All aspects of crowd activity in the early national period need much more study.

55. Madison quoted in Weigley, *United States Army*, 86. The point is also made in Bernard Donahoe and Marshall Smelser, "The Congressional Power to Raise Armies: The Constitutional and Ratifying Conventions, 1787–1788," *Review of Politics*, 33 (1971), 204.

56. Don Higginbotham, "The Debate Over National Military Institutions: An Issue Slowly Resolved, 1775–1815," in William M. Fowler, Jr. and Wallace Coyle, eds., *The American Revolution: Changing Perspectives* (Boston, 1979), 158; Kohn, *Eagle and Sword*, 76–80.

57. Constitution, art. I, sect. 8, cls. 11–16; art. II, sect. 2, in Samuel Eliot Morison, *Sources and Documents Illustrating the American Revolution, 1764–1788*, 2nd ed. (New York, 1965), 297–99.

58. Historians favoring the "bundle of compromises" interpretation include John K. Mahon, *The American Militia: Decade of Decision, 1789–1800* (Gainesville, Fla., 1960), 9–13; William Riker, *Soldiers of the States: The Role of the National Guard in American Democracy* (Washington, D.C., 1957), 14–17; Weigley, *United States Army*, 86–88; Millis, *Arms and Men*, 47–49.

59. "A Democratic Federalist," *Pennsylvania Herald*, 17 October 1787, in Merrill Jensen et al., eds., *The Documentary History of the Ratification of the States*, vol. 2: *Pennsylvania* (Madison, Wisc., 1976), 197. The letter, a reply to James Wilson's 6 October speech at the Pennsylvania ratifying convention, was reprinted in the *Pennsylvania Packet*, 23 October; New York *Morning Post*, 22 October; and the Baltimore *Maryland Gazette*, 26 October 1787.

60. Charles Warren, *The Making of the Constitution* (Boston, 1929), 517–20; Martin quotation on 519n. Jackson Turner Main, *The Antifederalists: Critics of the Constitution* (Chapel Hill, N.C., 1961), 146–48; Frederick R. Black, "The American Revolution as 'Yardstick' in Debates of the Constitution, 1787–1788," American Philosophical Society, *Proceedings*, 117 (1973), 176; Cress, *Citizens in Arms*, 98–102. Cecelia M. Kenyon, ed., *The Antifederalists* (Indianapolis, 1966), contains a good selection of Anti-Federalist writings denouncing the Constitution's military provisions. For a list of Anti-Federalist additions and amendments regarding the Constitution's military sections, see Higginbotham, *War of American Independence*, 458. James H. Hutson, "Country, Court, and Constitution: Antifederalism and the Historians," *William and Mary Quarterly*, 3rd ser., 38 (1981), is an excellent survey of the secondary material and integrates the Anti-Federalists into the Country/Real Whig tradition.

61. *Federalist* No. 25, in Jacob E. Cooke, ed., *The Federalist Papers*, (Middletown, Conn., 1961), 161–62. Other Federalist papers dealing with the Constitution's military clauses include numbers 3, 4, 5, 8, 11, 23, 41, and 46. See also Black, "American Revolution as 'Yardstick,' " APS, *Proc.*, 117 (1973), 174–75; Donahoe and Smelser, "Congressional Power to Raise Armies," *Rev. Pol.*, 33 (1971), 207, 209.

62. Kohn, *Eagle and Sword*, 83–85; Cress, *Citizens in Arms*, 103–109; quotation on 105.

63. For a superb historiographic essay of the early national period, see Jacob E. Cooke, "The Federalist Age: A Reappraisal," in George Athan Billias and Gerald N. Grob, eds., *American History: Retrospect and Prospect* (New York, 1971), 85–153.

64. Recent historians disagree whether or not the Second Amendment reflected a liberal or republican America. See Robert E. Shalhope, "The Ideological Origins of the Second

Amendment," *Journal of American History*, 69 (1982), 599–614; Lawrence Delbert Cress, "An Armed Community: The Origins and Meaning of the Right to Bear Arms," ibid., 71 (1984), 22–42; Shalhope and Cress, "The Second Amendment and the Right to Bear Arms: An Exchange," ibid., 587–93.

65. Cress, *Citizens in Arms*, 117–118; quotation on 118.

66. Knox quoted in ibid., 117.

67. Weigley, *United States Army*, 89–90.

68. The most detailed account of the Uniform Militia Act's evolution and provisions is in Mahon, *American Militia*, 14–20. See also Cress, *Citizens in Arms*, 120–21.

69. Mahon, *History of Militia*, 56. Upton, *Military Policy*, 85, called the Act, "a wild and impracticable scheme," though he applauded its proviso for universal military training, calling it "the truly democratic doctrine that every able-bodied male citizen owed military service to his country."

70. Riker, *Soldiers of the State*, 21; Weigley, *United States Army*, 94.

71. Kohn, *Eagle and Sword*, chap. 6 is excellent on the context surrounding the birth of the Legion. See also Francis Paul Prucha, *The Sword of the Republic: The United States Army on the Frontier, 1783–1846* (New York, 1969), chaps. 1–4; James R. Jacobs, *The Beginnings of the U.S. Army, 1783–1812* (Princeton, 1947), 50–188; Harry M. Ward, *The Department of War, 1781–1795* (Pittsburgh, 1962), 98–176. For the Indian perspective on these conflicts, see the essay by James H. Merrell in this volume.

72. This paragraph relies heavily on Kohn, *Eagle and Sword*, 175–86; quotation on 183. Stagg, *Mr. Madison's War*, 129–30, also emphasizes the importance of economic factors in shaping Republican military policy.

73. The next two paragraphs are based on the following works: Dumas Malone, *Jefferson and His Time*, vol. 5: *Jefferson the President: Second Term, 1805–1809* (Boston, 1974), chaps. 27–28; Reginald C. Stuart, *The Half-Way Pacifist: Thomas Jefferson's View of War* (Toronto, 1978); Stuart, "Thomas Jefferson and the Function of War: Policy or Principle," *Can. J. Hist.*, 11 (1976), 153–71; Theodore J. Crackel, "The Founding of West Point: Jefferson and the Politics of Security," *Armed Forces and Society*, 7 (1981), 529–43; Crackel, "Jefferson, Politics, and the Army: An Examination of the Peace Establishment Act of 1802," *Journal of the Early Republic*, 2 (1982), 21–38.

74. Stuart, "Thomas Jefferson and the Function of War," *Can. J. Hist.*, 11 (1976), 171. Henry Adams charged Jefferson with inconsistency in his *History of the United States During the Administrations of Jefferson and Madison* (New York, 1889–1891), IV, 212. For older views portraying Jefferson as a pacifist, see Louis M. Sears, *Jefferson and the Embargo* (New York, 1929); Charles M. Wiltse, *The Jeffersonian Tradition in American Democracy* (Chapel Hill, N.C., 1935), 196–200. Criticism of Jefferson's military policies is still common. See, for example, Frederick C. Leiner, "The 'Whimsical Phylosophic President' and His Gunboats," *American Neptune*, 43 (1983), 245–66.

75. Crackel, "Founding of West Point," *Armed Forces and Society*, 7 (1981), 532–35. Crackel discounts previous historians' interpretation that Jefferson founded West Point as a school for science and engineering. Ibid., 529–31.

76. In 1802 the army's authorized strength stood at 5,438 officers and men, while its actual strength was less than 3,600. The Military Peace Establishment Act reduced the army's authorized strength to 3,289, resulting in fewer than 300 actual dismissals. Nor did the Act cut military expenses to any degree. Some Republican congressmen estimated that as a result of the Act army reductions would result in an annual savings of $500,000. In reality the savings was closer to $35,000 annually. See Crackel, "Jefferson, Politics, and the Army," *J. Early Rep.*, 2 (1982), 22–23.

77. Inaugural Address, 4 March 1801, in Adrienne Koch and William Peden, eds., *The Life and Selected Writings of Thomas Jefferson* (New York, 1972), 324.

78. Malone, *Jefferson and His Time*, V, 512–14; quotation on 514. See also Merrill D. Peterson, *Thomas Jefferson and the New Nation: A Biography* (New York, 1970), 833–35; Stagg, *Mr. Madison's War*, 132–33.

79. Stagg, *Mr. Madison's War*, 130.

80. The phrase is from Charles Royster's stimulating article, "Founding a Nation in Blood: Military Conflict and American Nationality," in Hoffman and Albert, eds., *Arms and Independence*, 25–49.

CHAPTER 2

The Reintegration of the Loyalists and the Disaffected

Robert M. Calhoon

I. A DECENTRALIZED INFRASTRUCTURE

The reintegration of the Loyalists and the disaffected began with one of the earliest and most authentically revolutionary actions by the patriots—the First Continental Congress's recommendation that local committees enforce the nonimportation, nonexportation, and nonconsumption provisions of the Continental Association and publicly discredit "as the enemies of American liberty" violators of its provisions.[1] The astounding result of this clause in the Continental Association was the creation of a network of more than 7,000 committeemen by the spring of 1775, a virtually indestructible infrastructure of local revolutionary leadership. "The success of the Whigs in tying so substantial a group of local leaders to the enforcement of the Association," David Ammerman rightly emphasizes, "was a psychological victory of the first magnitude."[2]

These bodies quickly concluded that it would be futile to try to catch violators of nonimportation red-handed. Perhaps guided by the Manichaean language of Congress about "enemies" and "foes to the rights of British America," committees hit upon the dynamic tactic of collecting the

The author gratefully acknowledges the assistance of Peter J. Albert, Timothy M. Barnes, Carol Berkin, Jeffrey J. Crow, Eugene R. Fingerhut, Jack P. Greene, Harvey H. Jackson, David E. Maas, Gary D. Olson, Janice Potter, George A. Rawlyk, Arlene Phillips Shy, John Shy, Joseph S. Tiedemann, David H. Villers, and Robert M. Weir; part of a larger study of Southern evangelicalism and conservatism, this research was assisted by a fellowship from the American Council of Learned Societies. This chapter was also given as the Cincinnati Lecture at the Virginia Military Institute on April 23, 1986, where Colonel Willard M. Hays provided gracious hospitality.

names of potential or actual Crown supporters, summoning them for public interrogation, and thereby acting as protectors of the community as well as agents of resistance.

Exchanges between revolutionary committees and suspected Tories were part of what Peter Shaw calls "the ritual language" of the American Revolution, and ritualization of these proceedings was nowhere clearer than in the evolution of the Loyalist recantation as documents dramatizing the bonds holding revolutionary communities together as well as tensions threatening to shatter community unity.[3] When six men in Marblehead, Massachusetts, apologized in May 1775 for signing a farewell address to Thomas Hutchinson a year earlier, each admitted that he had unintentionally jeopardized the safety of the town by signing the address, and then each declared that the hostility of the community was a cleansing force which could restore his public reputation and render him once again a fit participant in the affairs of the body politic.[4]

"As My comfort in life does so much depend on the regard and good will of those among whom I live," wrote Enoch Bartlett of Haverhill, Massachusetts, in September 1774, "I hereby give it Under my Hand that I will not buy or Sell Tea or Act in Any public office Contrary to the Minds of the people in General . . . and will yet hope that all My errors in Judgment or Conduct meet with their forgiveness and favour which I humbly ask."[5] Similarly, when David Wardrobe, a British schoolmaster in Virginia, apologized to the Westmoreland Committee of Inspection on November 29, 1774, for having written an indiscreet letter to a correspondent in Scotland about Virginia politics, he "implor[ed] the forgiveness of this country for so ungrateful a return made for the advantages I have received from it, and the bread I have earned in it, and hope, from this contrition for my offence, . . . to subsist among the people I greatly esteem."[6]

There was a difference in tone between recantations from New England which were apologies to the whole community and those in the Chesapeake, where a newcomer and outsider admitted his dependence on the sufferance and hospitality of the aristocracy. Recantations reflected local patterns of deference and social control and, in the midst of revolutionary turmoil, an elaborate etiquette of superiority and inferiority. The use of ritualized public language as a means of admitting errant Loyalists into a republican polity indicated that the healing of political wounds was integral to the Revolution itself. The dramatization of political conflict, which Rhys Isaac has found at the core of the Revolution in Virginia, sprang directly from the manifold group antagonisms instigated and exacerbated by the Revolution.[7]

2. MORAL REPUBLICANISM

When the Continental Congress returned to Philadelphia on July 7, 1778, following British evacuation of the city, printer Benjamin Towne solicited several delegates for news and contributions to the *Philadelphia Evening Post*. One of the delegates, John Witherspoon of New Jersey, refused to cooperate unless Towne first publicly apologized for his collaboration with the British during General William Howe's occupation. Out of either naiveté or servility, Towne asked Witherspoon to compose a suitable apology for him. Later, when Towne saw what Witherspoon had written, he realized what a blunder he had made in entrusting the rehabilitation of his public image to so didactic and judgmental a figure as the Scottish Presbyterian and academic. Towne refused to sign Witherspoon's statement without substantial deletions. Witherspoon thereupon circulated the document in manuscript around Philadelphia, and it was published the following October in the Fishkill *New York Packet*. Over the following weeks Witherspoon then composed a wholly unsolicited recantation for another notorious Loyalist printer, James Rivington, which was even more elaborate and demeaning than Towne's.[8]

Witherspoon's Towne and Rivington recantations were, obviously, not authentic rituals of purgation and reintegration, but they did seek to educate a wide readership which enjoyed satire about the nature of republicanism, the fragile condition of republican virtue, and the ease with which scoundrels might sound plausible and innocent. Witherspoon was deeply suspicious of learning that was not grounded in personal virtue. It was not that he believed that people were capable of goodness—though he moved surprisingly close to this repudiation of Calvinism—but that he especially despised those contaminated by dependence on British favor and habituated to servility. Such Loyalists were, in Witherspoon's eyes, capable of insidious, chameleonlike mocking of republican virtues like sacrifice, duty, or the covenanted obligation to promote the common good. Witherspoon took special delight in exposing the intellectual emptiness of pro-British functionaries by having Towne and Rivington mouth parodies of Plutarch, Homer, and Samuel Johnson, which truly educated readers would recognize as shallow and obtuse. The superficiality and rhetorical excess of the Towne and Rivington recantations make them appear a minor episode in his career and a vacuous contribution to the discussion of reintegrating the Loyalists and the disaffected. Witherspoon was the earliest patriot to deal extensively with the issue of reintegration. He not only produced an elaborate depiction of what Samuel Adams called a "Christian Sparta," he endowed moral castigation of Loyalists, neutralists, and allegiance switchers with a kind of curative power. Like debased currency, condemnatory rhetoric was an asset the patriots possessed in abundance and could employ beneficially in the short term.

Loyalist reintegration arose as a political problem early in the war because of the existence of British garrison towns where people like Towne and Rivington—and their readers—could imbibe British corruption and arrogance. In Boston until March 1776, New York from September 1776 until November 1783, Newport from December 1776 until October 1779, Philadelphia from September 1777 until June 1778, Savannah from December 1778 until July 1782, Charles Town from May 1780 until December 1782, and Wilmington, North Carolina, from January to November 1781, Loyalist exiles found refuge, British military and economic power acquired a concentrated base, and an unstable culture of violence, deprivation amid wealth, and martial law pervaded the conduct of the war. In those towns which returned to American control during the war, those who had collaborated with the British but had not departed had to come to terms with the patriots. Surrounding each of these towns was a no man's land where illicit trade, crime, and patriot-Loyalist violence flourished. The British found administration of the garrison towns a vexing problem; indirectly, these towns nourished the Revolution by providing places to dispatch defiant Loyalists. Even illicit trade, which drained resources needed by the Continental Army, provided a valuable injection of British spending into the fringes of patriot-held territory. The garrison towns, therefore, created a large body of defectors for patriot justice to process back into American society as well as a visible demonstration of British power, corruption, and vulnerability.[9]

3. VOLITIONAL ALLEGIANCE

The most important scholarly discovery about the reintegration of the Loyalists and the disaffected is James H. Kettner's "idea of volitional allegiance" as a way of thinking about citizenship in Revolutionary America.[10] Simply stated, volitional allegiance was the notion that American citizenship should be a matter of "individual choice." This seemingly straightforward republican principle, however, was the product of a complex legal, political, and ethical situation—complexity central to the nature of the Revolution itself.

In the process of tracing the development of allegiance from *Calvin's Case* in 1608 to the Fifteenth Amendment in 1870, Kettner illuminates the conceptual problems peculiar to the study of allegiance. In Anglo-American tradition, he shows, concepts of allegiance have not taken the form of gradual accretions resulting from prolonged trial and error; rather, concepts of allegiance at any given time consisted of clusters of theory, practice, law, and tradition, which often coalesced suddenly under the pressure of events that thrust individuals and the state into new and ill-defined relationships. Very much like a Kuhnian paradigm, allegiance embodied contrasting and divergent elements complementary enough to meet the demands of specific situations and consequently fraught with potential internal stress—stress that became more pronounced as a particular definition of allegiance was applied to thorny political and legal cases.

Revolution and war disrupted the fragile web of suppositions undergirding obligation in British America. Drawing on traditional ideas, Revolutionary leaders insisted that George III had forfeited the allegiance of his colonial subjects and that their prior consent to British rule—expressed in the colonial charters—reserved ultimate constitutional authority to the whole body of the people as expressed by their representatives. But Anglo-American tradition provided little guidance in dealing with the question of individual allegiance in situations of Revolution and civil war. Could state governments impose American allegiance on all their inhabitants? Did the ultimate success of American arms by 1783 entitle the new nation to the allegiance of all the people by right of conquest? Republican principles and practical realities dictated a negative answer to both questions. The sheer impracticality of prosecuting large numbers of Loyalists for treason, the emerging conviction that in a civil war everyone should have a reasonable interval to decide which side to join, and the diplomatic need to strike a compromise between the sovereignty of the new nation and Britain's obligations to her Loyalist supporters were all among the constitutent elements of the concept of volitional allegiance.

Loyalists documented the formulation of volitional allegiance in two important instances. First, Peter Van Schaack privately expressed in the winter of 1775–1776 the view that "every individual has the right to choose the State of which he will become a member" when that person is caught up in the overthrow of an old government and formation of a new one. Van Schaack limited this right of personal choice of allegiance to the narrow interval between revolutionary overthrow and creation "for I admit that once a society *is* formed, the majority of its members undoubtedly conclude meaning to decide for the rest."[11] Chief Justice Thomas McKean of Pennsylvania took exactly the same position in 1781 when he ruled in the treason trial of Samuel Chapman that in Pennsylvania the interval of individual choice extended from May 14, 1776 (the day before Congress annulled the effect of the Penn charter) until February 11, 1777 (when the state enacted a treason statute making allegiance and protection reciprocal). At the time of Chapman's alleged offense of joining the British Legion in late December 1776, McKean ruled, "Pennsylvania was not a nation at war with another nation, but a country in a state of *civil war*."[12]

The presence in Pennsylvania of a variety of large communities of religious pacifists both provoked the radicals to a program of coercion and served as a moderating buffer against revolutionary zeal. Mennonites were willing to sell farm produce to the Continental Army and to pay commutation fees in lieu of military service, but they refused to take the oath prescribed by law in 1777 because they would not abjure allegiance to a king who had done nothing to forfeit his claim to their obedience and because they had no reason to trust the new regime in Philadelphia. Moravian pacifism did not proscribe any bearing of arms, but regarded military service as sinful if contrary to the conscience of the individual or performed under coercion. Schwenkfelders were the most apolitical and literalistic of the German pietist sects; one of their number, George Kriebel, told a judge that he could not take the oath of allegiance because the outcome of the war was still in doubt and therefore he did not yet know "upon what side God almighty would bestow the victory." The most visible pacifists and the most politically controversial were Quakers—a sect deeply split by the Revolution. Much of the traditional leadership of the Philadelphia Quaker merchant aristocracy refused on religious grounds "to join in any of the prevailing seditions and tumults," as one Quaker leader, Samuel R. Fisher, put it. Under Congressional pressure, Pennsylvania officials arrested more than forty prominent Philadelphia Quakers and sent them to detention in Winchester, Virginia, during the British occupation of Philadelphia. Beyond that harsh gesture, the discipline of the religious pacifists, the variety of the form of their noncompliance with Revolutionary dictates, and the weakness of coercive machinery all blunted punitive policies. Pluralism proved a powerful solvent of revolutionary persecution.[13] Volitional allegiance was the resulting equilibrium in this fluid situation.

A more complex and less studied setting for Revolutionary allegiance took shape in New York. Pressed to affirm allegiance to the Revolution in early 1777, Cadwallader Colden II told the New York Committee for Detecting and Defeating Conspiracies that "he conceived the former oath of allegiance which he had taken to the King of Great Britain to be binding upon him & professed a desire on being permitted to observe a state of neutrality." It took until the following October for the cumbersome machinery of revolutionary justice in New York to come to terms with this concept of allegiance. "No such state of neutrality can be known by the Council [of Safety]," Colden was told. Given time to reconsider his position, the stolid, apolitical son of New York's last royal lieutenant governor persevered in his claim to be "a faithful & true Subject to that State [New York] from which he receiv'd protection" and, while still bound by his allegiance to the king, he promised to be "a true and faithful Subject to the government of the Said State, So Long as it shall remain an independent State, and I reside therein."[14]

Colden's plight was emblematic of the situation of many Loyalists and neutralists in New York. "The contest between Whigs and Tories is not what was most important about Revolutionary Queens [County]," Joseph S. Tiedemann concludes in a detailed study of early Revolutionary mobilization across the East River from Manhattan; "the truly significant reality was that a decisive majority remained neutral in the contest between Great Britain and her thirteen colonies." These neutralists were "traditional agricultural people, . . . more concerned with the soil, the weather, and the prospects for the next crop than with debating the merits of Britain's imperial administration." Whig and Tory activists represented neither class nor generational constituencies; rather, they were a politicized minority already accustomed to elections, polemicism, public gatherings, and other forms of public display as ways of asserting virtue and denouncing vice.[15]

The keys to understanding most New York Loyalists are a sensitivity to apolitical language and gesture and an intimate knowledge of the local history. The late Jonathan Clark brought both qualities to his study of Loyalists and patriots in Poughkeepsie, New York. Clark tracked down personal and political data on nearly three-fourths of 329 male inhabitants of the town. He found 101 committed patriots and 61 staunch Loyalists; the remaining 69 "pristine fence sitters" included 29 "occasional patriots" and 40 "occasional loyalists." The people in these four categories knew one another and to a large extent were intermarried. Clark's 69 "occasional" Loyalists and patriots embodied the impulses and circumstances framing choices of allegiance. One occasional Loyalist, Peter Leroy, refused to sign the Association and had two sons fighting for the British, but under the influence of a patriot brother-in-law remained inactive in the struggle. Another, William Emmot, had agreed to take the oath of allegiance to the state and received, as a consequence, permission from Governor George Clinton to visit Long Island—behind enemy lines. That provoked a storm of protest from neighbors sceptical of Emmot's allegiance to the American cause. Known as a "sligh Designing fallow," Emmot took care to give no more offense and after the war emerged as a prosperous justice of the peace. In terms of wealth, both patriots and Loyalists spanned the social scale in Poughkeepsie, but on the average patriots had more wealth in 1775 and even more of them were among the very well-to-do. Supporting the Revolution was a gamble, but those who had the most to lose feared British victory more than they did independence. Forty of the 69 "occasional" Loyalists and patriots remained within the town and in possession of their property. "The resolution of the loyalist problem," Clark explains, "rested in the hands of men who, having made themselves noticeably large fish in a small pond, were as intent on saving their town as on saving their country. The destruction of their community, as they knew it, was not a price they would pay for victory."[16]

Finally, Michael Kammen's essay on "The American Revolution as a *Crise de Conscience:* The Case of New York," places the reintegration of the Loyalists within a spacious intellectual framework, which included an ironic subsection on "The Meaning and Consequences of an Oath"—one of the first mechanisms used in New York to validate citizenship. New Yorkers knew that oaths were often meaningless, that people swore allegiance insincerely to save themselves from injury or legal punishment, and that in an atmosphere of upheaval unprincipled opportunism flourished. Why then were oaths widely employed? In the first place, Kammen argues, because they were means of rehabilitating the disaffected and the disloyal. An oath could serve as a written record of submission to the new state; its imposition was a stern warning to behave well in the future; and the language of oaths summarized past behavior, including lapses of allegiance, and therefore as individualized prescriptions for conduct. An oath was a cheap, quick, uniform procedure that worked more often than it failed. Moreover, oaths gave individuals opportunities to verbalize and objectivize the hazards and pitfalls that entrapped the unprincipled and the naive in a revolutionary setting. As the Albany Committee of Safety discovered in late 1777, some people sided with Britain "thro' Fear, some thro' the persuasions of artful and designing Persons, others thro' the Allurements of Gain and the prospect of seeing their oppressed Country in the Hands of its base Invaders."[17] The clinical quality of such patriot diagnoses and Loyalist admissions resembled what Gordon S. Wood has called "the Whig science of politics"—the confident belief early in the Revolution that political behavior could be understood and handled by the careful discernment of virtue and corruption in the body politic. And the recognition of the contingent character of affiliation and even allegiance implicit in these documents was part of a "new emphasis on the piecemeal and the concrete in politics" which, according to Wood, soon replaced that body of classical principles.[18] In these terms, Loyalist reintegration was part of the interface between Whig assumptions and republican practice.

4. MILITARY TRIANGULARITY

During the mid-1960s two quantitative estimates put the maximum number of Loyalists at approximately 18 percent of the adult male population. Then in 1971 John Shy called attention to "the essential triangularity" of the War for Independence, that is, to the way British and American forces "contended less with each other than for support and control of the civilian population."[19] The triangularity hypothesis enables historians to make sense of a plethora of information about British frustration and American weakness. Despite the best efforts of conservative commanders on both sides, the war spilled off the formal battlefield and into the surrounding society in what the Rev. Samuel E. McCorkle called an "invasive" conflict. The politicizing and brutalizing of noncombatants hurt both sides but did far more damage to the British because it mocked their pretensions as protectors of the king's faithful subjects and guarantors of order in the colonies. The dual task of holding society together while conducting a socially divisive war, moreover, involved Revolutionary leaders in desperate experimentation, much of which ran counter to their basically conservative predilections. A sizable body of recent scholarship on local conflict during the war bears on the problem of Loyalist reintegration.[20]

In one of the best studies of the social dynamics of the war years, Ronald Hoffman discovered on the Eastern shore of Maryland, especially in Dorchester County, a kind of Tory populism among small farmers who defied the Whig elite that had overthrown the Proprietary government in 1775.[21] Harold B. Hancock identified the same sort of Loyalist defiance of a new state government in neighboring Sussex County, Delaware—for example, a bizarre episode in which a group of Tory refugees descended on the home of constable Robert Appleton in Bombay Hook, Delaware, and ordered him to read a Methodist sermon, destroy legal papers pertaining to Loyalists, and submit to being whipped by a black man.[22] The racial and religious references in the Appleton incident highlighted two intriguing features of Eastern Shore/Delaware Tory insurgency. News of Dunmore's appeal to Virginia slaves to join him in suppressing rebellion in 1775 reached the ears of Eastern Shore blacks and may have prompted fearful Maryland officials into over-reaction, which may have alerted yeoman farmers to the tenuous authority of the Revolutionary regime. As the war progressed, Loyalist activity became increasingly identified with the influence of Methodist preachers who seemed intent, as they did in Virginia, on building a new kind of spiritual order among poor whites and some slaves and free blacks and were oblivious to the patriots' presumptions to serving a divine purpose.[23]

Everywhere Loyalist deviance tested the discrimination and resiliency of patriot administration. Legislators, governors, and higher-level judges were conscious of the practical difficulties of drawing and enforcing tight legal norms; ordinary citizens and local officials were aware of the dangers to their safety from failing to do so. Two recent studies examine this process, one in Connecticut and the other in North Carolina. In both states, a legal vacuum existed at a critical moment in the Revolution. In Connecticut it occurred in 1774–1776; David H. Villers argues that local committees played their role to the hilt, but when committee authority proved insufficient, as it often did, they relied on what Villers calls " 'Liberty' gangs," which waylaid and terrorized suspects, extracted confessions, destroyed property, and in one sensational case broke into a jail to release patriot rioters convicted of illegally burning personal goods belonging to a New London customs collector. State officials, though uneasy about such vigilante justice, found these methods a useful supplement to the tenuous authority of the state and cumbersome machinery of the courts.[24] Jeffrey J. Crow found the same tension between official and popular justice in North Carolina. Here the vacuum occurred in the summer of 1781, when the government was exhausted by Cornwallis's invasion of the state and suppression of the Loyalists fell into the hands of individuals like Andrew Beard, "a person in the Practice of Shooting down peoples whom he is pleased to suppose disaffected to the . . . Government," in the words of Thomas Cabune, who nearly became one of Beard's victims. General Stephen Drayton saw events of this kind as part of a rough process of "convicting, reclaiming, or punishing of Tories" in which "our own imprudencies & irregular proceedings made more enemies than had ever become so from mere inclination."[25]

Both the Cabune and Drayton documents date from July 1781. Events in North Carolina during that summer provide a model for explaining regular and irregular warfare in the Revolution. Major James Craig occupied Wilmington in January 1781 and in July appointed David Fanning commander of Loyalist militia, already operating under Fanning's leadership. Craig and Fanning had finally learned how to fight irregular war in America successfully. Fanning devised a new guerilla strategy based on what John S. Watterson calls "quickness, mobility, deception, and improvisation." Fanning's raids concentrated on freeing Tory prisoners, capturing the most notorious persecutors of the Loyalists, operating widely in eastern North Carolina under cover of darkness, "plundering and destroying our stock of cattle and robbing our houses of everything they can get." Fanning's men were disciplined and violence was carefully targeted against key officials. Throughout Cumberland, Bladen, Anson, and Duplin counties, pockets of dispirited Loyalists felt emboldened by Fanning's exploits. General Nathanael Greene and Governor Thomas Burke sensed almost immediately what was happening. The only safe remedy was to hunker down and wait for events outside North Carolina to shift advantage away from the British irregulars. The use of retaliatory terror against known or suspected Loyalists only played into Craig's and Fanning's hands, enabling them to present themselves as agents of justice for the oppressed and targets of barbarity.[26] The Fanning-Burke duel in North Carolina in the summer of 1781 therefore pitted for the first time in the war adversaries who thoroughly understood military triangularity.

In South Carolina, Loyalist reintegration arose not only from patriot victory or from a stabilizing equipoise but from violence itself. The fierce civil war that convulsed South Carolina from late summer 1780 until the spring of 1782 played out memory of a previously learned experience with frontier lawlessness in the mid-1760s and harsh repression later in the decade by the South Carolina Regulators. The savagery employed by both Whigs and Tories in 1781 and 1782 frightened and shocked South Carolina patriot leaders. General William Moultrie did not exaggerate when he found, in early 1782, a shattered society of brutalized, frightened, impoverished people for whom "a dark melancholy gloom appears everywhere and the morals of the people are almost entirely extirpated." Even moderate, self-critical leaders like Aedanus Burke had felt an almost uncontrollable rage against the British and their Loyalist lackeys in South Carolina.[27]

All of these examples of military triangularity involved either geographical conditions hampering the establishment of Whig hegemony (as in Eastern Shore Maryland), or geopolitical fields of force giving Britain a competitive edge in dealing with the populace (as in areas adjacent to garrison towns in the middle states), or else the interplay of delicate social tensions making disaffection an understandable choice and reintegration a social and political imperative (as in South Carolina). One major variant remains: the state of Vermont, which lay beyond British or American control during the war and was for both sides an eagerly sought and finally elusive prize. Here military triangularity meant that the segment caught between Britain and America had the muscle to fight back. Within Vermont, patriots, Loyalists, and, among both groups, Vermont separatists, were bound together by common ties and interests that would make reintegration of the disaffected a natural consequence of the creation of a state independent of both Congress and Crown.

Peter S. Onuf places this story in the context of the jurisdictional territorial disputes of the Revolutionary era. Vermonters had to deal fundamentally with a problem that arose elsewhere in America only as an incidental feature of continental politics—the basis of statehood. The very existence of Vermont and the daily conduct of politics hinged on defining statehood in ways that would maintain cohesion within and cause the necessary degree of "havoc" in the affairs of grasping neighboring states. Vermont punished its Loyalists, then quickly forgave all but the most egregious of them, nearly negotiated its way back under British protection, and finally won a kind of reintegration into the American nation for Loyalists and separatists alike through admission as the fourteenth state.[28]

5. COSMOPOLITANS AND LOCALISTS

The severity or lenity of the treatment of the Loyalists at the conclusion of the Revolution has, for much of the twentieth century, been a test of the radicalism or moderation of the Revolution. That is not the only approach which can be taken to the postwar reintegration of the Loyalists. Paul H. Smith's article on General Guy Carleton as British commander in New York in 1782–83 selects a different perspective. Carleton believed with good reason that even after Yorktown, British possession of the port of New York was an immense asset. He proposed to the ministry that Britain simply refuse to budge unless the Americans agreed to some symbolic acknowledgment of allegiance to the king. The Rockingham ministry rejected Carleton's suggestion, not because the idea was faulty but because the capacity to pursue British interests in North America had been temporarily unhinged by the fall of the North government.[29]

Out of such divergent contingencies as London's unwillingness to let Carleton test the discipline and cohesiveness of the New York state government in 1782–83 and Britain's continued hold on the city during those two years, the Loyalists may have found the time and opportunity to make their way into republican society. Drawing on the sociology of conflict resolution, Joseph S. Tiedemann clusters those contigencies under four broad categories: withdrawal, imposition, compromise, and conversion. Using Queens County, New York, supposedly a Tory stronghold, as a test case, he estimates that no more than six percent of the adult males in the county went into exile and that the imposition of terms on those who remained was a matter of mutual adjustment rather than arbitrary prescription. New York's harsh anti-Tory legislation became in practice a kind of "psychic assurance" for the patriots "that their efforts had not been in vain" and haphazard enforcement an inducement to former Loyalists to accept the new order.[30]

The legislative search for such solutions, Jackson Turner Main demonstrates in his massive roll call analysis of the Confederation period, brought into the open and solidified two distinct orientations toward politics in the new republic, outlooks Main calls "localist" and "cosmopolitan." On roll call votes dealing with two major Loyalist issues, seventy-five percent of localists favored confiscation against only thirty-three percent of the cosmopolitans; sixty-one percent of localists opposed readmission of returning Loyalists as against sixteen percent of cosmopolitans.[31]

In her dissertation "The Treaty and the Tories: The Ideological Reaction to the Return of the Loyalists, 1783–1787," Roberta Tansman Jacobs generally concurs with Main's profile of the supporters and opponents of Loyalist reconciliation, although she suggests a strong surge of anti-Loyalist sentiment and legislation in 1783–84, a sharply focused and influential nationalist response in 1784, and a dismantling of barriers to Loyalist reintegration in 1785–86.[32]

David E. Maas's exhaustive study of Loyalist reintegration in Massachusetts confirms Jacobs's finding that localist hostility toward returning and remaining Loyalists in 1783 was short-lived.[33] Of 1,423 adult male Loyalists in Massachusetts (two percent of the population), Maas has identified 627 who remained in the state and 233 who returned. Approximately a quarter of physicians, whose occupational skills were in short supply, and Anglican ministers, who went into exile were able to return.[34] As in New York and Philadelphia, merchants possessed abilities needed to reinvigorate the economy, and those with friends among the patriots also found reintegration relatively easy. Maas attributed the tolerance of former Loyalists in Massachusetts to what he has called "honest graft"—the systematic plunder of Loyalist property by patriot politicians, creditors, and court officials during the War for Independence which substantially depleted the value of the estates returning Loyalists might have hoped to reclaim.[35] "Maryland's Samuel Chase . . . was an early advocate of leniency toward Loyalists," Norman K. Risjord notes in a similar instance, "even while he busily bought and sold their property."[36]

The most weighty contingency favoring Loyalist reintegration was the belief that strict compliance with Articles IV through VI of the Treaty of Paris was an essential precondition to establishment of a national reputation for justice and civility. The earliest and most complete linkage between the treatment of the Loyalists and the formation of a reputable national state appeared in Alexander Hamilton's defense of Joshua Waddington in a trespass action arising from a dispute over the rental of a brewery held by British merchants in New York City during the war. Hamilton's brief to the New York court in 1784 and his *Phocion* letters made justice and moderation toward the Loyalists and scrupulous observance of Articles IV to VI a unique opportunity to inculcate the right kind of civic habits. He set forth a theory of federalism that made state law clearly inferior to national law and treaty-making, and he lodged in the judiciary power to set aside state laws that contradicted national law or treaties. Other publicists followed Hamilton's lead. The need to attract capital to restimulate the economy, the useful entrepreneurial skills of many departed Loyalist merchants, the danger that persecuted Loyalists would provide Britain with a pretext for hostile intervention, and the conviction that a country "formed for commerce" had to open its market-place to British creditors and Loyalist merchants lest "Private Resent-ment . . . distract the Tranquility of Government, Trade forsake our Shores, and Contempt and Reproach . . . of consequence take [its] place" all appeared as themes in a well-orchestrated campaign. If Hamilton was the legal theorist of Loyalist reintegration, Benjamin Rush was its social interpreter. The Pennsylvania Test Acts of 1777–1779, Rush declared, were tyrannical measures reflecting the insecurity of the Constitutionalist regime because they denied nonjurors the right to grant or withhold assent to taxes imposed on them, offended conscientious pacifism, and damaged the prosperity of the community by excluding productive members of society from full citizenship.[37]

If the political reintegration of the Loyalists was a nationalist impera-tive, reconciliation of Loyalists, patriots, and neutralists within American churches was a necessary first step in the adjustment of the churches to a republican polity and culture. Each of the European religious traditions transplanted to the colonies in large or concentrated enough numbers to become a nascent denomination had members on both sides of the Revolu-tionary struggle—and some outside of it as well. One of the catalysts for the formation of Protestant denominations in the 1780s was the need to heal divisions arising from the Revolution within and between sects and confessional traditions.

No church had such a deep stake in legitimizing its place in American culture following the Revolution as the Anglicans. Anglicans in the South and around Philadelphia who had been predominantly patriots, or like the Rev. William Smith very passive Loyalists, were willing to accept lay participation in church governance and forego for the time being strict adherence to episcopal ordination. High Church traditionalists in Connecti-cut, led by Samuel Seabury, many of them staunch opponents of the Revolution, moved vigorously to secure sanction from the new state gov-ernment as a necessary prerequisite to consecration in England of a bishop. The Church of England shrank from any such intrusion into American civic life, though Seabury thereupon secured consecration as bishop of Connecticut from the Scottish Episcopal Church in 1783. Over the next six years, the two Anglican factions finally coalesced to form the Protestant Episcopal Church. What is not generally recognized in this familiar story is that Episcopalians, like other Protestant churches, opted for denominational polity as a way of resolving internal ecclesiastical problems and also establishing for themselves a stable position in the culture of the new republic.[38]

Quaker history contains another suggestive case of the origins of denominationalism. Torn like the Anglicans between English-based orthodoxy and acculturation in the new republic, the Revolution forced the Society of Friends to admit that it was not the True Church to which all believers would some day repair but rather a distinct kind of Protestant church. This movement toward a conventional definition of their sect was a positive reflection of American religious pluralism and a negative response to the hostility engendered by Quaker pacifism during the War for Independence. Similarly, the taint of Toryism among Methodists arose not only from John Wesley's harsh attacks on the Revolution or because the earliest preachers were apolitical Englishmen but also because Methodists disregarded social norms, shunned politicization, and alienated patriot elites. The potency of that impulse in a democratic society and the suitability of circuit-riding organization in an extensive, rural setting made what had been social liabilities before 1783 into cultural assets in the years which followed. A reputation for political intolerance may well have prompted Presbyterians to present a more moderate and congenial face to their fellow citizens as they sought to heal Old and New Side divisions and to identify national prosperity with the operation of divine providence.[39]

Scholarship on the Revolution has produced a fragmented but richly varied portrayal of Loyalist reintegration as a social and political process, but historians have been far less successful in recreating the interior experiences that underlay that process. There are isolated exceptions; of the serious biographies of Loyalists,[40] two of the best deal with men successfully integrated into the life of the new republic: Tench Coxe of Pennsylvania and William Samuel Johnson of Connecticut. Coxe sided with the British in 1776 and traded actively in Philadelphia during the British occupation. Johnson operated at the highest levels of the Whiggish provincial government in pre-Revolutionary Connecticut but temperamentally could not support independence and was jailed briefly in 1779 when his attempts to mediate between a British raiding force and frightened neighbors in Stratford were deemed "treasonous" by patriot officials. Both men had distinguished post-Revolutionary careers—Coxe as merchant, Treasury official under Hamilton, Jeffersonian publicist and journalist, and far-sighted advocate of industrialization; Johnson as influential delegate to the Constitutional Convention who was instrumental in the Great Compromise of July 1787, United States senator, and president of Columbia College.

Their parallel experiences were illuminating. Both were Anglicans, Johnson actively and Coxe inactively, but neither were doctrinaire in religion. Both secured political rehabilitation in 1779, well ahead of the charged and confusing atmosphere of 1783. Both had professional talents that were widely respected and not in overabundant supply in the new nation. Both had powerful friends within Revolutionary society and each handled himself with considerable discipline and sophistication at the crucial moment. "The Propriety, Modesty, and Prudence of your Conduct will probably in a little Time wholly remove the Impressions which have been made and fully restore you to your Friends and Country," Joseph Reed wrote to Coxe in early 1779, in a statement alluding to the delicacy of the task of winning forgiveness and understanding from moderate Pennsylvania patriots.[41] When Johnson came before the Connecticut Council of Safety on July 28, 1779, he saw only four familiar faces from his pre-Revolutionary days and nine newcomers to political power with whom he had never dealt. After three years of painful isolation, he took only two weeks to accept the Council's terms that he swear an oath of allegiance.[42] Opportunity, ability, and luck rank high in American success stories.

CONCLUSION: CAUSAL AND CONTEXTUAL HISTORY

A long tradition of Loyalist historiography has presented the Loyalists as a self-contained category of historical experience: victims of a popular seizure of power, exponents of a coherent philosophy of subordination and obedience, a military force willing to risk life itself in service of the Crown, and exiles who paid in concrete terms part of the human price for success of the Revolution.[43] A study of Loyalist reintegration, based on these assumptions, ought to be written. Conceptual insights favoring such an approach can be found in the novels of James Fenimore Cooper, William Gilmore Simms, Harold Frederic, and Kenneth Roberts, through which the Loyalists entered the literary consciousness of the United States;[44] in the gilded age historians' appreciation of the Loyalists, which Bernard Bailyn has brought to light;[45] and in Canadian nationalism, which has preserved the memory of Loyalist political philosophy carried to Nova Scotia and New Brunswick in the 1780s and 1790s.[46]

This chapter, in contrast, regards the Loyalists as fragments of historical experience within the larger context of the Revolution. The distinction between Loyalism as a subspecialty of scholarship and as a topic inextricably linked to the whole of the Revolution resembles the choice between what Ronald G. Walters calls "causal" and "contextual" history. Causal history identifies the participants in a historical event and studies what they did; contextual history asks what that event and those actions meant to affected individuals and to the people and culture surrounding them. "Contextual history," Walters explains, "is a history of commonality and structure rather than of distinctiveness and movement."[47] The scholarship examined in this chapter illuminates the shared social space inhabited by patriots and Loyalists and the common dilemmas they encountered. But neither a causal nor a contextual interpretation of Loyalist reintegration can be completely satisfactory, and historians need to devise a way of integrating the two approaches into a single, coherent vision of the subject.

The five interpretive insights employed here as organizing devices indicate both the utility and intrinsic limitation of a contextual treatment of Loyalist reintegration. The committee infrastructure in 1774–1775, the work of moral arbiters of republicanism in 1776–1777, the legal and political evolution of volitional allegiance in 1778–1779, the increasing military triangularity of the conflict in 1780–1781, and the cosmopolitan-localist dispute over treatment of the Loyalists in 1782–1785 emphasize that the social logic of the Revolution was unplanned and unanticipated and was shaped first by ideas and visions and next by social needs. In that sense, the treatment of the Loyalists served to reinforce and protect an initially fragile republican polity constructed from grassroots politics, moralistic revolutionary norms, philosophical and legal dilemmas, violence, and partisanship.

This formulation cannot contain all the complexities and paradoxes of the situation. The best town studies show many local leaders just as anxious as their cosmopolitan counterparts to ease the rehabilitation of the Loyalists.[48] Volitional allegiance was so egalitarian and libertarian in its implications that during the early nineteenth century the law of allegiance sharply curtailed free blacks, Indians, and women from the enjoyment of citizenship. Linda K. Kerber has shown that courts in New

York and Massachusetts refused to hold wives of male Loyalists accountable for their behavior on the ground that republican society had a transcendent interest in upholding the authority of husbands and preserving
wives in a state of political innocence and impotence.[49] Runaway slaves
and native American supporters of the Crown—and ultimately all blacks
and Indians—faced a post-Revolutionary regime that was much more
monolithic in its assertions of racial hegemony than pre-Revolutionary
British-Americans had thought of being.[50] The unexpected removal of
large numbers of British, French, and Spanish operatives from the lower
Mississippi valley and Great Lakes regions during the Napoleonic wars
deprived some former Loyalists of a potentially historic role in thwarting
manifest destiny.[51] Finally, the return of large numbers of the Canadian
descendants of Loyalist exiles to the United States during the nineteenth
century indicates that reintegration was a century-long rather than a
decade-long process.

NOTES

1. Merrill Jensen, ed., *American Colonial Documents to 1776* (London, 1955), 815.
2. David Ammerman, *In the Common Cause: American Response to the Coercive Acts of 1774* (Charlottesville, Va., 1974), 109.
3. Peter Shaw, *American Patriots and the Rituals of Revolution* (Cambridge, Mass., 1981), 2.
4. Quoted in Robert M. Calhoon, *The Loyalists in Revolutionary America, 1760–1781* (New York, 1973), 304.
5. Ibid., 305. Congress apparently distinguished between committees of inspection created in consequence of the Continental Association and the existing network of committees of correspondence that had existed in New England since early 1773.
6. *Virginia Gazette* (Pinckney), Feb. 9, 1775 in Robert L. Scribner, ed., *Revolutionary Virginia: The Road to Independence*, vol. 2, *The Committees and the Second Convention, 1773–1775: A Documentary Record* (Charlottesville, Va., 1975), 179–80.
7. Rhys Isaac, "Dramatizing the Ideology of Revolution: Popular Mobilization in Virginia, 1774 to 1776," *William and Mary Quarterly*, 3rd ser., 33 (1976), 357–85.
8. Timothy M. Barnes and Robert M. Calhoon, "John Witherspoon and Loyalist Recanta-tion," *American Presbyterians: The Journal of Presbyterian History*, 63 (1985), 273–83.
9. For a listing of scholarship on the British garrison towns, see Robert M. Calhoon, *Revolutionary America: An Interpretive Overview* (New York, 1976), 158–59; see also Janice Potter and Robert M. Calhoon, "The Character and Coherence of the Loyalist Press," in Bernard Bailyn and John B. Hench, eds., *The Press and the American Revolu-tion* (Worcester, Mass., 1980), 262–72; Robert Ernst, "Andrew Eliot, Forgotten Loyal-ist," *New York History*, 57 (1976), 284–320; Milton M. Klein, "An Experiment that Failed: General James Robertson and Civil Government in British New York, 1779–1783," *New York History*, 61 (1980), 228–254; Milton M. Klein and Ronald W. Howard,

eds., *The Twilight of British Rule in Revolutionary America: The New York Letterbook of General James Robertson, 1780–1783* (Cooperstown, N.Y., 1985); Elaine F. Crane, *A Dependent People: Newport, Rhode Island, in the Revolutionary Era,* (New York, 1985); and Barnes and Calhoon, "John Witherspoon and Loyalist Recantation."

10. James H. Kettner, *The Development of American Citizenship, 1608–1870* (Chapel Hill, N.C., 1978), chap. 7.

11. Ibid., 188–189.

12. Ibid., 195–96. See also G.S. Rowe, *Thomas McKean: The Shaping of an American Republicanism* (Boulder, Colo., 1978), 138–40; Henry J. Young, "Treason and Its Punishment in Revolutionary Pennsylvania," *Pennsylvania Magazine of History and Biography,* 90 (1966), 278.

13. Peter Brock, *Pacifism in the United States from the Colonial Era to the First World War* (Princeton, 1968), chap. 4; Henry J. Young, "The Treatment of the Loyalists in Pennsylvania," (Ph.D. diss., Johns Hopkins University, 1955), 267–71.

14. Eugene R. Fingerhut, *Survivor: Cadwallader Colden II in Revolutionary America* (Port Washington, N.Y., 1983), 58, 84–85. See also my review in *American Historical Review,* 89 (1984), 1388–89. For a similarly complex dilemma of a leading garrison town Loyalist leader, see Sheila L. Skemp, "William Franklin's Fight for Equality," paper read at the Southeastern American Society for Eighteenth-Century Studies, Columbia, South Carolina, February 28, 1985.

15. Joseph S. Tiedemann, "Communities in the Midst of the American Revolution: Queens County, New York," *Journal of Social History,* 18 (1984), 58–87.

16. Jonathan Clark, "The Problem of Allegiance in Revolutionary Poughkeepsie," in David D. Hall, John M. Murrin, and Thad W. Tate, eds., *Saints and Revolutionaries: Essays on Early American History* (New York, 1984), 285–317.

17. Jack P. Greene, Richard L. Bushman, and Michael Kammen, *Society, Freedom, and Conscience,* Richard M. Jellison, ed. (New York, 1976), 135, 139.

18. Gordon S. Wood, *The Creation of the American Republic, 1776–1787* (Chapel Hill, N.C., 1969), 606.

19. John Shy, "The American Revolution: The Military Conflict Considered as a Revolutionary War," in Stephen G. Kurtz and James H. Hutson, eds., *Essays on the American Revolution* (Chapel Hill, N.C., 1973), 126. This essay is conveniently available in John Shy, *A People Numerous and Armed: Reflections on the Military Struggle for American Independence* (New York, 1976), a book that contains several essays amplifying his views on the social configuration of the War for Independence; see chaps. I–II, VI–IX.

20. Samuel McCorkle, "The Curse and Crime of Plundering: A Sermon," McCorkle Papers, Duke University Library. Rob Sikorski and Thomas T. Taylor are preparing an edition of McCorkle's Revolutionary War sermons. See in general my review of Jeffrey J. Crow and Larry E. Tise, eds., *The Southern Experience in the American Revolution* and Don Higginbotham, ed., *Reconsiderations of the Revolutionary War: Selected Essays,* in *Journal of Interdisciplinary History,* 10 (1979), 367–70.

21. Ronald Hoffman, *A Spirit of Dissension: Economics, Politics, and the Revolution in Maryland* (Baltimore, 1973), 183–95, 223–41.

22. Harold B. Hancock, *The Loyalists of Revolutionary Delaware* (Newark, Del., 1977), 37, 82, 96 and Keith Mason, "Localism, Evangelicalism, and Loyalism: Popular Opposition to Elite Authority on the Eastern Shore of Maryland during the American Revolution," Conference on The Colonial Experience: The Eighteenth-Century Chesapeake, George Peabody Library, Baltimore, Maryland, Sept. 14, 1984.

23. Hoffman, *Spirit of Dissension,* 227–30; Hancock, *Loyalists of Delaware,* 80–86; Mason,

"Localism, Evangelicalism, and Loyalism," 20–23, 33–35; see also William Henry Williams, *The Garden of American Methodism: The Delmarva Peninsula, 1769–1820* (Wilmington, Del., 1984).

24. David H. Villers, "King Mob and the Rule of Law: Revolutionary Justice and the Supression of Loyalism in Connecticut, 1774–1783," unpublished paper based on Villers, "Loyalism in Connecticut, 1763–1787," (Ph.D. diss., University of Connecticut, 1976.)

25. Jeffrey J. Crow, "Liberty Men and Loyalists: Disorder and Disaffection in the North Carolina Backcountry," in Ronald Hoffman, Peter J. Albert, and Thad W. Tate, eds., *An Uncivil War: The Southern Backcountry during the American Revolution* (Charlottesville, Va., 1985), 129, 138, 140, 143–48, 161–62, 167–74. See also Paul D. Escott and Jeffrey J. Crow, "The Social Order and Violent Disorder: An Analysis of North Carolina in the Revolution and the Civil War," *Journal of Southern History*, 52 (1986), 373–402; Jeffrey J. Crow, "Tory Plots and Anglican Loyalty: The Llewelyn Conspiracy of 1777" and "What Price Loyalism? The Case of John Cruden, Commissioner of Sequestered Estates," *North Carolina Historical Review*, 55 (1978), 1–17 and 58 (1981), 215–33; and Clyde R. Ferguson, "Functions of the Partisan-Militia in the South during the American Revolution: An Interpretation," in W. Robert Higgins, ed., *The Revolutionary War in the South: Power, Conflict, and Leadership* (Durham, N.C., 1979), 239–58.

26. John S. Watterson III, "The Ordeal of Governor Burke," *North Carolina Historical Review*, 48 (1971), 95–102; Lindley S. Butler, ed., *The Narrative of Col. David Fanning* (Charleston, S.C. and Davidson, N.C., 1981), 6–10; Robert M. Calhoon, "Civil, Revolutionary, or Partisan: The Loyalists and the Nature of the War for Independence," *Military History of the American Revolution* (Washington, D.C., 1976), 93–108; Harry Eckstein, "On the Etiology of Internal Wars," *History and Theory*, 4 (1964), 133–163.

27. Robert M. Weir, " 'The Violent Spirit,' the Reestablishment of Order, and the Continuity of Leadership in Post-Revolutionary South Carolina," in Hoffman et al., eds., *An Uncivil War*, 76, 77, 85. Robert S. Lambert, *The South Carolina Loyalists* (Columbia, S.C., 1987), devotes a detailed chapter to Loyalist rehabilitation. See also the Loyalist recantations in the *Journals of the House of Representatives, 1783–1784*, Theodora J. Thompson and Rosa Lumpkin, eds. (Columbia, S.C., 1977), 39, 46, 127, 178–79; George C. Rogers, "Aedanus Burke, Nathanael Greene, Anthony Wayne and the British Merchants of Charleston," *South Carolina Historical Magazine*, 67 (1966), 76–83; and Jerome J. Nadelhaft, *The Disorders of War: The Revolution in South Carolina* (Orono, Me., 1981), chap. 4. Rebecca K. Starr, in "Loyalism on Daufuskie Island, South Carolina, 1775–1783," unpublished paper, explains the post-war reintegration of Loyalists who sought refuge on one of the sea islands as an extension of wartime "cultural memory, investing peace-keeping in authorized groups" among conflicting Loyalist and patriot communities in the islands. Cf. article by Joseph S. Tiedemann, note 30 below.

28. Peter J. Onuf, *The Origins of the Federal Republic: Jurisdictional Controversies in the United States, 1775–1787* (Philadelphia, 1983), chap. 6. For a discussion of earlier scholarship on the Vermont Loyalists, see Calhoon, *The Loyalists*, 330–34 and "The Floridas, the Western Frontier, and Vermont: Thoughts on the Hinterland Loyalists," in Samuel Proctor, ed., *Eighteenth-Century Florida: Life on the Frontier* (Gainesville, Fla., 1976), 1–15. A similar set of circumstances in Georgia produced the same narrow line between patriots and Loyalists. See Albert H. Tillson, Jr., "The Localist Roots of Upper Valley Loyalism: An Examination of Popular Political Culture," *Journal of Southern History*, forthcoming; George R. Lamplugh, "Up from the Depths: The Career of Thomas Gibbons, 1783–1789," *Atlanta Historical Journal*, 25 (1981), 37–44 and *Politics on the*

72 *Robert M. Calhoon*

Periphery: Factions and Parties in Georgia, 1776–1806 (Newark, Del., 1986); C. Ashley Ellefson, "Loyalists and Patriots in Georgia during the American Revolution," *The* *Historian*, 24 (1962), 347–56; Robert S. Lambert, "The Confiscation of Loyalist Prop-erty in Georgia, 1782–1786," *William and Mary Quarterly*, 20 (1963), 80–94; and James A. Henretta, "Southern Social Structure and the American War for Independence," in *The American Revolution: The Home Front, West Georgia College Studies in the Social* *Sciences*, 15 (1976), 1–14.

29. Paul H. Smith, "Sir Guy Carleton, Peace Negotiations, and the Evacuation of New York," *Canadian Historical Review*, 50 (1969), 245–64. See also Eldon Jones, "The British Withdrawal from the South, 1781–1785," in Higgins, ed., *Revolutionary War in* *the South*, 259–85.

30. Joseph S. Tiedemann, "Loyalism, Conflict Resolution, and New York Politics in the Critical Period, 1783–1787," *New York History*, 68 (1987), 27–43. Tiedemann's model applies closely to the dealings between patriot officials and native-born Virginia Loyalists studied in Adele Hast, *Loyalism in Revolutionary Virginia: The Norfolk Area and the* *Eastern Shore* (Ann Arbor, 1979), 140–188.

31. Jackson Turner Main, *Political Parties before the Constitution* (Chapel Hill, N.C., 1973), 32, 44–47, 348–53. Sigmund Diamond, in a prepared comment on a paper by Professor Main read at the Southern Historical Association in Memphis, Nov. 10, 1966, suggested the application of the cosmopolitan–localist concept to Confederation-period partisan-ship.

32. Roberta Tansman Jacobs, "The Treaty and the Tories: The Ideological Reaction to the Return of the Loyalists, 1783–1787," (Ph.D. diss., Cornell University, 1974), chapters III–VI. See the seminal and quite durable articles by Oscar Zeichner, "The Loyalist Problem in New York after the Revolution," *New York History*, 21 (1940), 284–302 and "The Rehabilitation of the Loyalists in Connecticut," *New England Quarterly*, 11 (1938), 324–29; and a fascinating case study, John M. Sheftall, "The Sheftalls of Savannah: Colonial Leaders and Founding Fathers of Georgia Judaism," in Samuel Proctor and Louis Schmier, eds., *Jews in the South* (Macon, Ga., 1984), 73–75.

33. David E. Maas, *Divided Hearts: Massachusetts Loyalists, 1765–1790, A Biographical Direc-tory* (Boston, 1980), xvi–xxvi.

34. David E. Maas, "The Massachusetts Loyalists and the Problem of Amnesty, 1775–1790," paper read at the American Historical Association, December 1975, Atlanta, tables 1 and 5. Another notorious Loyalist physician who secured quick readmission from American officials was Dr. John Pyle of North Carolina. See Carole Watterson Troxler, *The Loyalist Experience in North Carolina* (Raleigh, N.C., 1976), 28–29.

35. David E. Maas, "Honest Graft in Revolutionary Massachusetts," *Boston Bar Journal*, 23 (1979), 7–15.

36. Norman K. Risjord, *Chesapeake Politics, 1781–1800* (New York, 1978), 193, and R. Don Higginbotham, "James Iredell and the Revolutionary Politics of North Carolina," in Higgins, ed., *Revolutionary War in the South*, 79–97.

37. Jacobs, "The Treaty and the Tories," 117–121. See also Robert Michael Dructor, "The New York Commercial Community: the Revolutionary Experience," (Ph.D. diss., Uni-versity of Pittsburgh, 1975), and Philip Ranlet, *The New York Loyalists*, (Knoxville, 1986), and Hendrik Hartog, *Public Property and Private Power: The Corporation of the City of New York in American Law, 1730–1870* (Chapel Hill, N.C., 1983), 82–86, 103–105.

38. Bruce E. Steiner, "New England Anglicanism: A Genteel Faith?" *William and Mary* *Quarterly*, 27 (1970), 133–35 and *Samuel Seabury, 1729–1796: A Study in the High*

Church Tradition (Athens, Ohio, 1971) chap. 6. For an excellent analysis of the subject, and a valuable discussion of scholarship on post-Revolutionary Anglicanism, see David L. Holmes, "The Episcopal Church and the American Revolution," *Historical Magazine of the Protestant Episcopal Church*, 47 (1978), 283–88.

39. Sydney V. James, "The Impact of the American Revolution on Quakers' Ideas about Their Sect," *William and Mary Quarterly*, 19 (1962), 360–82; Donald G. Mathews, *Religion in the Old South* (Chicago, 1977), 29–37; Rhys Isaac, *The Transformation of Virginia, 1740–1790* (Chapel Hill, N.C., 1982), 260–64; Jonathan Powell, "Presbyterian Loyalists: A 'Chain of Interest' in Philadelphia," *Journal of Presbyterian History*, 57 (1979), 135–160; and Young, "Treatment of Loyalists in Pennsylvania," 294–304.

40. Bernard Bailyn, *The Ordeal of Thomas Hutchinson* (Cambridge, Mass., 1974); Carol Berkin, *Jonathan Sewall: Odyssey of an American Loyalist* (New York, 1976); Don R. Byrnes, "The Pre-Revolutionary Career of Provost William Smith, 1751–1778," (Ph.D. diss., Tulane University, 1969); John E. Ferling, *The Loyalist Mind: Joseph Galloway and the American Revolution* (University Park, Pa., 1977); Lawrence Henry Gipson, *American Loyalist: Jared Ingersoll* (New Haven, 1971); Leroy Hewlett, "James Rivington, Loyalist Printer, Publisher, and Bookseller of the American Revolution: A Biographical and Bibliographical Study, 1763–1783," (Ph.D. diss., University of Michigan, 1958); Albert Lawrence Lorenz, *Hugh Gaine: A Colonial Printer-Editor's Odyssey to Loyalism* (Carbondale, Ill., 1972); Alice M. Keys, *Cadwallader Colden* (New York, 1906); Eugene R. Fingerhut, *Survivor: Cadwallader Colden II in Revolutionary America*; Lawrence Shaw Mayo, *John Wentworth* (Cambridge, Mass., 1921); Bruce E. Steiner, *Samuel Seabury*; L.S.F. Upton, *The Loyal Whig: William Smith of New York and Quebec* (Toronto, 1969); and Anne Y. Zimmer, *Jonathan Boucher: Loyalist in Exile* (Detroit, 1978). As their titles suggest, not all of these books are biographies in a strict sense of the term, but all employ a biographical framework and define the genre of Loyalist biography against which the books by Cooke and McCaughey, below, are judged.

41. Jacob E. Cooke, *Tench Coxe and the Early Republic* (Chapel Hill, N.C., 1978), 45.

42. Elizabeth P. McCaughey, *From Loyalist to Founding Father: The Political Odyssey of William Samuel Johnson* (New York, 1980), 189.

43. For a discussion of this tradition, see Robert M. Calhoon, "Loyalist Studies at the Advent of the Loyalist Papers Project," *New England Quarterly*, 46 (1973), 284–85.

44. Donald G. Darnell, " 'Visions of Hereditary Rank': The Loyalist in the Fiction of Hawthorne, Cooper, and Frederic," *South Atlantic Bulletin*, 42 (1977), 45–54; Michael Kammen, *A Season of Youth: The American Revolution and the Historical Imagination* (New York, 1978), 24–26, 52, 154–56.

45. Bailyn, *Ordeal of Thomas Hutchinson*, 394–98.

46. Jane Errington and George Rawlyk, "The Loyalist–Federalist Alliance of Upper Canada," *American Review of Canadian Studies*, 14 (1984), 157–176 and Janice Potter, " 'Is This the Liberty We Seek?': Loyalist Ideology in Colonial New York and Massachusetts," (Ph.D. diss., Queen's University, 1977), 353–396.

47. Ronald G. Walters, *The Anti-Slavery Appeal: American Abolitionism after 1830* (Baltimore, 1976), 147.

48. Clark, "Problem of Allegiance in Poughkeepsie"; Fingerhut, *Survivor*, chap. 9; John J. Waters, *The Otis Family in Provincial and Revolutionary Massachusetts* (Chapel Hill, N.C., 1968), chap. 9; Calhoon, *Loyalists*, 292–94, 340–49; Francis T. Bowles, "The Loyalty of Barnstable in the Revolution," *Publications* of the Colonial Society of Massachusetts, 25 (1922–1924), 265–345; Nathaniel Freeman Papers, 1775–1785, William E. Clements Library, Ann Arbor, Michigan; and Robert J. Wilson, III, *The Benevolent*

Piety of Ebenezer Gay and the Rise of Rational Religion in New England, 1696–1787 (Philadelphia, 1984), 225–229.

49. Linda K. Kerber, *Women of the Republic: Intellect and Ideology in Revolutionary America* (Chapel Hill, N.C., 1980), 130–36.

50. Peter Marshall, "First Americans and Last Loyalists: An Indian Dilemma in War and Peace," in Esmond Wright, ed., *Red, White, and True Blue: The Loyalists in the Revolution* (New York, 1976), 33–53.

51. J. Leitch Wright, *Anglo-Spanish Rivalry in North America* (Athens, Ga., 1971); *Britain and the American Frontier* (Athens, Ga., 1975); and *William Augustus Bowles: Director General of the Creek Nation* (Athens, Ga., 1967). I am also indebted to Paula Perry, "They Did Not Wish Us Well: European Intrigues in America, 1782–1798," unpublished research paper, University of North Carolina at Greensboro, 1979.

CHAPTER 3

Force, Order, and Democracy in the American Revolution

John W. Shy

This comment may seem like one of those book reviews that discuss the subject rather than the book. So let me say that I accept virtually all that Robert M. Calhoon and E. Wayne Carp have told us about their respective subjects, and have been stimulated by their interpretations to make my own effort, treating their two subjects as parts of a single problem, to clarify and explain that problem.

Putting a paper on the subject of American counter-revolutionaries together with a paper on the subject of organizing a republican army suggests that the first item on the 1783 agenda was brute force; or, how to deal with Americans who failed to support the long armed struggle, and in many cases actually fought against it; and how to recruit and organize men who would fight for the republic without endangering it. Perhaps it is the elemental quality of the problem that puts it in first place. Perhaps also there is the desire to get it out of the way before moving on to more interesting items on the agenda. Not only is the subject of brute force somewhat limited and unedifying, it also turns out to be something like a non-subject in the early republic.

Nothing like the predicted violent attack on former Loyalists, no anti-Tory bloodbath, actually took place. Continued conflict in the North Carolina backcountry, and in a few other isolated areas, points up the general absence of either the need or the impulse to punish violently or coerce physically this large minority of Americans. Whatever they may have done during the war itself—and the ugly intensity of wartime violence between Whigs and Tories should not be underestimated—the new republic could get on with its agenda without using force against those who had dared to reject republicanism.

Similarly, the fears expressed in 1783 of either a military coup by an alienated, professionalized army, or the republic undefended by its cowardly, incompetent militia, led to nothing much. The Newburgh incident, the Society of the Cincinnati, and the military failures against the Ohio Indians end in the anticlimactic Militia Act of 1792—a dead letter before Washington signed it. Late in the decade the so-called Provisional Army, ostensibly raised for defense against French invasion, itself raised an interesting issue. Rumors circulated that this large new force would be used to smash the Republican opposition, as the Whiskey Rebellion had been smashed. More than 300 manuscript pages in the Washington papers record the pains taken by Alexander Hamilton to staff this army with "respectable" officers—men whose intelligence, courage, and sense of honor were matched by their hatred of Jacobinism. Had President Adams led the nation into war with France, and had Washington lived long enough to lend—once again—the benefit of his "aegis" to Hamilton (the real commander), the story of armed force in the new republic might have been very different indeed. But in the end nothing happened, and the Provisional Army, like the Newburgh coup and the Cincinnati menace, faded away.

Not even the War of 1812 has much to offer. Citizen soldiers proved to be inept aggressors (just as their ideologues had predicted), but were adequate defenders at Plattsburgh, New Orleans, and Baltimore, if not at Washington (but even Napoleon didn't win them all). Once more, in the end, Wellington judged the task of invading the United States as too risky and too expensive, thus confirming Jeffersonian arguments against large standing forces.

The problem, then, is not exactly brute force, but its relative absence or avoidance after 1783, and to that extent the problem exists mainly in our imagination. Revolutions are violent, and frequently have succumbed to violence. If 25,000 Americans suffered war-related deaths between 1775 and 1782, as Howard Peckham has estimated, that would be almost one percent of the population, and indicates a considerable amount of violence in the American Revolution. So we are led to expect that violence, threats of violence, and the general problem of violence in all its various forms would be a major aspect of American history after 1783. But they do not seem to have been very important. The real problem is what did *not* happen. For that nameless problem brute force is no more than a point by which we can triangulate the inquiry.

The other points for triangulation are *behavior*—what people did, and did not do, after 1783—and *mentality*—what they saw, thought, and believed. The overwhelming majority of Americans in 1783 did not attack Tories, or threaten to do so. It is much more difficult to know what they thought about them. A similar majority did not support the creation of a standing army or of a trained, effective militia force. Some political leaders, it is true, particularly from backcountry constituencies, opposed the lifting of legal and economic penalties against proscribed Tories. And some political leaders, particularly from New England, denounced the Society of the Cincinnati as aristocratic, militaristic, and un-American. But behavior, on the whole, indicates that brute force, except when deemed necessary against slaves and Indians, did not have an important place in the post-Revolutionary scheme of things. In 1838 Abraham Lincoln would deplore the various and widespread acts of violence threatening the American republic, but nothing comparable marks the period after 1783. Not Shays' Rebellion, which ended in flight and pardon, nor the Whiskey Rebellion, which ended in farce, came close in terms of bloodshed and bodily harm to the antiblack, anti-Mormon, anti-Catholic, vigilante excesses of antebellum America.

Mentality ought to be the key. Why the restraint toward traitors? Why the apathy about defending the republic? Or, more generally, why the disinclination to use force as a political instrument in a troubled society whose violent break-up was predicted by many observers? If we knew what people were thinking, we might answer the questions. Knowing little about mentality, and that little about a small number of articulate, politicized men, we naturally tend to guess—to make plausible inferences from what was done and not done. The most popular inference invokes some form of republican virtue: men unwilling to stain a noble experiment with blood, not even the blood of its opponents; men unwilling to believe that a corrupt institution—and army—might be a better way of defending the republic and enforcing its laws. Maybe this was the underlying, explanatory mentality of behavior that avoided brute force, but I doubt it. Too much in the citizenly behavior of Americans during and after the war suggests a lower level of consciousness and a less intense commitment.

If we are guessing—and I think we are—my guess leads back to behavior. Almost no one acts in a very concerned way about the problem, either in its anti-Tory form, its effective-army form, or any other form. My guess is that almost everyone understood two things so well that discussion, or the conscious inditement of what would serve historians as good evidence, was seldom necessary. The first thing is what every intelligent European statesman and soldier knew by 1783: the United States was too remote, too large, and too populous to be vulnerable to a serious military attack. The quality of American armed forces was far less important than the size and wealth of the nation. The other thing is less obvious, and more difficult to express clearly. American society, while fully armed and often violent (more than half of the three decades before 1783 were years of large-scale American warfare), had never depended much on the use of force to control its own (white) people. Wherever we look in the colonial period we find little reliance on organized force, or the threat of such force, to maintain order. There is violence, to be sure, from the Stono slave uprising to the Green Mountain Boys. But most of the time, in most places, the resolution of conflict and the prevention of disorder did not depend on the existence of a deterrent armed force—and Americans knew it.

Carp has emphasized localism in eighteenth-century American society, and Calhoon has stressed the "astounding" quality of the "decentralized infrastructure" created by the Continental Association. I will argue that just there, in the locality, lies the basic phenomenon of the problem. Except in parts of New England and other older, densely settled places, locality was nothing so pervasive and compelling as "community," with its close-knit web of values and relationships. Locality—like its correlative "-ism"—refers to no more than a delimited space, to the people residing in that space, and to a collective awareness of both the human and spatial entity. Whether defined administratively or geographically, the locality was the core of reality—the constituent element of any larger society and polity. Within the locality order was kept and power exerted, not by using force or threatening violence, but by clearly understood signals and rules. Here I diverge from Carp's emphasis on militia as an active, interventionist force in the life of the locality. Instead, I find more realism in Calhoon's account of taking and publishing names, and of the purgative ritual of recantation and oath-taking, as ways of dealing with local deviants. When organized force appeared, beyond the routine muster and training of militia, then the locality was at war, either with an outside enemy or within itself. Police, in any modern sense of the word, did not keep order; people—that is to say, social structure—kept order.

What this meant for Loyalism in 1783, and for military policy after 1783, can be traced through the two papers. Organizing and maintaining an armed force seemed unreal, and those who pressed the matter, like Hamilton, were viewed with some suspicion. War or insurrection, if they occurred, would provide enough time for society to respond, so that the diversion of time, energy, and money to military preparedness of any kind, whether standing army or trained militia, seemed a waste of valuable resources. If this can be called ideology, it is fairly latent and lethargic. For Loyalists, there were two choices: conform or leave. No more than one Loyalist in eight or nine left the United States, but many more left their localities or never returned to them. If there had been trouble during the war, it was easier to go to some new locality, perhaps not far from the old one, but far enough to facilitate a convenient forgetfulness. The process was not confined to Tories. Zealous and violent Whigs also could find mobility preferable to further confrontation; the option was usually available, and other incentives could make the choice painless. There were cases when implacable patriots were made to feel unwelcome by a majority who preferred a quick return to unforced order.

In short, the role of violence in this society—both its function and its frequency—may be misperceived. Disorder and violence existed, but there was far less than might be expected, given the lack of countervailing force. Organized force, even as a threat, was rare and exceptional; matters were worked out in other ways, which account for the lack of overt interest in the subject. The experience of the Revolutionary War had not sensitized people to the importance of the military issue; rather, it had reinforced their basic attitude toward it. That attitude was one part resignation, one part apprehension; resignation to the absence of any attractive alternative to doing nothing about an organized armed force, and apprehension of the likely dangers involved in forcing people to behave correctly. Individuals, families, and localities were simply too vulnerable if society and government were to make violence a normal and legitimate instrument. Where would it end? If there was a collective sensitivity to the problem, it was less to the political implications of the alternative forms of military organization than it was to the incipient anarchy of a society in transition from deference to democracy. Like the role of violence, the role of ideology, as a coherent set of explicit political beliefs, may have been exaggerated by modern historians.

CHAPTER 4

From One Agenda to Another: The Condition of American Federalism, 1783–1787

Jack N. Rakove

None of the members of the Revolutionary generation—save perhaps for Thomas Jefferson—better illustrates the multiple dimensions of republican culture than does Benjamin Rush, patriot, physician, and promoter of good causes ranging from penal reform to antislavery, from temperance to female education, from the revision of the Pennsylvania constitution to the restoration of Philadelphia as the national capital. Nor in the years after the Revolution did any of his contemporaries more succinctly express their shared aspirations for the improvement of American life, their awareness of challenges yet to be met, than did Rush in the familiar opening paragraph of his "Address to the People of the United States" in 1786. "There is nothing more common," Rush observed,

> than to confound the terms of *the American revolution* with those of *the late American war*. The American war is over: but this is far from being the case with the American revolution. On the contrary, nothing but the first act of the great drama is closed. It remains yet to establish and perfect our forms of government; and to prepare the principles, morals, and manners of our citizens, for those forms of government, after they are established and brought to perfection.

This evocative preamble can be lent to so many uses that it is easy to forget that the concerns Rush went on to address in this essay were narrowly drawn. His actual subject was "the defects of the confederation," which he described in such familiar terms as "the deficiency of coercive power" in Congress, the

This essay was written while the author held a Constitutional Fellowship from the National Endowment for the Humanities, whose generous support he wishes to acknowledge.

want of "exclusive" federal authority over paper money and commerce, the unicameral character of Congress, and "the too frequent rotation of its members." But if Rush was merely reciting a conventional litany of the failings of Congress, his emphasis on the priority of political reforms is striking nonetheless. For where others were wont to interpret failures in the public sphere as a reflection of deeper vices among the people, Rush inverted the relation between morals and politics by supposing that the work of improving the "morals, and manners of our citizens," had to begin with the resolution of more immediate and obvious problems of government.[1]

In the end, as Rush foresaw, the recasting of the federal system was the great work of the immedate post-Revolutionary period. At the close of the Revolutionary War, many problems and prospects confronted Americans eager to redirect their attention to private pursuits too long constrained by the burdens of a protracted war—to the restoration of old lines of commerce and the opening of new markets, to the extension of settlements both north and south of the Ohio River, and to a host of other concerns. But few of these matters constituted an agenda, unfinished or otherwise, in any strict sense of the term, a docket of proposals awaiting action by responsible authorities or concerned parties. In most areas, as Professor Bernard Bailyn has suggested, the Revolutionary legacy expressed itself in "a complicated interplay between the maturing of Revolutionary ideas and ideals and the involvements of everyday life," in a process in which, to use his favorite image, the "movement of thought" often carried Americans "past boundaries few had set out to cross, into regions few had wished to enter"[2]—and where, one might add, landmarks were unfamiliar and destinations uncertain. A few bold surveyors—like Rush, with his schemes for reform, and Jefferson, with his plan for the comprehensive revision of the laws of Virginia—did possess expansive views, but the activities that preoccupied most Americans in the years after 1783 do not reveal a national agenda being pursued with forethought and deliberation. After eight years of war and economic dislocation, Americans were too exhausted to do much more than put their own affairs, too long neglected, in order.

The one area in which the literal concept of an agenda does have an obvious relevance, however, is the subject that concerned Rush in 1786: the amendment of the Articles of Confederation. For from 1781 on, those who actively sought to strengthen the national government were forced to think in quite specific terms about just which further powers Congress needed, and which ones it was most likely to obtain. They had to ask, too, how the adoption or rejection of one proposal would affect the fate of others. Above all, they had to calculate how best to surmount the two obstacles that stood in the way of the adoption of any amendment: the preliminary hurdle of creating a substantial consensus within Congress, and the greater barrier of securing unanimous ratification by the states. Far more than was the case at the state level of politics, where the task of correcting the errors incorporated in the first constitutions seemed open-ended, reform of the confederation could proceed only through the pursuit of a carefully delineated agenda. So at least it seemed to James Madison, the most thoughtful and eventually the most influential of these reformers, and to the relatively small circle of like-minded men who shared his interest in national political problems.

But did the agenda that they were pursuing in the mid-1780s anticipate the transformation of the federal system that would begin to unfold with the Constitutional Convention of 1787? Since many leading Federalists had been seeking to amend the Articles of Confederation for some time, much of the historiography of the Revolution has treated the events of 1787–88 as the culmination of a struggle that had begun a decade earlier, when "radical" proponents of state sovereignty had vanquished "conservative" supporters of effective national power in the drafting of the first state constitutions and the Articles of Confederation.[3] That criticisms of the Articles were being voiced even before they were finally ratified certainly implies that they received less than a fair trial. Alexander Hamilton had prepared a devastating assessment of the assumptions under which the framers of the confederation had acted as early as September 1780.[4] Amendments were being discussed well before the Articles formally took effect on March 1, 1781; indeed, one (the first impost proposal) had been submitted to the states four weeks earlier. No sooner did the Articles go into operation than Congress began appointing a series of committees charged with considering what additional amendments and powers were necessary to discharge its responsibilities effectively. Madison himself was a member of the first of these committees, whose report proposed authorizing the union to use force against states that failed to meet their "federal engagements" for men, money, and supplies.[5] Six years later, he was still agonizing over the same issue.

Other telling similarities seem to link the various amendments discussed in the early 1780s and the actual changes the framers of the Constitution either effected or at least contemplated. The idea of holding a constitutional convention was itself broached as early as 1780. Even more striking, many historians believe, is the connection between the financial measures that Robert Morris urged Congress to adopt in 1782–83, and the comprehensive program that Hamilton later pursued, with greater success, as Secretary of the Treasury.[6] This nationalist upsurge failed when heavy-handed tactics and the coming of peace prevented the adoption of the Morris proposals. But in 1787, with the economic dislocations of the mid-1780s and Shays' Rebellion providing a convenient foil, the Federalists won the final round.

Certainly there is much to be said for attempting to identify which leaders and which groups would have favored or opposed a stronger national government at any point after 1776. Yet this emphasis on continuity in alignments makes it difficult to perceive the abrupt shifts in both tactics and goals that distinguished the gradual and modest amendments considered before 1786 from the radical measures pursued in 1787. It also ignores the enormous intellectual leap that enabled the framers of the Constitution to link the familiar problems of federalism with more complex and open-ended questions about republican government in general. Now and again, in the surviving records of these earlier years, one can find a document that foreshadows the full range of concerns that would preoccupy the framers in 1787.[7] But the historian who compares the actual debates at the Federal Convention with both the public and private discussions of the mid-1780s will be struck far more by their disparities than their similarities. By 1787, the framers of the Constitution could plausibly assume that their labors were meant to cure not only the palpable shortcomings of the Articles, but also the weaknesses of republican government within the states; many, like Madison and Hamilton, were even so bold as to believe that "we were now to decide for ever the fate of Republican Government."[8] Such presumption would have seemed entirely miscast only months earlier, when discussions of the plight of the confederation were still cast within far narrower limits. Only in 1787 did it become possible to believe that the movement to strengthen the confederation might address issues more fundamental than the mere augmentation of the powers of Congress.

What happened in 1787, then, was that one agenda was abandoned and another, both more innovative and expansive, substituted in its place. This transformation did not require the framers of the Constitution to cast themselves as the belated victors in a long struggle against their less enlightened predecessors,[9] but it was a transformation nonetheless. One of the great challenges inherent in explaining the making of the Constitution is thus to understand how the prosaic debates of the mid-1780s could give way to the enthusiasms of 1787–88. That is the subject of this chapter.

At the close of the Revolutionary War, the allocation of authority between Congress and the states constituted an unfinished agenda in at least two senses of the term. The first and more obvious set of problems arose from gaps between the broad responsibilities that had been delegated to Congress and the circumscribed powers with which it had to excercise its duties. Its most conspicuous weaknesses had become apparent during the final years of the war, when the states had proved incapable of raising the full quotas of men, money, and supplies that Congress had requisitioned. The framers of the Articles had indeed assumed, as Madison rightly observed in 1787, that "the justice, the good faith, the honor, [and] the sound policy" of the state legislatures would lead them to comply in good faith with such legitimate requests; but they had made no provision for instances when the states failed to act.[10] Congress could neither coerce the states into doing their duty nor act independently in the event of their default. The first years of peace revealed comparable problems in the realm of foreign affairs and in the management of the national domain, over which Congress had acquired effective title by 1784. National defense, foreign relations, and the development of the West were the three great responsibilities that were generally conceded to belong to Congress. No one of any consequence proposed a devolution of these functions upon the states. Yet in each of these areas the actual authority that Congress could exercise fell well short of what it needed. Most of the additional Articles that were proposed or merely discussed before 1786 were designed not to enhance its role but simply to enable it to operate within its alloted sphere.

But the federal agenda was unfinished in a second and more basic sense. In 1783, few were prepared to say just what additional functions could be safely or appropriately delegated to a national government. Would a confederation originally framed to deal with the exigencies of a revolutionary war prove adequate for a nation that, having gained its independence, was now evidently poised for a process of internal development and westward expansion? In 1777, more than a few members of Congress may have privately agreed, with Thomas Burke, that the drafting of the Articles was best delayed until war's end.[11] But other considerations had compelled them to complete a recognizably imperfect plan of confederation. Few then would have claimed that the Articles had been framed with an eye turned to the long-term development of the republic. Political exigencies had led its framers to establish a fairly simple division of authority between Congress and the states. Congress was given broad control over the conduct of war and foreign affairs, while the states were left responsible for almost everything that could be lumped under the broad heading of "internal police." Efforts to vest Congress with broad constitutional authority over Western lands had been decisively turned back by a bloc of "landed" states, led by Virginia, anxious to preserve their claims to vast expanses of territory lying beyond the existing perimeter of settlement. Congress received nothing more than the most carefully hedged authority over territorial matters, even though leaders of both landed and landless states understood that federal regulation of the American interior would ultimately prove necessary. In other matters of domestic concern—most notably commerce—the powers of Congress were so circumscribed as to be rendered nugatory.

Suppose, then, that the members of Congress had sat down in the summer of 1783—immediately after the comic opera mutiny of a group of unpaid Pennsylvania soldiers had convinced Congress to flee bustling Philadelphia for torpid Princeton—and attempted to draft an agenda defining outstanding issues of federal relations. What would this document have looked like? It would not be entirely facetious to suggest that such an agenda would have had two parts—continuing items and new business—and that the second of these headings would have been followed by a large question mark.[12]

What items would have appeared under the first heading of "unfinished business"? The principal federal concern in the summer of 1783, without doubt, was to see the states adopt the revenue plan that Congress had approved on April 18, 1783, following months of furious politicking marked by the threats and cajolings of Superintendent of Finance Morris and rumors of unrest (and worse) emanating from the army. After resisting these pressures, Congress forged a set of compromise resolutions that were to be presented to the states as a package—lest the partial adoption of particular proposals undo the collective accommodations so painfully secured. The comprehensive plan of April 1783 had three major elements: an impost lasting twenty-five years, to be collected by officials appointed by the states; a call upon the states to appropriate supplemental taxes for the payment of federal obligations; and a revision in Article 8 of the Confederation, altering the formula for apportioning the common expenses of the war among the states.

Robert Morris had sought far more. For almost a year he had conducted an aggressive campaign to convince Congress and interested parties "out-of-doors" that the union should be vested with authority to levy poll, land, and excise taxes as well as an impost. A few delegates, like the ideologue Arthur Lee of Virginia and David Howell of Rhode Island, opposed these measures—and the final compromise—out of a mixture of personal emnity against Morris and staunchly Whiggish convictions that liberty would be endangered if Congress enjoyed its own powers of taxation. "[N]o one who had ever opened a page or read a line on the subject of liberty," Lee declaimed, "could be insensible to the danger of surrendering the purse into the same hand which held the sword."[13] Such fears still echo—in milder language—in those historical accounts that portray Morris as a "nationalist" already intent on effecting a radical transfer of power from the states to the union. It would be more accurate to say that his own experience in both national and state government had convinced Morris that Congress would never be able to discharge its existing responsibilities until it enjoyed a degree of financial independence.[14] Bolder visions of empire were held by his assistant, Gouverneur Morris, and his two sturdiest allies in Congress, Alexander Hamilton and James Wilson, but the Superintendent was a man who preferred to confine his speculations to land, not politics.

The more telling objections against the Morris program were, in any case, political rather than ideological. Amendments to the Articles required the unanimous approval of the states, and after watching the original impost proposal of 1781 founder upon the lone opposition of Rhode Island, the delegates had no choice but to treat this condition with the utmost respect. A carefully framed compromise commanding the support of a substantial majority within Congress stood some reasonable chance of adoption by the states; a bolder and more controversial measure did not.

The idea that the states might be coaxed into approving a balanced and carefully explained compromise was not unrealistic. For in the second great item of unfinished business confronting Congress at war's end—the creation of a national domain northwest of the Ohio River—the delegates could have found some precedent for hoping that enlightened appeals could lead to the amicable adjustment of national and state interests. By agreeing to give Congress control over so vast an expanse of land, the states had indicated that it was not the financial autonomy of the union they objected to, but only a national power of taxation. Indeed, the same delegates who were most opposed to the idea of federal taxation on ideological grounds were first to exaggerate the windfall Congress would receive from the national domain. Transported by visions of the sale of millions of acres of land, they believed that its speedy exploitation would render schemes of taxation superfluous. "The western world opens an amazing prospect as a national fund," David Howell gushed in February 1784, "it is equal to our debt."[15] Moreover, despite the intense suspicion and animosity that the issue of Western lands had generated since 1776, by autumn 1783 most of the outstanding difficulties appeared close to solution. When Congress belatedly accepted the conditions that Virginia, the key landed state, had attached to its cession, the completion of this arduous process at last seemed at hand.[16]

Read in this way, then, the tortuous politics of the Western lands issue seemed to provide a great and hopeful lesson in the possibilities of interstate cooperation. More than that, as Peter S. Onuf has recently argued, it illuminated what might be called the necessities of federal government itself. For what the territorial controversies of the 1770s and 1780s revealed was that the individual states were hardly capable of exercising the panoply of sovereign rights with which they were presumably vested under both the Articles of Confederation and their own constitutions. They could neither secure their territorial limits—a minimal criterion of statehood—nor command the loyalty of all the communities lying within their claimed boundaries. Far from being the primordial sovereign units of which the union was composed, the individual states were themselves fragile governments whose authority was little less precarious than that of Congress. Individual states could hope to establish their legitimacy, Onuf concludes, only through a process of mutual recognition that presupposed the existence of a federal union. Federalism was thus the logical solution not only to problems involving demonstrably common interests, but also to the debilities of statehood itself.[17]

That was not, however, the only way the controversy over Western lands could be read. Its value as a precedent for the resolution of other difficult issues was unclear. Key advantages that Congress had enjoyed in bringing this dispute to an acceptable conclusion might not be replicable on other issues. The creation of a national domain had required neither the unanimous acquiescence of the states nor approval of a formal amendment to the Confederation. Instead, Congress had proceeded *politically*, seeking individual cessions from the states with claims to the land in question, while avoiding passing judgment on the merits of particular titles. Each of these states, in turn, had good reason to offer cessions to Congress (albeit under certain conditions), for all of their claims rested on tenuous theories of title.[18] Moreover, prominent leaders in the claimant states realized that governments already hard pressed to manage affairs within the existing perimeters of settlement would not be able to make their writ run to communities lying west of the Appalachian mountain chain. They were also well prepared to defer to genuine considerations of national interest. The movement for the Virginia cession was led, for example, by Madison, Thomas Jefferson, and Joseph Jones; while in New York, key roles were played by George Clinton, Philip Schuyler, Robert R. Livingston, and John Jay. In the end, the creation of the national domain was the result of a consensus to which the various parties to this dispute could subscribe. Whether similar agreement could be reached on other issues was, however, far from certain.

Revenue and land, then, were the two issues that headed the congressional agenda in 1783 and 1784. The relation between them was embarrassingly reciprocal. Congress was anxious to develop the national domain precisely because it saw the sale of these millions of acres of lands as a panacea for its financial woes, but its bankruptcy severely undermined its ability to settle the territory across the Ohio River in an orderly fashion. Congress was too poor both to maintain enough troops to restrain the frontiersmen who began spilling across the Ohio at war's end, and to afford to extinguish Indian claims to the lands in question through fair purchase. Instead, at the dictated treaties of Fort Stanwix (October 1784) and Fort McIntosh (January 1785), federal commissioners—including the intemperate Arthur Lee—followed congressional instructions and invoked a theory of conquest to justify dispossessing the four hostile tribes of the Iroquois and their allies to the west of their rights to the desired territory. These negotiations marked the beginning of the ill-advised policies that would lead to the Indian wars of the early 1790s.[19]

North of the Ohio River, Congress had only itself to blame for the deteriorating relations with the Indian tribes. Further south its intentions were better, but here the course of Indian relations provided a revealing case study in the "defects" of the Articles of Confederation. No clause of the Articles appeared more baffling than that which pertained to Indian affairs. Article IX gave Congress the "sole and exclusive right and power of . . . regulating the trade and managing all affairs with the Indians, not members of any of the States, provided that the legislative right of any States within its own limits be not infringed or violated." A broad grant of authority was thus immediately compromised by two substantial qualifications.[20] In 1783 and 1784, the ambiguity of this clause had sparked brief jurisdictional disputes between Congress and the states of New York and Pennsylvania, but once Congress acquired title to the Indian lands it sought, which lay beyond the claimed boundaries of either state, the basis for conflict evaporated. But there was no national domain south of the Ohio. Here North Carolina and Georgia were pursuing extremely aggressive policies designed to divest the Cherokees and Creeks of as much land as possible, and by adhering to a geographical definition of Indian "membership," they could plausibly claim to be exercising a valid "legislative right." Congress attempted to brake their policy in the Hopewell treaties of 1785–86, but by the summer of 1787, when war seemed imminent along the Southern frontier, Secretary of War Henry Knox and a congressional committee were forced to admit that effective federal jurisdiction could be created only if the Southern states completed cessions comparable to those that had led to the creation of the national domain.[21]

Of course, by the summer of 1787, the state of Indian affairs either north or south provided little more than an incidental illustration of the "imbecility" of Congress and the shortcomings of the Articles of Confederation. Well before then, additional and more disturbing items had begun to appear on the agenda of unfinished business, as the pervasive transition from war to peace allowed state and regional interests to be asserted with a new candor. During the first year of peace, the handful of itinerant delegates who continued to attend Congress while it wandered from Philadelphia to Princeton, Annapolis, and Trenton were preoccupied with matters of finance, Western lands, and the need to fix the location of a permanent national capital.[22] But by the time Congress reassembled in New York in January 1785, new concerns were becoming equally pressing.

The most serious doubts about the adequacy of the Articles of Confederation arose within the realm of foreign affairs. Indeed, it was the inability of Congress to frame and implement adequate foreign policies in the mid-1780s that originally provided nationally minded politicians with the most compelling set of reasons for contemplating major constitutional reform.[23]

Whatever uncertainty might have existed about the domestic responsibilities of Congress, there was general agreement that the conduct of foreign relations was a federal concern. Because this was the case, the emerging foreign policy dilemmas of the mid-1780s were doubly disturbing. They revealed, first, that Congress lacked the formal authority it needed to protect American commercial interests. Since most Americans assumed that the new republic's relations with Europe would be commercial rather than political in nature, this was a critical shortcoming. And, in the second place, the events of 1783–86 further demonstrated that, in matters of foreign policy, Congress could neither muster the same internal consensus nor command the same popular support that it had possessed in the early years of the Revolution, and which it still retained, though to a lesser extent, after 1779.[24] By the mid-1780s it was an open question whether there was, in fact, any longer a *national* interest that could be generally perceived or effectively pursued even by the relatively enlightened members of Congress, or to which the state governments and the larger public would readily defer.

Within a year of the conclusion of peace, Congress confronted three external challenges to the national welfare. American merchants, eager to restore pre-Revolutionary patterns of commerce, found early cause for disappointment in the measures that Britain quickly took to close both home island and West Indian ports to American shipping. At the same time, a stream of British ships sailed into American harbors, bringing goods that had been sorely missed during the wartime years of deprivation. In theory, the United States should have pursued a retaliatory strategy of limiting British access to American ports until British harbors were opened to American shipping. But such a policy stood to fail on two counts. Lacking authority to regulate interstate or foreign commerce, Congress could neither devise nor impose a uniform set of restrictions on British ships. This *constitutional* debility in turn diminished whatever prospects there might have been for advancing American trading interests through the negotiation of a satisfactory commercial treaty with Britain: what privileges could John Adams, the American minister, offer that British merchants did not already enjoy?

The second great issue of foreign relations was an outgrowth of the Treaty of Paris that had brought the Revolutionary War to a close. Article IV of the treaty provided that "creditors on either side shall meet with no lawful impediment" to the recovery of debts previously contracted in good faith. Under Article V, Congress was required to *recommend* that the states similarly permit British subjects and American Loyalists to sue for the recovery of confiscated property. Both articles placed Congress in the awkward position of guaranteeing what it lacked the constitutional authority to deliver: the compliance of state legislatures and courts with a national commitment made to a foreign power. When individual states, not unexpectedly, failed to abide by the terms of the treaty, Britain used their noncompliance as a pretext for retaining the Northwestern forts (Oswego, Niagara, and Detroit) whose surrender had also been part of the treaty of peace. This in turn further jeopardized the entire congressional policy for the national domain, since a continued British presence in the Northwest encouraged the hostile Western tribes to resist American encroachments on their lands.

The future of westward expansion was also implicated in the third major problem of foreign policy to arise with the coming of peace. In April 1784, Spain closed New Orleans and the lower Mississippi River to American navigation, in effect preventing frontier settlers living west of the mountain barrier from shipping their produce to the Gulf of Mexico and thence to other markets. This action, coupled with abortive separatist efforts to establish new states in Kentucky and what would become Tennessee, threatened to deprive the United States of the generous territorial settlement accorded by the Treaty of Paris. Should the weakness of the union force Western settlers to accommodate themselves to Spain, control of the regions lying between the mountains and the Mississippi would be lost to the United States. Furthermore, since the region below the Ohio was commonly viewed as an outpost of *Southern* expansion, acquiescence in the Spanish action threatened to exacerbate sectional tensions within Congress. Southern leaders grew particularly outraged in 1786, when John Jay, the secretary of foreign affairs, went so far as to propose that the United States abjure its navigational rights in exchange for a commercial treaty with Spain. Jay's proposal evoked a sharp and bitter sectional division within Congress, giving sudden validity to hitherto vague speculations about the eventual devolution of the United States into two or three regional confederacies.[25]

While the revenue plan of April 1783 continued its sluggish progress through the state assemblies, then, and while Congress continued its efforts to organize the national domain, it was this concern with aspects of foreign relations that dominated postwar efforts to strengthen the confederation. Proposals for reform developed along two lines. One involved *clarifying* the authority that might be presumed already to lie in Congress by virtue of its general power to make treaties with foreign nations. Here the great challenge was to provide a logic whereby national obligations could take precedence over the ostensibly legitimate actions of sovereign states. Thus in his seminal (though not unambiguous) decision in *Rutgers v. Waddington*, James Duane attempted to fashion an argument for the supremacy of federal treaties over state law, while simultaneously establishing a key precedent for the doctrine of judicial review of legislative acts.[26] The other avenue of reform centered on *enhancing* federal power in an area where experience indicated that the common welfare would be served by giving Congress what it currently lacked: greater authority to regulate commerce both among the states and with foreign nations. In 1784 Congress did ask the states to give it limited authority over foreign commerce; in 1785 and 1786 it considered committee reports proposing additional powers in the same areas; and in September 1786 the Annapolis Convention was called to ponder the same issue.

Revenue, Western land, the protection of American commerce, and state violations of the Treaty of Paris: these were the principal concerns of the relatively small group of leaders who supported the movement to strengthen the Articles of Confederation. Their ideas of what was desirable in theory did not transcend their awareness of what they hoped might prove feasible in practice. Their thoughts centered naturally on the specific additional powers that Congress would need if national interests were to be effectively asserted and national responsibilities effectively discharged. What was largely missing from their discussions and proposals was the larger array of concerns that we associate with the debates at the Constitutional Convention, with the Federalism of 1787–88, and with the central theory that even today arguably provides the dominant paradigm of American political science: James Madison's conception of the extended republic.

For the reformers of the mid-1780s were not thinking of using the amendment of the Confederation as a means for curing the vices of republican government within the states. Nor did their discussions more than incidentally consider the relevance of such aspects of constitutional theory as the separation of powers or the nature of representation to the existing problems of the union. The various amendments to the Articles that were proposed during these years did not anticipate the theoretical concerns that would acquire so prominent a place in the debates of 1787. They were designed, first and foremost, to free Congress from its dependence on the states, to enable it to resolve problems that fell within its existing sphere of responsibility. The improved conduct of national affairs, it was hoped, would gradually elevate the character of public life within the states as well, but that would be a secondary and deferred benefit. Concerns about what might be called the internal efficiency of Congress were similarly relegated for later consideration. John Jay may have already concluded that "To vest legislative, judicial and executive Powers in one and the same Body of Men, and that too in a Body daily changing its members, can never be wise," but proposals to alter the structure of the federal government were mere suggestions at best.[27]

It was not, of course, a lack of imagination or interest in issues of constitutional theory that discouraged efforts to conceive of the problem of federalism in terms that went beyond identifying the specific additional powers that Congress needed. Rather, all such matters were rendered merely speculative by the requirement that amendments to the Articles receive the unanimous ratification of the states. This was the first and dominant condition to which the supporters of a stronger federal union had to accede. Instead of contemplating the calling of a general convention, they pursued a prudent strategy of proposing discrete and limited amendments in the hope that their piecemeal adoption and implementation would make Americans less wary of the dangers of a more efficient national government. The desultory and ultimately fruitless histories of *all* the amendments that Congress had requested since 1781 indicated that proposals envisioning a more radical transfer of power from states to union stood little if any chance of adoption. If measures as carefully framed as the limited commercial amendments of 1784 failed of adoption, there seemed little chance that bolder proposals would fare better. Nor, for the same reason, did major changes in the political structure of the union appear any more likely. Almost certainly the first of these would involve implementing some form of proportional representation in Congress—a measure the small states would obviously wish to block.

To say that the nationally minded reformers of the mid-1780s had little reason to anticipate the larger theoretical problems that would confront the Federal Convention of 1787 does not mean, however, that such issues were not being considered in a different context. For at a lower level of politics, questions about the proper distribution of power among the branches of government and the obligations of representatives were becoming subjects of thoughtful controversy during these years. The experience of republican government within the states was indeed leading many to reconsider the validity of the assumptions of 1776. The most important and novel lessons that brought James Madison to fashion his doctrine of the extended republic were not, after all, those he had learned during his four years at Congress, but rather the result of the three succeeding years of frustration in the Virginia legislature. The basis for rethinking basic principles of republican government was being laid within the states; what was missing, until late 1786, was an occasion for recognizing that these lessons could be usefully or realistically applied to the problem of federalism.[28]

This transposition became possible only when the abortive Annapolis Convention of September 1786 left the reformers with no other option than the risky gamble of a general constitutional assembly. The Annapolis meeting marked a final effort to salvage the strategy of piecemeal, gradual reform. It was called to consider the sole issue of commerce, and convened under the authority of the states to avoid the taint that would henceforth afflict any amendment emanating from Congress itself. The hopes underlying that strategy were exploded when the Annapolis Convention failed to muster the quorum needed to bestow weight on the amendment it was expected to propose. Rather than adjourn and admit that this final tactic had proved bankrupt, the handful of delegates present agreed to issue a call for a plenary convention to assemble the following spring. Their act was the work not of a group of political conspirators stealing a march on their slumbering opponents, but of like-minded men who had now realized that further caution carried no prospect of victory. The call issued by the Annapolis delegates was the result more of political desperation than anything else.

Desperation, it turned out, had its rewards. Now that the other alternatives for reform had been discredited—and once it became clear that a majority of states were responding favorably to the call—the very fact of the Convention became significant in its own right. With good reason, skeptics still doubted whether such a body could reach agreement on any set of proposals that stood a realistic chance of adoption. But others, especially those leaders aware of the extent of sectional tensions within Congress, sensed that they could no longer count upon enjoying an indefinite period of time for amending the Articles. During the nine months that separated the dispersion from Annapolis and the gathering at Philadelphia, it at last became both politically and intellectually possible to link the debilities of the union with the vices of republican government within the states.

No one illustrates this transition more dramatically or significantly than James Madison. Throughout the mid-1780s, Madison had been deeply committed to the strategy of piecemeal reform. In 1785 he had warned James Monroe, his replacement at Congress, against pursuing the idea of a general convention. By 1786, recognizing that any amendment emanating from Congress itself would be fatally tainted, he changed his mind and placed his hope in the meeting at Annapolis, but in doing so he still insisted on the need for gradual reform. Now, however, he set himself to the task of rethinking the entire problem of federal government, and in the paper he distilled from his researches—his pre-Convention memorandum on "The Vices of the Political System"—he forged an explicit link between federalism and republicanism. The connection between the two was made, quietly but powerfully, only after Madison had completed his summary of the manifest shortcomings of the Articles of Confederation. "In developing the evils which viciate the political system of the U.S.," he wrote, "it is proper to include those which are found within the States individually, as well as those which directly affect the States collectively, since the former class have an indirect influence on the general malady and must not be overlooked in forming a compleat remedy." It was from this transition that Madison went on to explain how the establishment of an extended federal republic could serve to secure the great object of protecting individual liberty against the dangers it faced within the states. It would do so, first, by obstructing the formation of factious majorities intent on pursuing private interests in the guise of the public good, and second, by encouraging power to pass from the demagogues dominant at the state level of politics into the hands of a better class of men.[29]

Some historians resist according so great an importance to the merely intellectual labors of Madison. Certainly had Shays' Rebellion and its aftermath in the Massachusetts elections of 1787 not provided impressive evidence in support of his thesis, his argument, by itself, might well have proved unavailing. Nor should we treat the Convention itself as a sort of referendum on Madison's theory; were we to do so, it would be difficult to claim that its logic had carried the day.[30] Yet it would be wrong to dismiss the theory of the extended republic solely as a text in political philosophy. In at least one vital sense, its aims were immediate, pragmatic, and consciously designed to influence the politics of the Convention.

Madison had made it possible to cast the agenda of national reform in terms that went well beyond anything that had been seriously considered before the spring of 1787.[31] Many of his colleagues in the Convention had probably come to Philadelphia imagining that their deliberations would extend no further than compiling and endorsing a comprehensive list of the various proposals for additional powers that had circulated during the mid-1780s—perhaps something akin to the final set of amendments that a committee chaired by Charles Pinckney had reported to Congress in the summer of 1786.[32] Madison had mapped higher ground. The Virginia Plan—which arguably was the next extension of his thought—did not assume that the Convention had to begin its work by identifying which additional powers the union needed. Instead, it presumed that the national government would receive a general grant of legislative authority, and moved ahead to ask how that government should be designed. It thus diverted the attention of the delegates away from the stock concerns of the mid-1780s, and forced them to begin to confront a range of issues that hitherto had not seemed pertinent to the context of national politics. Now lessons drawn from the experience of the states could be applied to the problems of the union, and serve, at the same time, as a generalized commentary on how a republican government, at any level of the polity, should be constituted. During the opening weeks of the Convention, it seemed less important to determine what role the federal government was actually to play in American life than to decide how it was to be organized and (of course) whom and what it would represent.

The irony of this situation is that the Convention could never have succeeded had contemporaries been able to grasp just how easily or sweepingly the standing agenda of the mid-1780s could be altered, had they foreseen just how far the Convention would be prepared to go. True, more adventurous and radical ideas were perhaps being aired in private than the modest proposals that occasionally appeared in the public prints during the months leading up to May 1787. Writing to John Adams in the late fall of 1786, Samuel Osgood reported that it was not "uncommon to hear the principles of Government stated in common Conversation. Emperors, Kings, Stadtholders, Governors General, with a Senate, or House of Lords, & House of Commons, are frequently the topics of Conversation."[33] Yet in the early months of 1787, these discussions were not brought to anything resembling a clear focus; nor did they produce anything like the relatively surprising degree of consensus that had coalesced just prior to another momentous gathering in Philadelphia thirteen years earlier: the First Continental Congress.[34] Even Madison—customarily regarded by everyone except William Crosskey[35] as the best prepared of the delegates—did not begin to pull his specific ideas together until March 1787; while the actual preparation of the Virginia Plan was only made possible by the failure of the Convention to muster a quorum on the appointed date of May 14, which gave the Virginians the time to frame their proposals. Against such a background, the intellectual task of bridging the gap between the limited proposals of the mid-1780s and the Federalist platform of 1787 proved too difficult for parochial leaders to perform—even if Patrick Henry did smell a rat. It was because the delegates came to Philadelphia largely unencumbered by instructions or binding positions that they were able to accept the Virginia Plan, in its full scope, as an appropriate framework for discussion.

There was, however, a second irony that would require decades rather than months to unveil. The shift in perspective that led the framers to focus on the architecture of government rather than its functions was, in a sense, a distraction. The Convention may well have come to believe that the entire future of republican government hinged on its debates. But the original concerns of the mid-1780s remained intact; at the core of the new government's powers one would still find the preeminent worries of the immediate postwar years: foreign affairs, commerce, and the disposition of Western lands. Whether it would have significant duties beyond these familiar areas seemed, by the later weeks of the Convention, to be very much of an open question. The rhetoric of the earlier weeks of conflict between the small and large states had led partisans on both sides to project the responsibilities of the new regime in exaggerated terms: if the new government were to be so powerful, one could argue with equal plausibility either that justice to the large states required a system of proportional representation in both houses, or that the security of the small states warranted giving them an equal vote in at least one chamber. Yet once this issue was surmounted, and passions had begun to cool, many delegates were even prepared to admit that the new government might not, after all, have that much to do. "The most numerous objects of legislation belong to the States," Rufus King observed on August 7; "Those of the National Legislature were but few. The chief of them were commerce & Revenue. When these should be once settled, alterations would be rarely necessary & easily made."[36]

This may have been a more accurate prediction than King privately suspected. No one observing the operations of the federal government during much of the next century could have concluded that the Convention had in fact established a political leviathan. In the realm of what might be called public policy, its principal business remained consistent with the concerns that had comprised the unfinished agenda of national politics at the close of the Revolution; at the more prosaic level of daily activity, its most vital service, arguably, was the delivery of the mail. In many ways, the United States was not much less of a confederation in 1836, when Madison, the last of the framers, passed away, than it had been half a century earlier. The federal government remained, in John Murrin's phrase, "a midget institution in a giant land"—an establishment in which, as James Sterling Young has wryly noted, "there were more people making the law than enforcing it."[37]

None of these observations detracts from the significance of the framers' achievement in 1787; but they do need to be borne in mind by historians whose own agenda—spurred by a vestigial mysticism that has us commemorate events in roundly numbered intervals—currently includes understanding the making of the Constitution. By placing an entirely new agenda before the American people in 1787, the framers were able to surmount all the obstacles that in the first years of peace had seemingly consigned the confederation to a condition of "imbecility." From that point on, the Federalists of 1787–88 held a political initiative that their opponents were never able to reverse, allowing them, as most accounts of the ratification campaign have agreed, to prevail in critical situations where they entered the convention chambers as a distinct minority.

Yet when one attempts to locate the constitutional politics of the late 1780s in a larger context—the development of the liberal state in the nineteenth century—the assessment of this remarkable episode becomes more puzzling. In its experimental combination of hopeful aspirations and pragmatic accommodations, the Constitution may indeed be seen as "the prototypical creation of the age."[38] But when one sets the political expectations of 1787 against the developments of the decades to follow—especially the contrast between the quietude of the federal government and the relative vigor of the states—a different and rather more ironic perspective emerges. What now stands out is the mood of exceptional enthusiasm and heightened expectations, both hopeful and fearful, that swept the politically active segments of the American population while the Constitution was suspended in judgment. Few Americans could view it with relative dispassion. Alternately believing that the fate of the union or the preservation of liberty respectively required either its adoption or rejection, they could not be expected to determine just how well it anticipated the agenda upon which they would be acting individually and collectively in the years ahead.

One is left to wonder whether the adoption of the Constitution owed more to the contingent political factors operating in 1786–88 than to any great structural imperatives demanding the establishment of a stronger union. Indeed, had the requirement of unanimous state ratification not obstructed every effort at reform, a good case could be made that the adoption of even one amendment to the Articles might have rendered the gradual process to which Madison and others were originally committed workable, permitting the United States to remain a confederation in name as well as substance. But the failure of all previous efforts at amendment, coupled with a sense of approaching crisis evoked by such events as Shays' Rebellion and the debate over the Mississippi, concentrated the minds of the delegates wonderfully, preparing them to entertain ideas that might have been dismissed as either absurd or at least impracticable only months earlier.

Within this context, it is only appropriate to offer a concluding reflection on the one member of the Federal Convention whose thought and activity have stood at the center of recent interpretations of the making of the Constitution. James Madison did not leave Philadelphia entirely pleased with the work he had done so much to promote. He was especially disappointed that the Convention had rejected his pet scheme for a federal veto over state legislation, and that the small states had managed to uphold their indefensible claim to equal representation in the Senate. Yet notwithstanding these disappointments and the other ironies of constitutional and political change he would observe during his remaining half century of life, the course of the Convention owed much to his distinctive approach to politics. In 1787, despite a decade of public life, Madison was still neither a forceful speaker nor a commanding personality. What he had learned to do instead was to prepare himself more thoroughly for debate than anyone else, to analyze alternative courses of action with characteristic rigor, and to understand the advantages that fell to the legislator who could convert his particular understanding of a problem into a framework for general discussion. More than any of his colleagues, Madison grasped the uses to which a well-prepared agenda could be put; and the general course of the Convention—though not (admittedly) all of its decisions—owed much to that understanding.

NOTES

1. [Benjamin Rush], "Address to the People of the United States," reprinted in John P. Kaminski and Gaspare J. Saladino, eds., *The Documentary History of the Ratification of the Constitution* (Madison, 1976–), XIII, 46–9. The editors incorrectly attribute a February 1787 date to this essay, which is when it appeared in the first issue of Matthew Carey's *American Museum;* it was originally published, however, in the Philadelphia *Independent Gazetteer* for June 3, 1786.

2. Bernard Bailyn, "The Central Themes of the American Revolution: An Interpretation," in Stephen G. Kurtz and James H. Hutson, eds., *Essays on the American Revolution* (Chapel Hill, N.C., 1973), 19; and *The Ideological Origins of the American Revolution* (Cambridge, Mass., 1967), 232.

3. In somewhat simplified form, this summarizes the interpretation that runs through the principal works of the late Merrill Jensen and which still informs the writing of his numerous students. See especially Jensen's most influential books, *The Articles of Confederation: An Interpretation of the Social-Constitutional History of the American Revolution, 1774–1781* (Madison, 1940), and *The New Nation: A History of the United States During the Confederation, 1781–1789* (New York, 1950).

4. Hamilton to James Duane, September 3, 1780, in Harold Syrett and Jacob Cooke, eds., *The Papers of Alexander Hamilton* (New York, 1960–78), II, 400–418.

5. Jack N. Rakove, *The Beginnings of National Politics: An Interpretive History of the Continental Congress* (New York, 1979), 288–291.

6. E. James Ferguson, "The Nationalists of 1781–1783 and the Economic Interpretation of the Constitution," *Journal of American History*, 56 (1969), 241–261; and see the more detailed treatment in Ferguson, *The Power of the Purse: A History of American Public Finance, 1776–1790* (Chapel Hill, N.C., 1961). E. Wayne Carp has similarly invoked a concept of a "nationalist" upsurge to describe the politics of the early 1780s, but places greater emphasis on problems of military logistics rather than finance; see Carp, *"To Starve the Army at Pleasure": Continental Army Administration and American Political Culture, 1775–1783* (Chapel Hill, N.C., 1984), 191–217. More cautious assessments of the political implications of the Morris program are found in Clarence L. Ver Steeg, *Robert Morris: Revolutionary Financier* (Philadelphia, 1954); and Rakove, *Beginnings of National Politics*, 297–329. Lance Banning, "James Madison and the Nationalists, 1780–1783," *William and Mary Quarterly*, 3rd ser., 40 (1983), 227–55, offers an interpretation of Madison's role that seems to straddle the two positions.

7. One remarkable example of this is a letter from Jonathan Jackson, a Newburyport (Mass.) merchant who had briefly served in Congress to Secretary of War Benjamin Lincoln, April 19, 1783, Fogg Collection, vol. 19, Maine Historical Society.

8. Farrand, *Records*, I, 423–4 (June 26).

9. Thus when Edmund Randolph introduced the Virginia Plan on May 29, 1787, he took care to note that the "defects" of the Articles were not to be traced to their framers, who a decade earlier had "done all that patriots could do, in the then infancy of the science, of constitutions, & of confederacies." Farrand, *Records*, I, 18–19.

10. "Vices of the Political System of the U. States," in William T. Hutchinson, William M.E. Rachal, and Robert A. Rutland et al., eds., *The Papers of James Madison* (Chicago and Charlottesville, 1962–), IX, 351.

11. Thomas Burke to Governor Richard Caswell, November 4, 1777, in Paul H. Smith, ed., *Letters of Delegates to Congress, 1774–1789* (Washington, D.C., 1976–), VIII, 227. The drafting of the confederation is analyzed in Rakove, *Beginnings of National Politics*, chaps. VII–VIII.

12. Notice ought to be taken, however, of the resolutions that Alexander Hamilton had prepared in April 1783, while serving as delegate from New York, and which in fact contemplated calling a constitutional convention to propose major reforms in the structure of the union; Syrett and Cooke, eds., *Papers of Hamilton*, III, 420–426. But as Hamilton himself noted, his resolutions had to be "abandoned for want of support."

13. Lee's remarks were recorded by Madison in his notes of debates for January 28, 1783; see Hutchinson and Rachal, eds., *Papers of Madison*, VI, 149. Our sources for these debates are perhaps more complete than those for any other major issue in the history of the Continental Congress. The most important are Madison's notes of debates, reprinted ibid., V and VI, passim, and the documents in E. James Ferguson et al., eds., *The Papers of Robert Morris, 1781–1784* (Pittsburgh, 1973–).

14. Compare the account in Ferguson, *Power of the Purse*, 125–45, with the treatments in Ver Steeg, *Robert Morris*, 78–110, and Rakove, *Beginnings of National Politics*, 297–324. While much has also been made of the Newburgh incident and the purported danger of a military mutiny, there is little evidence that the unrest at camp exercised any significant influence on the deliberations of Congress. See the incisive comments in Henry Knox to Alexander McDougall, West Point, February 21, 1783, Henry Knox Papers, XI, Massachusetts Historical Society.

15. David Howell to Jonathan Arnold, February 21, 1784, in William R. Staples, ed., *Rhode Island in the Continental Congress* (Providence, 1870), 479.

16. Thomas Abernethy, *Western Lands and the American Revolution* (New York, 1937) remains the standard account; but to understand the relation between the settlement of boundary disputes and land claims, on the other hand, and the establishment of a federal regime, on the other, one needs to read Peter S. Onuf, *The Origins of the Federal Republic: Jurisdictional Controversies in the United States, 1775–1787* (Philadelphia, 1983).

17. Onuf, *Origins of the Federal Republic*, chaps. 1–2. The essays collected in Ronald Hoffman and Peter J. Albert, eds., *Sovereign States in an Age of Uncertainty* (Charlottesville, VA, 1981), provide a useful introduction to the range of difficulties the states encountered during the war years proper. Among the best studies of individual states are Ronald Hoffman, *A Spirit of Dissension: Economics, Politics, and the Revolution in Maryland* (Baltimore, 1973), and Edward Countryman, *A People in Revolution: The American Revolution and Political Society in New York, 1760–1790* (Baltimore, 1981). There is still ample room for research into the question of how the states attempted to mobilize their resources—among which one could include the political commitments of their citizenry—to deal with the demands of the war. Studies of state politics in the 1780s have tended to stress the emergence of coherent factions anticipating both alignments vis-à-vis adoption of the Constitution and the formation of the first party system. See, most notably, Jackson T. Main, *Political Parties before the Constitution* (Chapel Hill, 1973), and Norman K. Risjord, *Chesapeake Politics, 1781–1800* (New York, 1978).

18. The best and, in political terms, the most weighty of these claims belonged to Virginia, but even its title defense depended in large measure on an "ancient charter" that the

crown had revoked a century and a half earlier. The Massachusetts and Connecticut claims required a similarly loose reading of their charters, while New York, the first of the ceding states, rested its title on the history of its relations with the Iroquois and the hazy notion of Iroquois "suzerainty" over the tribes of the Ohio Valley.

19. The best introductory account is Reginald Horsman, *Expansion and American Indian Policy, 1783–1812* (East Lansing, Mich., 1967), chap. 1.

20. In its final debate on the Indian affairs clause in October 1777, Congress had refused to accept amendments that would have clarified the meaning of "not members" by giving the term either a territorial or a jurisdictional gloss; at the same time, it added the "legislative right" proviso at the behest of the landed states. See Worthington C. Ford, ed., *Journals of the Continental Congress, 1774–1789* (Washington, D.C., 1904–37), IX, 844–5. Since the landed states held the upper hand throughout the final debates on the confederation, whatever ambiguity exists within the Indian affairs clause seems to have been contrived to protect their claims by preventing Congress from acquiring broad jurisdiction until the process of territorial cessions was at least well under way.

21. See the report of Henry Knox to Congress, July 18, 1787; and the report on Indian affairs in the Southern department, August 3, 1787, ibid., XXXII, 365–69; XXXIII, 455–63. The committee report, in fact, did attempt to interpret the language of Article IX in a way favorable to federal authority, but it undercut that effort by conceding that unequivocal national jurisdiction required a cession from the concerned states. The post-Revolutionary history of Indian relations along the southern frontier deserves fresh attention.

22. Lawrence D. Cress, "Whither Columbia: Congressional Residence and the Politics of the New Nation, 1776–1787," *William and Mary Quarterly*, 3rd ser., 32 (1975), 581–600.

23. Frederick W. Marks, III, *Independence on Trial: Foreign Affairs and the Making of the Constitution* (Baton Rouge, La., 1973), 3–95.

24. The relation between the conduct of foreign relations and the preservation of congressional authority is discussed in Rakove, *Beginnings of National Politics*, 112–119, 243–274.

25. See the account in H. James Henderson, *Party Politics in the Continental Congress* (New York, 1974), 387–99. Madison remained deeply concerned with the political fallout of the Mississippi question well into 1788, when the issue figured prominently in the Virginia ratification convention. Its constitutional implications are examined in Jack N. Rakove, "Solving a Constitutional Puzzle: The Treatymaking Clause as a Case Study," *Perspectives in American History*, n.s., 1 (1984), 272–81.

26. The surviving record of *Rutgers v. Waddington* is reprinted, with an excellent introduction, in Julius Goebel, ed., *The Law Practice of Alexander Hamilton* (New York, 1964–81), I, 282–419; also see the still valuable essay of E.S. Corwin, "The Progress of Constitutional Theory between the Declaration of Independence and the Meeting of the Philadelphia Convention," *American Historical Review*, 30 (1924–25), 511–36.

27. Jay to Jefferson, August 18, 1786, in Henry P. Johnston, ed., *The Correspondence and Public Papers of John Jay* (New York, 1890–93), III, 210.

28. Gordon S. Wood, *The Creation of the American Republic, 1776–1787* (Chapel Hill, N.C., 1969), 393–467.

29. Rutland, ed., *Papers of Madison*, IX, 353–58; for a general discussion of Madison's evolving position, see Rakove, *Beginnings of National Politics*, 368–80, 392–95.

30. This is especially the implication to be drawn from the rejection of Madison's pet scheme of a federal veto on all state laws, a proposal whose significance is ably analyzed in Charles Hobson, "The Negative on State Laws: James Madison and the Crisis of Republi-

can Government," *William and Mary Quarterly*, 3rd ser., 36 (1979), 215–35. It is worth noting, however, that Madison's general theory was very much the subject of debate during the opening seven weeks of the Federal Convention—in other words, down to the key decision of July 16 giving the states an equal vote in the Senate. For a detailed analysis of this point, see Jack N. Rakove, "The Great Compromise: Ideas, Interests, and the Politics of Constitution Making," ibid., 44.

31. I do not mean to imply that only Madison was capable of making this leap; other members of the Convention were working toward the same conclusions and moving beyond the limited agenda of previous years. Yet in terms of the actual politics of the Convention, the Virginia Plan provided something more than an incidental starting point for discussion. In a manner analogous to the deadlock over apportioning representation among the states, it helped to structure both the course of debate and the range of alternatives the delegates were prepared to consider.

32. Ford, ed., *Journals*, XXXI, 494–98.

33. Osgood to Adams, November 14, 1786, Adams Family Papers, microfilm reel 368, Massachusetts Historical Society.

34. A contrast explicitly noted in Stephen Mix Mitchell to William Samuel Johnson, July 26, 1787, in William Samuel Johnson Papers, vol. II, Connecticut Historical Society; also see Rakove, *Beginnings of National Politics*, chap. II.

35. See the idiosyncratic analysis of the period preceding the Convention in William Winslow Crosskey and William Jeffrey, Jr., *Politics and the Constitution in the History of the United States*, vol. III, *The Political Background of the Federal Convention* (Chicago, 1980), 368–462.

36. Farrand, *Records*, II, 197–99; also see the general discussion in Jack N. Rakove, "The Legacy of the Articles of Confederation," *Publius*, 12 (1982–83), 45–66.

37. John Murrin, "The Great Inversion, or Court versus Country: A Comparison of the Revolution Settlements in England (1688–1721) and America (1776–1816)," in J.G.A. Pocock, ed., *Three British Revolutions* (Princeton, 1980), 425; James Sterling Young, *The Washington Community, 1800–1828* (New York, 1966), 30.

38. Bailyn, "Central Themes," 23.

CHAPTER 5

The Problem of Power: Parties, Aristocracy, and Democracy in Revolutionary Thought

Lance Banning

Power is a hand that can caress as well as crush, provide as well as punish. It cannot say yes to some without denying others. It may lack capacity to nourish if it cannot also grip. Properly directed, nonetheless, the might of a community, concentrated in its government, can increase the happiness and nurture the prosperity of the society it shields. If it were otherwise—if the fist could not be opened, if everyone possessed the same ideas and interests, or if the revolutionary generation had not expected government to promote the general welfare as well as to protect the citizenry from lawlessness within and dangers from without—power might have proved a less persistent problem than it did.

Power puzzled revolutionary leaders longer and more deeply than older histories suggested because the revolutionaries did not consistently conceive of government as no more than a necessary evil, which should be limited to the protection of the individual in his pursuit of private goods. Nor did they always think of their society in terms of the relationships between an aggregate of solitary social atoms.[1] Living in an age of commerce, the revolutionary generation wanted benefits, not just protection, from their governments. Heirs to neo-classical and civic-humanist political ideas, as well as to the English libertarian tradition, they were accustomed to regarding man both as an individual involved in a relationship with other individuals and as a member of persistent social groups. In consequence, although the Revolution started with a fear of unresponsive central power, it produced a general government whose reach and grasp were more impressive than the claims that generated the American rebellion, and it involved the revolutionaries in a lifelong argument not only over ways in which great power might be rendered safe, but also over ways in which it could be shared and exercised so as to take advantage of its positive potential. Recent histories have focused scholarly attention on dimensions of the revolutionaries' thinking that were long neglected. A better understanding of the sources of their thought has thrown new light on how it changed and made it possible to see the federal Constitution as an incident in an extended effort to resolve a set of problems that the Founders redefined, but neither solved nor ceased debating.[2]

From this new perspective, it is helpful to approach the Revolution as a moment in our past when circumstances forced the nation's leaders to consider fundamentals. The moment was a long one. Historians today seem more and more inclined to think of this consideration of the fundamentals as a process that began as early as 1763 and may have reached a partial resolution only after the conclusion of the War of 1812.[3] The circumstances were the sort that pressed the revolutionaries to probe continuously deeper into all the basic concepts: virtue and self-interest; the many and the few; parties and the public good; liberty and power. The institution of our present federal government came roughly halfway through the course of this collective effort. The writing and approval of the Constitution ultimately altered nearly all the terms of the continuing debate, but it did not do so at once, nor did it solve all of the problems that the argument involved.

In 1763, most articulate American colonials identified themselves as English and shared with other Englishmen a reasonably coherent way of thinking about political society and power. Government, they thought, originated in the consent of the society it served and exercised a legitimate authority only when it faithfully protected the indefeasible rights of those it sheltered. But as power naturally inclined to turn against the liberties it was intended to defend and individuals were equal only in their right to hold their lives and property secure, the most effective way to guarantee that all would be protected and that government would stay within its proper bounds was to divide the sovereign authority (or legislative power) among three different branches, each representing different segments of society and all combining to provide the three essential characteristics that just, enduring governments require.[4] On both sides of the ocean, the history of seventeenth-century England was remembered as the story of the nation's struggle to confine the government within due limits and to forge effective links between the exercise of power and society's consent.[5] On both sides, by the middle of the eighteenth century, Englishmen complacently and boastfully agreed that their complicated government of king-in-parliament had solved this problem in a manner that was properly the envy of the enlightened world.[6] With power shared among the Crown, the House of Lords, and the House of Commons, every major segment of society possessed sufficient power to protect its vital interests, and the state reflected all the finest qualities of every simpler form of government without the risks and limitations which simpler governments entailed: the unity and vigor of a monarch; the wisdom commonly associated with a leisured, well-born few; and the responsiveness to common good that flows from the participation of the body of the people.[7]

Coherent as it seemed, eighteenth-century thinking was in fact a very complicated blend of elements that did not blend as smoothly as contemporaries thought. When British thinkers asked about the origins and limits of governmental power, their reasoning began with individuals. In the manner of John Locke, they emphasized a natural equality of rights, the limitations of legitimate authority, and the logical necessity that any aggregate of equals must be guided by the largest number.[8] When they thought about *good* government, by contrast, eighteenth-century Englishmen and their colonial cousins concerned themselves primarily with the relationships between two fundamentally *unequal* social groups: the many, and the few who are distinguishable from the majority by their greater leisure, better birth, and superior possessions.[9] This second line of reasoning, which may be traced back through the Renaissance to ancient Greek and Roman thinkers, was more preoccupied with the achievement of a stable mixture of the virtues of two social groups than with the rights of individuals. Where Locke assumed a sharp distinction between society and government, the neo-classical tradition was inclined to merge the two, conceiving of society as *embodied in* the different parts of government and worrying less frequently about the limits of governmental power than about the maintenance of its internal equilibrium.

Logically, these different modes of thought involved some rather contradictory assumptions and suggested inconsistent attitudes toward power. Historically, they had converged so neatly during the seventeenth-century struggle to confine the Stuart kings that eighteenth-century Englishmen were seldom conscious of the tensions.[10] Men had sometimes to be thought of in their individual capacities and sometimes as constituents of persistent and potentially conflicting groups. Regarded either way, their liberties seemed safest when power was divided among the few, the many, and the one. The governmental equilibrium that guaranteed security for every segment of society seemed simultaneously to shield the individual from grasping power. This seemed more certainly the case because the course of English history suggested that dangers to the governmental balance and the liberties of subjects both ordinarily issued from the usurpations of the one (or the executive) and because habitual association of liberty with property encouraged an assumption that the whole political society was present in the Lords and Commons, which confined the Crown and linked the exercise of power with consent.[11]

For colonials, however, the crisis in imperial relations which ground its way inexorably toward independence in the decade after 1765, severely shook this integrated way of thinking. The Revolution pitted its constituent ideas against each other, wrenched them into different shapes, and forced the altered elements into a new configuration. Half a century later, power was a different sort of problem. If this was less apparent to contemporaries than it seems to us, that was in part because Americans still feared the possibility of its abuse and still expressed this fear in eighteenth-century language, condemning "aristocracy" and "influence" and the like, employing terms that were increasingly ill-suited to contemporary practices and needs. But the persistence of such terms was also a reflection of the fact that older structures of ideas had not abruptly crumbled. While the Revolution and the Constitution rapidly produced a new consensus about the character and limits of legitimate authority, the problem of good government was not so readily resolved; newer worries over parties and the public good could not be easily disjoined from more traditional concerns about relationships between the many and the few. Aristocracy, democracy, and parties troubled revolutionary leaders in succession. Successive grapplings with these problems significantly reshaped the country's thought and institutions, but the hardest questions raised by the determination of the Founders to secure a government at once responsible and wise were not so much resolved as thoroughly rephrased.

Crisis came upon the empire in the aftermath of Britain's brilliant victory in the last and largest of four eighteenth-century wars with France. Struggling with a swollen national debt, obliged to govern conquered Canada, and conscious of a gathering concern with the irrationality and looseness of imperial relations, the ministry began to tighten its control and initiated parliamentary legislation intended to require the older colonies to pay a portion of the costs of their administration and defense. The colonies rebelled, proclaiming that it was the right of English peoples to be taxed only by their own elected representatives and that it was the custom of the British empire to confide internal regulation of the colonies' affairs to their provincial governments, in all of which the people's representative assemblies had come to hold the largest share of power. So serious and uniform was the colonial resistance that the Stamp Act had to be repealed. Yet Parliament insisted on its sovereign right to leglislate in every case for all the British peoples, and the need for a colonial revenue remained. Different taxes followed. More colonial resistance ensued. In 1774, the spiral of resistance and reaction culminated in the punitive Coercive Acts, the meeting of a Continental Congress, and the ministry's decision to resort to force.

Independence, in a sense, resulted from the empire's inability to reach agreement on the character and limits of legitimate authority. Not directly represented in the British Parliament (and aware from the beginning that even the admission of a few colonial representatives would not make Parliament responsive to colonial desires), Americans repeatedly attempted in the decade after 1765 to pressure and persuade the English to accept new definitions of the limits of its power. Early in the crisis, it was not unreasonable for them to think they could succeed. From their perspective, Parliament's attempt to levy taxes obviously threatened not only the accepted right of Englishmen to hold their property secure, but all of the traditional (or "constitutional") arrangements linking power with consent. The House of Commons, they conceded, guarded liberty "at home." Parliament was rightfully the ultimate authority within the empire. But Parliament's encroachment on the local legislatures' customary right to hold the purse strings challenged the assemblies' very place within the governmental structure, disputing their control of just the power that the Commons had itself employed to win a vital and continuous role within the central government. Colonials expected Englishmen to recognize that they were asking only for security against the claims of arbitrary, irresponsive power, which was no more than Englishmen demanded for themselves. The arguments they wielded were grounded firmly in the English libertarian tradition. The limits they insisted on were moderate at first: Parliament should leave taxation in the hands of the colonials' own representatives, which would continue to protect their other rights; the central government should check its growing inclination to intrude on the provincial governments' conventional or "constitutional" autonomy in local matters.[12]

These arguments, of course, did not persuade the English. Parliament would not agree that its authority was constitutionally limited by the traditional prerogatives of the colonial assemblies. The ministry decided to respond to extra-legal pressure with coercion, and coercion drove the Continental Congress to deny that the colonials were obligated to submit to *any* legislation to which they had not assented. From this point, the path ran straight to arms and independence. And when Americans had reached its end, they found themselves committed to a revolution. Although a decade's argument had not convinced the English, it had radically transformed their own ideas.

It did so in two ways. First, the lengthy effort to define the "constitutional" extent of parliamentary control resulted in a powerful new emphasis upon an active and continuous relationship between legitimate authority and popular approval, as well as on a newly literal insistence on inherent, equal rights, which governments could challenge only at their peril.[13] In their attempt to bind a distant, unresponsive central government, colonials recurred repeatedly to Locke and other theorists who traced the purposes and limits of political authority to pre-governmental compacts. Thousands of colonials became accustomed to assuming that, as individuals were the parties to these compacts, every individual (or, as the eighteenth century conceived it, each responsible, white male) is equally entitled to protection and personally entitled to an active voice in political decisions. Although some English writers tried to argue that colonials were "virtually" represented in the House of Commons, along with other Englishmen who lacked the right to vote, the confrontation with an uncontrollable imperial authority hammered home the lesson that power-wielders will respond primarily to those to whom they owe their places and with whom they share a fundamental unity of interests. In the colonies, where unprecedented numbers had the right to vote, the governmental officers and branches most immediately dependent on the people were valiant in the defense of liberty, while the appointive branches often lagged behind. Meanwhile, the distant House of Commons, which rested on a more restricted franchise, seemed ever more apparently a feeble guardian of liberty, or even part of the increasing danger. Popular election and political responsibility, accountability and a direct dependence on the body of the people, increasingly appeared as one.[14]

They seemed the more identical, by 1776, because colonials no longer trusted that the House of Commons genuinely protected even the majority in England. This was the second way in which the crisis had disrupted older modes of thinking. Compelled to understand why the imperial government, which was supposed to be ideally designed for the defense of freedom, repeatedly refused to stay within its limits—and more and more inclined to link responsibility with popular election—colonials immersed themselves in English writers who believed that recent economic and political developments had undermined the equilibrium between the parts of government and washed away the barriers against abuse. Emphasizing the dependence of the Lords (and bishops) on the Crown, together with the ministry's control of rotten boroughs and ability to influence independently elected members of the Commons through awards of offices or pensions, English opposition writers warned that all effective power was devolving on an uncontrollable executive. The apparent danger to the independence of the House of Commons was particularly disturbing to writers whose ideas still carried traces of their origins in the republican assumptions of the English interregnum—and to Americans, who had no native aristocracy, decreasing trust in nonelective officers, a rising inclination to insist on individual equality, and growing reason to associate their unity in the defense of liberty with uncorrupted local houses of assembly and the uniformity of interests among the equals on whose votes these representatives depended.[15]

Common Sense became the most effective pamphlet the world had ever witnessed because it joined and made explicit both of the conclusions toward which thinking had begun to point. If independence was the only logical response to failure to compel the mother country to accept the limitations necessary for colonial security, that failure was a consequence in turn, Paine argued, of England's governmental structure. The vaunted English constitution actually combined "the base remains of two ancient tyrannies," aristocracy and monarchy, with "some new republican materials." Mixed of such discordant elements, it functioned only when the Crown corrupted its republican component, rendered it a hidden tyranny, and issued English freedom "warning to depart." In order to "receive the fugitive," the pamphlet finished, America would have to link its separation from the peril with destruction of the remnants of those tyrannies, creating a new order in which power would depend entirely on the people and liberty might permanently endure.[16]

To Paine, creation of a revolutionary order seemed a relatively simple task: power should be limited by written charters and made to rest exclusively on popular election. To the majority of revolutionary leaders, though, the reconstruction never seemed that easy; and time revealed additional dimensions of the problem. Power, it developed, was a many-headed creature, and as soon as it seemed tamed, another fearsome head escaped the bonds. Indeed, the earliest attempts to make it safe were cause for rising worry before the war was through.

The early theater of the American Revolution was the thirteen states. Distant, unresponsive power had proved dangerous, so power was brought home and grounded firmly on the democratic body of the people. The Continental Congress, which did not receive a formal charter of authority until 1781, was trusted only with responsibilities that Parliament had not abused: it did the nation's diplomatic business and oversaw the war, but was denied an independent power of taxation or even the authority to regulate external trade. The general government, in practice, became the instrument of thirteen wary, revolutionary states, and all these states except Rhode Island and Connecticut (whose governments had always been entirely elective) formalized the lessons of the recent crisis by preparing new, more democratic frames of government. Written constitutions, usually including bills of rights, expressed the revolutionary understanding that governments were servants of the people, attempted to define the limits of their power, and distributed responsibilities among their different parts.

Separate parts for different functions. Although they shared Paine's opposition to hereditary privilege and contrasted the identity of interests between the people and their democratic representatives with the irresponsibility of aristocrats and kings, most revolutionary leaders disagreed with Paine's conclusion that the simplest form of government was best. Chartered limitations of authority, they argued, would not be automatically and universally respected. Power tended naturally to overflow its proper limits and could not be safely trusted to a single set of servants, not even to the annually elected representatives of an undifferentiated people. Good government, moreover, demanded qualities not found in representative assemblies: unity, consistency, and wisdom, as well as a reflection of majority demands and needs. And even in societies without hereditary ranks, there were still differences between the many and the few, each of whom required protection. Therefore, nearly all the states established complex governments, and most of them attempted, by various expedients, to make the upper house of legislature counterpoise the popular assembly, assuming that the wisdom and stability imparted by a second branch would counterbalance the impetuosity of the people's immediate representatives. Many revolutionary leaders hoped to make the second house the special guardian—if not the representative—of property. All insisted on a rigid separation of executive and legislative powers.[17]

The new state constitutions were the written evidence of the ambivalence of revolutionary minds. Most revolutionary leaders were natural aristocrats, products of a deferential world who simultaneously gloried in their unity with lesser people and continually betrayed their caution in the face of revolutionary agitation. A train of thought as old as Aristotle reinforced their consciousness of the potentially conflicting interests of the great and small and justified their feeling that a sound and stable polity demanded qualities which they could not associate with governments invariably responsive to majority demands. They had resisted British measures in order to protect their liberties, their property, and their traditional ability to make most day-to-day political decisions. They knew that these could also be endangered from below. Although they were beginning to believe that even the unpropertied had rights—a genuine respect for the essential dignity of every individual was among the most important contributions of the Revolution—they did not forget that their societies were made up of distinctive groups, among which men of property and talents (they themselves) comprised the most conspicuous minority. Thus, bills of rights and written constitutions, which derived all power from the people, also demonstrated a conviction that no government should be entirely sovereign, and constitutional divisions of governmental power were meant to guarantee that even the majority would be restrained.

It is easy to exaggerate these reservations. It is clear, in fact, that older histories unduly minimized the transformation that accompanied independence. Most revolutionary leaders were emotionally, irrevocably committed to a democratic social order, to the eradication of hereditary privilege in favor of a reconstructed world where power would derive from talent and public service. Most were not more fearful of the people than they were committed to the concept that legitimate authority can have no other source than popular election. Recent scholarship has shown that revolutionary thinking called not merely for a distant, abstract social contract, but for continuous and active, vigilant participation by the body of the people, for governments not only limited but genuinely responsive to popular control. The crisis of the empire had suggested that liberty was safest where power rested most immediately upon the people. Accordingly, the new state constitutions all provided for annual elections of the popular assemblies and usually for annual elections of the senates and executives as well. Many lowered the amount of property required to exercise the franchise. Nearly all placed stringent limitations on the powers of executives, which were almost always to be chosen by the legislative branch. Most revolutionaries traced the origins of the imperial dispute—and the subversion of the British constitution—to bloated, grasping ministries and a corrupted House of Commons. Severe restrictions on appointive powers and a denial of the right to veto legislation were intended to exclude executives from legislative matters and put an end to their capacity to wedge themselves between the people and their representatives. In all the states but two, the only institutional restraint on the assembly was the second house of legislature, and the second house was commonly inclined to let the first assume the lead.[18] On balance, the departures from colonial tradition were as striking as the continuities and more impressive than the reservations evident in the establishment of bicameral regimes.

The reservations warrant serious attention because they did so much to shape and render comprehensible the discontents that characterized the middle 1780s and prepared the way for truly sweeping constitutional reform. A constitutional convention met, of course, primarily because of the debility of the confederation government. By 1786, a huge majority of revolutionary leaders recognized a crisis of the union. Few denied that power had been inappropriately divided between the states and general government or that the Articles of Confederation were inadequate to national needs. But constitutional reform assumed the character it did because the Constitutional Convention refused to limit its attention to the weaknesses of the confederation. Most members of the great Convention were equally dissatisfied with the way in which the problem of power had been handled in the revolutionary states. And once they had decided that amendment of the Articles could not suffice to cure the nation's ills, they turned their minds as well to thorough reconsideration of the structure of a sound republic.

The framers' discontents can be described in a variety of ways. The Revolution, we might say, had solved the problem of the character and sources of political authority. America's rejection of hereditary power was permanent and fierce. So was the conviction that government should have its origins in a literal agreement of the people, embodied in a written charter. Nearly all the members of the Constitutional Convention shared the popular revulsion with aristocrats and kings, and the tiny number who did not immediately admit that even a revival of lifetime terms of office was impracticable in the United States. Monarchy and aristocracy, in any literal definition of those terms, no longer posed real dangers. On the other hand, nearly all the delegates agreed that, everywhere, the country suffered from "an excess of democracy."[9] There was a general consensus that the revolutionary constitutions had confided too much power to the lower houses of assembly, which could not effectively be checked by governmental branches less immediately responsive to popular demands. Rule by the assemblies seemed to demonstrate that unrestrained majorities were dangerous custodians of private rights and public good. Liberty, defined as popular control of power, no longer seemed a certain guarantee of liberty defined as the inherent rights of all—or even of the well-considered, long-term interests of the whole community. Good government, in short, appeared to have been sacrificed to revolutionary fear of unresponsive power.[20]

As its members understood it, then, the Constitutional Convention was confronted with two fundamental problems, not just one. The first and more apparent was the revolutionary fear of concentrated, central power, which had resulted in a general government unable to advance the nation's interests or even to fulfill its legal obligations. This problem the Convention sought to solve by reconstructing the confederation as a federal republic. In a sense, the delegates decided to attack the problem that had wrecked the empire and was on the verge of wrecking the new union by calling on the people to create a limited, safe substitute for Parliament and King: a general government that might be trusted with taxation, regulation of the country's commerce, and other positive responsibilities because all of its officers would owe their places to the people or the states, with whom political responsibilities would be carefully divided. But the decision to erect a great republic was accompanied by a determination to avoid the vices that the delegates associated with the structure of power in the revolutionary states, and this immediately involved them in a second problem, which demanded every bit as much imagination as the first. The members meant to build into their great republic additional security for the few against the powers and the passions of the many, but most of them remained unwilling to confide authority to officers entirely independent of the many. All believed that any such expedient would be rejected by the public. The delegates could not entrust the powers they intended for the new regime to nonelected agents, and yet they were determined to create a government that would display the virtues they considered lacking in the states: consistency, the wisdom to discern the long-term interests of the community, and the vigor to defend the greater good whenever it appeared at odds with partial or more immediate considerations.

Once again, the great Convention's ingenuity was equal to the task. It provided that the three great branches of the federal government would derive in different ways, for different terms, and sometimes more and sometimes less directly from the people: the House of Representatives would be elected every other year by all those qualified to vote for members of the lower houses in the states; the senators would be selected by the local legislatures; and the president, rearmed with several of the powers commonly denied to state executives, would also be elected indirectly. No branch would be dependent on another. Different duties, varied terms of office, and different degrees of distance from the people would guarantee the equilibrium between the parts, provide security for both the many and the few, and assure attention to the long-term public good as well as to the people's current needs. In effect, the Constitution was intended to secure the characteristic qualities or "principles" of aristocracy and monarchy, but without resorting to hereditary power or departing from the democratic principle that, in the end, the majority must rule.[21]

Not everyone, of course, admired the framers' ingenuity. The Constitution was approved by hairsbreadth margins in the larger states, and only after its supporters promised subsequent amendments, which became the Bill of Rights.[22] Nor was this narrow victory merely an expectable result of fear of change and popular distrust of central government. Rather, the opponents of the Constitution recognized the framers' fear of popular majorities, understood that the Convention had deliberately attempted to distance power from the people, and at once condemned the "squinting" of the plan toward aristocracy and monarchy. George Mason, who attended till the end and then refused to sign, insisted from the first that the Convention could not have its cake and eat it too, that the attempt to introduce the benefits of aristocracy and monarchy would sooner or later result in the real thing.[23] Anti-Federalists generally maintained that so much power, so well shielded from majority demands, would quickly prove unsafe for both the people and the states. Most believed the plan was inconsistent with democracy, and many claimed that it had been deliberately concocted by a conclave of aspiring lords to lay the groundwork for a gradual reintroduction of hereditary rule.[24] Federalists could denounce extravagent suspicions and insist that the new government was both republican and safely limited to tasks that did not call for intimate familiarity with the people's local needs and situations.[25] Such arguments by no means conquered Anti-Federalist fears of unresponsive power.

Neither did the quick addition of a bill of rights. While it is true that absence of the guarantees afforded by the first amendments had been among the loudest, most consistent Anti-Federalist complaints, most Federalists regarded the amendments as redundant: they denied the federal government powers it had not been granted in the first place: they effected no substantial alteration of the federal system. The Bill of Rights, it can be said in hindsight, confirmed a preexisting understanding that the Constitution transferred only limited authority to the general government from the states and people. It thus contributed importantly to rapid, general recognition of the legitimacy of the new regime. But its adoption left abundant room for further argument about the limits of federal powers, and this argument immediately became entangled with an equally important controversy that the Bill of Rights did not address. During the ratification controversy, Federalists and Anti-Federalists had generally agreed that governments can be created or abolished by the people, that the people have a right at any time to redistribute power as they please, that popular approval of a written constitution represents an exercise of this authority, and even that a federal republic should incorporate effective checks and balances between the branches of the general government, together with a rational division of responsibilities between the federal government and states. But Federalists and Anti-Federalists had disagreed profoundly over how much power could be placed at a considerable remove from popular control without encountering an unacceptable risk that rulers would entirely slip their bonds, becoming—first in fact, but then perhaps in form as well—entirely independent of the people. The amended Constitution did not settle this dispute. It rearranged the parties and moved it to a different ground.

In 1787 and 1788, the ratification contest divided revolutionary leaders who condemned an excess of democracy and a crippling fear of central power from those who were more fearful of a concentration of authority in distant officers who would be subject only indirectly or infrequently to popular election. Concerned that power so remote from popular control might be monopolized by an elite, manipulated by the great at the majority's expense, and turned in time against the liberties as well as the interests of ordinary people, Anti-Federalists entered on the federal experiment with apprehensions that were only partly eased by the adoption of the Bill of Rights.[26] And while most Federalists had favored constitutional devices intended to restrain tyrannical majorities, not all of them dismissed the dangers that transfixed the opposition. Among the most important advocates of constitutional reform were leaders who had never meant to place as much authority as possible in rulers only distantly responsive to majority demands, men whose fear of interested majorities was fully counterbalanced by the revolutionary memory of rulers whose independence from the people had released a governing minority to pursue ambitions of its own. For Federalists like these, whose most important spokesman was James Madison, the Constitution was a necessary, democratic remedy for democratic ills, but the multiple divisions of authority established by the charter were as critical to preservation of the Revolution as any other feature of the great reform.[27] After 1789, such Federalists soon joined with former Anti-Federalists to identify the Constitution as a threatened boundary beyond which further concentration of authority would indeed prove inconsistent with a democratic sympathy of interests between the rulers and the ruled. Within three years, revolutionary leaders had divided once again, this time into warring parties whose appearance had been unanticipated by the framers of the Constitution and whose disagreement reached an ideological intensity without real parallel in subsequent American history.

The policy disputes and sectional antagonisms which divided the first political parties cannot be covered in this chapter.[28] What bears remarking is the very great degree to which their bitter argument about the use of power was inseparably entangled with continuing disputes about its proper distribution. The rapid triumph of the Constitution was accompanied and even speeded by a fierce debate about its meaning,[29] an argument compounded almost equally of new concerns about relationships between the nation's economic groups and sections and of old, unanswered questions about liberty and power.

Parties had their origins within the infant federal government, when congressmen and cabinet members quarreled sharply over the morality and social consequences of Alexander Hamilton's political economy. Madison and Thomas Jefferson, as well as many former Anti-Federalists, realized that Hamilton's proposals for managing the revolutionary debt would involve a major shift of wealth from South to North, from West to East, and from the many to a few whose fortunes would expand dramatically as a result of federal largesse—all of which seemed inconsistent with republican morality, with harmony between the nation's sections, with a sound commercial policy, and with the relatively modest distances between the rich and poor that seemed most consonant with political democracy. No less importantly, however, Hamilton's proposals, together with the broad construction of the Constitution advanced in their defense, threatened to entail a major shift of power from the states to the general government and from the House of Representatives to the federal executive. The economic program and the disregard of constitutional restraints both seemed to center power at a level and in governmental branches least responsive to the people, while creating in the congressmen and private citizens who were enriched by governmental payments an interest fundamentally at odds with the majority's.[30] In this direction, many warned, lay an eventual reintroduction of hereditary privilege and the immediate oppression of the body of the people.[31]

How much power, of what sort, had been confided to the general government? Which responsibilities could safely be entrusted to a government so distant from the people, and which would have to stay within the firm control of their immediate representatives in the several states? What degree of leadership should be permitted to the federal executive? How intimate should be the link between the rulers and the ruled? Throughout the long, uncompromising course of their ferocious party war, the Federalists and Jeffersonian Republicans struggled with the problems that the Revolution had not solved, and none of these divided them more clearly than the effort to define a level of continuing popular involvement in

political decisions that would be sufficient to assure a government responsive to the people's needs without reintroducing popular misrule.[32]

The clashing groups within the infant government both quickly pledged
allegiance to the Constitution. Each accused the other of a settled wish to
see it overturned. Madison and Jefferson and their supporters detected an
increasing danger to the constitutional devices that controlled the risks
associated with great power, along with an increasing danger to the social
foundations of democracy. The Hamiltonians, still preoccupied with localism and an excess of democracy, denounced the opposition's efforts to
arouse the people and accused the Jeffersonians of trying to reverse the
recent constitutional reform. After 1793, the choices forced upon the country by the wars of the French Revolution, together with conflicting sympathies about the Revolution itself, polarized the national electorate behind
the contending governmental factions and encouraged both emerging parties to regard the other in virtually apocalyptic terms. The Jeffersonian
Republicans condemned a Federalist conspiracy to undermine the balance
of the federal system, revive hereditary privilege, and prepare the way for a
reunion with Great Britain. Federalists charged the Jeffersonians with
slavish admiration of the atheistic, levelling democracy being pioneered in
France, insisting that continual suspicion of elected rulers was incompatible with liberty and order.[33]

These accusations were sincere expressions of the deepest fears of the
contending parties. They were also efforts to contend with more immediate developments and issues that could not be easily encompassed by
familiar ways of thinking. Persistent party conflict was itself a new phenomenon, for which contemporaries had no ready, well-developed justification.[34] The absence of a concept of a party system, of a theory of the
public benefits of party competition, favored a conspiratorial interpretation of opponents' motives. So did the country's peripheral involvement in
Europe's revolutionary wars, which reminded both new parties of the
immediacy and fragility of America's own revolutionary settlement. Only
gradually, therefore, were old preoccupations with relationships between
the many and the few distinguished more consistently from newer arguments about the nature of a sound relationship, in a republic, between the
rulers and the ruled.

Over time, the stubborn presence of competing parties and the lengthen-
ing experience with federal institutions did encourage a rephrasing of traditional concerns. Condemnations of aristocratic plots or radical democracy

were joined and partially displaced by newer worries over the relationship between the whole and the parts in an established federal republic. In the years between the great embargo and the declaration of the War of 1812, the really urgent questions were those concerning the relationship between the nation and its sections, between political parties and the public good; it began to be a bit more common for issues to be stated in such language. But the first years of the new republic were an age of difficult transition, never quite complete. The old concerns did not entirely lose their urgency until the revolutionary generation was replaced by younger leaders and party conflict temporarily disappeared. Even then, the newer questions, concerning the relationship between the people and their agents, party loyalty and public interest, or the nature of a sound division of responsibilities between the federal government and states, would reappear within the context of a new legitimation of two-party conflict. Through a civil war and many other changes, most of them persist today.

NOTES

1. Classic statements of the older view include Louis Hartz, *The Liberal Tradition in America: An Interpretation of American Political Thought since the Revolution* (New York, 1955) and Daniel J. Boorstin, *The Lost World of Thomas Jefferson* (Boston, 1948).
2. Useful reviews of the recent literature are Robert E. Shalhope, "Toward a Republican Synthesis: The Emergence of an Understanding of Republicanism in American Historiography," *William and Mary Quarterly*, 3rd ser., XXIX (1972), 49–80; Shalhope, "Republicanism and Early American Historiography," ibid., XXXIX (1982), 334–356; and Daniel Walker Howe, "European Sources of Political Ideas in Jeffersonian America," *Reviews in American History*, X (1982), 28–44.
3. A particularly good, recent argument that the revolutionary era extended through the War of 1812 is John M. Murrin, "The Great Inversion, or Court versus Country: A Comparison of the Revolution Settlements in England (1688–1721) and America (1776–1816)," in J.G.A. Pocock, ed., *Three British Revolutions: 1641, 1688, 1776* (Princeton, 1980), 368–453.
4. Classic statements of this eighteenth-century synthesis included, in order of their appearance: Algernon Sidney, *Discourses Concerning Government* (London, 1698); [John Trenchard and Thomas Gordon], *Cato's Letters: or Essays on Liberty, Civil and Religious, and other Important Subjects*, 4 vols. (London, 1733 [Org. pub., 1720–23]); and [James Burgh], *Political Disquisitions*, 3 vols. (London, 1774–1775).
5. For the dominance of Whiggish views of history, see H. Trevor Colbourn, *The Lamp of Experience: Whig History and the Intellectual Origins of the American Revolution* (Chapel Hill, N.C., 1965).
6. Corinne Comstock Weston, *English Constitutional Theory and the House of Lords, 1556–1832* (New York, 1965); Bernard Bailyn, *The Ideological Origins of the American Revolution* (Cambridge, Mass., 1967).

7. "As with us the executive power of the laws is lodged in a single person, they have all the advantages of strength and dispatch that are to be found in the most absolute monarchy; and as the legislature of the kingdom is entrusted to three distinct powers . . . actuated by different springs and attentive to different interests, . . . there can be no inconvenience be attempted by either of the three branches but will be withstood by one of the other two.

Here then is lodged the sovereignty of the British constitution, and lodged as beneficially as is possible for society. For in no other shape could we be so certain of finding the three great qualities of government [wisdom, virtue, and strength] so well and so happily united. . . . Like three distinct powers in mechanics, they jointly impel the machine of government in a direction different from what either, acting by itself, would have done, but at the same time in a direction which constitutes the true line of the liberty and happiness of the community." William Blackstone, *Commentaries on the Laws of England*, John Taylor Coleridge, ed., 4 vols. (16th ed.; London, 1825), I, 49–50, 154–155.

8. John Locke, *Two Treatises of Government*, Peter Laslett, ed., rev. ed. (New York, 1965).

9. J.G.A. Pocock, *The Machiavellian Moment: Florentine Political Thought and the Atlantic Republican Tradition* (Princeton, 1975).

10. Locke and Sidney contributed alike to the development of a contractual philosophy and to the English modification of classical ideas. The blending of the two was complete by the time of *Cato's Letters*. For the persistence and transmission to the colonies of this blend, see Caroline Robbins, *The Eighteenth Century Commonwealthman: Studies in the Transmission, Development, and Circumstance of English Liberal Thought from the Restoration of Charles II until the War with the Thirteen Colonies* (Cambridge, Mass., 1959).

11. Libertarian philosophers regarded men as owners, both of property and of their other rights. Civic humanists regarded ownership, especially of land, as the prerequisite for the independence of will that was the precondition for participation with other owners in political relationships. In both England and the colonies, the right to vote ordinarily rested on property qualifications. On the link between liberty and property, besides Pocock, see C.B. Macpherson, *The Political Theory of Possessive Individualism: Hobbes to Locke* (Oxford, 1962) and H.T. Dickinson, *Liberty and Property: Political Ideology in Eighteenth-Century Britain* (New York, 1977).

12. My discussion of the Revolution rests throughout on the body of recent literature reviewed in the articles cited in note 2 above. But for the argument over sovereignty, see particularly Edmund S. Morgan, "Colonial Ideas of Parliamentary Power, 1764–1766," *William and Mary Quarterly*, 3rd ser., V (1948), and Edmund S. and Helen M. Morgan, *The Stamp Act Crisis: Prologue to Revolution*, rev. ed. (New York, 1963). Older, but also useful in this respect, is Charles Howard McIlwain, *The American Revolution: A Constitutional Interpretation* (New York, 1923). For the rise of the assemblies and their attempt to replicate the powers of the House of Commons, see Jack P. Greene, *The Quest for Power: The Lower House of Assembly in the Southern Royal Colonies, 1689–1776* (Chapel Hill, N.C., 1963) and "Political Mimesis: A Consideration of the Historical and Cultural Roots of Legislative Behavior in the British Colonies in the Eighteenth Century," *American Historical Review*, LXXV (1969), 337–367.

13. The transforming effect of an individualistic, natural-rights philosophy is a major theme for Bailyn, *Ideological Origins of the American Revolution*, and Gordon S. Wood, *The Creation of the American Republic, 1776–1787* (Chapel Hill, N.C., 1969), the two works that have become the starting points for current views of revolutionary thinking.

14. When British proponents of the theory of virtual representation pointed out that a

majority in England also lacked the right to participate in parliamentary elections, colonials were quick to answer that two wrongs did not make a right. English radicals, who supported the colonials, increasingly agreed. For evidence that English radical thinking was moving in similar directions, see John Brewer, *Party Ideology and Popular Politics at the Accession of George III* (Cambridge, 1976) and Colin Bonwick, *English Radicals and the American Revolution* (Chapel Hill, N.C., 1977).

15. This is a major theme of Bailyn as modified in Pauline Maier, *From Resistance to Revolution: Colonial Radicals and the Development of American Opposition to Britain, 1765–1776* (New York, 1972).

16. *The Complete Writings of Thomas Paine*, Philip S. Foner, ed., 2 vols. (New York, 1945), I, 6–9 and below. A superb discussion of the pamphlet is Bernard Bailyn, "Common Sense," in *Fundamental Testaments of the American Revolution*, Library of Congress Symposia on the American Revolution, no. 2 (Washington, D.C., 1973), 7–22.

17. The provisions of the revolutionary constitutions are discussed most fully in Willi Paul Adams, *The First American Constitutions: Republican Ideology and the Making of the State Constitutions in the Revolutionary Era*, trans. Rita and Robert Kimber (Chapel Hill, N.C., 1980). But my discussion of constitutional thought and developments from 1776 to 1787 rests especially on Wood and my own reading in primary and secondary sources. As in *The Jeffersonian Persuasion: Evolution of a Party Ideology* (Ithaca, 1978), I do suggest that American thinking departed more slowly from its British sources than Wood believes.

18. Revolutionary hostility to privilege, the role played by the assemblies in resisting Britain, and many other factors contributed to this result, but annual elections, similar electoral bases, similar property qualifications for members, and (in several states) clauses giving the origination of money bills to the lower house were particularly influential in making the second house a pale reflection of the first. Massachusetts (followed by New Hampshire after 1784) was the only state to grant its governor a provisional veto. New York's governor participated in the exercise of a similar power as a member of a special council of revision.

19. Elbridge Gerry's phrase. Max Farrand, ed., *The Records of the Federal Convention of 1787*, 4 vols. (1937 ed.; New Haven, 1966), I, 48.

20. The last three sentences paraphrase the major argument of "Vices of the Political System of the United States," in *The Papers of James Madison*, Robert A. Rutland, et al., eds., 14 vols. (Chicago and Charlottesville, Va., 1962–), IX, 354–357. See also Madison's speech of June 19 in Farrand, *Records*, I, 318–319.

21. In Britain, wrote Thomas Jefferson, who may have remembered the passage from Blackstone quoted in note 7 above, "their constitution [supposedly] relies on the House of Commons for honesty and the Lords for wisdom, which would be a rational reliance if honesty were to be bought with money and if wisdom were hereditary." Jefferson despised hereditary lords (and corrupted representatives), yet praised a system that attempted to produce a "proper complication of principles," contrasting it with the situation in Virginia, where "173 despots," the number in the lower house, ruled honestly but unwisely. *Notes on the State of Virginia* (1785; New York, 1964), 113–124. A reading of the records of the Convention or *The Federalist* leaves little doubt that the framers sought an executive and upper house that would impart the unity and wisdom traditionally associated with a king and an aristocracy.

22. Robert Allen Rutland, *The Ordeal of the Constitution: The Antifederalists and the Ratification Struggle of 1787–1788* (Norman, OK, 1966).

23. "Objections to the Proposed Federal Constitution," in Cecilia M. Kenyon, ed., *The Antifederalists* (Indianapolis, 1966), 195.

24. For Antifederalist thinking, see Kenyon's introduction to *The Antifederalists;* Jackson Turner Main, *The Antifederalists: Critics of the Constitution, 1781–1788* (Chicago, 1961); Herbert J. Storing, *What the Anti-Federalists were FOR: The Political Thought of the Opponents of the Constitution* (Chicago, 1981); James H. Hutson, "Country, Court, and Constitution: Antifederalism and the Historians," *William and Mary Quarterly,* XXXVIII (1981), 337–368.

25. These were the major themes of *The Federalist,* especially of Madison's numbers.

26. Banning, *The Jeffersonian Persuasion,* chap. 4.

27. I have elaborated a revisionary view of Madison's thought and conduct during the later 1780s and early 1790s in three recent essays: "James Madison and the Nationalists, 1780–1783," *William and Mary Quarterly,* 3rd ser., XL (1983), 227–255; "The Hamiltonian Madison: A Reconsideration," *Virginia Magazine of History and Biography,* XCII (1984), 3–28; and "The Practicable Sphere of a Republic: James Madison, the Constitutional Convention, and the Emergence of Revolutionary Federalism," in Richard Beeman, et al., eds., *Beyond Confederation: Origins of the Constitution and American National Identity* (Chapel Hill, 1987), 162–87.

28. The interpretation follows Banning, *The Jeffersonian Persuasion,* Murrin, "The Great Inversion," Drew R. McCoy, *The Elusive Republic: Political Economy in Jeffersonian America* (Chapel Hill, N.C., 1980), and other recent works emphasizing the parallels between the first party conflict and eighteenth-century British arguments between the Court and the Country. For a review of this literature and a response to its critics, see my "Jeffersonian Ideology Revisited: Liberal and Classical Ideas in the New American Republic," *William and Mary Quarterly,* 3rd ser., XLIII (1986), 3–19.

29. See also Banning, "Republican Ideology and the Triumph of the Constitution, 1789–1793," *William and Mary Quarterly,* 3rd ser., XXXI (1974), 167–188.

30. This paraphrases remarks of Jefferson to George Washington recorded in "Anas," in Paul Leicester Ford, ed., *The Works of Thomas Jefferson,* 12 vols. (New York, 1904), I, 192–198 and above.

31. Among the most systematic explanations of the antidemocratic consequences of consolidation was Madison's report to the House of Delegates on the responses to the Virginia Resolutions of 1798. See Gaillard Hunt, ed., *The Writings of James Madison,* 9 vols. (New York, 1906), VI, 357–359.

32. Also helpful for contrasting party attitudes toward a politically active population is Richard Buel, Jr., *Securing the Revolution: Ideology in American Politics, 1789–1815* (Ithaca, 1972).

33. On Federalist political thought, see also James M. Banner, Jr., *To the Hartford Convention: The Federalists and the Origins of Party Politics in Massachusetts, 1789–1815* (New York, 1970); Linda K. Kerber, *Federalists in Dissent: Imagery and Ideology in Jeffersonian America* (Ithaca, 1970); and Gerald Stourzh, *Alexander Hamilton and the Idea of Republican Government* (Stanford, 1970).

34. Richard Hofstadter, *The Idea of a Party System: The Rise of Legitimate Opposition in the United States, 1780–1840* (Berkeley, 1969).

CHAPTER 6

The Ambiguities of Power

J.R. Pole

It is something of a paradox of the American Revolution that its leaders knew what they were against before they were absolutely sure about what they were for. The issue, certainly, was sovereignty; the British left them in no doubt about that, and sovereignty involved not merely the location of power but its legitimacy. Lawless power lost authority and therefore forfeited the vital claim to sovereignty. The Americans agreed to throw off British power and agreed that it was unconstitutional before they could agree as to where power should be located among themselves and before they could agree as to what constituted lawful power in America.

Very few would have dissented from the view that the assemblies exercised lawful power within their own jurisdictions, though this assertion meant that the assemblies had to occupy space previously taken by the recognized authority of royal governors. The chapters by Jack Rakove and Lance Banning suggest the value of focusing on two areas where the revolutionary situation not only presented new power conflicts but opened new ambiguities in both the location and the legitimacy of power. How and on whose authority was power to be distributed between the states and the Congress? On whose authority, again, was power to be exercised *within* the states? Banning approaches the American side of the problem by way of the quarrel with Parliament, observing that power was linked with consent in all the traditional (or "constitutional") arrangements. This was true enough of the representative element in British government, which in principle included the power to tax, but it had never been true of the whole of British government, which included a powerful element of royal prerogative; the prerogative had in fact frequently made its authority felt in the colonies. American society may not have been as simple or "unmixed" as its spokesmen liked to proclaim, but it certainly contained no indigenous element of prerogative power. This was what presented Americans with an inherently "republican" political order, which they achieved without having to plan or debate it and almost without thinking about it.

As early as 1776, however, when John Adams derived from the great writers on politics the consensus that "all good government is republican,"[1] he meant something rather more complicated, and certainly included the idea that many different forms of government could come within that ambit. Adams believed in the existence of such a thing as a natural aristocracy, as did many of his contemporaries, and he certainly thought that whether one liked it or not, such an element would inevitably—by its nature—take a large part in government. Banning goes as far as to say that "most revolutionary leaders were natural aristocrats." But a moment later he seems to contradict himself by saying that "most revolutionary leaders" (the same phrase: the same people?) were "emotionally, irrevocably committed to a democratic social order." Certainly they believed in eliminating the vestiges of formal aristocracy endowed by law with hereditary privileges, but it is stretching their views—or rather, those on which they agreed—to insist that they all wanted to establish a political system that represented a sort of incorporation of social democracy, a concept of which many of them were distinctly apprehensive.

To grasp these matters in the proportions in which they appeared to contemporaries, we shall do well to reestablish some ground that has long been familiar to historians. The social order in which these men held their positions of leadership was based on property. Banning takes his stand for the novelty rather than the traditionality of the new state constitutions, observing modestly that many reduced the property qualifications for the suffrage franchise. It is hardly less relevant to point out that they all retained the foundation of some sort of property qualification; even in Pennsylvania, the most radically democratic of these constitutions linked suffrage with tax payment. We should not lose sight of the fact that whole communities sometimes petitioned for tax relief on grounds of extreme hardship. In Massachusetts, where the draft constitution was subjected to the scrutiny of the towns in the winter of 1779–80, a close examination of the monetary requirements has revealed that, while the general aim was continuity with the old colonial qualifications, the figures were rounded up rather than down.[2] The main point to grasp here is that this was a society that took for granted the connection between property and responsibility; to the leaders and apparently to most of the common people, it seemed no impropriety, certainly no violation of anyone's rights, to withhold the suffrage from those who were idle, indigent, or lacking in the attributes that would bind them to the permanent interests of the society *as* a society of property owners.

The really effective cause of the extension of the suffrage in the revolutionary period was not so much reform of the election laws enacting democratic intentions as something quite adventitious—the wartime inflation. The steep and rapid drop in the value of money devalued the currencies in which the property qualifications were expressed. It is true that when this was seen to be happening, legislators, who had other things to think about, and an interest in retaining the sympathies of the populace, did not interfere by raising these values in line with inflation. By the 1780s, the reintroduction of earlier values does not seem to have been part of any party's program. But suffrage reform was not one of the more dynamic forces in any of the plans that led up to the Revolution. Events rather than ideology re-made the political order.

The suffrage is of very little value unless it is considered within the wider context of representation, and here Professor Banning's chapter, as a statement about the relocation of political power, contains a notable omission. In colonial government the basis of representation conformed to no consistent principle, but in modern political democracy, we accept the general rule of one man (or one person), one vote. By far the most important development in American political arrangements in the revolutionary period was the introduction of this very principle of majority rule on a personal basis. As is characteristic of political rather than ideological events it happened bit by bit, unsystematically and according to no complete plan; it was left incomplete in the Constitution when the states were given equal strength in the Senate. But it owed its inception more to this period than any other, and recent judgments of the Supreme Court have confirmed it as a principle.

The explanation of this historical process has been known for nearly twenty years and I do not think I ought to go into it in any great detail. To put the matter in outline, the irregular distribution of representation operated to the acute disadvantage of the major interests of property. The most striking example occurred in Massachusetts, where Boston, which had the most massive concentration of property in the province, was entitled under the old laws to only four representatives. As soon as the majority principle was introduced, Boston's representation in the assembly rose to twelve. It is tempting to think that this far-reaching change came about because it was in line with good Whig principles, and some historians have fallen for the temptation, but the truth is that it came about because it was in the interests of the great merchants to secure a political representation proportionate to their property. It came about also because Boston contained the greatest single concentration of persons.[3]

The confluence of the interests of persons and property conspired to produce a reform that was to have lasting consequences not only for Massachusetts but for American political science. This in turn tells us something about social or "class" relationships. The merchant-capitalists obviously did not feel threatened by the political power of numbers; they did not perceive any clash of interests. Similar convergences produced similar results elsewhere, and not least in the political processes that worked for the introduction of representation by numbers in the House of Representatives under the Constitution of the United States.[4] As far as I am aware, these conclusions have never been challenged—although I would not claim that the forces I have outlined worked smoothly or produced uniform results. I have noticed, however, that more recent research both on the broader and on the more local scale has confirmed them.

If we are to understand the power relationships of the revolutionary era, we have to revert to the elementary point that American leaders were not democrats in the modern sense. The world of Whig ideas in which they lived and which most of them wanted to preserve was one in which political institutions existed primarily for the protection of property. These ideas can be seen in action very clearly in pre-Revolutionary American town and county demands for extension of representation. A "modernist" would obviously expect to find underrepresentation of *persons* as the chief grievance complained of. But this was never the case. These petitions invariably begin by reporting the *wealth* of the county or district, usually noting its tax payments, and only secondarily referring to the numbers of persons unrepresented. Very little in this complex of principles looked toward the development of modern democracy. But Whig principles were vulnerable to events, and those of the Revolution exerted themselves on the Whig framework in a manner that brought forward the more democratic elements and gave them their moment of political opportunity.

Americans were heirs to a long and recently reinforced tradition of distrust of power, and a word should be said here about the separation of powers in principle, if not in practice. It is easy to confuse the concept of separation of powers with that of mixed government, but they are different. Separation of powers refers to the *structure* of government, which in the United States consists of three parts—executive, legislative, and judicial. The theory is that a danger of abuse occurs when any one branch is able to exercise undue influence over another; a particularly important principle, deriving from English experience from the Stuart monarchy, maintains that the judiciary must be separate from the executive. The separation of powers has not had a very favorable press with American political scientists, since in a pure form it obviously cannot work, and much time and energy have to be spent in finding ways to circumvent it.

Mixed government, on the other hand, arises from the relationship of the government to the underlying *social* structure. England after the Glorious Revolution was agreed to be a "mixed monarchy" or sometimes a "limited monarchy." There were, of course, earlier precedents for other views of the constitution. The principle here was that the monarchy governed in conjunction with the official representatives of the three estates, which were supposed to consist of the peers spiritual (i.e., the bishops of the Church of England), the peers temporal, both sitting in the House of Lords; and the commons, sitting in their own house. By mid-eighteenth century the idea had gained ground that the Crown was one of the estates, and I have even seen Lord Mansfield subscribing to it, but historically it is an error, and it is sufficient to say that it was condemned by Maitland.[5]

In theory, because of the absence of a hereditary aristocracy, America did not need separate chambers to reflect the interests of different estates of the realm. But there was a residue of that type of thinking in the original plans for the Senate, and in most of the state constitutions the upper house was regarded as the formal representative of property as opposed to numbers in the lower house, an arrangement that distinctly echoed the idea of separate "estates."

A further point, and here again my comment arises from an omission, must refer to religion. The separation of church and state was on the agenda of the Enlightenment in Europe, and French *philosophes* had reason to admire and envy the Americans for their achievement in the First Amendment. Only a few years earlier had come the famous Virginia statute for religious liberty, which was in fact an act of disestablishment of the prevailing church. Jefferson, who first introduced it, said that it brought on the severest contests he had known. It was by no means a foregone conclusion and was bitterly contested every inch of the way. The purpose of the constitutional amendment was twofold: to keep the state's hands off religion and to keep the church's hands off the state. But it applied only to the federal government, leaving the states free to retain their own establishments. Only gradually did the federal example spread to the states, but the effect in the end was to establish, not the church, or any one church, but the principle that in the United States the political arm of the people was neutral in matters of religious conviction. In our own day we have frequent reasons to be mindful of the political force of religion. It might have been more formidable, and religious politics would certainly have been much more divisive, if the United States had not incorporated the principle of religious neutrality into its constitution.

As Rakove argues, the movement toward a new constitutional framework was associated with an increasingly strong conviction in the minds of the future Federalists that something had to be done about power within the states—a conviction that had never been associated with either the construction or earlier plans for the reform of the Articles of Confederation. The Articles were intended to give the individual states, united for certain common purposes, the best available framework for their own security and integrity. If state legislators had known in advance that the Philadelphia Convention would be taken over by a group of men who were bent on making a new constitution, with power to influence the character of state government, it is very unlikely that enough delegations would have been appointed to make the Convention possible.

Professor Rakove's book, *The Beginnings of National Politics* (New York, 1979) emphasized the multitudinous practical problems that faced the Continental Congress for urgent decision, and tended to diminish the stress placed by some earlier historians on ideological forces in the making of policy. His present chapter makes clear that a more ideological intention entered into the prehistory of the Constitution as well as into the work of the Convention—an intention to define the character of government as well as to empower and coordinate. This purpose, of course, was not lost on the Anti-Federalists. Their appreciation of the issues was enough to determine the nature of their opposition to the Constitution and goes far to explain the controversies that flared up over Federal policies in the administrations of Washington and Adams.

Some popular leaders may have gone into the Revolution with the undeclared aim of introducing more democratic changes into the political life of their own colonies; they were hardly in a position to have aims for America as a whole. Nor could any such avowed program have united Americans. More concrete and purposeful aims were formed during and after the War of Independence and went into the making of the Constitution. The locus of power shifted, and so did its uses. The context of these changes was the experience of the Revolution itself. They were its result, not its cause.

NOTES

1. Paul H. Smith, ed., *Letters of Delegates to Congress, 1774–1789* (Washington, D.C., 1976), III, 402.
2. J.R. Pole, *Political Representation in England and the Origins of the American Republic* (Berkeley, 1971), 207–11.
3. Pole, *Political Representation*, 170–72, 248, 317–19, 323–24, 325–26, 333–34, 350, 352n, 372–73, 535–36, 538.
4. Merrill Jensen, *The American Revolution within America* (New York, 1974), Stephen D. Patterson, "The Roots of Massachusetts Federalism," in Ronald Hoffman and Peter J. Albert, eds., *Sovereign States in an Age of Uncertainty* (Charlottesville, VA, 1981); and unpublished research on South Carolina by Mark D. Kaplanoff. For excessive confidence in the power of ideology, see Gordon S. Wood, *The Creation of the American Republic* (Chapel Hill, N.C., 1969), 170–72.
5. F.W. Maitland, *The Constitutional History of England* (Cambridge, 1919), 75.

CHAPTER 7

An Unfinished Revolution: The Quest for Economic Independence in the Early Republic

Drew R. McCoy

Born during the war for American independence, Henry Clay knew nothing of formal colonial subjugation. Yet almost four decades after the Treaty of Paris, in the wake of a second war for independence that he had judged largely successful, the speaker of the House of Representatives talked as if little had really changed since the time of his birth. Try as they might to disguise the truth, his fellow Americans remained a curious hybrid of a nation. They formed, in fact, "independent colonies of England"—"politically free," to be sure, yet "commercially slaves." As Clay so eloquently and urgently pleaded in 1820, it was high time for the United States to forge the economic autonomy it had long sought but was still denied.[1]

As Edmund S. Morgan suggested almost twenty years ago, the quest for national economic independence that culminated in Clay's vision of an "American System" actually began before the Revolutionary war for political independence. The nonimportation movements of the 1760s and 1770s were significant in part because they "obliged the colonists to think about the possibility of an economy that would not be colonial," and in the ideology that informed them could be found "the glimmerings of a future national economic policy." After the Revolution a consensus, anchored to a value system that Morgan defined as "the Puritan Ethic," gradually emerged and gave impetus to the successful movement for national political reform in the late 1780s. Visionaries such as Alexander Hamilton and James Madison wanted "to transform the still colonial economy of the United States by directing the industry and productivity of its citizens" toward the "balanced self-sufficiency" that would provide the security that mere political independence had not. Stimulating the development of domestic manufactures was, of course, the key, and Morgan's continentalists of 1787 hoped to promote this end by a judicious regulation of foreign commerce. Their vision of a balanced economy, Morgan concluded, stretched backward and forward through time; rooted in pre-Revolutionary protest, it looked ahead to the Whig program of the antebellum era. Indeed, the economy sought by these Founding Fathers "would not be a northern economy or a southern economy but an American economy, of the kind described some decades later by Henry Clay."[2]

Morgan said very little about the post-1789 period, noting only that the story was replete with ironies, but the large sweep of his interpretation, with its emphasis on incipient nationalism and on ideological continuity across generations, would undoubtedly have pleased Clay. Much to his chagrin, the Kentuckian's notion of an "American System" proved controversial enough to shape the contours of political debate for almost three decades, as he quickly discovered the difficulty of persuading his fellow citizens that his proposals were not all that innovative, that they built, in fact, on a Revolutionary tradition that reached back to the founding generation's quest for economic autonomy. Why had the Constitution been adopted at all, Clay repeatedly asked, if not to promote the national well-being that political independence alone had not? Modern historians might say that the Constitution was indeed indispensable to the ultimate creation of a strong national economy. It laid the necessary legal foundations for a national market, and it offered the means of reviving public credit and generating capital for investment.[3] As Clay understood, however, the mere existence of the Constitution would not suffice. To promote economic independence the document had to be liberally interpreted and constructively employed, which posed no small problem given the old-fashioned timidity of many constitutional theorists. Even more important, Americans had to recognize that at least some traditional notions and habits were best relinquished. If Clay appealed to Morgan's Revolutionary tradition, in other words, he described a complex, even ambiguous, past and a republican heritage that contributed to, as well as identified, the dilemma of persistent economic dependence. Without arguing that Clay was uniformly astute in his judgments, I wish to suggest that his "second-generation" perspective offers a useful way of approaching the broader subject of the post-Revolutionary quest for American economic independence.

Clay offered a simple and compelling definition of national economic independence by first citing "the three great wants of man"—food, raiment, and the means of defense. Since the earliest colonial days, he averred, Americans "have always had, in great abundance, the means of subsistence" while they have "derived chiefly from other countries" both their clothes and the necessary instruments of defense.[4] On balance, this arrangement had worked rather well. No one could dispute the monumental significance of abundant sustenance. As republican tradition taught, only the man who could feed himself was politically free. Having direct access to the productive resources of nature conferred the necessary measure of individual independence that defined the republican citizen.[5] As a people, moreover, Americans had never suffered famine or had to rely on others, either in England or elsewhere, for life-sustaining nourishment. In this fundamental sense, as Clay suggested, they had long enjoyed independence. On the other side of the ledger, though, the pattern of American commerce in the 1820s suggested another long-standing reality: Americans still had to import, to a great extent, both their finer clothing and many of the vital materials of public defense. Since at least the 1760s they had boasted of the abundant potential of household industry to provide adequate if crude apparel, and beyond the family sphere public manufacturing had grown in fits and bursts, culminating in the unprecedented expansion during the recent period of embargo and war. But if progress had occurred, it had not been sufficient, as the republic's daunting experience during the War of 1812 had made manifest. National security thus demanded, Clay asserted, that Americans invigorate the manufacturing sector of the economy and generate the requisite sources of internal supply.[6]

This hardly sounds controversial, and indeed it was not. Aside from disagreement about the constitutionality of certain measures, American leaders appeared to concur in the years just after the War of 1812 that the promotion of domestic manufactures (and the internal improvements that might reinforce national economic independence) was sound policy that was long overdue. The outline of Clay's vaunted "American System" took clear legislative shape in the chartering of the Second Bank of the United

States, the passage of a higher protective tariff, and the near success of an ambitious internal improvements bill. Clay wanted in the 1820s to build on these triumphs, to get both what he hadn't gotten and more of what he had. But it is essential to understand that his analysis of America's economic dependence went considerably beyond the familiar concern with food, clothing, and defense. That the United States still had to import at least some "necessaries" was only part, and perhaps the lesser part, of the problem. As Clay saw it, the quest for economic independence led squarely to an inescapable concern with the persistent, ever more ominous, dilemma of insufficient employment for the republic's burgeoning population. Here he cut to the heart of the issue of economic autonomy, reviving and illuminating a vital strain of republican culture that can be traced back at least to the 1780s.

Clay's renowned two-day speech on the tariff in March 1824 contained a thorough and succinct analysis of the problem of economic stagnation in the American republic that summarized long-standing concerns. He did not have to remind his fellow congressmen of the current hard times; the symptoms, if not the causes, were incontrovertible. Why was the economy depressed, and so many Americans dangerously idle? "The greatest want of civilized society," Clay observed, "is a market for the sale and exchange of the surplus of the produce of the labor of its members."[7] In the case of an overwhelmingly agricultural society like the youthful United States, the surplus of produce and raw material was simply too large to be absorbed by available markets at home and abroad. Glutted markets for American tobacco, grain, and cotton drove prices down, discouraged production, and sapped the industry of republican citizens. According to Clay, the failure of Americans to adjust to changed conditions in Europe was largely responsible for the present crisis. During the more than two decades of upheaval that attended the French Revolution they had produced for a capacious but necessarily transient market; after 1815, when Europe stabilized and became less dependent on external supply, they continued to produce "in reference to an extraordinary war in Europe, and to foreign markets" that no longer existed.[8] What the ensuing catastrophe made painfully evident was that the United States could no longer employ its republican citizenry, fully and profitably, on the land. A republican economy predicated on agriculture and foreign commerce had apparently reached a deadend.

Clay understood what a bitter pill this was for Americans to swallow. But simple logic reinforced hard evidence. Since population was growing far more quickly at home than in Europe, the gap between the volume of the republic's agricultural surplus and the number of potential consumers abroad, he reasoned, would steadily widen if the present structure of the economy were not altered.[9] Matters could only get worse, and they were bad enough already. "All the existing employments of society," Clay concluded, "are now overflowing. We stand in each other's way." The desperate search for employment could be seen, for instance, in "the eager pursuit after public stations." Alternately shocked and amused during this session of Congress by the barrage of office-seekers who applied for places before they became vacant, Clay wryly noted that he had first learned of the indisposition of the House doorkeeper a few weeks earlier when someone abruptly put in for the job. He was happy to find, in this case, that "the eagerness of succession, outstripped the progress of disease;" but it was a curious society, indeed, in which "the pulse of incumbents, who happen to be taken ill, is not marked by more anxiety by the attending physicians, than by those who desire to succeed them, though with very opposite feelings."[10]

Thus the quest for national economic independence, as Clay defined it, ultimately focused on the issue of employment. No country that depended on precarious—or even worse, fictitious—foreign markets for the requisite stimulus to productivity was either healthy or entirely free. Employment had to be generated at home, and Americans must ponder carefully their options. One path was foreclosed by principled commitment. "In Europe, particularly in Great Britain," Clay observed, "their large standing armies, large navies, large even on their peace arrangement, their established church, afford to their population employments which, in that respect, the happier constitution of our government, does not tolerate, but in a very limited degree." America's sudden abundance of morbid office-seekers might be accommodated by increasing the number of available positions—but not in a country dedicated to a republican revolution that repudiated patronage and swollen bureaucracies. It would be quixotic indeed to address the problem of economic dependence by compromising the substantive thrust of political independence. "In proportion as the enterprise of our citizens, in public employments, is circumscribed," Clay observed, "should we excite and invigorate it in private pursuits."[11] His solution, of course, was to develop manufactures on a scale that would bring about economic independence in all respects, including the excitement of industrious productivity among a chronically depressed and lethargic citizenry.

Clay's analysis vividly recalled the experience of Americans in an earlier period of economic distress, when quite similar concerns had been voiced and a comparable solution proposed. During the 1780s idleness and the underemployment of resources, human and otherwise, had been prevalent enough to provoke thoughtful analysis of the young republic's unexpected predicament. Following independence, American expectations of unparalleled prosperity, which had often been euphoric, were abruptly dashed. The inevitable adjustment of the economy to the new conditions of independence was fraught with difficulties. The foreign demand for many American products, including wheat and tobacco, proved highly unstable; even more important, perhaps, the markets for American exports, most notably in the British West Indies, were heavily encumbered by the mercantilist regulations of foreign governments. When Americans appeared to compound their problem by gorging themselves with imported British manufactures, critical attention was focused on the so-called "unfavorable balance of trade." There were two ways to readjust that balance: one was to expand exports, either by driving open closed markets or discovering new ones, and the other was to reduce imports by adopting more austere habits and substituting domestic manufactures for imported goods. Thus in the midst of the crisis of the confederation period, the idea of a more balanced economy, with increased attention to the development of native manufacturing that might revive the industry of idle hands, caught the fancy of many disillusioned republicans.[12]

To many observers, indeed, America's problem appeared to be that it could not profitably dispose of its agricultural surplus abroad, which resulted in stagnation, idleness, and severe unemployment at home. If the republic did in fact have a surplus of farmers with no available markets to consume their produce, the promotion of manufactures might serve a dual purpose: they would employ those who could no longer make a living in agriculture and the export trade and at the same time create a more secure market for surplus American produce that could not be exported. This vision of internal development caught the spirit of the English observer Richard Price's contention that the American states were "spread over a great continent, and make a world within themselves." Since Americans were capable of producing everything they needed at home, Price asserted in 1784, they were in a position to spurn foreign commerce, which all too often brought with it luxury, corruption, and the constant risk of war.[13] Even more important, an economy of this shape promised true independence, in that Americans would no longer have to depend on favorable conditions in other parts of the world to sustain their well-being.

Price's model of an isolated and self-sufficient republic was no doubt an appealing vision to Americans caught in the throes of commercial depression and moral despair during the first decade of independence. Yet most Americans understood that this insular political economy would require either the introduction of new and potentially dangerous forms of manufacturing or the acceptance of a very primitive, Spartan way of life that could easily degenerate into barbaric savagery. Moreover, Price's suggestion appeared hopelessly at odds with the realities of American life. The young republic did not have the requisite infrastructure for the highly developed domestic commerce that would necessarily anchor his vision, and too many Americans already had too strong an interest in foreign commerce to abandon it. "It has long been a speculative question among Philosophers and wise men," George Washington commented in 1785, "whether foreign Commerce is of real advantage to any Country; that is, whether the luxury, effeminacy, and corruptions which are introduced along with it; are counterbalanced by the convenience and wealth which it brings with it." The important point, however, was that "the decision of this question" was "of very little importance" to American public officials, since they had "abundant reason to be convinced, that the spirit for Trade which pervades these States is not to be restrained."[14] No one questioned the need to overcome an unfavorable balance of trade and its adverse social consequences, and all recognized the potential benefits of developing at least some forms of manufacturing. But Americans differed significantly in their approaches to rectifying the problems of the confederation period, as the important example of James Madison clearly suggests.

Madison's analysis of the crisis of the 1780s bore a striking resemblance to Clay's formulation of the republic's dilemma almost forty years later. Like Clay, Madison zeroed in on the problem of employment and on its peculiar intensity in a republican society like the United States. In any civilized society where there was "a surplus of subsistence," Madison noted, there was always a corresponding "surplus of inhabitants" in need of employment, which raised the inescapable and most vexing question in the science of political economy: "What is to be done with this [human] surplus?" In the old countries of Europe, these unfortunate people were traditionally "distributed into manufacturers of superfluities, idle proprietors of productive funds, domestics, soldiers, merchants, mariners," and the like. Even so, there were never enough jobs to go around, and all too often this solution to the dearth of employment formed part of the larger problem of social and political corruption. Since republican reforms— including a more equal division of land and a "juster government"— eliminated most of these customary avenues of escape for an idle, surplus population, the dilemma of employment, as Clay would later note, was ironically more intense in an enlightened country like America. Pursued to their ultimate conclusion, Madison's assumptions, grounded in the post-Revolutionary crisis of the 1780s, appeared to offer little cause for optimism.[15]

Yet Madison did not succumb to pessimism, nor did he rush to embrace Clay's later formula for an "American System." Rather, he envisioned a republican system of political economy that was predicated on the seemingly unlimited potential for the expansion of agriculture and the export trade. Acutely conscious of population growth and diffusion, Madison imagined an independent economy tied more to vigorous landed and commercial expansion than to the promotion of extensive and advanced forms of manufacturing. Geographical expansion was necessary to offset the pressure of America's demographic explosion, which always threatened to create conditions of heightened population density with dangerous levels of inequality and landless poverty. Just as important, an expansive commerce was necessary to supply sufficient markets that might absorb the republic's ever-burgeoning agricultural surplus. For Madison, resolving the economic crisis of the 1780s thus required a revolution in international commerce and continued territorial expansion. Since political reform at the national level was essential to both ends, his support of the new Constitution was linked directly to the quest for economic independence— though not in the precise sense that Professor Morgan has suggested or that Clay would imply in the 1820s.[16]

Madison's conception of economic independence was largely one of gaining positive control over the marketing of America's productions abroad. He sought to create a marketing system independent of the British empire, one that would finally liberate the republic's commerce from the oppressive shackles of a pre-Revolutionary system that artificially confined trade to less lucrative channels than would otherwise exist. Here he drew, as so many other Americans had at the height of the Revolution, on the heady vision of a world of free trade that Adam Smith had been only one of many theorists to articulate formally. British mercantilism exemplified the evils to be overcome. Until Americans were able to break free from the system, they would continue to import more than they should from England, they would be heavily restricted in their access to "natural" and essential markets in the West Indies, and they would continue to market the bulk of their exportable surplus through the highly disadvantageous mechanism of the British entrepôt for American staples. The fundamental idea, in short, was that open competition and free trade must replace the British monopoly sustained by traditional mercantilist practices. Unlike some other Americans, including Alexander Hamilton, Madison had not lost faith in the prospects for substantial—and immediate—progress toward the Revolutionary vision of a more liberal international commercial order.[17]

Madison's formulation of American economic independence was thus fully consistent with a larger vision of an international division of labor that would assign to the United States a specialized role as the producer of "necessaries." He was not entirely insensitive to the potential dependence such a relationship implied; indeed, one can find occasional evidence of his concern that British capital and credit were so powerful that any system of free exchange might, from the perspective of the less developed partner, be inherently exploitative. But Madison was too firmly committed to the ideology of commercial freedom and to faith in the presence of abundant untapped markets outside the British empire to fret about any dangers that might be lurking in his ideal world. He tended not to fear British power, anyway. Given his assumptions about economic dependence and independence, a young country like the United States, as the exporter of necessaries, held the upper hand in any test of commercial strength with an old, highly developed society like England that relied on the exportation of "superfluities," or luxury manufactures, to employ its surplus population. Indeed, Madison was confident that the American republic, once blessed with a competent federal government, held sufficient power to smash the British system and destroy the commercial conditions that spawned the chronic idleness and instability of the 1780s.[18]

He was wrong. Madison's pursuit of this heady but elusive vision over the next twenty-five years formed an integral part of both the Jeffersonian movement and the history of the early republic. His efforts to implement a program of commercial retaliation against England, one that he confidently believed would force that country to adopt a more liberal posture, were consistently thwarted, at first by the initiative of his new rival in the Treasury Department. Hamilton, of course, had a very different approach to political economy and a definition of economic independence appreciably closer to Clay's later formulation. The Secretary of the Treasury viewed the Madisonian vision of a world of free trade as chimerical, and he vigorously disputed the notion that a young, undeveloped country like the United States possessed sufficient "natural" power to coerce an end to mercantilism. He therefore spurned aggressive commercial legislation, calling instead for temporary acquiescence in British maritime domination and the prompt creation of a more balanced national economy with advanced manufactures.[19]

As Madison and his fellow Jeffersonians later discovered when they were finally able to give their system a sustained test, Hamilton's thinking was less unsound that they had originally thought. The failure of commercial coercion, most vividly in the great embargo of 1807–09, was largely responsible for a gradual but significant shift in the emphasis and orientation of the Madisonian vision of economic independence. Although the promotion of manufactures had never been the primary goal of Jeffersonian commercial policy, no one objected to household manufactures and other forms of small-scale industry. If retaliatory commercial legislation (which would always be temporary) had the effect of stimulating these forms of production, that was all to the good, since an increase in this sector of the American economy would help reduce the heavy flow of British imports that contributed to the chronically unfavorable balance of trade. Initially, however, the idea of promoting extensive domestic manufacturing through commercial legislation had served principally as a threat to the British that might hasten their abandonment of unsound practices; gradually it emerged as a secondary but increasingly important goal of commercial retaliation; and finally, in the wake of the embargo, it assumed a position of significance for many moderate Jeffersonians in a revised, but not all that drastically revised, conception of economic independence.[20]

Madison's initial formulation foundered on more than the simple failure of Jeffersonian commercial policy. Certainly the external obstacles to the fulfillment of the vision were formidable enough; as Jefferson so aptly remarked in 1816, he and other Americans had come to accept what they had not believed possible thirty years earlier, "that there exist both profligacy and power enough to exclude us from the field of interchange with other nations."[21] But as Madison also discovered, the vision contained internal tensions and even contradictions of a kind that ultimately could not be ignored. Indeed, toward the end of his long career, following his retirement from public life in 1817, he was forced to think through more deeply than he ever had the issues that had preoccupied him for the previous half-century. In doing so he moved steadily closer to Clay's vision of economic independence.

In Madison's correspondence we find ample expression—and development—of a point that Clay adverted to in his speeches on the tariff. To the extent that the American economy had thrived during the twenty-five years after the creation of the new federal government, it had profited directly from extraordinary circumstances and from the distress of others. The long war in Europe had of course created a host of vexing diplomatic problems for the neutral United States, problems that eventually dragged the young republic into the war. But it had also provided a basis for the unparalleled expansion of American commerce. Indeed, the hard times of the 1780s had abruptly ended with the explosion of trade in the early 1790s. By the early years of the nineteenth century the carrying and reexport trades had mushroomed to dizzying heights, while the value of America's direct export trade tripled.[22] As Clay so emphatically asserted, however, the conditions that underwrote this buoyant prosperity were not permanent—and who could wish that they were? He noted the irony in the midst of the sluggish economy of 1824: all it would take to unleash the American dynamo yet again was the eruption of "such a general war as recently raged" throughout Europe and her dominions. "Instantly there would arise a greedy demand for the surplus produce of our industry, for our commerce, for our navigation. The languor which now prevails in our cities, and in our sea-ports, would give way to an animated activity. Our roads and rivers would be crowded with the produce of the interior. Every where," he concluded, "we should witness excited industry."[23]

Clay's point, of course, was not that his fellow countrymen should root for a renewal of the horrid conflagration that had afflicted Europe for the bulk of two decades. Madison had expressed the idea well enough in a letter to Tench Coxe in 1819, even before the onset of an economic panic that would lend greater urgency to his concern. A Europe at peace simply would not absorb the same volume of American exports that it had at war, and this spelled trouble for an American economy predicated on agriculture and foreign commerce. Glutted markets for the American surplus meant falling prices and flagging industry at home, and if peace continued in Europe, "as ought to be the wish of all, nothing but seasons extensively unfavorable [i.e., in Europe] can give us an adequate market for . . . our grain crop."[24] No matter how Americans weighed the situation, apparently it took catastrophe—either civil or natural—to make their economy work. "These prospects merit general attention," Madison mused to Coxe, for they clearly pointed to "the consequent necessity of directing our labour to other objects."[25]

The other objects included, of course, manufacturing, "for which the labor turned off from the soil will be a ready fund."[26] If happy events in Europe gave impetus to this necessary shift in the American economy, so too did recent salutary developments in the southern part of the Western hemisphere. The revolutions for independence in Spanish America warmed the hearts of many proud republicans to the north, but with his characteristically sharp eye Madison saw potential linkages and ramifications that were truly global. As "young nations which are entering into the commerce of the world," these new republics of Latin America were "still more agricultural than the U.S."; and by "narrowing the room for our present staples in foreign markets," they would "hasten and extend the application of our industry to manufactured articles." Political revolution in this oppressed part of the world, in short, would unleash the productive energy of potentially formidable rivals to the United States in the agricultural export trade. In a curious sense, the Hispanic-American republics would now occupy the former role of the youthful United States, and an older America, ironically, would assume a posture toward them that resembled Britain's relationship to its former colonies. The "growing markets" of these new republics would call for manufactures, and Madison believed that "our comparative vicinity will favor supplies from our workshops." "Whatever advantage therefore may accrue to a nation from a combination of manufacturing with agricultural industry," he concluded, "will in our case be forwarded by the independent rank assumed by our fellow inhabitants of this hemisphere."[27]

Earlier in his career Madison would have been considerably less willing to acknowledge any such advantage—in 1792, for instance, he had typically argued that a resort to manufacturing in the United States ought "to be seen with regret as long as occupations more friendly to human happiness, lie vacant."[28] Now he was convinced of both the necessity and the advantage of building a more diversified economy. Back in the early 1790s he had talked confidently of the superior strength of a young agricultural nation in relation to an older manufacturing country. The American republic, he had then asserted, was all the more independent because its exports consisted of "necessaries" upon which its customers depended for their very survival; England, by contrast, exported frivolous luxuries the consumption of which fluctuated wildly with, and hence was dependent upon, every whimsical shift of fashion and fancy.[29] Now his position appeared quite different and considerably more complex. As he noted repeatedly to several different correspondents in the 1820s and 1830s, the very nature of American trade generally put the young republic at a disadvantage. The demand for its exports never exceeded "what may be deemed real and definite wants," but its manufactured imports were often "objects neither of necessity, nor utility; but merely of fancy and fashion, wants of a nature altogether indefinite."[30] Although a nation exchanging necessary and useful articles for the luxuries of another had a manifest advantage under such exceptional circumstances as war or "a contest of prohibitions and restrictions," the advantage was reversed in "the ordinary freedom of intercourse."[31] Beyond a point, in other words, there was nothing an agricultural nation like the United States could do to increase the demand for its surplus. The demand for the surplus of a manufacturing nation like England, however, was potentially boundless and could therefore sustain the industry and employment of an ever-greater number of its citizens.

Madison's reflections always returned to this issue of glutted markets and a surplus for which there was no longer an effective demand. His preoccupation exposed yet another contradiction in his original conception of economic independence. Rather than being compatible elements of a coherent vision, territorial and commercial expansion, in practice, existed in serious tension with one another. Rapid settlement of the American frontier served the invaluable purpose of accommodating the surge in population growth that might otherwise undermine the republican character of the United States. But the "safety valve" of westward expansion also hastened and exacerbated the dilemma of glutted markets in an agricultural republic. Bringing more and more fresh land under cultivation only increased the size of an ever more unmanageable surplus, which prompted Madison to flirt with the notion that it was time to apply the brakes.[32] That he could actually call into question the wisdom of continued, rapid territorial expansion is a revealing measure of how far he had traveled since the immediate post-Revolutionary era. A young visitor to Montpelier in 1827 reported Madison's observation, for instance, that it was much more to the interest of Virginia and the other Southern states "that the Northern people should turn to manufactures and eat our corn and wheat, and consume our products, than be induced from overstocked population at home to emigrate to the West, there to make for market rival produce to ours, to glut the foreign markets." "The encouragement to Western emigration," it now seemed, "had gone quite far enough."[33]

Several years later Madison speculated that even Virginia was destined to move quickly into manufacturing. Initially, at least, Clay had suggested that his American System would defuse sectional tensions by forging strong ties of interdependence among specialized regional economies. Madison's vision appears to have been somewhat different: regional accommodation would occur as the present sectional differences in the employment of capital gradually vanished. That the Old Dominion, as much as the Northeastern states, "must be speedily a manufacturing as well as an agricultural State" reflected the larger dynamic that Madison saw to be at work throughout the republic.[34] In perhaps the most thorough and mature statement of his political economy, Madison explained clearly in 1833 just why his original vision of an agricultural republic was no longer, and perhaps never had been, viable. Everyone understood that in the "thickly-settled countries" of the Old World "the application of labour" to manufactures resulted "from the surplus beyond what is required for a full cultivation of a limited soil." Yet contrary to conventional wisdom, the presence of a vast expanse of fertile land in North America generated its own momentum toward the same end. "In the United States, notwithstanding the sparseness of the population compared with the extent of the vacant soil," Madison reflected, "there is found to be a growing surplus of laborers beyond a profitable culture of it; a peculiarity which baffles the reasonings of foreigners concerning our country, and is not sufficiently adverted to by our own theoretic politicians."[35] One must note that Madison emphasized the notion of *profitable* cultivation. In theory, given the continuing abundance of land, the overwhelmingly majority of Americans might happily remain farmers for ages to come; but they would necessarily be primitive, even barbaric, subsistence farmers, not the industrious, surplus-producing republican farmers that had always graced Madison's vision. "Whatever be the abundance or fertility of the soil, it will not be cultivated when its fruits must perish on hand for want of a market."[36] Here, again, was the rub: the inescapable need for markets to sustain the industry and full employment of a large population, no matter how much land it had to exploit. "Our country must be a manufacturing as well as an agricultural one, without waiting for a crowded population," Madison concluded, "unless some revolution in the world or the discovery of new products of the earth, demanded at home and abroad, should unexpectedly interpose."[37] He was not holding his breath.

Representing two distinctive generations of Jeffersonian leadership, Clay and Madison made a principled effort in the 1820s to understand one another fully. While Madison did not brand the author of the American System a heretic, as many Republicans who suddenly become doctrinaire free traders, including a geriatric Jefferson, emphatically did, neither did he embrace the full spirit or principle of Clay's legislative program. As early as 1820 Madison expressed the desire to push "a middle course" between the pure free traders and the zealous protectionists, calling for a spirit of judicious compromise both "in the National Councils and in the public opinion."[38] As he wrote to Clay in 1824, after perusing a copy of the Kentuckian's celebrated speech on the tariff, he had always believed in necessary "exceptions to the general rule" that "leaves to the judgment of individuals the choice of profitable employments for their labour & capital." Hence Madison supported, as he had since 1789, a moderate tariff. But in his enthusiasm for the development of a more balanced, independent national economy, Clay appeared to forget that these exceptions— such as in the case of articles necessary for public defense or "of a use too indispensable to be subjected to foreign contingencies"—were limited.[39] Madison staunchly defended the constitutionality of a protective tariff; contrary to the assertions of an increasing number of militant free traders among his fellow Virginians in the 1820s, he did not question the legitimate power of the federal government to provide the kind of stimulus to domestic industry that Clay desired. What Madison disputed was the expediency of such an extreme policy of protection (which was bound, he believed, to inflame sectional acrimony) as well as its necessity. Given his assumptions about the logic of social and economic development, he simply believed that many of the changes sought by Clay would take place anyway, "without a legislative interference."[40]

Although Madison had traveled much of the distance toward Clay's understanding of economic independence, in sum, he remained delicately perched between the alternative positions that were ultimately attached to the two national parties of the antebellum era. Madison did not live to see the final defeat of Clay's vision of an American System in the 1840s, but we may be sure that he would have taken no joy in its demise. By weakening the authority of national institutions, especially the federal government, the successful Jacksonian revolution inadvertently laid the groundwork for exactly what Clay had feared it would: the tragic dissolution of the Union that Madison's generation had labored, against formidable odds, to make viable and permanent.

During these same years that saw the erosion of political nationality, however, the American economy, even without the guidance of Clay's integrative system, grew both stronger and more balanced. Even so, one might well argue that despite its success it fell considerably short of the full measure of independence that the Revolutionary generation of the late eighteenth century had aspired to. What underwrote the economic growth of the antebellum era was British credit and British capital; and as the panics of 1819 and 1837 made clear, the American economy was largely at the mercy of the vicissitudes of the capital markets of London. The republic's commerce, moreover, remained fundamentally neocolonial, locked in the classic imperial relationship defined by the familiar exchange of agricultural products, now led by cotton, for manufactured goods. Indeed, as Robert Wiebe has recently noted, if economic autonomy measured independence, as the Revolutionary generation had always believed it should, America's freedom in Henry Clay's day, and even well beyond, "remained as elusive as ever."[41]

NOTES

1. Henry Clay, "Speech on the Tariff," April 26, 1820, in James F. Hopkins and Mary W. M. Hargreaves, eds., *The Papers of Henry Clay* (Lexington, 1963), II, 828.

2. Edmund S. Morgan, "The Puritan Ethic and the American Revolution," in Morgan, *The Challenge of the American Revolution* (New York, 1976), 101, 134–35. This essay was originally published in the *William and Mary Quarterly*, 3rd ser., XXIV (Jan. 1967), 3–43.

3. See, for example, Stuart Bruchey, *The Roots of American Economic Growth, 1607–1861: An Essay in Social Causation* (New York, 1965), especially chaps. 4 and 5, and Forrest McDonald, "The Constitution and Hamiltonian Capitalism," in Robert A. Goldwin and William A. Schambra, eds., *How Capitalistic is the Constitution?* (Washington, D.C., and London, 1982), 49–74.

4. Clay, "Speech on Tariff," April 26, 1820, in Hopkins and Hargreaves, eds., *Clay Papers*, II, 826–828.

5. See Drew R. McCoy, *The Elusive Republic: Political Economy in Jeffersonian America* (Chapel Hill, N.C., 1980), chaps. 2 and 3.

6. Henry Clay, "Speech on the Tariff," March 30–31, 1824, in Hopkins and Hargreaves, eds., *Clay Papers*, III, 683–730.

7. Ibid., 687.

8. Ibid., 684–85.

9. Clay, "Speech on Tariff," April 26, 1820, ibid., II, 826–27.

10. Clay, "Speech on Tariff," March 30–31, 1824, ibid., III, 692–93.

11. Ibid., 693.

12. For elaboration and citations see McCoy, *Elusive Republic*, chaps. 3–5.

13. Richard Price, *Observations on the Importance of the American Revolution . . .* (London, 1784), 62–63.

14. Washington to James Warren, Oct. 7, 1785, John C. Fitzpatrick, ed., *The Writings of George Washington* (Washington, D.C., 1931–1944), XXVIII, 290–91. See also, Washington to Benjamin Harrison, Oct. 10, 1784, ibid., XXVII, 473–74. For a similar statement from Thomas Jefferson at about the same time, see Jefferson to G.K. van Hogendorp, Oct. 13, 1785, Julian P. Boyd et al., eds., *The Papers of Thomas Jefferson* (Princeton, 1950–), VIII, 633. See also Jefferson to John Jay, Aug. 23, 1785, ibid., 426–27, and Jefferson to Washington, Mar. 15, 1784, ibid., VII, 26.

15. Madison to Thomas Jefferson, June 19, 1786, in Julian P. Boyd et al., eds., *The Papers of Thomas Jefferson* (Princeton, 1950–), IX, 659–60. See also McCoy, *Elusive Republic*, chap. 5.

16. McCoy, *Elusive Republic*, chap. 5.

17. Ibid., chaps. 2–5. See also, for broad context, two relevant dissertations: Robert Bruce Bittner, "The Definition of Economic Independence and the New Nation" (Ph.D. diss., University of Wisconsin, 1970), and William Dyer Grampp, "Mercantilism and Laisser Faire in American Political Discourse, 1789–1829" (Ph.D. diss., University of Chicago, 1944).

18. See McCoy, *Elusive Republic*, chaps. 5 and 6.

19. Ibid., chap. 6.

20. Ibid., chaps. 8–10. For a relevant discussion of political economy and moderate Jeffersonianism with a somewhat different interpretive emphasis, see the appropriate sections of Richard E. Ellis, *The Jeffersonian Crisis: Courts and Politics in the Young Republic* (New York, 1971).

21. Jefferson to Benjamin Austin, January 9, 1816, Andrew A. Lipscomb and Albert Ellery Bergh, eds., *The Writings of Thomas Jefferson* (Washington, D.C., 1903–1904), XIV, 391.

22. See, for instance, Douglass C. North, *The Economic Growth of the United States, 1790–1860* (New York, 1961), 36–38, 221, 249, and Curtis P. Nettels, *The Emergence of a National Economy, 1775–1815* (New York, 1962), esp. chaps. 3–6 and 10–11. For background on the 1780s see also Gordon C. Bjork, "The Weaning of the American Economy: Independence, Market Changes, and Economic Development," *Journal of Economic History*, XXIV (December 1964), 541–60, and above all, John J. McCusker and Russell R. Menard, *The Economy of British America, 1607–1789: Needs and Opportunities for Study* (Chapel Hill, N.C., 1985).

23. Clay, "Speech on Tariff," March 30–31, 1824, Hopkins and Hargreaves, eds., *Clay Papers*, III, 687.

24. Madison to Tench Coxe, February 12, 1819, in *Letters and Other Writings of James Madison* (Philadelphia, 1865), III, 116–117.

25. Ibid., 117, and Madison to Coxe, March 20, 1820, ibid., 170.
26. Madison to George Joy, November 25, 1820, James Madison Papers, Library of Congress, Series 2 (microfilm).
27. Madison to Mathew Carey, October 25, 1822, ibid.
28. Madison, "Republican Distribution of Citizens," March 5, 1792, in Gaillard Hunt, ed., *The Writings of James Madison* (New York, 1900–1910), VI, 99.
29. See McCoy, *Elusive Republic*, chap. 6.
30. Madison to Clarkson Crolius, December 1819, in Hunt, ed., *Writings of Madison*, IX, 17.
31. Madison to Richard Rush, May 1, 1822, in *Letters and Other Writings*, III, 266, and Madison to Henry Clay, April 24, 1824, in Hunt, ed., *Writings of Madison*, IX, 187.
32. See, for instance, Madison to Nicholas P. Trist, January 26, 1828, in Hunt, ed., *Writings of Madison*, IX, 304–305.
33. Jesse Burton Harrison, "Private Notes of Conversation with Mr. Madison in 1827," Burton Harrison Papers, Library of Congress, Series III, Box 6.
34. Madison, "Majority Governments," 1833, in Hunt, ed., *Writings of Madison*, IX, 526.
35. Madison to Professor Davis (not sent), 1832 [1833], in *Letters and Other Writings*, IV, 265.
36. Madison, "Majority Governments," in Hunt, ed., *Writings of Madison*, IX, 525.
37. Madison to Davis, 1832 [1833], in *Letters and Other Writings*, IV, 265. See also McCoy, *Elusive Republic*, chap. 10, and "Jefferson and Madison on Malthus: Population Growth in Jeffersonian Political Economy," *Virginia Magazine of History and Biography*, 88 (July 1980), 288–303.
38. Madison to Coxe, March 20, 1820, in *Letters and Other Writings*, III, 171.
39. Madison to Clay, April 24, 1824, in Hunt, ed., *Writings of Madison*, IX, 186.
40. Ibid. See also Madison to Thomas Cooper, March 22, 1824, in *Letters and Other Writings*, III, 429–430.
41. Robert H. Wiebe, *The Opening of American Society: From the Adoption of the Constitution to the Eve of Disunion* (New York, 1984), 191–92.

CHAPTER 8

Two Republics in a Hostile World: The United States and the Netherlands in the 1780s

Jonathan R. Dull

John Adams must have been in a pugnacious mood that first day of March in 1776. His diary for that day contains a warning that if France were not willing to help his fellow Americans it should beware for the security of its West Indian colonies. He went on to brag of how warlike and powerful America had become, of how skilled and disciplined were its armies. Were it to join forces with Britain the two in combination, Adams claimed, could conquer the French colonies within six months.[1]

Twelve days later the count de Vergennes, the French foreign minister, presented his king a memoir warning of precisely that danger. There is little evidence, however, that Vergennes took seriously the possibility of an Anglo-American reconciliation.[2] He soon presented an argument for aiding the Americans that portrayed them very differently. This argument virtually ignored any hypothetical threat to the West Indies. Instead it was based on considerations of the balance of power, particularly of the importance of America to the continuation of Britain's strength. To the possible objection that the Americans themselves might pose a threat to French interests, Vergennes argued that the current war would exhaust them. Moreover, he said,

There is every reason to believe that if the Colonies attain their end, they will give to their new government the republican form, and that there will even be as many small republics as there are at present provinces: now, republics rarely have the spirit of conquest, and those which will be formed in America will have it all the less, as they know the pleasures and advantages of commerce, and have need of industry, and consequently of peace, to procure for themselves the commodities of life, and even a quantity of things of prime necessity. It may, then, be said that the fear of seeing the Americans sooner or later make invasions on their neighbors has no apparent foundation, and that this fear deserves no consideration.[3]

The prediction that American unity would not survive the war, although widely shared in Europe,[4] would not have met agreement among Adams and his friends, but Vergennes's other points—that republics were basically peaceful and that a desire for commerce and a desire for conquest were mutually exclusive—already were clichés in America as well as Europe.[5] Events of the next few years seemed to confirm that even if the United States survived it was hardly likely to be much of a threat to its neighbors. The United States lacked the resources to expel the British from its own territory, let alone to renew its attempts to add Canada to the union. Massive infusions of French capital proved necessary to prevent the collapse of American currency and subsequent government bankruptcy,[6] and French troops and warships were needed before the military stalemate with Britain was finally broken in 1781. Although American confederation was approved the same year, political unity remained elusive. Even peace failed to resolve the problems of weakness and disunity, problems that both contributed to the postwar anxiety so evident in other chapters of this book and helped to lead to the constitutional convention.[7]

European statesmen naturally saw little reason to change their opinion of the new republic during these years. Even the brilliant peace of 1782–83 offered little evidence of any real American power. France, which had provided indispensable financial, naval, and military support to the United States, nevertheless left the American negotiators free to reach their own agreement with Great Britain. The British government, anxious to split the Franco-American alliance, showered concessions on the Americans in hope they would make a compromise peace.[8] Franklin, Jay, and Adams, the American peace commissioners, happily obliged (the agreement they signed in November 1782 being conditional in theory, although not in practice).[9] While the American triumph reflected the shrewdness of its diplomats, it was a measure of neither present nor potential military strength. Indeed, the earl of Shelburne, whose government had made the agreement, was soon driven from office in punishment for what Parliament perceived as needless surrender of British interests. Succeeding governments showed little inclination to conciliate the United States, refusing full compliance with the terms of the peace treaty and inflicting severe damage on American trade.

The statesmen of the major European powers could hardly have been surprised by America's difficulties. They generally were accustomed to associating republics with weakness and disunity. Europe's own republics, such as the Swiss cantons, the Mediterranean trading states of Genoa, Venice, and Ragusa, and, most important of these, the United Provinces of the Netherlands, cut a poor figure in international affairs. Americans were far less likely to see the similarity, generally viewing their country as far different than any European state and associating Europe with decadence and corruption. Notwithstanding this sense of superiority, Americans nonetheless occasionally displayed a sense of solidarity with the republics of Europe, particularly the Netherlands.[10] This was particularly true during the early years of the Revolution, when the Dutch experience was regarded as an example to be emulated. Thomas Paine, for example, in arguing for American independence cited the Netherlands as a model of successful foreign policy: "Holland, without a king hath enjoyed more peace for this last century than any of the monarchical governments in Europe."[11] Paine had good reason for his praise. The Dutch had escaped the brunt of the War of Austrian Succession (1740–48) and had remained neutral throughout the entire Seven Years' War (1756–63).[12] Americans, believing their trade vital to the European balance of power, thought that they too could remain neutral in future wars and prosper through trade with all the belligerents. Indeed, initially they thought their trade so valuable that France would come to their aid without even requiring a treaty of military alliance.[13]

The War for American Independence soon introduced Americans to the realities of power politics. The war demonstrated not only American weakness, but also that of the Netherlands. Both Britain and France exerted great pressure to procure Dutch support in the war. The British interrupted Dutch trade in hope of intercepting naval stores being sent to France or munitions being sent to America via the Dutch colonies in the Caribbean. France in turn applied selective pressure on Dutch towns and provinces so they would form a common front against British demands. When the Dutch tried to find an escape in a league of neutral shippers led by Russia, the British in 1780 declared war on them. By war's end the Dutch found most of their colonies occupied by either their British enemies or their French allies. The peace negotiations largely ignored them until finally the French foreign minister arranged terms with Britain on their behalf and forced their compliance.[14]

Their failings in war and diplomacy were in part the result of serious flaws in the Dutch political and social system, flaws which were observed at first hand by statesmen like John Adams. By 1787 the Netherlands had come to serve a cautionary purpose for American political thinkers. During the constitutional convention the Dutch political system was a subject of discussion; later, in *Federalist* Number 20, James Madison used the Netherlands as an example of the failings of a confederacy of republics, implying that the American confederacy faced similar dangers unless it could achieve greater unity through the newly drafted constitution.[15]

The comparison between the Netherlands and the United States can serve purposes beyond the study of American political thought, however. It also can help us place in clearer perspective the relative strengths and weaknesses of the new republic. By showing us how America's problems resembled or differed from those of the Netherlands it can help us better differentiate between problems stemming from America's political institutions and those coming from other causes. Finally, it can help to explain why pessimists about the American experiment eventually were confounded by America's survival and growth to world power.

At first glance the comparison may seem far-fetched. The Netherlands was a tiny country compared even to the United States of 1783. Slightly smaller than it is today, it occupied an area comparable to Connecticut, Rhode Island, and Massachusetts combined (not counting Maine, then a part of Massachusetts). Its population of approximately two million was somewhat more than half that of the United States.[16] Like the thirteen American states, the seven provinces of the Netherlands varied enormously in population; the most powerful and populous, Holland, dominated the country to a much greater extent than did any of the American states. (Indeed, the Netherlands as a whole frequently was called by the name of this province.) In spite of its smaller size and population, the Netherlands appeared in many ways more advanced than the United States. It was more developed economically, more powerful militarily, and more sophisticated politically. As we shall see, these advantages were more apparent than real and were counterbalanced by American advantages that eventually proved more important.

Perhaps the most striking difference between the two countries was the relative development of their economies. The Netherlands had been the most economically powerful state of mid–seventeenth-century Europe. During the intervening century and a quarter its position relative to larger neighbors like France and Britain had deteriorated, but the Netherlands still was more advanced than most of Europe. It was heavily urbanized, contained a large and sophisticated mercantile community, and was both a major shipper and exporter of finished goods. It was still one of the world's great banking centers and by the mid-1780s had become one of the leading creditors of the United States.[17]

By contrast, the United States was chiefly an exporter of food and raw materials to Europe and the Caribbean (although it did have a respectable merchant marine and a sizable mercantile community scattered among the small cities of the Atlantic seaboard). As such it was extremely vulnerable to foreign market conditions (except, of course, in times of war or scarcity). True, America was self-sufficient in food and in many other needs of a predominantly rural economy. On the other hand, American agriculture, fisheries, timber, and shipbuilding were dependent on access to foreign markets, particularly the European colonies in the West Indies. Moreover, the United States, unlike the Netherlands, produced few manufactured goods and could provide little credit for its merchants. The part of the American population that lived in small cities along the Atlantic coast was highly dependent on foreign trade, but even many plantation owners and farmers needed foreign manufactured goods or credit.

To compound the difficulty, America was more dependent than the Netherlands on a single trading partner. Despite its political independence, the United States remained an economic satellite of Great Britain. During the decade after the war American statesmen like Thomas Jefferson attempted with little success to foster trade with France and other European states.[18] In 1790 America was still dependent on Britain and the British West Indies for the bulk of its imports and sent them nearly half of its exports.[19] Britain did not hesitate to use this dominance in its own interest, severely restricting American trade with Britain, Ireland, Canada, and the West Indies and thereby inflicting great damage on American merchants, fishermen, farmers, and shipbuilders. The problem of American dependence on Britain, unresolved by the adoption of the new constitution, was largely responsible for the fierce debate between the followers of Jefferson and those of Hamilton, as well as for the War of 1812. In today's terminology, the United States was in a neocolonial relationship to Britain that did not end until the American industrial revolution in the decades preceding the Civil War (and in the case of the American South that relationship was still existent in 1861).

In spite of their differences, the United States and the Netherlands had much in common. Neither possessed the economic basis for an independent foreign policy. The same was true of their military situation. Each lacked the military and naval strength to participate with full autonomy in international affairs. The Dutch did possess a peacetime army comparable in size to Britain's,[20] but it lacked the British army's capacity for wartime expansion. Moreover, unlike Americans, the Dutch were not protected by an ocean's distance from potential enemies. They proved unable to defend themselves at the approach of foreign armies, like those of France in 1748 and 1794 and those of Prussia in 1787. Their navy, the fifth largest in Europe (behind that of Britain, France, Spain, and Russia) was theoretically more respectable. In spite of extraordinary Dutch bravery, however, it performed abysmally in the war of 1780–83. The Dutch could hope for safety only by balancing between competing great powers.

The United States had even less military strength. Depending on America's geographical isolation, Congress at war's end reduced the army to negligible size and eliminated the navy altogether. This step led to humiliations like those suffered by the Dutch. In order to pressure Americans to pay their debts to British creditors, the government of Great Britain refused to evacuate nine frontier forts within the United States, including such posts as Niagara and Detroit.[21] The United States was helpless to compel their evacuation. The American Army also proved unable either to coerce Indian tribes along the frontier or to prevent tens of thousands of settlers from overrunning Indian hunting grounds.[22] Although Britain showed restraint in its dealings with the Indians, the combination of British-held frontier posts, angry Indian tribes, and uncontrolled American settlers posed an obvious danger.[23] The United States also was unable to prevent Spanish closure of the Mississippi River to American shipping, a move that created severe economic and political repercussions along the frontier. Fortunately, the Spanish military presence in Florida and Louisiana was very weak, but the Spanish held close contacts with the dangerous Indian tribes along the Georgia and Carolina borders.[24] At sea the United States was unable to defend its shipping from Barbary pirates, let alone any European power in case of war.[25]

The lack of an effective army or navy or even of the funds to establish them mocked America's claims to an autonomous place among the powers of the Western world. During the war the French diplomatic representatives in Philadelphia had been able to exercise great influence over Congress, dependent as it was on France for financial and military support.[26] Had any European state declared war in the 1780s, America, unable to pay its debts to France (and barely able to pay the interest on loans from the Netherlands), would have found it difficult to raise the funds to defend itself. Instead, its failure to pay its debts might have given America's creditors an excuse to intervene against it. (By the end of the decade the French minister to the United States was entertaining such ideas.)[27] Only its distance from Europe, its difficult and extensive terrain, and the previous example of British failure gave the United States any greater security than the Netherlands.

In theory, the Netherlands even possessed considerable political advantages over America. The Dutch had a well-established government bureaucracy, the United States only the most rudimentary. (The American foreign office, for example, resembled in size and complexity that of a European state of the seventeenth century.) The Netherlands had a fixed capital at The Hague, while Congress suffered the humiliation of wandering from city to city.[28] Whereas during the Confederation period the presidency of Congress was a largely ceremonial office with a rapid turnover of occupants (fifteen men in an equal number of years),[29] the Dutch possessed a hereditary chief executive, the stadholder, with powers exceeding those the new American constitution would give the president. In spite of all these advantages, however, the Netherlands suffered from many of the same problems that plagued its sister republic. The major European powers treated the Dutch with contempt, deriding not only their economic dependence and military weakness, but also their acute political divisions and their cumbersome and ineffectual system of government. The Dutch were deeply divided by competition among cities, among provinces, and among social classes. In the battle for political and economic dominance, the merchants of Amsterdam held great advantages, but they met bitter opposition from other cities such as Rotterdam, provinces such as Zeeland, and classes such as the nobility, which dominated the inland provinces. Eventually the battle between the conservatives and the "patriots" led by Amsterdam resulted in armed Prussian intervention—in 1787 the king of Prussia, brother-in-law of the stadholder, felt compelled to terminate the budding Dutch revolution.[30]

The United States, too, was marked by political, social, and sectional disagreements. Competition among the states, for example, undercut American resistance to British bullying. Here Connecticut was particularly blameworthy, frustrating attempts to form a common front on trade policy by its desire to surpass neighboring states.[31] Entire geographical sections were divided by conflicting value systems, habits, and economic interests. The most obvious split was between the plantation (staple) economies of the South and the farming and fishing economies of the North. There were significant variations, however, even within these larger regions. The interests of New England, for example, differed from those even of its most immediate neighbors. Another basic split, evident even within individual states, was between East and West. The frontier and seaboard held differing views on subjects ranging from currency to Indian relations (a divergence not totally dissimilar from that between the Netherlands' coastal region and its agricultural hinterland). One historian has seen in these differences the embryonic development of American political parties.[32] The split between newer and more established areas led to separatist movements, whose leaders sometimes flirted with the idea of foreign assistance, Vermonters looking toward British Canada, inhabitants of Kentucky toward either Spain or Britain. A movement for independence from the United States even developed on tiny Nantucket.[33]

The political divisions threatening America often were manifestations of underlying social tensions—between debtor and creditor, merchant and farmer, the landed and the landless. At least America was spared the battle over the privileges of a hereditary nobility that helped embitter Dutch political life, although this was counterbalanced by the problem of the growing number of slaves and their increasing concentration in the American South. The United States also held a second advantage; the bitter battle between patriot and Loyalist during the Revolution had ended with the departure of perhaps 60,000 to 100,000 supporters of Great Britain[34] and the reintegration of the remainder. In spite of the human costs, Americans could find a bond of unity in their support of the Revolution, however they might interpret the meaning of that Revolution.

The effects of disunity and conflict were worsened in both the Netherlands and the United States by the lack of an effective central government. The States General of the Netherlands and the American Continental Congress were each almost paralyzed by severe limits on their authority. In theory, and often in practice, the States General could proceed only with the concurrence of all seven of the Dutch provinces. Affairs moved with maddening slowness as issues were referred to the assemblies of the various provinces for debate and decision. The Continental Congress faced a nearly identical problem. After years of effort, the opposition of New York blocked its attempt to secure an independent revenue.[35] The Dutch advantage in having the stadholder as a central authority was nullified in practice because the stadholder during this period, William V, was weak, unpopular, and a source of political discord.[36]

The disunity and disorganization of the Dutch and American political systems profoundly affected their conduct of foreign policy. Factions in the Netherlands characteristically divided into pro-British and pro-French parties, a situation that would be duplicated in the United States of the 1790s. Debates on foreign policy in the States General retarded negotiations, as was shown by the ridiculous figure cast by the Dutch representatives at the 1782–83 peace negotiations. Luckily, the American peace commissioners were far enough distant from America to negotiate for themselves. Congress had been deeply divided over foreign policy as different factions contended over who would occupy various diplomatic posts and as representatives of different regions of the country debated war objectives. Worst of all, America had been so dependent on French assistance that in 1781 Congress had ordered the commissioners to acquiesce to French desires about negotiation of the peace. Franklin, Adams, and Jay largely ignored their orders and, rather apprehensively, took advantage of the opportunities of the moment. As already mentioned, the Dutch lacked a similar opportunity and saw the French make peace on their behalf. The advantageous American peace of 1783 was less a triumph of American foreign policy than the result of good fortune and the individual abilities of the American negotiators. Indeed, Congress failed to ratify and return the treaty by the prescribed time and had to depend on British willingness to look the other way.[37]

The postwar period demonstrated that the United States could no longer depend on good fortune. We have already seen some of the results of American disunity, as state rivalries blocked formation of a common front against British trade policies. Congressional weakness permitted the states to act almost as individual sovereign governments. Virginia itself ratified individually the peace treaty with Britain, Georgia undertook negotiations with Spain about border issues involving Spanish Florida, and various states negotiated with Indian tribes and contracted foreign loans. The 1778 Franco-American treaty of commerce was violated by Massachusetts and

New Hampshire, which levied tonnage duties on French goods.[38] Most dangerously, the terms of the peace were violated repeatedly by state restrictions on payment of debts to British merchants and by evasions of the provisions relating to Loyalists.[39] These violations gave Britain an excuse to retain frontier posts within the United States. Not even the States General could be defied with such impunity.

It is not surprising that the United States, like the Netherlands, was the object of the contempt of such foreign powers as France and Britain. Both America and the Netherlands were characterized by a divided polity, inefficient government, backward economy, military weakness, social conflict, and lack of leadership. With considerable justification, Hamilton described the United States as reaching "almost the last stage of national humiliation."[40] Nevertheless the fate of the two countries would be far different. The Dutch soon lost their independence and remained under French control for almost twenty years. During most of the same period the United States managed to balance between Britain and France. The brief War of 1812 with Britain, however ill-considered, at least resulted in neither diminution of American independence nor loss of American territory. During the succeeding half century, the United States industrialized, expanded to the Pacific, survived a civil war, and entered, at least potentially, the ranks of the great powers. The Netherlands, restored to independence in 1815, resumed its lackluster role among the secondary powers of Europe. Why, in spite of their similarities in the 1780s, did the history of the United States and the Netherlands diverge so drastically? What advantages of the United States proved so decisive?

The answers in hindsight are fairly obvious. The greatest of America's advantages was its virtually limitless extent of territory. By European standards, even the land east of the Mississippi was gigantic. America's size alone gave it relative immunity from conquest. Britain had tried unsuccessfully for more than six years to solve the logistics of conquering so vast a country.[41] Protected by its great distance from Europe, a mountainous and wooded terrain, and a dispersed population, the United States had survived the attacks of one of Europe's most wealthy and powerful states. America's greatest vulnerability had been its economy. Its trade was disrupted greatly by the war, its currency saved from collapse only by massive French loans and grants, its people subjected to severe privation.[42] In case of future hostilities America might again lose its foreign trade, might even be driven by economic pressure or internal division to make a disadvantageous peace, but there was relatively little danger of wholesale foreign occupation. The Netherlands, protected only by obsolete forts and a small army, was far more vulnerable; its last resort was to open its dikes and flood the countryside (as it had done in 1672), but nothing was able to protect it from the armies of revolutionary France.

America's great size also meant that the United States could support an increasing population without social dislocation. The Europe of the 1780s contained perhaps fifty times the population of the United States in only four times the area.[43] The favorable climate and soil of the United States also added to America's promise. Benjamin Franklin had predicted, not unrealistically, a doubling of population every twenty-five years;[44] by 1860 the United States surpassed Great Britain in numbers and had almost caught up to France. A population of thirty-one and a half million permitted it to raise armies comparable to those of the major powers of Europe, although sadly these American armies were raised to be used against each other. The Netherlands of 1860 contained fewer than three and a half million people.[45] While the United States had tripled in area and reached the Pacific Ocean, the Netherlands had made only tiny gains against its neighbors, the Germans and the waters of the North Sea. America, moreover, had well begun its rise to become the greatest industrial power in the world.

America's growth in area, population, resources, and industry was still a dream in the 1780s, however. For the moment, its survival was based less on its ability to compete with the states of Europe than on its capacity to be useful to them. As a still predominantly agricultural country, it was a source of raw materials and markets for Britain and, to a far smaller extent, France. (This economic usefulness would alter British attitudes in America's favor, particularly after the outbreak of a new war with France.) America's agricultural surplus, moreover, was extremely important to the wealthy sugar-producing European colonies of the Caribbean and, in time of need, to Canada.[46] Even though the United States itself posed little immediate military threat to the West Indies, American bases could be a great aid to any European forces operating in the Caribbean.[47] In 1782, for example, a French fleet had sailed to Boston to escape the Caribbean hurricane season.[48] America's usefulness to both France and Britain helped it to balance between the two great powers. In contrast, the Netherlands had little to offer as an ally and a huge and virtually undefended colonial empire to pillage as an enemy. Hence, both Britain and France bullied it. Divided by factionalism, the Dutch could barely resist, let alone extract diplomatic advantage from a policy of neutrality.

America's political situation, moreover, was not as similar to that of the Netherlands as had appeared in the 1780s. Its political problems proved less intractable and its political divisions less unbridgeable than many had expected. The debate over the adoption of the Constitution and social upheavals like Shays' rebellion obscure the degree of political consensus in the early United States. The power of the hereditary executive was a bitter issue in the Netherlands; the power of the American presidency proved far less divisive. Americans also were spared the Dutch debate over the privileges of the aristocracy. Divisions between American social classes were muted by the existence of almost unlimited cheap land, political divisions by common consent on issues like the validity of the recent Revolution and the desirability of republican institutions. Because of this relative consensus, a political change of revolutionary scope could occur in 1787–88 without bloodshed or the summoning of foreign troops, as happened in 1787 in the Netherlands.

Finally, the United States survived in a hostile world in part by good fortune. As we have seen, the American peace commissioners of 1782 had benefited from the British desire for separate peace. It was America's good fortune that during the 1780s, when it was most vulnerable, its potential enemies were exhausted from the recent war. The French Revolution then diverted Europe's attention and led France and Britain to court America's support. Wise statesmanship by Washington, Adams, and Jefferson helped the United States take advantage of its neutrality and avoid war. Madison, less prudent, led America into war against Britain, but again good fortune aided it in avoiding any permanent damage.[49] The Netherlands, neither lucky nor well-led, became for twenty years a French puppet state, as did such other European republics as Genoa, Venice, Ragusa, and the cantons of Switzerland.

America thus possessed advantages that the Netherlands and the other republics of Europe did not. We must not assume, however, that America's survival in a hostile world was inevitable. The failure of America to reform its political institutions, its entrance into an unwise war, or its failure to resolve its internal disputes could have greatly altered American history. Its greatest danger came not from foreign threat, but from internal weakness and division. In overcoming that danger, the wisdom of its people proved to be America's greatest strength.

NOTES

1. L.H. Butterfield, ed., *Diary and Autobiography of John Adams*, 4 vols. (Cambridge, Mass., 1961), II, 235.
2. I have argued this point in *The French Navy and American Independence: A Study of Arms and Diplomacy, 1774–1787* (Princeton, 1975), 33–35.
3. Benjamin Franklin Stevens, ed., *Facsimiles of Manuscripts in European Archives Relating to America, 1773–1783*, 25 vols. (London, 1889–98), 13: no. 1310, p. 13 (Stevens' translation).
4. Charles R. Ritcheson, *Aftermath of Revolution: British Policy toward the United States, 1783–1795* (Dallas, 1969), 33.
5. See, for example, John Jay's comments in John Joseph Meng, ed., *Conrad Alexandre Gérard: Despatches and Instructions* (Baltimore, 1939), 434.
6. E. James Ferguson, *The Power of the Purse: A History of American Public Finance, 1776–1790* (Chapel Hill, N.C., 1961), 40–47, 125–30.
7. The best study of postwar diplomatic problems and their political consequences is Frederick W. Marks, III, *Independence on Trial: Foreign Affairs and the Making of the Constitution* (Baton Rouge, 1973).
8. Jonathan R. Dull, *Franklin the Diplomat: The French Mission* (Philadelphia, 1982) [American Philosophical Society, *Transactions* 72: part 1], 53–64; Vincent T. Harlow, *The Founding of the Second British Empire*, 2 vols. (London, 1952–64), I, 146–311. In addition to his immediate aims Shelburne may have hoped a liberal treaty would further his aims of recapturing Britain's share of American trade.
9. For the general disregard by the American public of the conditional nature of the agreement see William C. Stinchcombe, *The American Revolution and the French Alliance* (Syracuse, 1969), 197.
10. See, for example, Butterfield, *John Adams Diary and Autobiography* IV, 45.
11. The quotation is from *Common Sense* in Philip S. Foner, ed., *The Complete Writings of Thomas Paine*, 2 vols. (New York, 1945), I, 10.
12. Alice Clare Carter, *The Dutch Republic in Europe in the Seven Years' War* (London, 1971).
13. William C. Stinchcombe, "John Adams and the Model Treaty," in Lawrence S. Kaplan, ed., *The American Revolution and "A Candid World"* (Kent, Ohio, 1977), 69–84.
14. Two general histories of the Dutch experience are Friedrich Edler, *The Dutch Republic and the American Revolution* (Baltimore, 1911) and Jan Willem Schulte Nordholt, *The Dutch Republic and American Independence*, trans. Herbert H. Rowen (Chapel Hill, N.C., 1982).
15. See index under "Netherlands" in Max Farrand, ed., *The Records of the Federal Convention of 1787*, rev. ed., 4 vols. (New Haven, 1937) and Benjamin Fletcher Wright, ed., *The Federalist: By Alexander Hamilton, James Madison, and John Jay* (Cambridge, Mass., 1961), 182–86.
16. For the population of the Netherlands see Jack Babuscio and Richard Minta Dunn, *European Political Facts, 1648–1789* (London, 1984), 342. Between 1780 and 1790 American population rose from 2.8 million to 3.9 million: *Historical Statistics, Colonial Times to 1970*, 2 vols. (Washington, D.C., 1975), II, 1168. For further discussion see Lester J. Cappon, ed., *Atlas of Early American History: The Revolutionary Era, 1760–1790* (Princeton, 1976), 102.
17. Ferguson, *Power of the Purse*, 235–38. For the Dutch economy see Fernand Braudel, *Civilization and Capitalism, 15th–18th Century*, vol. III, *The Perspective of the World*, trans. Siân Reynolds (New York, 1984), 175–276.

18. See Merrill Peterson, "Thomas Jefferson and Commercial Policy, 1783–1793," *William and Mary Quarterly*, 3rd ser., 22 (1965), 584–610.

19. *Historical Statistics of the United States* II, 905, 907, 1176; John H. Coatsworth, "American Trade with European Colonies in the Caribbean and South America, 1790–1812," *William and Mary Quarterly*, 3rd ser., 24 (1967), 247.

20. The Dutch army by the 1770s had dropped to below 30,000 men: Simon Schama, *Patriots and Liberators: Revolution in the Netherlands, 1780–1813* (New York, 1977), 57.

21. For the posts and their strategic significance see Marks, *Independence on Trial*, 5–6. The decision not to surrender them is discussed in Ritcheson, *Aftermath of Revolution*, 76 and in J. Leitch Wright, Jr., *Britain and the American Frontier, 1783–1815* (Athens, Ga., 1975), 20–49.

22. Marks, *Independence on Trial*, 15–19.

23. Ritcheson, *Aftermath of Revolution*, 164–84; Wright, *Britain and the American Frontier*, 12–14, 28–31, 36–41; Isabel Thompson Kelsay, *Joseph Brant, 1743–1807: Man of Two Worlds* (Syracuse, 1984), 349–414.

24. Arthur Preston Whitaker, *The Spanish-American Frontier, 1783–1795: The Westward Movement and the Spanish Retreat in the Mississippi Valley* (Boston, 1927), 42–43 and passim.

25. James A. Field, Jr., *America and the Mediterranean World, 1776–1882* (Princeton, 1969), 27–36; William M. Fowler, Jr., *Jack Tars and Commodores: The American Navy, 1783–1815* (Boston, 1984), 1–16.

26. Stinchcombe, *American Revolution and the French Alliance*, 62–76, 153–69.

27. Marks, *Independence on Trial*, 107–08. For an earlier and friendlier French diplomat see Paul Sifton, "Otto's Memoire to Vergennes, 1785," *William and Mary Quarterly*, 3rd ser., 22 (1965), 626–45.

28. Jack N. Rakove, *The Beginnings of National Politics: An Interpretive History of the Continental Congress* (New York, 1979), 334–37.

29. For a listing see Mark Mayo Boatner, III, *Encyclopedia of the American Revolution* (New York, 1966), 274.

30. The best study of Dutch political life in the period is Schama, *Patriots and Liberators;* see especially 121–35.

31. Marks, *Independence on Trial*, 80–82. For a brief survey of the effects of sectionalism see Joseph L. Davis, *Sectionalism in American Politics, 1774–1787* (Madison, Wisc., 1977).

32. Jackson Turner Main, *Political Parties before the Constitution* (Chapel Hill, N.C., 1973).

33. Ritcheson, *Aftermath of Revolution*, 151–63; Whitaker, *Spanish-American Frontier*, 94–107; Marks, *Independence on Trial*, 130–31; Wright, *Britain and the American Frontier*, 7–8, 32–35, 41–49.

34. Ritcheson, *Aftermath of Revolution*, 53.

35. Rakove, *Beginnings of National Politics*, 337–42.

36. Schama, *Patriots and Liberators*, passim.

37. Richard B. Morris, *The Peacemakers: The Great Powers and American Independence* (New York, 1965), 447–48.

38. Marks, *Independence on Trial*, 3–4; Lawrence S. Kaplan, *Colonies into Nation: American Diplomacy, 1763–1801* (New York, 1972), 156.

39, Ritcheson, *Aftermath of Revolution*, 63–64.

40. Wright, *The Federalist*, 156.

41. See R. Arthur Bowler, *Logistics and the Failure of the British Army in America, 1775–1783* (Princeton, 1975).

42. For an example see Richard Buel, Jr., *Dear Liberty: Connecticut's Mobilization for the Revolutionary War* (Middletown, Conn., 1980).

43. Europe's population in the mid-1780s was perhaps 180,000,000 while that of the United States was still well under 4,000,000. See note 16 above.

44. Leonard W. Labaree, William B. Willcox et al., eds., *The Papers of Benjamin Franklin*, 25 vols. to date (New Haven, 1959–), IV, 233.

45. B.R. Mitchell, ed., *European Historical Statistics, 1750–1979*, 2nd ed. (New York, 1980), 32.

46. Ritcheson, *Aftermath of Revolution*, 185–203.

47. For British fears of the danger America posed to the West Indies see ibid., 3–4.

48. Dull, *French Navy and American Independence*, 299–300.

49. See John Charles Anderson Stagg, *Mr. Madison's War: Politics, Diplomacy and Warfare in the Early American Republic, 1783–1830* (Princeton, 1983).

CHAPTER 9

The American Republic in a Wider World

Don Higginbotham

The nature of an independent America was almost as important to many of its citizens as the fact of independence itself, and it was also a subject of no little interest to Europeans as well. In both the New World and the Old a multitude of thoughtful individuals reflected on how America's republican character would influence its role in the family of Western nations. If the republics of antiquity had not survived into the early modern era, a few republican political entities had reappeared since the Renaissance, usually as autonomous city-states or as leagues or confederacies. European republics were thought of in connection with energetic commercial activity—Genoa, Venice, Ragusa, the Swiss cantons, and especially the United Provinces of the Netherlands, which, like the United States in the Confederation period of the 1780s, was seen as a league of loosely joined republics. But they were also considered politically unstable and militarily vulnerable to the pressures of outside powers. Those very weaknesses had converted the United Provinces to second-rate power status, which was only confirmed for the Dutch as a result of their humiliation at the hands of Britain during the American War of Independence. The United Provinces—and republics generally—were described as peace-loving states whose objectives in time of international strife were to engage in economic intercourse with belligerent and nonbelligerent kingdoms alike on a fair and impartial basis. That was why the Netherlands had enthusiastically supported Catherine the Great's League of Armed Neutrality in 1780.

America, too, it was predicted, after winning its independence would seek only trade and pacific relations with the governments of Europe. If that was the opinion of French foreign minister Vergennes and the British diplomat David Hartley, it was also the fervent wish of the American commissioners who concluded the Treaty of Paris in 1783. While the optimism of a Benjamin Franklin on those prospects, when examined from a later perspective, seems naive, we should remember that it was a widely held view at the time that Britain's supremacy in the galaxy of empires rested in large part on her monopoly of the raw materials of her American provinces. To be sure, during the Revolutionary War itself the European crowned heads had responded cautiously, even negatively, to the offers of liberal trade treaties extended by American missionary diplomats, who appeared spouting the ideas embodied in Adam Smith's recently published *Wealth of Nations*. But it was relatively easy for Congressional emissaries to rationalize their failures, attributing them to European fears of British retaliation and predicting that more positive responses to American appeals would be forthcoming after 1783. Europe as well as America would reap handsome dividends from a new day in economic affairs. In their most enthusiastic moments, some American diplomats went so far as to hope that the Revolutionary struggle had been "a war to end all wars." For if mercantilism, that aged instigator of internal strife and imperial bloodlettings, could be replaced by more open trading relationships, nations would have far less to generate tensions and rivalries between them, and peoples would find through free and frequent contact that their common interests exceeded their differences. Franklin, a complex blend of pragmatist and idealist, declared—in language that has a modern ring—that no labor was as rewarding as the work of peace and that there was no such thing as a "good war" or a "bad peace."

The interpretation of American world-mindedness thus far expressed is of a piece with the predominant school of diplomatic historians of the past generation, including Felix Gilbert, Paul Varg, Gerald Stourzh, and Richard B. Morris, and their writings are partly reflected in this volume's essays by Jonathan R. Dull and Drew R. McCoy. Another recent investigator, James A. Hutson, discloses another strain of American internationalist thought, and in fact argues that it was the dominant one throughout the Revolutionary era. Whether a majority of articulate Americans really wished "to seal the country off completely from Europe in the interest of preserving republican purity" and consequently to repudiate "idealistic internationalism" is debatable, but one cannot deny Hutson's contention that some of Franklin's countrymen were less than sanguine about European business connections.[1] Even if the British monopoly were broken and intercourse more broadly diffused by forging links with continental principalities, the result would be the insertion of corrupting European influences, leading to a preoccupation with luxuries, to an attended laziness at the expense of the traditional work ethic, and ultimately to a pervasive immorality.

Yet apprehension about commerce should not be analyzed solely as an American phenomenon. Catherine of Russia, who sometimes referred to herself as a republican (she clearly attests to the imprecision in Europe attached to that term), was ambivalent like her idol Montesquieu as to the plusses and minuses of foreign imports. But she not infrequently sounded as dogmatically negative as Hutson finds many Americans to have been, especially when she adverted that the decline of Venice, Genoa, and the United Provinces could be traced directly to an undue accumulation of wealth in private hands and the concomitant evisceration of civic virtue.

If Americans, like Europeans such as Catherine, were of different minds about commerce, most would probably have agreed with Franklin and Madison that commerce that involved the export of surplus agricultural products to a variety of foreign markets was desirable and that specified European imports need not necessarily shred the moral fiber of the republic. The Jeffersonians did not wish a return to the age of "primitive, even barbaric, subsistence farmers," as McCoy phrases it. Americans continued to require from the outside—in Henry Clay's later words—two of the "great wants of man": raiments and the tools of protection and self defense. Nor was there deep disagreement about the idea of domestic manufactures itself, a recognized need since the nonimportation movement in the decade before Lexington and Concord. Household manufactures and small-unit industries would lessen America's dependence on the Old World.

The question was not one of whether America should be economically independent, but rather how the nation should achieve it. To what extent should the central government stimulate manufactures by bounties, internal improvements, and tariffs, and should it retaliate against those kingdoms that refused to accept American agricultural exports? The question—one of political economy—was tied to the movement for a stronger political union, for until the adoption and ratification of the federal Constitution of 1787 it was impossible for Congress to energize the economic sector. Broadly speaking, Hamilton's solution was to use government to stimulate manufactures and to keep America economically linked with Britain, which, for the foreseeable future, would continue to be its natural trading partner as it had been in the days when colonial commerce had been controlled by the mercantilist laws and policies of the parent country. The Jeffersonians, especially Madison, continued to espouse the liberal idealism of Revolutionary foreign-policy thinking, scarcely sobered by the country's failure to secure trade treaties during the Confederation years and by Secretary of State Jefferson's similar frustrations in the early 1790s.

Perhaps only a new nation not yet terribly set in its ways and blessed with an abundant public domain could debate its economic options as did Americans between the 1780s and the 1830s. By the terms of the peace of 1783 America stretched westward to the Mississippi; it was a republic, as the Anti-Federalists were wont to say, of unparalleled proportions. Assuredly the Dutch, blessed in the seventeenth century but cursed in the eighteenth by their geographical limits, did not have the real estate, nor, for that matter, did they have a centralized republican political system as republicanism was shaped and defined by the American federal Constitution. In 1787, the year that Americans set about putting their political house in order, the Dutch political edifice was falling apart: Prussian troops entered the United Provinces to silence factional divisions and bolster the authority of the stadholder.

Both Dull and McCoy call attention to what the American West afforded the new nation. Dull sees it as giving America untold advantages for growth and prosperity denied to the Dutch and the other republics of Europe, while McCoy tells us that for Madison it held the answer to the question of how to provide employment in agriculture for a burgeoning population and at the same time use those products of the American farms to force open the trading ports of Europe and to smash Britain's economic domination of the United States. In the long course of American history, at any rate, we can agree with Dull that the New World republic derived immeasurable benefits from its "limitless extent of territory." Near the end of his half-century career in journalism Walter Lippmann penned a brilliant analysis of that very point. Lippmann put this comparative dimension in even wider focus. He maintained that the North American interior provided the United States not only a unique advantage over small countries like Holland without vast holdings beyond their settled areas; America also had opportunities far greater than most of those states that did have expansive inland regions within their boundaries. He was referring to the great central mass of those world continents that have been almost totally undeveloped because of jungles, deserts, or other near impenetrable barriers. He particularly singled out South America, where an intractable core helped to account for crowded settlement areas, economic retardation, and trade relationships dominated by foreign interests.

Yet those blessings of the American frontier did not all come instantaneously and in the form sought by Madison. In time, of course, the ports of Britain, France, and other parts of Europe and the West Indies were opened to American bottoms, since the belligerents on both sides needed American produce during the international conflict that raged for over two decades following the onset of the French Revolution. But these war-induced opportunities did not lead to enlightened commercial pacts that would transcend the struggle. European statesmen were no more inclined to adopt liberal American principles of international intercourse than they had been in the 1780s. Madison and Clay would look back on those prosperous if tumultuous years between 1792 and the War of 1812 and agree that the original Jeffersonian economic strategy had worked—or performed as well as it did—owing to unprecedented international conditions and Europe's wartime distress. (This world crisis would not be the last time that a foreign upheaval would be seen as a shot in the arm for a troubled economy—such sentiments were scarcely hidden in 1914–1915 and 1939–1940.) Only after 1815 would a considerable element of the party of Jefferson led by Clay and other second-generation Republicans (with some help from Madison, not Jefferson himself) think of using the national domain in somewhat Hamiltonian terms—that is, to stimulate manufactures, create sectional interdependence, and promote national self-sufficiency.

The Revolutionary generation's concept of republicanism contained certain imperatives relating to the outside world. First, the American republic should pursue the path of peace, eschewing the blood-drenched rivalries of the Old World, rivalries that invariably had dragged the English colonials into the maelstrom of European warfare before 1763. The War of 1812 proved that hope short-lived, although subsequently America profited from the absence of a truly international war until 1914, after which the United States' preoccupation with neutral trading rights was perhaps the major factor in entering World War I in 1917, the same preoccupation that figured so prominently in the declaration of war against Britain in 1812. Whatever the nature of Wilsonian objectives, foreign policy under the Jeffersonians was aggressive, not only in its relentless pursuit of foreign trade but also in its quest for territorial expansion. Though commercial and landed expansion had been central to the Jeffersonian vision of a preeminently agrarian republic, McCoy shows that by the 1820s the Virginian's political party had pulled back from both—Madison said they should "put on the brakes." But the rhetoric of expansionism, once set loose, may have developed an internal dynamic that could be adopted by still other parties or interest groups in after years. Such advocates could cite Jeffersonian precedents, not Federalist or Hamiltonian ones. The Jeffersonians bought Louisiana, made war in 1812, seized west Florida, and then pressured Spain into giving up east Florida, all of which were justified in terms of preserving or strengthening the American experiment in republicanism. The rhetoric of Manifest Destiny in the 1840s sounds far more Jeffersonian than Hamiltonian; and in one form or another, according to George Kennan, most Americans' wars since then have been sold to the public as moral causes or crusades. With such fervor aroused, it is hardly surprising that John Shy and Russell Weigley have found Americans obsessed with total victory, with what Weigley terms "a strategy of annihilation."

A second imperative, economic independence, proved as elusive as the initial republican vision of perpetual peace, regardless of whether the nation sought to stand on its own feet by means of Republican or Federalist strategies. Even if Hamilton's economic thinking was more realistic than that of Jefferson and Madison, and even if Clay's American System constituted at least a tacit acknowledgment of Hamilton's wisdom, Clay had little success in implementing his ambitious program. Even so, after 1840 American industrial development was not insignificant, but it could hardly be compared to the accelerated pace of the Industrial Revolution in England, and British exports to America increased rather than decreased. Furthermore, American business advances owed much to British capitalists, who turned from declining opportunities in continental Europe to the United States. Ironically, vast sums of pounds sterling went into the development of the American West during the canal age—the region farthest removed from Europe and from Eastern cities that all too often reflected demoralizing Old World influences in Jefferson's view. Even Jefferson's idealized agricultural hinterland could not escape the Britain that he and his party had hoped to expel from the American scene. With good reason both McCoy and Dull say that the antebellum economy continued to be neocolonial.

A third imperative, though not relevant to the objectives of McCoy and Dull, was intellectual independence, a dream elegantly espoused by Jefferson, Noah Webster, and, most inspiringly, by Ralph Waldo Emerson in his 1837 Phi Beta Kappa address at Harvard College. That, too, was not to be as American culture continued to be highly derivative of its older British model. A good measure of the explanation appears to be contained in Joseph J. Ellis's *After the Revolution: Profiles of Early American Culture,* where the argument is advanced that political, economic, and demographic concerns—with their emphasis on individual autonomy and self-expression—proved an inhospitable rather than a nurturing environment for the flowering of high culture.[2]

Americans willing to look beneath their patriotic effusions might nonetheless have found another imperative that, on balance, had worked extremely well by the middle period, and that was their constitutional system, although the richness of their political accomplishments would no more convert the world to their political principles than it had to their economic notions. Withal, Americans have rarely been bereft of optimism for fresh beginnings—for world peace, for unencumbered commerce, for enduring prosperity, and so on. World tensions, trade deficits, and sparkling technological achievements elsewhere in the 1980s serve as a reminder that the new day remains elusive. It is also true, however, that the liberal, internationalist ideas of the young Madison and the elderly Franklin in the 1780s have never been entirely abandoned.

NOTES

1. "Early American Diplomacy: A Reappraisal," in Lawrence S. Kaplan, ed., *The American Revolution and "A Candid World"* (Kent, Ohio, 1977), 40–68, especially 49.
2. Joseph J. Ellis, *After the Revolution: Profiles of Early American Culture* (New York, 1979).

CHAPTER 10

Settlers, Settlements, and New States

Peter S. Onuf

The key to the new nation's future greatness lay in the West. But the key could easily be lost. With this in mind, congressmen articulated and attempted to implement principles that would open the West to settlement while preserving and strengthening the union.[1] During the period from the adoption of the first territorial government ordinance in 1784 to the passage of the Northwest Ordinance in 1787, they worked out the main features of a system that would govern subsequent American territorial expansion. They pledged Congress to guarantee the eventual equality of new western states and, by laying out their boundaries in advance, attempted to preempt future jurisdictional controversy. At the same time, they sought to sell national land on terms that would help relieve the nation's financial burdens while guaranteeing orderly expansion and economic growth. These measures were all designed to secure and to extend the union: the underlying concern of each was with the character, interests, and loyalties of prospective settlers.

Congress's revenue needs converged with contemporary prescriptions for western economic and political development. The relatively high price of land—set at a dollar per acre in 1785—would screen out speculators as well as poor, subsistence farmers and put a premium on commercial agriculture.[2] New settlers would be prevented from spreading too far and thin by the gradual, progressive survey and sale of national lands. Thus they would be clustered into neighborhoods that could be controlled and protected with much less difficulty than scattered settlements. The predetermination of private property lines and state boundaries would eliminate the leading sources of conflict on earlier frontiers. Industrious immigrants from the old states and from Europe were also assured that they would eventually enjoy the full benefits of American citizenship as new western states were organized and admitted into the union.

Yet the success of congressional western policy was by no means certain. Dissatisfaction with the initial version of the territorial system—embodied in the 1784 government ordinance and the 1785 land ordinance—mounted after its first general publication in mid-1785. Critics of the land ordinance charged that the system was too restrictive: they said the high price of federal lands and the requirement of advance surveys would retard settlement.[3] Meanwhile, critics of the government ordinance charged that it was too permissive: it did not provide adequate guarantees for the preservation of law and order before statehood.[4] The passage of the Northwest Ordinance in July 1787 and the coincidental sale of 1,500,000 acres to the Ohio Company reflected Congress's response to these attacks as well as its problems in bringing its lands to market and finding sufficient numbers of worthy purchasers and settlers. Instead of solving the nation's financial woes, the western lands had constituted a further drain on the treasury. Keeping the national domain clear of squatters and speculators may have been imperative for promoting land sales and orderly development, but the resulting expense was enormous.

The result was a radical revision of the means employed to achieve the goals of American western policy. But it does not follow that these policy changes signified a cynical capitulation to financial exigencies or a betrayal of "liberal" principles embodied in the 1784 territorial government ordinance. Local autonomy and frontier democracy were not vital issues to potential settlers—at least to those Congress hoped to recruit.

Whatever credit Manasseh Cutler of the Ohio Company deserves for the specific provisions—and even the passage—of the 1787 ordinance for territorial government, it is clear that it was drafted with the intention of attracting "robust and industrious" settlers from New England.[5] Many of these settlers were only willing to venture westward under the company's aegis and with the promises of law and order written into the ordinance: the inducements to emigrate under the existing land and government ordinances were inadequate. The real issue—for settlers and policy-makers alike—was land. The enjoyment and productive use of the land depended on clear title, protection from "savage" neighbors—Indian or white—and access to markets. These conditions required the effective exercise of congressional power during the territorial period. The settlers' concern with political rights was prospective: once their new communities were successfully founded, could they look forward to joining the union on an equal footing? In the meantime, provisions for "colonial" government were not only an administrative necessity: they were a necessary inducement to potential settlers.

I. FIRST PRINCIPLES

In April 1786 James Monroe wrote John Jay, Secretary for Foreign Affairs, that Congress was about to decide whether it would establish a territorial government for the Northwest "upon Colonial principles" before the new states to be organized there were "admitted to a vote in Congress with the common rights of the other States." The alternative was that westerners "be left to themselves until that event."[6] At the same time, Congress was faced with other momentous questions that would shape the future history of the Northwest. How would the new states be bounded? What populations would qualify them for statehood?

When Monroe presented this choice to Jay he was serving on a congressional committee charged with reconsidering the principles of territorial government set forth in the ordinance of April 23, 1784. The drafters of the ordinance, including Monroe's mentor Thomas Jefferson, specified boundaries for sixteen new states, conforming with the requirement of the Virginia land cession that Congress sponsor the creation of new western states not to exceed 150 miles square each.[7] The proposed new states covered the new national domain north of the Ohio (the so-called "ten new states") as well as the transmontane regions of old states that had not yet relinquished their claims. Under the ordinance, the new states were promised admission to the union when their respective populations equalled that of the smallest existing state.

Pressure for enlarging new state boundaries and for raising the population threshold grew out of difficulties encountered by Congress in organizing land sales and settlement in the national domain. Many congressmen feared that small, lightly populated states would not qualify for admission or that, if they did, they would never equal the original members in population and wealth. The revisions eventually proposed by Monroe's committee—and ultimately incorporated in the Northwest Ordinance—were supposed to attract industrious farmers to the Ohio country and guarantee the orderly expansion of settlement.[8] Policymakers became convinced that the large measure of local autonomy permitted by Jefferson's ordinance was incompatible with these goals. As a result, within weeks of Monroe's letter, Congress moved to establish a "colonial" system for the temporary government of its western lands.

From Jefferson's vantage point in Paris, Congress's choices on the issue of state size and population and temporary territorial government looked like a rejection of his liberal principles in favor of a more restrictive and conservative system. These polarities have also dominated historical writing.[9] On one hand, Congress could allow settlers to manage their own affairs within relatively small "states" that could anticipate early admission into the union. On the other, it could enlarge the new states to the point of jeopardizing their republican character while, by raising the population requirement, protracting the period of "colonial" control indefinitely.

But if congressional decisions on these issues were to be of far-reaching significance to the future of the republic, they were not particularly controversial at the time. Jefferson worried about how westerners would react to changing state size and to the imposition of a more "strong-toned" territorial government. Monroe and his colleagues were more concerned that the process of settlement might never begin unless changes securing law, order, and land titles were instituted. Given Congress's poor start in promoting western settlement, there was also good reason to fear that small states would fail to meet the population requirement, and thus be barred from the union indefinitely. Thus, Monroe reasoned, Jefferson's overarching goal of promoting the expansion of the union on the basis of new state equality would be jeopardized unless his proposals for temporary government and small states were discarded.

The formation of frontier settlements and preparation for statehood presented no problems for Jefferson when he propounded the founding principles of the territorial system in 1784. Impressed with the mushrooming growth of Virginia's Kentucky District, he assumed that the region across the Ohio River would also settle rapidly. As he later told the French encyclopedist Jean Nicolas Demeunier: "We have seen lately a single person [Daniel Boone] go and decide on a settlement at Kentucky, many hundred miles from any white inhabitants, remove thither with his family and a few neighbors, and though perpetually harrassed by the Indians, that settlement in the course of 10 years has acquired 30,000 inhabitants. . . ."[10] When the Kentucky lands filled up, and Congress opened the national domain to settlement, the frontier would push beyond the Ohio. Then, predicted George Washington, the western country "will settle faster than any other ever did."[11]

Because Jefferson, with other contemporary commentators, assumed the continuing growth and spread of population to the West, he concluded that Congress's main task was to connect old and new settlements on equitable terms. The major contribution of his ordinance was to establish the principle of new state equality. For the same reasons, the ordinance did not deal with the problem of creating and organizing new settlements. Jefferson thought private initiatives, rationalized and directed by the congressional land system, would suffice.

The scope of the 1784 ordinance suggests that Jefferson did not consider the distinction between unsettled and settled areas significant: he expected new frontier regions to fill in rapidly once opened to settlement. He also expected future state land cessions to establish Congress's jurisdiction over rapidly developing areas that would soon qualify for statehood.[12] The ordinance set forth the terms on which these areas—most notably Kentucky—would join the union. Separatists advocating the division of the old states subsequently read the 1784 ordinance as an invitation to organize their own new states.[13] Though the separatists overlooked the necessity in Jefferson's scheme for prior jurisdictional cessions by the states and for an amendment to the Articles, they did grasp his central concern: "compacts" between old and new states would preclude an exploitative, colonial regime in the West and thus constitute the basis of an enduring union. The existence of those new states—or of settlements that could plausibly aspire to statehood—was taken for granted.

Jefferson failed to anticipate obstacles Congress would face in organizing new settlements across the Ohio. Assuming the inevitability of frontier expansion, he concluded that settlers would bitterly resist being degraded from self-government to colonial dependency. Far from the United States—and from the complications of congressional politics—Jefferson was also inclined to theorize from republican first principles: thus, he told Monroe, westerners "will not only be happier in states of a moderate size, but it is the only way in which they can exist as a regular society"; only a "tractable people"—which frontier settlers assuredly were not—"may be governed in large bodies."[14] But Monroe was convinced that the new states would have to be enlarged, invoking his own experience during his recent "rout[e]s westward" as well as his reading of the current state of

national and sectional politics.[15] Because of the requirements of the congressional land system, variations in the quality of the land itself (Monroe
predicted that the extensive prairies would remain poor and sparsely settled), and the region's strategic vulnerability, the future development of
the Northwest would not follow the pattern of the southern frontier. In
fact, the only legitimate settlers in the national territory, the Illinois
French, showed little enthusiasm for local autonomy. Instead, they
pressed Congress to confirm their land titles and establish effective territorial government, complaining about being left "in a state of nature, with-
[ou]t law government or protection" ever since the Virginia cession.[16]
Meanwhile, as Congress faltered in its efforts to implement the 1785 land
ordinance, the anticipated emigration of American settlers and formation
of new settlements was delayed.

Jefferson's mistake was not to overestimate the capacity of frontier settlers to manage their own affairs, but rather to expect too much from the
new land system. The land and government ordinances were paired in
Jefferson's thinking. In 1784 he and Hugh Williamson of North Carolina
had been the chief authors of a proposed land ordinance designed as
companion legislation to the government ordinance.[17] Though Congress
rejected Jefferson's and Williamson's proposals, their idea of organizing
the western lands under a grid became central to congressional policy. The
ordinance finally adopted in May 1785 differed in important respects from
the 1784 plan, notably in combining provisions for prior survey and compact sale and settlement by township with the grid. But Jefferson applauded these changes. He wrote Monroe from Paris that the adopted
ordinance improved on the earlier proposals "in the most material circumstances." He had the most "sanguine . . . expectations" that the national
lands would find a ready sale.[18]

The land ordinance was supposed to produce revenue while rationaliz-
ing settlement patterns and providing the basis for social order in the
national domain. It would guarantee the rapid creation of a class of orderly, industrious landholders with a common interest in defending their
titles and upholding national authority. In effect, order would be superim-
posed on the vast, seemingly irresistible westward migration, thus securing landholdings and eliminating title conflicts. For Jefferson, then, the
definition of property rights in the land ordinance would provide the
foundation of social order. The government ordinance therefore could
focus on the rights of these frontier communities in relation to the union

and to each other. The delineation of state boundaries would maintain order among the new states just as the definition of property rights in the land ordinance would secure orderly settlement.

The goals of fixing state boundaries and private property lines were intimately related, as geographer William Pattison has demonstrated in his fine study of the origins of the rectangular survey system.[19] State lines would constitute a kind of supergrid: surveys within each new state were supposed to begin at its southeast corner, so providing periodic correction for accumulated deviations from meridian lines (which tended to converge as they ran north). Because each new state had its own grid, the common rights of local property-holders would reinforce political divisions. The government ordinance was designed to remove any uncertainty about an area's future jurisdictional status: as congressman David Howell reported, "settlers will always readily know in which of the states they are." The jurisdictional confusion that characterized earlier frontier settlements, jeopardizing national security and the survival of the union, would be avoided.[20] The land ordinance would provide the same certainty and security for purchasers of federal lands. "Emigrants from all parts of the world" would be attracted to the Northwest, William Grayson predicted, because the ordinance guaranteed an "exemption from controversy on account of bounds to the latest ages."[21]

The land and government ordinances thus were intended to be complementary. After transmission to the states, they were printed together in newspapers throughout the country in June and July 1785. This was the first publication of the government ordinance as it was finally adopted.[22] The link between the land system and provisions for territorial government remained crucial for policymakers after 1785. But the fit between the two ordinances became increasingly problematic. The "invisible hand" in the land market became more and more visible as Congress moved to protect its property from squatters and speculators and to locate legitimate buyers. The surveys required by the land ordinance multiplied Congress's costs. Delays in bringing federal lands to market and sluggish sales soon showed that the national domain would not be the hoped-for panacea for a depleted treasury. Complaints about the high price of federal land and continuing threats of Indian war discouraged prospective settlers; straggling settlements, lacking numbers sufficient for self-defense or self-government, looked to the national government for protection.

It was clear by 1787 that Congress would not be able to sell its lands unless it could provide "criminal and civil justice," thus securing "Peace and property among the rude people who will probably be the first settlers there."[23] As Richard Henry Lee explained, the Northwest Ordinance established a "temporary Government . . . preparatory to the sale of that Country."[24] In effect, the relationship Jefferson had posited between the land system and territorial government was reversed: territorial government facilitated the sales that in Jefferson's scheme would have made government unnecessary. But changes in western policy should not be seen as a rejection of Jefferson's vision of an expanding union. Instead, confronted with new, largely unanticipated complications, policymakers began to come to grips with contradictions implicit in plans for orderly expansion and economic development in the national West.

2. SETTLERS AND SETTLEMENTS

Between 1784 and 1787 assessments of the demand for national property became less and less optimistic. At the outset, many observers assumed the rapid, continuous flow of settlement. Congress only had to screen out undesirable settlers from a continuing westward flow. The human "torrent" seemed irresistible: in Washington's memorable language, "you might as well attempt . . . to prevent the reflux of the tide, when you had got it into your rivers," as to try to stop it.[25] As the river image suggested, that movement might be channelled—indeed, if it could not be, there was no point in developing a western policy at all. But subsequent experience called expansionist assumptions into question: the demand for national land—on Congress's terms—proved disappointing. It became clear that Congress would have to devise other means to attract purchasers if it hoped to reap any benefit from its property. This realization set the stage for the Ohio Company deal.

But Congress's concern with the character of potential settlers, however they were recruited, was constant. Congressmen knew that decisions about how to distribute and organize the public lands would determine the kind of people who would settle in the national domain. The first settlers would set a pattern for their successors. In turn, the character of these settlers and of their settlements would help define Congress's role in providing temporary, territorial government.

Rhapsodic descriptions of the western lands encouraged thousands of easterners, many suffering the effects of local land shortages, to look westward for new homes. In a typical effusion, soldier-poet David Humphreys held forth on the Arcadian delights of the western country:

> Then let us go where happier climes invite,
> To midland seas and regions of delight;
> With all that's ours, together let us rise,
> Seek brighter plains, and more indulgent skies;
> Where fair Ohio rolls his amber tide,
> And nature blossoms in her virgin pride;
> Where all that beauty's hand can form to please,
> Shall crown the toils of war, with rural ease.[26]

Other writers were at a loss to describe the bounty of western nature: "words would fail to give you a just idea of its riches."[27] According to a report from Kentucky, "any description I can possibly give, would fall infinitely short."[28] A visitor to the Ohio country called on "industrious farmer[s] from the eastern states" to emigrate to "this delightful country": "struggle no longer with the devouring embarrassments of cold and frost, in the barren regions of the north, but embrace the invitations of peace and plenty in a temperate climate."[29]

The western lands promised great things for an enterprising people. In the words of Richard Henry Lee, the western "country is fine beyond description both in soil and climate—abounding with all those primary and essential materials for human industry to work upon, in order to produce the comfort and happiness of mankind."[30] But if these new lands were potentially very productive—crop yields were said to be "amazing"—Lee and like-minded commentators feared that subsistence could be so easily obtained that settlers would have little incentive to work, particularly as long as markets for surpluses remained inaccessible. A rhetorical solution to the dilemma was to describe the West as a "savage wilderness" that "laudable industry" might transform into "a civilized field that shall blossom like the rose."[31] But a little work went a long way. The "savage wilderness" was really more like "a perfect paradise," according to one member of Col. Thomas Hutchins's team of surveyors—at least if "a few select friends" could be recruited to provide company. There would be plenty of time to socialize. "The people of this country"—the lands bordering on the national domain—were, he reported, "the most indolent in the world."[32]

Mankind generally—and the United States in particular—stood to benefit little from the spread of subsistence farming and a general regression to semisavage indolence. The lure of fertile land and easy living threatened to draw multitudes from productive pursuits in eastern communities into lives of laziness and sloth. Expansion thus would unleash centrifugal forces that would undermine the prosperity and power of the new republic.[33] Congress's answer to this threat was the 1785 land ordinance. The cost of federal lands would block out poor, lazy squatters; instead, the territory would attract industrious settlers determined to recoup their investment by developing their property and finding markets for their products. Under the new land system, settlers would be clustered in adjacent townships, thus facilitating the development of local markets; internal improvements would link East and West.

The emphasis on commercial agriculture and economic development reflected Congress's overriding concern with revenue. Its goal was to create a national domain that would produce revenue through land sales. The idea that the sale of the West would help pay for the Revolution became fixed in congressional thinking, particularly as prospects for developing other revenue sources dimmed. Consequently, Congress showed little enthusiasm for proposals that called for extensive, free land grants, even when they promised to satisfy soldiers' bounty claims or secure the frontiers.[34] The commitment to a commercial frontier was incompatible with propositions to rusticate old soldiers, or with pastoral fantasies about sustaining a balance at a "middle stage" between nature and civilization most propitious for the preservation of republican liberty. The economic and political independence that were supposed to be essential props to republican virtue in long-settled areas were difficult to distinguish from the "independence" of lazy, lawless, and improvident frontier squatters.

These themes were developed in a satirical blast against pastoralism and republicanism that appeared in the *Connecticut Magazine* in April 1786. "Lycurgus" mockingly claimed that Jefferson's 1784 territorial government ordinance was a blueprint for "universal liberty and universal poverty." Congress's new states would be "an asylum for decayed patriots." "Embosomed in academic groves, and surrounded by the wild magnificence of nature," old soldiers would *"sit each under his own tree . . .* cultivating peace with the beasts and the savages." Thus would "commence that glorious millenium, so often predicted by the American Poets."[35] "Lycurgus's" satire underscored concerns about the character of western settlers and settlements that pointed the way toward a more elaborate scheme of territorial government. He mocked the idea of the West as an asylum or refuge, suggesting that if escape were the leading impulse, western expansion would be ruinous both for the survival of the union and the development of the national economy. "Lycurgus" further suggested that the line between civilization and savagery would be blurred in a pastoral landscape. Once assimilated to his new environment, the refugee would regress to the level of the "beasts and savages," or even to the vegetable condition of "his own tree."

For "Lycurgus," the republican pastorale was nothing less than a formula for disuniting the states and betraying the new nation's promise. The climax of his vision was the emergence on the frontiers of a new, shadow union of thirteen antistates, including the illegal, unrecognized new states of Vermont, Kentucky, and Wyoming, in addition to the ten new western states. According to "Lycurgus," strict republicans suspected that the United States was "already much too large": they must also fear, he concluded in one of his most extravagantly satirical passages, that the new nation might become too prosperous: "It is evident that the inland parts and western frontiers of the country are by far the most healthful and fertile portion of our dominions; and therefore, if we hold them in possession, they certainly ought never to be settled. Poverty,—hard labour—and shortness of life are essential to the preservation of our liberties."[36] Disunion, "Lycurgus" suggested, was the logical, republican solution to the danger of American prosperity.

Other, less playful writers also predicted that the new states would break off from the union and, following Vermont's example, become "rich and happy" by escaping the old states' burdens of debt and taxes.[37] Malcontents of all sorts would seek refuge on the frontiers, "Primitive Whig" told readers of the *New-Jersey Gazette,* including those "running away from publick taxes, and private debts." Thus, he concluded, "we diminish our internal strength under the notion of extending our dominion."[38]

Depopulation—the loss of productive workers, taxpayers, and potential purchasers of state lands—was the eastern analogue of western settlement run amuck. Theorists offered reciprocal solutions to both problems. Economic revival in the East would end the "waste of people," banished to the wilderness by lack of work and indebtedness.[39] Meanwhile, development of the productive potential of the West would open up new markets, sustaining the growth of population and prosperity throughout the union.

At the same time, frontier development would drive up western land prices, thus blocking the escape of the improvident and unproductive to "free" land, subsistence farming, and a reversion to savagery. A vigorous, integrated national economy would accelerate population growth while attracting industrious immigrants from abroad. According to a writer in the *Maryland Gazette*, a large and growing population was the key to national "strength and riches"—provided the "great majority of those numbers are usefully employed."[40]

Visions of western economic development were premised on the extension of market relations, transportation routes, and a union of eastern and western interests. These visions precluded conceptions of the West as a refuge for old soldiers or virtuous republicans, or as an "asylum for the poor."[41] Implicit in such conceptions was the idea that East and West were utterly different and distinct places. But development depended on an intersectional harmony of interests and a common commitment to pursue happiness in similar ways. The crucial issue was the westerner's relation to the natural world. "Cato" warned his readers that it was a great mistake to believe that "the advantages with which Nature blesses an infant empire . . . constitute[d] the sum of its happiness." If this were true, America could turn its back on the world—and Americans could turn their backs on each other—in order to live off the bounties of nature. Instead, "Cato" argued, the gifts of nature "are the instruments of greatness, and the earnest of future felicity: they form the basis of the glorious edifice. . . . In a people so enlightened as ours, advantages should seem to call forcibly for improvement, and to inspire a generous ambition."[42] A New Yorker elaborated on this theme in an apostrophe to the new nation's potential for development. The "spectacle" of this "laborious nation" transforming the virgin landscape was "interesting, noble and august." God Himself must be "delighted" to see the Americans "animate, by the invigorating breath of industry, all the regenerating powers of nature," to see them "improve the mysterious system of destruction and reproduction, [and] stir up, enrich, and meliorate the earth, rendering the appearance of nature still more beautiful."[43]

An instrumental attitude toward nature, enlarging "all streams of population, opulence and pleasure," created bonds of interest between easterners and westerners. It also defined the boundary between civilized, enterprising whites and "savages," white as well as red. Indeed, the "higher use" argument for expropriating Indian land depended on the settlers'

distinctive capacity to develop its full agricultural and commercial potential. The problem, as "Lycurgus" and other commentators saw it, was that
white settlers were all too ready to revert to savagery and thus fail to
exploit "the instruments of greatness" presented for their use.

The idea that settlers who moved beyond the restraints of civilized
society—and the incentives of the marketplace—would become Indianized
was a familiar one.[44] The squatters who moved onto the federal lands were
easily confused with "savages." One of the federal surveyors wrote from
Fort Harmar, in July 1786, that this "lawless set of fellows . . . are more
our enemies than the most brutal savages of the country." The surveyors
anticipated continuing interference "from a few rascally yellow fellows,
that are outcasts of all the tribes, and the whites who have been dispos-
sessed of fine bottoms."[45] Renegade Indians and white "banditti" were
seen forming unholy alliances, or spurring each other on to bloody atrocities. The consequence of illegal settlement and resulting troubles with the
Indians, real and imagined, was that policymakers came to see that the
implementation of land policy depended on establishing an effective military presence across the Ohio.

Frontier violence raised questions about Congress's role in fostering
settlement on the national domain. First, it was no longer clear that the
progress of settlement was irresistible; indeed, unauthorized encroachments on Indian lands north of the Ohio threatened to provoke a bloody
resistance that would roll back the white frontier. Further, the prevalance
of violence deterred industrious easterners from purchasing federal lands.
In the words of a Boston writer, "the terror of savages would deter the
people of *this country* even from Paradise."[46] Western development thus
hinged on Congress's determination to clear the ground of squatters, Indian traders, speculators, and other interlopers with an interest in foment-
ing "uneasiness" among the tribes.[47] By acting decisively, Congress would
select the kind of settlers who would guarantee the region's future
development—and the increasing value of its remaining property.

Speculators were seen lurking behind the rumor and reality of frontier
violence. With ambitions to become "petty princes in the western country," speculators were interested in discouraging potential purchasers of
the Ohio lands until they had gained control of extensive tracts.[48] According to "Cincinnatus," reports of savage conditions would "lessen the number of buyers" and thus the "price of [federal] land," and, by emphasizing
the need for security, encourage Congress to "grant the lands in that

quarter on condition of settlement only." "Cincinnatus" traced a widely published letter warning of the imminence of full-scale conflict with the Indians and criticizing congressional land policy to the machinations of Nathaniel Sackett and a company of New York land speculators.[49] The Sackett group promised to defend the frontier by organizing a new state at its own expense, if Congress would grant it an enormous tract of land bounded by Lake Erie and the Ohio, Muskingum, and Scioto rivers. "Cincinnatus" hoped "Congress and the Savages together, will be able to keep them and all others out."[50]

Congress rejected the Sackett proposal, demonstrating its determination to protect its property interests and implement the 1785 land ordinance. Policymakers attempted to solve the problem of frontier disorder by driving off squatters and speculators and recruiting orderly immigrants. By setting up land auctions in each of the old states, the land system would draw industrious, market-oriented purchasers directly from the sources of population growth. Thus the national domain would bypass the usual course of lawless landgrabbing that one Kentucky writer characterized as a virtual law of American frontier development. "It is well known," he asserted, that "every part of America that has hitherto been settled, has flowed in blood for a long time."[51] But industrious eastern farmers would be less likely to provoke their Indian neighbors than the semisavage predators who usually arrived first in a new country. At the same time, George Washington confidently predicted, "the gradual extension of our Settlements will as certainly cause the Savage as the Wolf to retire."[52]

The recruitment of worthy settlers continued to be a leading concern of territorial policymakers throughout the Confederation period. Washington, William Grayson, and other commentators hoped to see a large influx of foreigners settle the West—thus, incidentally, answering antiexpansionist anxieties about the depopulation of the old states.[53] But the new land system was better designed to exploit the rising demand for lands in the eastern states. Jefferson thought the land ordinance would guarantee that the national domain would be settled by a "proper mixture of the citizens from the different states."[54] In either case, it was agreed that Congress should look beyond the frontier itself for purchasers: the least eligible settlers were the large numbers of western "adventurers" said to be waiting ("as it were on tip toe") for permission to move into the Ohio country.[55]

Yet the land system was not simply a means of attracting worthy, easily governed settlers. It was also supposed to be a means of educating new settlers—in the broadest sense—to know and pursue their true private interests while fulfilling their public responsibilities. "We live at the origin of things," wrote "P.W." Every decision respecting the founding of these new western societies, even the choice of their names, would have momentous consequences. "Let us engrave the names of our brave Gallican friends on the first beginnings . . . of our great labour," he counseled, so that future generations would learn from these lasting "monuments of gratitude."[56] Inspired by similar logic, Jefferson had proposed neoclassical names, suitable for the new western republics, in a draft of the original government ordinance. At the same time, he thought that the land system presented "an happy opportunity . . . of introducing into general use the geometrical Mile, in such a manner as that it cannot possibly fail of forcing its way on the people."[57] Jefferson's premise was that settlers would "go to school" by moving west.

The principle had more significant and enduring applications. The land system itself would teach settlers to "see" the western landscape—and their own opportunities within it—through the pattern of the grid that defined specific property holdings.[58] Rational, systematic settlement would help create enlightened communities. As Manasseh Cutler wrote, shortly after the Northwest Ordinance was adopted, the great advantage of the new territory over any "other part of the earth" was "that, in order to begin *right*, there will be no *wrong* habits to combat, and no inveterate systems to overturn—there is no rubbish to remove, before you can lay the foundation."[59] The ordinance's provision for the public support of education complemented the rationality of geometrical survey, clear property titles, and predefined boundaries. Settlers on the national frontiers would not be the ignorant, degraded frontiersmen who, by common report, are "every day turning their backs upon all the benefits of cultivated society." Cutler's new westerners were turning their backs on "rubbish," not civilization. The result of a "systematic" territorial policy would be that "the whole territory of the United States [would be] settled by an enlightened people."[60]

The relative compactness of settlement that would result from the sale of land by lot or township was also seen as a crucial means of socializing new settlers. In 1782, well before Congress had any lands to administer, Pelatiah Webster advocated controlled expansion so that "we can *extend our laws, customs,* and *civil police* as *fast* and as *far* as we extend our *settlements.*"[61] Washington also endorsed the idea of "progressive seating." An artificially limited supply would keep land prices up while "extending the benefits, and deriving all the advantages of Law and Government from them at once; neither of which can be done in sparse Settlements, where nothing is thought of but scrambling for Land, which more than probably would involve confusion and bloodshed."[62] In March 1785, shortly before the adoption of the land ordinance, Timothy Pickering agreed that "dispersed" settlers would be "impossible to govern"[63] Tightly clustered in compact settlements directly contiguous to longer-settled regions in neighboring states, settlers on the national frontier would be held in check by common interests and associations. They would soon develop civic competence.

The township system incorporated in the land ordinance appealed to southerners, even though they were accustomed to acquiring lands for themselves by indiscriminate occupation. Not only did townships appear to guarantee a population density that facilitated the maintenance of law and order, they also promised to attract groups of immigrants with prior communal bonds. Thus, Grayson explained to Washington, "the idea of a towhship with the temptation of a support for religion and education, holds forth an inducement for neighborhoods of the same religious sentiments to confederate for the purpose of purchasing and settling together."[64] Though "support for religion" was eliminated from the adopted land ordinance, and Congress agreed to offer alternative townships for sale by individual lot, the new system was designed to promote group migration. The high price of land would deter land speculation while encouraging potential settlers to pool their resources in order to purchase whole townships.

An orderly frontier thus depended on a land system that directed settlement into neighborhood clusters—imposing order on private initiatives—while inducing existing neighborhoods to relocate from the settled parts of the country. These effects were reciprocal: large numbers of industrious farmers would hesitate to venture into the wilderness without assurances that they would soon enjoy the benefits of local institutions—including courts, schools, and churches—convenient neighbors, and easy access to the outside world.

Images of order imposed on the land by the grid system, reinforced by expectations of rapid and orderly development, would thus attract the most orderly settlers. It was a neat formula—at least in theory. But it soon became clear that large numbers of foreigners or easterners would not be bidding for federal lands, even when offered for sale at a single site, according to a revision of the ordinance. When lands from the first surveys were finally brought to auction late in 1787, only 72,934 acres were sold, providing the government a mere $117,108.22 in revenue.[65] Congress therefore was compelled to consider alternative means to achieve its policy goals. Accepting congressional responsibility for maintaining order in the new settlements, the drafters of the Northwest Ordinance moved to fill a vacuum left by the 1784 government ordinance. The origins of these new provisions for territorial government are to be found in the 1785 land ordinance in which Congress first extended the promise of system and order to prospective settlers. By 1787 it was clear that buyers would settle for nothing less than a fully developed "colonial" government, qualified by appropriate compact guarantees, during the territorial period.

Agent Manasseh Cutler received a sympathetic hearing when he promised that the Ohio Company would mobilize "an actual, a large, and immediate settlement of the most robust and industrious people in America."[66] Congressmen understood that Cutler was offering to settle the region with New Englanders. (Cutler judiciously confined explicit comparisons between northern and southern settlers to his private correspondence. He wrote Nathan Dane of Massachusetts, one of the authors of the Northwest Ordinance, that northerners were "undoubtedly preferable"; "They will be men of more robust constitutions, inured to labor, and free from the habits of idleness.")[67] For his part, Virginian Edward Carrington was pleased to report that the Ohio Company included "the best men in Connecticut and Massachusetts." Congress's contract with the company "will be a means of introducing into the Country, in the first instance, a discription of Men who will fix the character and politics throughout the whole territory, and which will probably endure to the latest period of time."[68]

3. NEW STATES

Between 1784 and 1787, the ideas of "state" and "settlement" became distinct in American western policy. The two ideas were closely linked in Jefferson's original conception of the territorial system: Kentucky and other existing settlements could anticipate admission to the union at an early date; new settlements, formed according to the pattern set by the land ordinance and within state lines specified by the government ordinance, would soon join them. In a sense, statehood was coexistent with settlement itself. Thus, in 1785, a Richmond writer could refer to Spanish threats against "settlers in the new States," as if those states already existed.[69]

But there were problems with imputing social order, political competence, and distinct "state" interests to new frontier settlements. As we have seen, the expansion of settlement in a manner compatible with revenue needs and national security was itself problematic. Further, as Congress assumed the responsibility of preparing its land for sale and maintaining law and order thereafter, the role of the new states became less and less apparent. Congress's decision to employ base lines for its surveys independent of the new state boundaries reflected this development.[70] The split between settlement and statehood was completed in the Northwest Ordinance: all the "states" would be governed as one (or two) territories prior to the final stages of state-making.

The major contribution of the Northwest Ordinance was to reject the notion of territorial "statehood" that was central to the 1784 ordinance. The state boundaries described in the new ordinance were prospective and (to some, unclear extent) variable: they did not govern the settlement process. In the later history of the Northwest the old idea that the new "states" existed from the founding of the territory was occasionally revived in response to proposed boundary changes. Otherwise, statehood was simply a more or less distant promise: it had no relevance for the organization and government of the first settlements.

The emerging distinction between settlement and state also helped resolve a variety of related misgivings about continental expansion. As long as it was equated with the addition of new states, expansion seemed fraught with danger. An overextended union might give rise to despotic government, or disintegrate into anarchy and confusion—or both. In any case, as Abbé Raynal warned his American friends, "The tranquillity of empire decreases as it is extended."[71]

The same logic applied to the separate states. These "republics" should "never desire an extended dominion," a Philadelphia writer explained, because "it has always proved inconsistent with the preservation of their liberties."[72] Yet it was also true that states could be too small. Another Philadelphian denounced the "baneful influence" of agitation for small, new states.[73] The process of state division tended toward complete atomization and the end of all government. The common ground for both writers was that states—small or large, for better or worse—were conceived of as distinct political societies.

Beginning with the premise that frontier settlements were "states," at some early stage of development, it was logical for Jefferson to worry about their relative size. The same principles that controlled political development elsewhere would operate in the new western states; due regard for these principles was imperative during the period of state founding. If the new states "can be retained til their governments become settled and wise," he told Madison, "they will remain with us always."[74]

Jefferson's insistence on equitable "compacts" between the original states and the western states as a necessary condition for continuing union also reflected his assumption that new settlements were "states" from the outset. Other commentators, arguing from the same premises, were less optimistic. In Rufus King's opinion, "no paper engagements . . . can be formed" which would guarantee union "between the Atlantic States, and those which will be erected to the Northwestward."[75] King's pessimism reflected a new, post-Jeffersonian awareness of divergent sectional interests. But the way he framed the problem showed that he continued to accept Jeffersonian assumptions about frontier statehood. These assumptions made it difficult to imagine an expanding union.

James Madison grappled repeatedly with the dilemmas presented by expansion. In August 1784, in a letter to Jefferson discussing the Mississippi crisis, he wrote of "the danger to the Confederacy" that would result from "multiplying the parts of the Machine."[76] Assuming that each new state would represent a distinct new interest, it was difficult not to conclude that the union inevitably would collapse. These progressive complications, he wrote Lafayette a few months later, should teach the Spanish not to fear the growth of new western settlements that free navigation of the Mississippi would encourage. He explained: "As [settlements] become extended the members of the Confederacy must be multiplied, and along with them the Wills which are to direct the machine. And as the wills multiply, so will the chances against a dangerous union of them. We experience every day the difficulty of drawing thirteen States into the same plans. Let the number be doubled & so will the difficulty."[77] Whatever comfort the Spanish might derive from these possibilities, they also suggested strongly that expansion and new state creation were *not* in the new nation's best interests. Given the legendary imbecility of the existing union, Congress might well follow "Lycurgus's" advice and close off the frontiers altogether.[78] Otherwise, a British writer predicted, the addition of "ten infant states" and Vermont would surely overtax the feeble machinery of national government: "What degree of unanimity may be expected among such a number of states, may be easily imagined."[79]

But these conceptual difficulties could be cleared away if the collective interests of westerners were distinguished from the separate, disaggregated interests of a large number of new western states. During the mid-1780s, sectional political conflict led many Americans to devalue state interests. Interest, they argued, was not always neatly defined by state boundaries but could be regional—and even continental—in scope. This was clearly true in the West, where the phantom new "states" lacked governments, land offices, or any other plausible focus of interest. Transmontane settlers understood their common interests, displaying a highly developed sectional consciousness during the Mississippi crisis. According to one report, the threat of a treaty blocking the Mississippi produced "political phrenzy" across the frontiers. "The general voice of the western community . . . is, EQUAL LIBERTY with the thirteen states, or a *breach of peace*, and a *new alliance!*"[80]

Sectional politics reinforced some of the lessons congressmen had been learning in the process of implementing and revising territorial policy. By necessity, Congress directed more and more attention to selling its lands, recruiting settlers, and organizing new settlements. This reorientation had far-reaching implications. First, the focus on the settlement frontier displaced the earlier concern with the status and interests of new western "states." The maintenance of law and order at the local level, which potential settlers demanded, depended on the effective exercise of national authority: "states" did not figure in the equation, at least until some future date. The problem of territorial government thus was transposed from the level of the "state" to that of the local community. The attainment of statehood—that is, self-government and membership in the union—would mark the culmination of a protracted process of building frontier communities from the ground up. Republicanism would flourish not because these states were smaller or larger, but because their foundations—communities of orderly, industrious settlers—were well laid.

In seeking to attract settlers, Congress had to respond to the individual and associated interests of prospective purchasers, further undercutting the assumption that the new states, as such, had distinctive interests of their own. As settlers' interests were cut loose from the assumption of parochial, mutually exclusive state loyalties, they could be seen as providing potential connections between frontier settlements and the wider world. The expanding scope of interest thus offered a solution to the conundrum of union: its survival would not have to depend on "paper engagements"—or on the exercise of despotic power—*if* the interests of easterners and westerners were developed reciprocally. This was the implicit message of the Mississippi furor. It was the explicit premise of promoters of internal improvements like George Washington who argued that "strong commercial bands" alone could prevent the loss of the West.[81]

By clearly distinguishing the first frontier settlements from the states they would eventually become, the Northwest Ordinance reflected a new way of thinking about territorial expansion. Settlement and economic development would come first, enabling Americans to exploit the vast new opportunities opening to their west while promoting the wealth and power of the entire nation. The success of their enterprises—measured by crossing a population threshold now set at 60,000—would conjure new states into existence. Then westerners would enjoy the full benefits of American citizenship.

The emphasis on economic development in American thinking about the West made it possible to see territorial expansion as a unifying project. Manasseh Cutler and other publicists claimed that all interests converged in the new settlements: "The advantages of almost every climate are here blended together; every considerable commodity, that is cultivated in any part of the United States, is here produced in the greatest plenty and perfection."[82] These great natural endowments, rightly used, would guarantee the nation's greatness. A New York writer thus chided his countrymen: "all nations but the Americans know the value and abilities of America; we have those resources within ourselves which no other nation can boast." But, he complained, "we totter about like infants, afraid to venture beyond the length of our leading-strings. . . . Youth is the time for exertion and enterprise, in the political as well as the natural constitution. The seeds must be sown in infancy, and they will be rooted in age."[83] Significantly, this writer thought the new nation's "constitution" would be written in the works of enterprising Americans. So too, in pursuit of their own interests, western settlers would advance the interest of all. Prosperity and abundance would be the true cement of union.

In late 1791 Madison returned to the problem of union in an essay titled "Consolidation," written for the *National Gazette*. By extricating "states" from distinct, mutually exclusive "interests," he was now able to argue for a stronger union—*and* for states' rights. "If a consolidation of the states into one government be an event so justly to be avoided, it is not less to be desired . . . that a consolidation should prevail in their interests and affections." The states would be bastions of liberty in the continuing struggle against incipient despotism. Yet the states could not survive if guided by "local prejudices and mistaken rivalships." Therefore it was the patriotic duty of all Americans "to consolidate the affairs of the states into one harmonious interest."[84]

Madison's argument may seem disingenuous, or at least paradoxical. But such logic suggested a solution to the problem of the extended republic. Indeed, expansion across space would serve to control and perhaps one day eliminate the factional discord that republicans found so vexing. Inspired by prospects for boundless national wealth and happiness in an expanding union of interests, Americans could also be confident that republican liberty would be well secured in an expanding union of states.

NOTES

1. The April 23, 1784 Ordinance is in Worthington C. Ford, ed., *Journals of the Continental Congress* (hereafter *JCC*), 34 vols. (Washington, D.C., 1904–37), XXVI, 274–79. The land ordinance of May 20, 1785, and the Northwest Ordinance of July 13, 1787, are in ibid., XXVIII, 375–81 and XXXII, 334–43.

2. These themes are elaborated in Peter S. Onuf, "Liberty, Development, and Union: Visions of the West in the 1780s," *William and Mary Quarterly*, 3rd ser., 43(1986), 179–213.

3. For instance, Letter from a gentleman in the Western Country, December 1785, *Massachusetts Spy* (Worcester), Jan. 26, 1786. See the discussion in note 50 below. According to Washington, in a letter to Lafayette, July 25, 1785, "Many think the price which they have fixed upon for the Lands too high" and that the sale by townships would be "a great let to the sale." In John C. Fitzpatrick, ed., *The Writings of George Washington*, 39 vols. (Washington, D.C., 1931–44), XXVIII, 208.

4. Congress received frequent complaints from settlers in the Illinois region who "wish to be under the protection" of the United States. Extract of a letter, d. New York, June 22, 1785, *New-Haven Gazette*, Sept. 8, 1785. See also Secretary of Congress to Kaskaskia Inhabitants, Aug. 24, 1786 promising that Congress would soon adopt a new "plan of a temporary government." In Edmund Cody Burnett, *Letters of the Members of the Continental Congress* (hereafter *LMCC*), 8 vols. (Washington, D.C., 1921–36), VIII, 450.

5. Manasseh Cutler Journal, entry for July 21, 1787, in William Parker Cutler and Julia Perkins Cutler, *Life Journals and Correspondence of Rev. Manasseh Cutler, LL.D.*, 2 vols. (Cincinnati, 1888), I, 296.

6. Monroe to Jay, April 20, 1786, *LMCC*, VIII, 342.

7. The Virginia cession, March 1, 1784, is reprinted in Clarence E. Carter, ed., *The*

Territorial Papers of the United States, 34 vols. (Washington, D.C., 1934–), II, 6–9. See the discussion in Peter S. Onuf, *The Origins of the Federal Republic: Jurisdictional Controversies in the United States, 1775–1787* (Philadelphia, 1983), 41–46, 75–102, 166–68.

8. Committee reports of Feb. 14, March 24, May 10, July 13, Sept. 21, 1786, *JCC*, XXX, 68–70, 131–35, 251–55, 402–406, XXXI, 669–72. See the account of these deliberations in Jack Ericson Eblen, *The First and Second United States Empires: Governors and Territorial Government, 1784–1912* (Pittsburgh, 1968), 28–32.

9. Notably Eblen, *First and Second Empires*, 17–51. The historiography is discussed in Ray Billington, "The Historians of the Northwest Ordinance," *Illinois State Historical Society Journal*, 40 (1947), 397–413, and Philip R. Shriver, "America's Other Bicentennial," *The Old Northwest*, 9 (1983), 219–35.

10. "Jefferson's Observations on Demeunier's Ms. [1786]," Julian Boyd, ed., *The Papers of Thomas Jefferson*, 21 vols. (Princeton, 1950–), X, 57.

11. Washington to Henry Knox, Dec. 5, 1784, in Fitzpatrick, ed., *Washington Writings*, XXVIII, 3–4.

12. Jefferson's "Answers to Demeunier's First Queries," Jan. 24, 1786, in Boyd, ed., *Jefferson Papers*, X, 14. See also Jefferson to Madison, April 25, 1784, ibid., VII, 118, and Madison to Jefferson, March 16, 1784, in Robert Rutland et al., eds., *The Papers of James Madison*, 14 vols. (Chicago and Charlottesville, Va., 1962–), VIII, 9, and the discussion in Onuf, *Origins of the Federal Republic*, 161–62.

13. Petition to Virginia Assembly, n.d., reprinted in *Freeman's Journal* (Philadelphia), Jan. 12, 1785; "Address to the Western Inhabitants," enclosed in Charles Cummings to the Pres. of Congress, April 7, 1785, Papers of the Continental Congress (National Archives, Washington, D.C.) XLVIII, 289; extract of a letter from a gentlemen in Frankland, Aug. 17, 1785, *The Times* (London), Dec. 31, 1785; "Impartialis Secundus," *Falmouth Gazette* (Portland, Mass.), July 9, 1785.

14. Jefferson to Monroe, July 9, 1786, and to Madison, Dec. 16, 1786, Boyd, ed., *Jefferson Papers*, X, 112, 603.

15. Monroe to Jefferson, Jan. 19, 1786, ibid., IX, 189.

16. According to William Grayson's report, in a letter to Lt. Gov. Beverley Randolph, June 12, 1787, *LMCC*, VIII, 610.

17. Report of April 30, 1784, *JCC*, XXVI, 324–30. See the discussion in William Pattison, *Beginnings of the American Rectangular Land Survey System, 1784–1800* (Chicago, 1957), 38–39.

18. Jefferson to Monroe, Aug. 28, 1785, Boyd, ed., *Jefferson Papers*, VIII, 445.

19. Pattison, *American Rectangular Survey*, 15–36, 53–55.

20. David Howell to Gov. Jonathan Arnold, Feb. 21, 1784, William R. Staples, ed., *Rhode Island and the Continental Congress* (Providence, 1870), 480.

21. Grayson to Washington, April 15, 1785, *LMCC*, VIII, 95–96.

22. The report of March 1, 1784, *JCC*, XXVI, 118–20, including Jefferson's suggested state names, was widely published in 1784 as "Resolutions of Congress." See for instance, *Virginia Gazette* (Richmond), May 15, 1784, and *Virginia Journal* (Alexandria), June 3, 1784. The adopted government ordinance and land ordinance were printed together in *New-Jersey Gazette* (Trenton) and *Connecticut Courant* (Hartford), both June 6, 1785, and in numerous other papers in all parts of the country in the following weeks.

23. Madison to Edmund Randolph, April 22, 1787, in Rutland, ed., *Madison Papers*, IX, 397; Richard Henry Lee to William Lee, July 30, 1787, *LMCC*, VIII, 629.

24. Lee to Francis Lightfoot Lee, July 14, 1787, ibid., VIII, 619.

25. Washington to Grayson, April 25, 1787, in Fitzpatrick, ed., *Washington Writings*, XXVIII, 138.

26. Humphreys, "Address to the armies of the united states of America," [1782], *American Museum*, 1 (March 1787), 238.

27. A letter from a gentleman in the western country, to his friend in Connecticut, Nov. 5, 1785, *Maryland Gazette* (Baltimore), Feb. 28, 1786.

28. Extract of a letter from a gentleman in Kentucky, to his friend in Philadelphia, Oct. 28, 1784, *New-Jersey Gazette*, Feb. 7, 1785.

29. Extract of a letter from a gentleman in the western country, to his friend in Connecticut, d. Fort Harmar, Feb. 7, 1786, ibid., May 8, 1786.

30. Lee to John Adams, May 28, 1785, *LMCC*, VIII, 128.

31. A correspondent, d. Nov. 3, 1785, *Connecticut Courant*, Nov. 7, 1785. The theme—and language—was frequently invoked. See for instance, Jonathan Loring Austin, *An Oration, Delivered July 4, 1786* (in Boston) (Boston, 1786), 15.

32. Extract of a letter from a gentleman in the western region to his friend in Boston, Aug. 8, 1786, *New Haven Gazette and Connecticut Magazine*, Sept. 28, 1786.

33. Writing as "Nestor," Benjamin Rush asserted that "there is but one path that can lead the United States to destruction; and that is their extent of territory. It was probably to effect this, that Great Britain ceded to us so much waste land." *Independent Gazetteer* (Philadelphia), June 3, 1786. See the discussion in Onuf, *Origins of the Federal Republic* 159–60.

34. Rudolph Freund, "Military Bounty Lands and the Origins of the Public Domain," in Vernon Carstensen, ed., *The Public Lands: Studies in the History of the Public Domain* (Madison, WI, 1963), 15–34. See the new state plan devised by Rufus Putnam and associates in Octavius Pickering, ed., *The Life of Timothy Pickering*, 4 vols. (Boston, 1867–73), I, 457–59, 546–49.

35. "Lycurgus," no. 10, *New Haven Gazette and Connecticut Magazine*, April 20, 1786.

36. "Lycurgus," no. 2, ibid., Feb. 23, 1786. "Lycurgus's" first number (ibid., Feb. 16, 1786), a straight argument for development, was picked up by other papers (*Connecticut Courant*, Feb. 27; *Maryland Gazette*, March 24). *Connecticut Courant* reprinted the satirical no. 2 on March 8, but as far as I can tell, no other numbers—all in the satirical mode—were reprinted.

37. Item in *Maryland Gazette*, May 4, 1787; item in *Independent Chronicle* (Boston), April 19, 1787. For discussion of the connection between Vermont and the western settlements see also Madison to Washington, March 18, 1787, in Rutland, ed., *Madison Papers*, IX, 314–17, and Washington to Madison, March 31, 1787, in Fitzpatrick, ed., *Washington Writings*, XXIX, 188–92.

38. "Primitive Whig," no. V, *New-Jersey Gazette*, Feb. 6, 1786.

39. "Amicus," *Freeman's Journal*, Dec. 13, 1786. See also "A Plain, but Real, Friend to America," d. Baltimore, Aug. 9, 1785, *Maryland Journal* (Baltimore), Aug. 16, 1785.

40. Item in *Maryland Gazette*, April 17, 1787.

41. Austin, *An Oration*, 15. See also "Celadon," *The Golden Age; or Future Glory of North-America Discovered* (n.p., 1785), 9, for an elaboration of the asylum theme: "The poor, the oppressed, and the persecuted will fly to America as doves to their windows.—This Western-World will be the dernier resort, the last refuge, and asylum for afflicted merit."

42. "Cato," To the Public, *Connecticut Magazine*, Jan. 25, 1787.

43. Item d. New York, July 20, 1786, *Freeman's Journal*, July 26, 1786.

44. See item in ibid., May 24, 1786, citing Abbé Raynal on the degeneration of "Europe-

ans . . . when arrived at the regions of the new world," and the comments in "An Account of the progress of the Population, Agriculture, Manners, and Government in Pennsylvania," *Columbian Magazine*, 1 (November 1786), 117–22. See also Roy Harvey Pearce, *Savagism and Civilization: A Study of the Indian and the American Mind* (Baltimore, 1965; orig. pub., Baltimore, 1953, as *The Savages of America*), esp. 53–104.

45. Extract of a letter from a gentleman at Ft. Harmar . . . to his friend in this town [Boston], July 26, 1786, *New Haven Gazette and Connecticut Magazine*, Oct. 5, 1786.

46. Item reprinted from *Boston Gazette*, Feb. 27, 1786, *Maryland Gazette*, March 24, 1786.

47. A letter from a gentleman of eminence in the state of Connecticut . . . to his friend in Chesterfield, May 15, 1786, *New-Jersey Gazette*, July 3, 1786; Nathan Dane's Address to the Massachusetts House [Nov. 9, 1786], *LMCC*, VIII, 503.

48. "Primitive Whig," *New-Jersey Gazette*, Feb. 6, 1786. See the discussion in Onuf, "Liberty, Development, and Union," 189–93.

49. Nathaniel Sackett et al., *A Memorial &c* [to Congress] (New York, Sept. 27, 1785); Papers of the Continental Congress, 41, IX, 349; Aug. 23, 1785, *JCC*, XXVII, 651.

50. "Cincinnatus," *Massachusetts Spy*, Feb. 16, 1786, also printed in *Connecticut Magazine*, March 9, 1786. "Cincinnatus" questioned the authenticity of a "Letter from a gentleman in the Western country," December 1785, first printed in New York in early January and republished throughout the country (including *Pennsylvania Gazette*, Jan. 11; *Columbian Herald* [Boston], Jan. 19; *Massachusetts Spy*, Jan. 26, 1786).

51. Extract of a letter from a gentleman residing in Kentucky to his friend in Chester co., Dec. 8, 1786, *Freeman's Journal*, April 11, 1787.

52. Washington to Duane, Sept. 7, 1783, in Fitzpatrick, ed., *Washington Writings*, XXVII, 140.

53. Washington to Knox, Dec. 5, 1784, and to Richard Henry Lee, Aug. 22, 1785, ibid., XXVIII, 4, 231; Grayson to Washington, April 15, 1785, ibid., VIII, 95–97, and to William Short, June 15, 1785, *LMCC*, VIII, 141–42. On the eastern states' fears of depopulation see Rufus Putnam to Washington, April 5, 1784, in Cutler and Cutler, *Life of Cutler*, I, 174–75, and Rufus King to Elbridge Gerry, June 4, 1786, in *LMCC*, VIII, 380–82.

54. Jefferson to David Hartley, Sept. 5, 1785, in Boyd, ed., *Jefferson Papers*, VIII, 482–83.

55. See the "Letter from a gentleman," cited in note 50 above.

56. "P.W.," Extract of a letter from Bedford, Pa., n.d., *Independent Chronicle* (Boston), Aug. 25, 1785.

57. Jefferson to Francis Hopkinson, May 3, 1784, in Boyd, ed., *Jefferson Papers*, VII, 205.

58. John R. Stilgoe, *Common Landscape in America, 1580 to 1845* (New Haven, 1982), 99–107, passim.

59. Cutler, *An Explanation of the Map which Delineates . . . the Federal Lands* (Salem, 1787), reprinted in Cutler and Cutler, *Life of Cutler*, II, 393–406, quotation at 404.

60. Item attributed to a "physician of some eminence," *Maryland Gazette*, March 13, 1787; Manasseh Cutler's Journal, entries for July 21, 24–25, 1787, reprinted in Cutler and Cutler, *Life of Cutler*, I, 296, 299.

61. Webster, "An Essay on the Extent and Value of our Western Unlocated Lands" (Philadelphia, April 25, 1782), reprinted in *Political Essays on the Nature and Operation of Money, Public Finances, and Other Subjects* (Philadelphia, 1791), 485–500, quotation at 495.

62. Washington to Jacob Read, Nov. 3, 1784, Fitzpatrick, ed., *Washington Writings*, XXVII, 487. See also Washington to Hugh Williamson, March 15, 1785, ibid., XXVIII, 107–108.

63. Pickering to Elbridge Gerry, March 1, 1785, in Pickering, *Life of Pickering*, I, 505.

64. Grayson to Washington, April 15, 1785, *LMCC*, VIII, 95.

65. April 21, 1787, *JCC*, XXXII, 225–27; Madison to Randolph, April 22, 1787, in Rutland, ed., *Madison Papers*, IX, 397. For a concise account of the early history of the land system see Malcolm Rohrbough, *The Land Office Business: The Settlement and Administration of American Public Lands, 1789–1837* (New York, 1968), 3–25.

66. Cutler Journal, entry for July 21, 1787, in Cutler and Cutler, *Life of Cutler*, I, 296.

67. Cutler to Nathan Dane, March 16, 1787, ibid., I, 194.

68. Carrington to James Monroe, Aug. 7, 1787, in *LMCC*, VIII, 631.

69. Item d. Richmond, *Virginia Journal*, March 31, 1785.

70. The grid laid down in the land ordinance was altered by Congress May 12, 1786, *JCC*, XXX, 262, by omitting the requirement that lines be run according to the "true meridian." At the same time the territorial government committee was abandoning Jefferson's proposed boundaries (see note 8 above). See Pattison, *American Rectangular Survey*, 19–36, 53–55, 90–92.

71. "Address from the Abbé Raynal to the Independent Citizens of America," *Freeman's Journal*, April 12, 1786.

72. Item in ibid., June 15, 1785.

73. Item d. Philadelphia, Jan. 26, 1786, *Maryland Gazette*, Feb. 3, 1786. For further discussion of the state size question see Onuf, *Origins of the Federal Republic*, 34–36.

74. Jefferson to Madison, June 20, 1787, in Boyd, ed., *Jefferson Papers*, XI, 480.

75. King to Gerry, June 4, 1786, in *LMCC*, VIII, 380.

76. Madison to Jefferson, Aug. 20, 1784, in Rutland, ed., *Madison Papers*, VIII, 108.

77. Madison to Lafayette, March 20, 1785, ibid., VIII, 252.

78. "Lycurgus," no. 2, *New Haven Gazette and Connecticut Magazine*, Feb. 23, 1786.

79. Extract of a letter from London, Oct. 14, 1784, *New York Gazetteer*, Jan. 11, 1785. See also Richard Champion, *Considerations on the Present Situation of Great Britain and the United States of America* (London, 1784), 238–39, for a prediction that the union would break up into "three great Republicks."

80. From a Correspondent, d. New York, July 12, 1787, *Independent Chronicle*, July 19, 1787.

81. Washington to Knox, Dec. 5, 1784, in Fitzpatrick, ed., *Washington Writings*, XXVIII, 3. Opening of the Potomac "will be one of the grandest Chains for preserving the federal Union," item, d. Alexandria, Nov. 15, 1784, *Virginia Journal*, Nov. 25, 1784.

82. Cutler, *Explanation of the Map*, in Cutler and Cutler, *Life of Cutler*, II, 400.

83. Item d. New York, Nov. 4, 1785, *Virginia Journal*, Nov. 17, 1785.

84. [Madison], "Consolidation," d. Dec. 3, 1791, *National Gazette* (Philadelphia), Dec. 5, 1791.

CHAPTER II

Declarations of Independence:
Indian–White Relations in the New Nation

James H. Merrell

In the spring of 1783 word reached Philadelphia that the war with Great Britain was over at last. As news of the treaty signed at Paris spread, Americans greeted it with booming cannons and tolling bells, official speeches and roaring bonfires, the "Mirth and Jollity" helped along by healthy doses of liquor. There were no celebrations in the Indian villages of America, however. Most native peoples living east of the Mississippi River had sided with Great Britain in the recent conflict. Now King George III had abandoned and betrayed them, signing a peace treaty that, without so much as mentioning his Indian allies, ceded to the United States all of the land between the Appalachians and the Mississippi. The Indians were said to be "Thunder Struck" when they learned of the agreement. If so, they quickly found their voices. A Wabash delegation that visited Detroit to demand an explanation was, according to the British commander, "very impertinent," and used "expressions not proper to be committed to paper." Others were more polite if scarcely less impertinent. The Six Nations are "a free People subject to no Power upon Earth," the Iroquois spokesman Aaron Hill (Kanonraron) proclaimed, and in the South Creeks, Cherokees, and Chickasaws also denied having done anything "to forfeit our Independance and natural Rights . . . ."[1]

Few today remember these declarations of independence.[2] The general scholarly consensus holds that for Indians the American Revolution was a "catastrophe," a "disaster" of "incalculable" magnitude that left natives "demoralized" and their "world turned upside down." With natives teetering on the brink of extinction, Americans driven westward by a sense of mission and at last unchecked by French resistance or British proclamation lines took the "initiative." In the space of fifty years they swept halfway across the continent, trampling Indians every step of the way and finally removing them from the East altogether.[3]

The habit of focusing on American attitudes, policies, and actions in the post-Revolutionary era makes the Indians' talk of independence sound absurd. In fact, however, their words serve as a useful reminder that the native was not a pathetic victim being hustled down the road from Revolution to Removal by frontiersmen after blood, government agents after land, or missionaries after souls. The shadow of Removal should not be allowed to obscure the degree to which the Indian still had a hand in shaping his own destiny. The Wabash at Detroit, the spokesmen for the Iroquois and the Southern nations—these and other Eastern Indians were accustomed by long and often painful experience to dealing with people from Europe. After 1783 that experience enabled them not only to assert their freedom but to defend it. Careful attention to native voices reveals that the story of the new nation's efforts to find a place for its aboriginal neighbors cannot be told without some understanding of what place those neighbors would accept.

The Revolutionary generation's plans for the Indian were succinctly expressed by a band of intoxicated soldiers in 1779. At a Fourth of July banquet held during General John Sullivan's march into Iroquois territory, the officers' tenth toast was to "Civilization or death to all American Savages."[4] After the war the phrase would become common among those interested in Indian affairs. "[C]ivilized or extinct," "moralized or exterminated," "Civilization or extinction," "war or civilization"—the refrain runs through private correspondence, public speeches, and official records well into the nineteenth century.[5] If Indians did not become white they soon would be extinct, wiped out either by force of arms or in a less violent war of attrition in which peoples unable to cope were, as Crèvecoeur put it, "doomed to recede and disappear before the superior genius of the Europeans."[6]

At first, most citizens of the new nation preferred death to civilization. During the War for Independence some smaller native groups had supported the rebel cause, but the majority—lured by gifts and British promises of protection from land-hungry colonists—ended up on the other side, and the rebels were furious. John Adams called them "blood Hounds,"

George Washington equated them with wolves—"both being beasts of prey tho' they differ in shape"—and the Declaration of Independence condemned them as "merciless Indian Savages."[7] Nor were the victors willing to forgive and forget once the war was over. "The white Americans have the most rancorous antipathy to the whole race of Indians," an Englishman recently returned from America wrote in 1784; "and nothing is more common than to hear them talk of extirpating them from the face of the earth, men, women, and children."[8]

Feelings ran so deep that it made little difference which side Indians had chosen. The Catawbas, who supplied food to patriot forces and shrewdly began calling their chief "General" instead of "King," nonetheless found their reservation boundaries and their hunting privileges under attack during the 1780s. Oneidas and Tuscaroras broke away from their Loyalist Iroquois brethren, suffered countless indignities at the hands of their American allies during the war, and were the first of the Six Nations to lose their lands once peace returned. In Massachusetts the faithful Stockbridge suffered a similar fate, and Mashpees, after sending a higher percentage of their men to serve in the army than any other community on Cape Cod, lost the power of self-government. Further west a frontier mob killed several Delawares—including two who were officers in the Continental Army.[9]

If this was the way Americans treated their friends, it was hard to imagine how they would treat their enemies. Some Indians did not wait around to find out. Many Iroquois accepted Britain's invitation to move to Canada. At the opposite end of the country British officials and American Loyalists crowding aboard emigration vessels at St. Augustine were astonished to find Southern Indians in their midst, begging to be allowed a berth. "However chimerical it may appear to us," wrote the garrison's commandant, "they have very seriously proposed to abandon their country and accompany us, having made all the world their enemies by their attachment to us."[10]

Those who stayed behind confronted a nation determined to take its pound of flesh one way or another. On the frontier, rumors of real or imagined atrocities committed during the war raised the longstanding hatred of Indians to a fever pitch. North and South, it was open season on natives. Some assaults were dignified as a campaign or an "informal war;" others, like the massacre of ninety-six Moravian Delawares at Gnadenhutten in 1782, were more difficult to disguise.[11] But few needed a disguise when, as Indiana's territorial governor William Henry Harrison admitted in 1801, frontier folk "consider the murdering of the Indians in the highest degree meritorious."[12] A man like John Steele, one of North Carolina's Indian commissioners in the 1780s, risked political suicide by suggesting that natives be treated fairly. This was no time for someone in a position of authority to be thought soft on Indians.[13]

Few were. In fact, officials in the frontier states were entirely sympathetic to the notion that the Indian must pay for his sins, though they generally preferred payment in land, not lives. The war gave Georgians—already called "Ecunnaunuxulgee" by the Creeks, which meant "People greedily grasping after the lands of the red people"—a new excuse to use an old ploy and demand territory in compensation for "the many injuries done that virtuous state. . . ."[14] The land market in North Carolina was even more active. Cherokees had been paying retribution since 1777; after the war the pace of cessions accelerated, the line between state agent and private speculator blurred, and whites made off with vast slices of coveted territory.[15] The masterminds of these deals—including one William Blount, whose hunger for the soil earned him the Indian sobriquet "dirt king"[16]—would have found kindred spirits in Pennsylvania and New York. There, state commissioners competed with land companies to see who could snatch the most acreage from the Six Nations. Fifteen treaties made between 1784 and 1796 left a tangled thicket of claims to the area. Only one thing was clear: almost none of the land belonged to the Indians any more.[17]

Not to be outdone, soon after the war the national government entered the Indian sweepstakes. Eschewing the crude methods of the frontier and the cloak of compensation donned by the states, Congress came up with a theory of conquest to push tribes west. By defeating Great Britain, the argument went, the United States had also conquered Britain's Indian allies, and by the Treaty of Paris now owned all of the land east of the Mississippi. The natives had lost, Congress proclaimed in 1783, and "with a less generous people than Americans, they might be compelled to retire beyond the lakes, but as we prefer clemency to rigor . . . and as we are disposed to be kind to them, . . . we from these considerations and from motives of compassion draw a veil over what is passed, and will establish a boundary line between them and us. . . ."[18]

Within a year agents were on their way to inform the Indians. The Americans made their new position clear from the very outset of each meeting by ignoring the body of ritual that had traditionally governed diplomatic contacts. Gone were the customary belts of wampum and the elaborate Indian speeches. In their place Americans substituted blunt talk and a habit of driving each article home by pointing a finger at the assembled natives.[19] "You are mistaken," commissioners treating with the Iroquois at Fort Stanwix in 1784 announced, "in supposing that . . . you are become a free and independent nation, and may make what terms you please. . . . You are a subdued people. . . . We shall now, therefore declare to you the condition, on which alone you can be received into the peace and protection of the United States." "[W]e claim the country by conquest," federal spokesmen told another council the following year; "and are to give not to receive. It is of this that it behooves you to have a clear and distinct comprehension."[20] "[I]t made the Indians stare," wrote one witness of American behavior at Fort Stanwix.[21] For the second time in as many years, they had been struck dumb.

American arrogance—whether expressed in an "informal war" by settlers, forced land cessions to a state, or the federal conquest theory—rested upon more than hatred of Indians and a desire for revenge. There was reason to believe that the United States could indeed subdue the native nations on its borders. The patriots had just defeated the most powerful country on earth; if necessary, could they not turn around and score a similar success against Indians? Arrayed against approximately 2.4 million inhabitants of the new nation were perhaps 150,000 natives, and it was unlikely that these scattered peoples could ever coordinate an effective defense, divided as they were into some eighty-five different tribes. Ancient cultural differences distinguished Creek from Cherokee, Cherokee from Shawnee, Shawnee from Iroquois. Even within each group, unity was at best an occasional thing. None had any form of central government to speak of. All were riven by bitter factional disputes arising out of longstanding divisions, the debate over the alliance with Britain, or the wisdom of adopting Euro-American customs. Americans surveying the tenuous ties between Creek Upper and Lower Towns, the Cherokees and their estranged Chickamauga kinfolk, or the ruins of the Six Nations Confederacy could perhaps be forgiven if they felt confident of imposing their will upon their politically disorganized and widely dispersed neighbors.[22]

Had the United States been successful, there would have been a real revolution in Indian–white relations. As it turned out, however, Indian resistance made the Americans eat their words. Government commissioners or land companies generally found natives to listen to a harangue or sign a treaty. Someone was always willing to do that much, from fear or greed or a genuine hope that peace would last. A few might even tell an agent what he wanted to hear, agreeing that "you have every thing in your power—you are great, and we see you own all the country."[23] But most refused to sit still for the verbal or physical pounding. Great Britain had lost to the Americans; her allies most certainly had not, for despite rebel invasions of Cherokee and Iroquois territories, Indians more than held their own against American forces, especially in the Ohio region.[24] Moreover, they had never signed a peace treaty, and without that consent the King "had no right Whatever to grant away to the States of America, their Rights or properties. . . ."[25]

Indians had a number of weapons at their disposal to back up their words. In Florida Spanish officials stood ready to do whatever they could to discomfit the new nation, including aiding its native neighbors. The British in Canada had an even bigger score to settle, and to stir up trouble they kept a string of forts on the American frontier in violation of the Treaty of Paris.[26] Among the natives, leaders such as Alexander McGillivray of the Creeks and the Mohawk Joseph Brant emerged who were ideally suited to make the most of the situation.[27] Both had been educated in colonial schools and could slip easily across the cultural divide to bargain with Europeans. In 1784 McGillivray struck deals with the Spanish that made him Commissary among the Creeks and guaranteed the nation, among other things, the goods needed to defend itself "from the Bears and other fierce Animals."[28] Meanwhile Brant led the Iroquois exodus to Canada, received a commission as Captain of the Northern Confederate Indians, and worked hand in hand with the British to stiffen native resistance.[29]

Fancy titles and fluent English would have gotten the two leaders nowhere without native support. Both were as well-connected among their own people as they were well-versed in European ways. McGillivray threaded his way cautiously through the intricate web of Creek politics, never claiming a higher title than was due him by custom, manipulating the traditional forum of the National Council to forge an unprecedented unity in Creek society.[30] Brant set his sights even higher, aiming at nothing less than a pan-Indian confederacy to resist the Americans. "[W]hat is the reason why we are not Still in possession of our forefathers birth Rights?" he asked an intertribal council at Detroit in 1786. "You may Safely Say because they wanted that Unanimity which we now So Strongly and Repeatedly recommend to you. . . . Therefore let us . . . be unanimous. . . . The Interests of Any One Nation Should be the Interests of us all, the Welfare of the one Should be the Welfare of all the others."[31] Throughout the 1780s and early 1790s, men of many nations who shared Brant's vision criss-crossed the eastern half of the continent to carry out this mission.[32] The prospects appeared so bright that one British agent looked forward to the day when he could turn "our friends the *United Indian Americans* against our friends the United States."[33]

Hopes for national or international unity ultimately foundered on the rocks of traditional localism and cultural diversity. Nonetheless, even temporary alliances and partial confederacies that were encouraged by Britain or Spain proved more than a match for the Americans. In 1786 and again in 1787, Creek and Cherokee war parties armed by Spaniards and assisted by Shawnees drove settlers out of disputed territories in Tennessee and Georgia. In 1790 and 1791 Ohio Indians with help from southern nations destroyed American armies marching to subdue them. A delegation sent by President Washington a year later to warn that "[t]he warriors of the United States number like the Trees in the woods" was unable to get the message across before Indians killed or captured most of the party.[34]

These were only the more embarrassing in a long series of reverses that gave the talk of conquest, compensation, and extermination a rather hollow ring. Americans could lay claim to the entire continent if they wished; it was theirs only on paper.[35] The Indian nations insisted that they were sovereign, that American independence did not mean native American dependence, and the United States was unable to make them change their minds. Defeating the greatest military power in the world obviously did not guarantee success against people determined to resist the invasion of their homelands. It was time to try another approach.

The United States began to feel its way toward a different policy even before the Constitution was ratified. After his appointment as Secretary of War in 1785, Henry Knox peppered Congressional committees with report after report outlining the dismal state of Indian relations, warning of the disastrous consequences of a general Indian war, and arguing that it was no disgrace to follow the British example of negotiating with rather than bullying native leaders. Under his prodding Congress began to wonder whether "instead of a language of superiority and command; may it not be politic and Just to treat with the Indians more on a footing of equality, . . . and instead of attempting to give lands to the Indians to proceed on the principle of fairly purchasing of them and taking the usual deeds?" The Northwest Ordinance of 1787, reflecting this change of heart, pledged that "[t]he utmost good faith shall always be observed towards the Indians; their land and property shall never be taken from them without their consent . . . ."[36]

Before long United States commissioners dropped the bluster common in the mid-1780s and conformed to native custom once again, opening talks with the "black drink" ceremony and closing them with token gifts and songs of peace. In between, they admitted that their predecessors had "put an erroneous construction" on the Treaty of Paris. "As he [the king] had not purchased the country of you," they assured the Indians, "of course he could not give it away . . . ."[37] The national government now offered to pay for territory taken in earlier treaties; if a tribe refused to sell, Americans occasionally proved willing to relinquish their claims. In 1790 McGillivray got some Creek land back, and four years later the new nation handed over 1,600 square miles of western New York to the Six Nations. The agreement "appears like a great light to us," an Iroquois headman told the American negotiator, Timothy Pickering. "And to me," Pickering agreed, "it seems like a new era."[38]

Pickering was not alone. By the time he sat down with the Iroquois sachems, many Americans had begun to view the Indian in a different light. Civilization, not death, was again on their minds. As articulated by Knox and other leaders, America's mission came to include not only recognition of native rights to the soil but also a concerted effort to confer "the Blessings of Civilization" upon the Indians.[39] Missionaries—Knox's "instruments to work on the Indians"[40]—would join government agents to effect the great change. Under their supervision natives would be "Americanized": men would drop the bow or musket and pick up the hoe or plow, women would abandon the field for the home, children would forsake the bush for the classroom, and all would give up their heathen ways for Christ. Eventually (Knox guessed it would take fifty years) the tribe itself would wither away and the Indians would be absorbed into American society. Instead of taking Indian lives and Indian lands, then, the new nation proposed to take Indian culture and Indian lands. Conversion rather than coercion was to free western territory from the natives' grasp, for policymakers expected that peoples weaned from the chase would part willingly with their vast hunting grounds, thereby allowing the United States to advance rapidly westward. To us it may seem nothing more than conquest by other means. To Knox, Jefferson, and many of their contemporaries, extraneous land for "the Blessings of Civilization" seemed like a fair trade.[41]

The idea of rescuing the Indians from themselves had preoccupied Englishmen and their American cousins since the days of the Hakluyts.[42] Despite repeated failures, the dream endured, even during the darkest days of the Revolution. In the early stages of the conflict, while Adams was calling them "blood Hounds," Congress considered spreading the gospel and "the civil arts" among the natives. At the war's conclusion a triumphal arch erected in Philadelphia to commemorate the Treaty of Paris was adorned with paintings suitable to the occasion, including one that depicted the conversion of the Indians. Thereafter some treaties promised certain Indian nations statehood, and at least one state legislature debated the wisdom of offering bounties to citizens who would marry natives. That even Sullivan's officers on their way to destroy Iroquois villages would pause to consider an alternative to extermination testifies to the enduring power of the old dream.[43]

Such sentiments might well have remained submerged had the United States managed to prove its theory of conquest. When Indians made a mockery of American claims, the ideology of conversion and coexistence was available to justify, even sanctify, a different approach. The plan made sense for several reasons. First, the new nation was acutely sensitive to its image, both among contemporaries and in the eyes of generations yet unborn. "Indians have their rights and our Justice is called on to support them," Virginia governor Benjamin Harrison argued in 1782. "Whilst we are nobly contending for liberty will it not be an eternal blot on our National character if we deprive others of it who ought to be as free as ourselves."[44] Harrison penned his comments to his North Carolina counterpart, Alexander Martin—not a very receptive audience. By the end of the decade, however, more people echoed Harrison's remarks, and more listened. If unfair treatment of the Indian continued, Knox feared, "the disinterested part of mankind and posterity will be apt to class the effects of our Conduct and that of the Spaniards in Mexico and Peru together—." A policy grounded in justice and civilization, on the other hand, would "reflect permanent honor upon the national character." No country determined to set an example for all humankind could afford to start off on the wrong foot by mistreating its own neighbors.[45]

Quite apart from a concern with appearances, there was good reason to believe that the scheme would work. In the heady days of the postwar era, when America had thrown off the yoke of tyranny and France appeared to be following suit, anything seemed possible, even success in an enterprise that had known little but failure.[46] Moreover, the design seemed to rest on sound philosophical foundations. From the Revolution to the Jacksonian era, thoughtful Americans agreed that societies progressed along the same path (a path which reached "its present state of perfection" with Euro-American culture), that differences among peoples could be attributed to environmental influences, and that therefore native Americans could be guided along the path toward "civilization." When Jefferson argued that the "proofs of genius given by the Indians of N. America, place them on a level with Whites in the same uncultivated state," others were quick to concur and make plans to cultivate them.[47] Indians might be an unformed mass of stone, but Americans eager to become sculptors were convinced, as a Cherokee agent said, that "the Statue is in the Block and that by the repeated strokes of the means, the desired effect will be produced."[48]

Success seemed all the more likely because deep fissures appeared to be opening in the "Block" of traditional native culture. During the 1780s armed resistance to American pretensions had forced the United States to back down, but Indians paid a terrible price. By 1794, when Anthony Wayne shattered the Ohio Indian confederacy at Fallen Timbers and the last of the Cherokee opposition crumbled, the cost was becoming painfully clear. For twenty years Cherokees, Iroquois, and other Indians had endured invasions of their homelands and the destruction of towns, crops, and orchards. To purchase peace Cherokees had given up more than half of their 40,000 square miles of territory between 1776 and 1794, the Iroquois even more. Every cession entailed painful uprooting from ancient homes and resettlement in an ever-smaller circle. Worse still, dislocation had combined with warfare and disease to reduce native population. In the last quarter of the eighteenth century the Six Nations lost half of its eight to ten thousand people, and Cherokee numbers fell from sixteen thousand to ten thousand.[49]

Cultural disorientation followed close on the heels of physical devastation. As hunting lands vanished under the plow, game disappeared from the forests that remained, and warfare became less common, the customary avenues that native men had followed to acquire social status and vital merchandise began to close. They compensated in various ways—hiring themselves out to whites, displaying their skills in early versions of a wild west show, stealing horses in search of the risks and rewards once provided by the hunt—but nothing was a satisfactory substitute for more traditional endeavors.[50] At the same time, the tribal elder began to feel as obsolete as the hunter and warrior, for the changes in native existence threatened to make his vast knowledge of ancient lore irrelevant to future generations. The erosion of the past can also be traced in the annual calendar of ritual. Among the Cherokees, hunting songs were no longer meaningful, war dances lost their power, and the yearly round of ceremonies fell from six to two, with even these last survivals becoming mere caricatures of their former solemn purpose.[51]

Small wonder that symptoms of social stress were more evident in native America. In the Six Nations the suicide rate climbed, and drunkenness, long a problem among Indians everywhere, reached epidemic proportions. Townspeople and families turned against each other in violent communal binges that often left several dead. Others began to drink alone, withdrawing from society to seek solace in the bottle and lose themselves in an alcoholic haze. Still others blamed their troubles on supernatural forces, and a rash of witchcraft accusations broke out in many communities.[52]

As if the signs of demoralization were not promising enough, American hopes of changing Indians received another boost from vocal natives who wanted to avoid destruction and combat despair by embracing white ways. During the Revolution Delawares had made instruction in American customs part of the price of their support for the rebels. Thereafter some Indians from virtually every nation pestered the government for education and urged their people to take advantage of it. Cornplanter of the Senecas, the Shawnee chief Black Hoof, Cherokees like James Vann and Charles Hicks, a Catawba named John Nettles, Hendrick Aupaumut of the Stockbridge—these and many more believed that the only chance of survival lay in abandoning the old ways, and they complained about "people who have hardly any holes in their heads" to let in new ideas.[53]

Thus the time seemed ripe to erase the dismal record of frustration and failure that had marked efforts to win Indians over in the past, and during Washington's administration the federal government set to work with its chisels. Its first move was to pry Indian affairs from the clutches of the states, where much of the initiative had lain during the Confederation period. Next it charted the course the nation should follow, passing laws to recognize native sovereignty, forbid trespassers on Indian land, regulate trade, and provide technology along with lessons in its proper use. For a generation these policies and their underlying philosophy remained remarkably consistent, shaping intercultural relations from George Washington to John Quincy Adams. They persisted after American victories in 1794 temporarily broke the Indians' will to fight, after treaties that year and the next substantially reduced the mischief Britain and Spain could make, after the Louisiana Purchase prompted President Jefferson to toy with the idea of moving Indians across the Mississippi River. They even expanded, as missionary organizations committed more energy to the Lord's—and Henry Knox's—work, encouraged by tax dollars the government provided.[54]

In retrospect it seems surprising that the dream of assimilating Indians did not die sooner than it did, for it met opposition from every corner of American society. As usual, distance made the heart grow fonder: men far removed from daily contact with another world, men like Knox or Pickering, could talk all they wished about justice, Americanization, and assimilation. People on the frontier still spoke a radically different language, a language learned in childhood from the gruesome tales of savage exploits popular at the time.[55] In 1818 a missionary in Tennessee found that ideas about the Indians' innate equality had not penetrated very far inland. "[T]he sentiment very generally prevails among the white people near the southern tribes (and perhaps with some farther to the north)," he reported, "that the Indian is by nature radically different from all other men and that this difference presents an insurmountable barrier to his civilization."[56] Frontier hatred of Indians was so common, so intense, so deepseated that no policy or proclamation could root it out, and it fueled the indifference to Indian lives and Indian lands against which the federal government struggled.

Controlling western officials proved as difficult as taming settlers. Most governors of the states bordering on Indian nations stood closer to the frontiersman than to the national government, for these men were themselves heavily involved in western expansion. William Blount, the "dirt king," became governor of the Territory South of the Ohio and superintendent of Indian affairs in the region, responsible for controlling the very settlement he was promoting.[57] When Tennessee achieved statehood in 1796 John Sevier succeeded Blount, again combining the offices of governor and federal Indian agent. For natives it was like going from the frying pan into the fire. Blount hated Indians because they were in the way; Sevier simply hated them. As governor of the state of Franklin in 1785, he had refused to jail Major James Hubbard, who had murdered a Cherokee, arguing that "had any other person met with the same insult from one of those bloody savages, . . . I say had they been possessed of that manly and soldierly spirit that becomes an American, they must have acted like Hubbard." Between 1780 and 1793 Sevier demonstrated his own spirit by leading thirty-five attacks on Indians.[58]

Placing men of this stripe in prominent positions was akin to posting a fox to guard the henhouse. Blount took it upon himself to bully the Cherokees into pulling their border westward, then expressed disappointment that "[t]he boundary is not extended as far as I wished and hoped it would be." Governor and agent Sevier justified his westward thrust by voicing the common view that "no people shall be entitled to more land than they can cultivate. Of course no people will sit and starve for want of land to work, when a neighboring nation has much more than they can make use of." Neither had much use for the idea of incorporating Indians. Both complained loudly when the national government tried to slow the westward advance or respect Indians' rights.[59]

Natives with few friends nearby looked to the nation's capital for protection. But even there, where the policies originated, there was deep ambivalence about the native American. If the talk of "blood Hounds" and "beasts of prey" had died down, it could readily be adopted again if circumstances warranted. Nor could the clamor for making Indians white drown out the whispers of doubt. If anything, the whispers grew louder, for Americans were gradually coming to adopt a color scheme that made assimilation all but impossible. The old belief that beneath the layer of bear grease, dirt, or sunburn was a white person yearning to be cleaned up was slowly being replaced by the notion that Indians were "redskins." This ominous shift from nurture to nature, from cultural stains that could be wiped off to racial tones that were impossible to eradicate, undermined the serene confidence behind the effort to drag the Indians across the cultural divide. Seen in this context, the plan to Americanize natives was the last glimmer of a setting sun, not the dawn of a new day that some took it to be.[60]

The limits of America's commitment to federal policy were clear in the failure of the government to practice what it preached. Enforcement of the law on the fringes of settlement lay in the hands of men like Sevier, an army too small for the task and often unsympathetic to official policy, militias that were more part of the problem than of the solution, and local juries that routinely sided with any white person against any Indian. The situation seemed hopeless. "I believe scarcely any thing short of a Chinese Wall, or a line of Troops will restrain Land Jobbers, and the Incroachment of Settlers, upon the Indian Territory," wrote a dejected President Washington in 1796.[61]

But if implementation of national policy was a thorny problem, federal officials made it all the more difficult by giving it low priority. Fulfilling promises to Indians invariably took second place to western expansion. The Revolutionary generation fervently believed that it was America's destiny to people the continent, and nothing could be permitted to stand in the way. Thus the government promised that Indians could keep their lands, yet quickly stopped returning territory fraudulently acquired and sent delegations to bring "to reason" those who refused to sell more—approaching Choctaws, for example, no less than forty times in thirty years.[62] Thus the government established public factories to eliminate trade abuses, yet proposed that the debts accumulated at these trading posts be used to coerce recalcitrant leaders.[63] Thus the government promised to supply the personnel and funds necessary to teach Indians white ways, yet appropriated little money, sent few teachers, and often abandoned the projects it did undertake.[64] It was a sorry record by any standard of measurement.

Last but by no means least, a federal government busy battling its own doubts and stiff opposition from the states and the frontier also confronted native peoples even less enthusiastic about the program than their white neighbors.[65] The Indian response varied from time to time and tribe to tribe, but few were willing to don the physical and cultural straitjacket whites had fashioned for them. Native doubts about the old ways were matched by equally grave misgivings about the white people's path to salvation. For every Cornplanter or Black Hoof preaching conversion, there were many more who were appalled at the idea. Men plant, tend, and harvest crops? Only "squaws and hedgehogs are made to scratch the ground," scoffed one Oneida man. A Delaware based his skepticism on religious grounds, arguing that the Great Spirit had given "the white man a plough, and the red man a bow and arrow, and sent them into the world by different paths." Not only different paths, an Iroquois sachem claimed, but "a different complexion, and different customs." A Cherokee went further still, asserting that the two cultures "are not derived from the same stock" and "that *they* are the favorites of the great spirit . . . ." Appearances were deceiving: in the face of defeat, and even of despair, the rock of native culture that policy makers hoped to fashion in their own image was substantially intact. It would require a sharp chisel and a large hammer indeed to sculpt "civilized" people out of such unyielding stone.[66]

Some natives blunted the white man's offensive with indifference. Catawbas, for example, proved enormously frustrating to their would-be saviors. Here was a people that had been wholly surrounded by settlers for more than a generation, a people loyal to the patriot cause, a people already taking on the trappings of Euro-American culture. Many spoke English, answered to names like Brown, Harris, or Ayers, lived in log cabins, and dressed much like everyone else in the Carolina uplands. It seemed almost too easy to finish the job already begun: shortly after 1800 a series of missionaries set up shop near the Nation, built a school, and preached God's word. Their message fell on barren ground. The Indians listened politely enough (some children even trooped into the schoolroom), but after a while they "Became unattentive" and drifted off. Whites were baffled and angry. "These wretched Indians," wrote one of their neighbors in 1826, "though they live in the midst of an industrious people, and in an improved state of society, will be Indians still." Catawbas readily adopted the superficial customs of an alien culture; they drew the line when an outsider tried to tamper with the fundamental wellsprings of their existence.[67]

While some peoples met the vanguard of European culture with indifference, others counterattacked. Between 1800 and 1812 many natives developed a world view that served as an antidote to the poisons injected by close encounters with whites. The excitement began when certain individuals among Creeks, Cherokees, Shawnees, Iroquois, and other tribes experienced a dramatic vision of a better way. Virtually all of these holy men were from obscure, even corrupt, backgrounds. The Creek Josiah Francis (Hilis Hadjo, or "Crazy Medicine") was exceptional only in his deeply superstitious nature. The Shawnee Prophet (Tenskwatawa) was a poor hunter and worse warrior, a corpulent, quarrelsome man whose forte seemed to be drinking. Handsome Lake of the Senecas was a more prominent member of his nation, but he, too, was a notorious drunkard whose alcoholic excesses shattered the peace of his village.[68] Each emerged from these depths a changed man, bearing a message of hope that had enormous appeal in native America and sparked a series of revitalization movements. It was, as one observer among the Creeks later recalled, "the age and time of prophecy."[69]

The Indians who flocked to hear the new messiahs were responding to a deeply felt need for answers to the confusion of their times. Men like Handsome Lake or Tenskwatawa commonly rise to prominence when people feel that they have lost their way, when the accepted theories of how the world should be can no longer account for the world as it actually is.[70] While the movement may be considered a sign of desperation,[71] it can also be construed as a creative response to rapid change, an attempt to bring theory and reality into line again. Indians in the new nation accomplished this by stressing certain themes, themes that focused upon a return to traditional ways. Prophets uniformly condemned the consumption of alcohol, the outbreaks of violence in the village, and the accumulation of private property, urging their listeners to restore communal harmony, familiar ceremonies, and customary respect for tribal elders. No prophet's message was blindly devoted to tradition or entirely devoid of European influence. Both Handsome Lake and Tenskwatawa condemned the ancient medicine societies and customary marriage practices while incorporating Christian notions of sin and confession.[72] Nonetheless, the thrust of the movement ran directly counter to American culture.

If the visions and visionaries had common origins and stressed common themes, they assumed very different shapes. Those who visited Prophetstown in present Indiana after 1805 to hear the gospel according to Tenskwatawa, and the Creeks who later listened with approval to the Prophet's brother, Tecumseh, imbibed a powerfully nativistic, explicitly anti-American doctrine. Indians were to have nothing to do with the Americans, "the children of the Evil Spirit," "the scum of the great Water," who were like a great ugly crab that had crawled from the sea. Hunters were to pay only half of their debts to the traders, women were not to marry whites, anyone meeting an American in the forest was to greet him from a distance but never shake hands. Avoidance would prevent further pollution. To root out the contamination that had already occurred, natives must forsake the plow and the loom, kill the cattle, hogs, and fowl, shed the clothing and weapons, and stop eating the white man's bread.[73]

The Prophet's potent message became explosive when Tecumseh translated it from the spiritual to the political realm. Disgusted by the seemingly endless series of land cessions extracted from Indians, Tecumseh grafted onto Tenskwatawa's words the old talk of a pan-Indian confederacy that would halt American encroachment and prevent—by force if need be—further land deals. Before 1810 he had eclipsed his brother and attracted followers from Ohio to the Mississippi River. To add to this core of support he ventured to Canada to receive assurance of British aid and south of the Ohio River to enlist the backing of the Southern nations. Choctaws and Chickasaws proved unreceptive, but among the Creeks, where he had kinfolk and where the rift between traditional and "progressive" factions was widening, Tecumseh received a more enthusiastic welcome. He taught people there the new war songs, instructed them in the "Dance of the Lakes," and returned north in the fall of 1811 with high hopes of making his dream a reality. In only three years, however, war with the Americans would destroy both dream and dreamer, and the Prophet, who survived the conflict, sank back into the obscurity from which he had come.[74]

By then the Creek movement Tecumseh had helped nurture had also met a violent death. What started out as a civil war between traditionalists (termed Red Sticks) and those under the influence of the United States became a general conflict when Creek prophets led the Red Sticks in an attack on Americans holed up in Fort Mims in August 1813. Armies from Tennessee, Georgia, and the Mississippi Territory allied with Choctaws, Cherokees, and non-nativist Creeks and headed into the nation. The Red Stick prophets met them with an arsenal that included dyed cow tails, medicine bags, magic rods, a "Holy Ground Town" protected by an invisible barrier no white person could cross, and a belief that the enemy's bullets could be rendered harmless by native medicine. It was not enough; within a year three thousand Creeks lay dead and Andrew Jackson was dictating a harsh peace.[75]

Elsewhere the age and time of prophecy took a very different course. Among the Cherokees and the Iroquois the calls for reform stopped short of wholesale condemnation of whites. These people were not like Indians; they might even be inferior; they were not necessarily evil. Their way of life was alien, but Indians might adopt some customs without fear of pollution. Followers of Handsome Lake and his counterparts in the Cherokee nation sought to regain control of their destiny without directly challenging white dominance or altogether abandoning white ways. The aim was to return to old values but not necessarily old practices, to place what cultural change did occur within a traditional, explicitly native context in order to combat the drift (some said the headlong rush) toward total acceptance of foreign habits. Perhaps the Christian missionaries living in these nations since 1800 had exposed the inhabitants to another side of Euro-American culture and left them less prepared to dismiss white ways outright. Whatever the reason, there was less talk of white men as scum, of a magic barrier around a village, of shunning everything foreign.[76]

Whether they responded with quiet indifference, open violence, or something in between, it was increasingly clear that most of these native groups were never going to be a showcase for government policies. Hopes came to focus more and more on the Cherokees, who, despite their short-lived revival, were generally considered "the most civilized tribe in America."[77] Here, if anywhere, the seeds of white culture would take root and flourish. A visitor to the nation in the early decades of the nineteenth century found it easy to agree with missionary claims that "Cherokees are rapidly adopting the laws and manners of the whites."[78] Family farms replaced communal holdings, and on those farms were cattle and hogs, plows and spinning wheels, slaves and wagons, the whole supported by a large and growing network of roads, mills, and blacksmith shops. The political achievement was no less impressive. After 1800 the nation's leaders had developed a representative government and a judicial system modeled closely on American practices that gave them centralized authority and enabled them to touch every corner of Cherokee life, from inheritance patterns to clan revenge to marriage customs. From their lofty heights of "civilization," Cherokees themselves began to look down upon "the wretched Creeks" and "the wild savage Indians" beyond the Mississippi.[79]

Confident claims by satisfied missionary boards could not disguise the fact that something was going terribly wrong in the Cherokee mountains. It was not so much that many remained outside the circle of Christianity and civilization, sniping at missionaries and complaining about the web of alien laws spun by the nation's leaders; these skeptics would be won over in time. It was not so much that people who did avidly embrace white ways saw nothing wrong with consulting conjurors as well as clergymen or pulling their children out of school to attend ballplays or dances; that, too, would pass. The real problem was that even those most willing to follow the missionaries' lead in everything still did not care to follow their mentors into white society. Instead, Cherokees used the skills taught them to develop a powerful national spirit along new lines and beat the white man at his own game in the courts, the Congress, and the forum of public opinion. The limits of Cherokee enthusiasm were clear in 1817 when the United States offered each of them citizenship and 640 acres. Only 311 of

3,200 heads of household took the government up on its offer, and before long many of these had repented and returned to the Cherokee fold.[80]

The most obvious expression of this reluctance to change came in 1827 when leading Cherokees met to draft a national constitution akin to state and federal versions. In one sense they were doing nothing more than codifying the laws passed over the previous two decades. Yet their deliberations also represented an emphatic rejection of the campaign to assimilate them into American society. The constitution was an assertion of sovereignty, a claim that Cherokees were an independent people and chose to remain so. It was, in short, a declaration of independence. Lest anyone miss the point, the nation's leaders scheduled the constitutional convention to convene on July 4.[81]

By then the tide against federal policy was running so strong that neither assimilation nor national sovereignty was likely. The frontiersman's opinions were the same. What had changed was the stance of the states, the view of the federal government, and the climate of opinion. Southern governors had never liked the Indian policies drafted in Washington; after the War of 1812 they went a step further, declaring that even if those policies were successful and the Indian thoroughly Americanized, under no circumstances would he be accepted as a citizen. A free person of color, perhaps, but equal to whites, never. To make their point more forcefully, states like Georgia and Tennessee stepped up their lobbying campaign at the national level, working in Congress to garner support for their views. The effort was successful: even as the United States established a small Civilization Fund for missionary efforts, it halved the annual budget for Indian affairs, ignoring recommendations from the War Department that the sum be doubled.[82]

Washington went along now because the number of people committed to the old policies dwindled rapidly after 1815. In 1818 John C. Calhoun, one of Henry Knox's successors as Secretary of War, announced that "[t]he time seems to have arrived when our policy towards them should undergo an important change. . . . Our views of their interest, and not their own, ought to govern them." A year later he told a Cherokee delegation to become white or "become extinct as a people. You see that the Great Spirit has made our form of society stronger than yours, and you must submit to adopt ours." James Barbour, Secretary of War under John Quincy Adams and one of the last of the Jeffersonians, was amazed to hear his counterpart in the State Department, Henry Clay, dismiss the very idea of assimilating Indians. "He believed they were destined to extinction," Barbour wrote, "and, although he would never use or countenance inhumanity towards them, he did not think them, as a race, worth preserving. . . . They were not an improvable breed, and their disappearance from the human family will be no great loss to the world." "Governor Barbour was somewhat shocked at these opinions," President Adams remarked, "for which I fear there is too much foundation."[83]

Barbour's isolation from his colleagues reflected a profound shift in the "style of thought" regarding America's aboriginal inhabitants.[84] The notion that Indians were by nature equal to whites and could be improved was out of fashion. In its place was a growing sense that the two peoples were fundamentally different, that an impenetrable racial barrier divided them and doomed every reform effort. This, of course, was precisely what inhabitants of the frontier—both white and Indian—had been saying all along. But now authorities on both sides of the Atlantic were taking anatomical measurements and offering "scientific" theories that gave innate racial differences an aura of respectability.[85]

Thus Andrew Jackson's election to the presidency in 1828 was the logical culmination of a radical change in the sentiments of the nation as a whole. Educated in the same rough school as John Sevier, the new president had built his career on Indian-hating, and he made no secret of his views.[86] For ten years he had been trying to convince Americans to break their habit of negotiating with natives. Treaties were necessary only when the government was weak and the Indian strong. Now that the situation was reversed, the United States should dispense with such nonsense and dictate terms.[87] As president, Jackson resurrected the old argument that the Treaty of Paris gave the United States all of the Indians' land. The natives remained there, his administration insisted, by the "mere grace of the conqueror."[88]

In the 1780s Indians had rallied to shatter such illusions. But much had changed since Brant and McGillivray were on the scene. The British and Spanish had at last been swept off the board altogether, Tecumseh and the Red Sticks had demonstrated the futility of open resistance, and removing these dangers had boosted the new nation's self-confidence. At the same time, opposition to men like Jackson weakened, frustrated by the failure of Indians to live up to expectations. The frontiersman's hatred, legitimized by "scientific" racism, had the stage largely to itself, and removal followed swiftly.

By 1830 most Americans had forgotten the promises made to Indians in the 1790s. When expansion with honor proved impossible, the country chose expansion without,[89] and in the process changed forever the native's place in American life. A few rough yardsticks help measure the distance Indians had come since the Revolution. While it had taken European immigrants almost two centuries to push inland as far as the Appalachians, within the span of a single lifetime their descendants swept all the way to the Mississippi, and by 1844 less than one-fourth of the 150,000 Indians living in the East in 1783 remained there.[90] During the eighteenth century the native was so much a part of the American scene that as young men George Washington, John Adams, and Thomas Jefferson were accustomed to seeing Indians regularly; few of their successors would rub shoulders with a native in any but an official capacity.[91] Reflecting this central place in American existence, in the late colonial era the native had been the most common—almost the only—symbol used to represent Anglo-America, yet within a generation it had given pride of place to a variety of other figures.[92] America was removing Indians in more ways than one.

Still, if Removal was the end of the beginning for Indians in historic times, it was not the beginning of the end. Natives avoided either of the fates General Sullivan's officers had in store for them, navigating between the treacherous shoals of extinction on one side and civilization on the other. Americans haunted by the words of Benjamin Harrison or Henry Knox, by the gap between the ideals expressed in the Declaration of Independence and the reality of Indian treatment, could never bring themselves to destroy native Americans outright. This hesitation has given native groups the opening they needed to maintain a distinct culture and a separate identity. Cherokees, Choctaws, Chickasaws, Creeks, and Seminoles rebuilt their societies west of the Mississippi. In the East, bands of Cherokees and Seminoles were still holed up in the North Carolina mountains or the Florida swamps, while the Iroquois found refuge of another sort in the religion of Handsome Lake. And on Cape Cod during the darkest days of Removal, the Mashpees fought a successful battle to regain some of the rights Massachusetts had revoked after the Revolution. They pressed their case through the newspapers, the courts, and the legislature, arguing "that we, as a tribe, will rule ourselves, and have a right to do so; for all men are born free and equal, says the Constitution of the country."[93] They had the wrong document but the right idea, and in the years to come many more tribes would make the same argument. These declarations of independence, issued across the years from Aaron Hill's day to our own, have blunted efforts to make Indians into something they were not or, failing that, to get rid of them altogether. The determination to be "Indians still," to maintain some say in their destiny, is the triumph hidden within the tragedy that stretched from the Treaty of Paris to the Trail of Tears.

NOTES

1. For the Americans' celebrations, see Jackson Turner Main, *The Sovereign States, 1775–1783* (New York, 1973), 439–41, quotation on 440. The reports of the Indians' reactions are quoted in Randolph C. Downes, *Council Fires on the Upper Ohio: A Narrative of Indian Affairs in the Upper Ohio Valley until 1795* (Pittsburgh, 1940), 278; Dorothy V. Jones, *License for Empire: Colonialism by Treaty in Early America* (Chicago, 1982), 143; Barbara Graymont, *The Iroquois in the American Revolution* (Syracuse, 1972), 260. For similar statements, see Jones, *License for Empire*, 145; Graymont, *Iroquois in the Revolution*, 280; Michael D. Green, "Alexander McGillivray," in R. David Edmunds, ed., *American Indian Leaders: Studies in Diversity* (Lincoln, Neb., 1980), 46.
2. For an earlier native "declaration of independence," see Francis Jennings, "The Indians' Revolution," in Alfred F. Young, ed., *The American Revolution: Explorations in the History of American Radicalism* (DeKalb, Ill., 1976), 325–26. See also Gary Nash, "The Forgotten Experience: Indians, Blacks, and the American Revolution," in William M. Fowler, Jr., and Wallace Coyle, eds., *The American Revolution: Changing Perspectives* (Boston, 1979), 29–46. Dorothy Jones (*License for Empire*) is also careful to note the role Indians played in shaping the course of events.
3. James H. O'Donnell, "The World Turned Upside Down: The American Revolution As a Catastrophe for Native Americans," in Francis P. Jennings, ed., *The American Indian and the American Revolution*, The Newberry Library Center for the History of the American Indian, Occasional Papers Series, No. 6 (Chicago, 1983), 80–93; Reginald Horsman, *Expansion and American Indian Policy, 1783–1812* (East Lansing, Mich., 1967), 3; James Axtell, "The Unbroken Twig: The Revolution in Indian Education," in Jennings, ed., *American Indian and American Revolution*, 74; Francis Paul Prucha, "The American Indian and the Revolution," Milwaukee County Historical Society, *Historical Messenger*, XXX (1974), 51; Bernard W. Sheehan, *Seeds of Extinction: Jeffersonian Philanthropy and the American Indian* (Chapel Hill, N.C., 1973). Axtell, who wrote of the "incalculable damage" done by the Revolution, also pointed out that from the perspective of education the conflict "was only a brief skirmish" in a longer war. Axtell, "The Unbroken Twig," in Jennings, ed., *American Indian and American Revolution*, 74.
4. Quoted in Roy Harvey Pearce, *The Savages of America: A Study of the Indian and the Idea of Civilization*, rev. ed., (Baltimore, 1965), 55.
5. Ibid., 68; Michael Paul Rogin, *Fathers and Children: Andrew Jackson and the Subjugation of the American Indian* (New York, 1975), 210; Alexis de Tocqueville, *Democracy in America*, ed. J.P. Mayer, trans. George Lawrence (Garden City, N.Y., 1969), 326.
6. J. Hector St. John de Crèvecoeur, *Letters from an American Farmer and Sketches of Eighteenth-Century America*, ed. Albert E. Stone (New York, 1981), 122.
7. Quoted in Richard Drinnon, *Facing West: The Metaphysics of Indian-Hating and Empire-*

Building (New York, 1980), 70, and Horsman, *Expansion and Indian Policy*, 9. For the Declaration of Independence, see Drinnon, *Facing West*, 97–99, 102–03. The Indians' role in the Revolutionary War may be followed in Downes, *Council Fires*, chaps. 8–11; Jones, *License for Empire*, chap. 6; Graymont, *Iroquois in the Revolution;* James H. O'Donnell, *The Southern Indians in the American Revolution* (Knoxville, Tenn., 1973). A good brief summary of the literature is Wilcomb E. Washburn, "Indians and the American Revolution," in John R. Brumgardt, ed., *The Revolutionary Era: A Variety of Perspectives* (Riverside, Ca., 1976), 26–40.

8. Quoted in Alden T. Vaughan, "From White Man to Redskin: Changing Anglo-American Perceptions of the American Indian," *American Historical Review*, LXXXVII (1982), 942. See also Reginald Horsman, *Race and Manifest Destiny: The Origins of Racial Anglo-Saxonism* (Cambridge, Mass., 1981), 108–14.

9. See James H. Merrell, "Natives in a New World: The Catawba Indians of Carolina, 1650–1800," (Ph.D. diss., The Johns Hopkins University, 1982), 542, n. 81, 555–63, 636; Graymont, *Iroquois in the Revolution*, 241–44, 285–90; Jeanne Ronda and James P. Ronda, " 'As They Were Faithful': Chief Hendrick Aupaumut and the Struggle for Stockbridge Survival," *American Indian Culture and Research Journal*, III (1979), 51; Kim McQuaid, "William Apes, Pequot: An Indian Reformer in the Jacksonian Era," *New England Quarterly*, L (1977), 615; Russel Lawrence Barsh, "Native American Loyalists and Patriots: Reflections on the American Revolution in Native American History," *The Indian Historian*, X (1977), 13.

10. Graymont, *Iroquois in the Revolution*, 263–64, 284–85. Quoted in O'Donnell, *Southern Indians in the Revolution*, 131.

11. The phrase "informal war" is Henry Knox's, quoted in Francis Paul Prucha, *American Indian Policy in the Formative Years: The Indian Trade and Intercourse Acts, 1790–1834* (Cambridge, Mass., 1962), 39. (Recently Prucha has placed much of this work into a larger context. See *The Great Father: The United States Government and the American Indians*, 2 vols. [Lincoln, Neb., and London, 1984].) For examples of the conflict, see Downes, *Council Fires*, 271–76, and chap. 12. The situation in the southeast is explored in R.S. Cotterill, *The Southern Indians: The Five Civilized Tribes Before Removal* (Norman, Okla., 1954), chap. 4. For Gnadenhutten, see Sheehan, *Seeds of Extinction*, 187–88; Graymont, *Iroquois in the Revolution*, 252–53.

12. Quoted in R. David Edmunds, *The Shawnee Prophet* (Lincoln, Neb., 1983), 5.

13. See Walter H. Mohr, *Federal Indian Relations, 1774–1788* (Philadelphia, 1933), 167–70, 174–75.

14. Michael D. Green, *The Politics of Indian Removal: Creek Government and Society in Crisis* (Lincoln, Neb., 1982), 26; O'Donnell, *Southern Indians in the Revolution*, 131. For Georgia's actions, see Green, *Politics of Removal*, 34; Helen Hornbeck Tanner, "Pipesmoke and Muskets: Florida Indian Intrigues of the Revolutionary Era," in Samuel Proctor, ed., *Eighteenth-Century Florida and Its Borderlands* (Gainesville, Fla., 1975), 28, 31–32, 33.

15. O'Donnell, *Southern Indians in the Revolution*, 54–59, 134–35; Rogin, *Fathers and Children*, 81–85; Cotterill, *Southern Indians*, 57–59, 63–64.

16. Rogin, *Fathers and Children*, 82.

17. Barbara Graymont, "New York State Indian Policy after the Revolution," *New York History*, LVII (1976), 438–74; Anthony F. C. Wallace, *The Death and Rebirth of the Seneca* (New York, 1969), 150–54, 179–83; Jones, *License for Empire*, 175–85. A list of the treaties may be found in Jones, *License for Empire*, table 14, 181.

18. Quoted in Downes, *Council Fires*, 285. For the conquest theory, see Horsman, *Expansion and Indian Policy*, chap. 1.

19. Wallace, *Death and Rebirth of the Seneca*, 197–98.

20. Quoted in Downes, *Council Fires*, 291, 294.

21. Quoted in Wallace, *Death and Rebirth of the Seneca*, 198.

22. The population figures are from J. Leitch Wright, Jr., *Britain and the American Frontier, 1783–1815* (Athens, Ga., 1975), 2–3. For the lack of strong central government and the power of factions, see Wallace, *Death and Rebirth of the Seneca*, 39–44, 162–68; Green, *Politics of Removal*, chap. 1; William G. McLoughlin, *Cherokees and Missionaries, 1789–1839* (New Haven, 1984), 30–32; Grace Steele Woodward, *The Cherokees* (Norman, Okla., 1962), 97–116; Charles M. Hudson, *The Southeastern Indians* (Knoxville, Tenn., 1976), 223–39.

23. Downes, *Council Fires*, 297.

24. Ibid., chaps. 8–11; Wallace, *Death and Rebirth of the Seneca*, 134–41.

25. Quoted in Graymont, *Iroquois in the Revolution*, 260. Similar sentiments are in Jones, *License for Empire*, 145, Downes, *Council Fires*, 308, and Green, "McGillivray," in Edmunds, ed., *Indian Leaders*, 46.

26. For Spain, see Jack D.L. Holmes, "Spanish Policy toward the Southeastern Indians in the 1790s," in Charles M. Hudson, ed., *Four Centuries of Southern Indians* (Athens, Ga., 1975), 65–82. For Great Britain, see Wright, *Britain and the American Frontier*; Robert F. Berkhofer, Jr., "Barrier to Settlement: British Indian Policy in the Old Northwest, 1783–1794," in David M. Ellis, ed., *The Frontier in American Development: Essays in Honor of Paul Wallace Gates* (Ithaca, 1969), 249–76.

27. Their careers may be followed in Green, "McGillivray," in Edmunds, ed., *Indian Leaders*, 41–63; James H. O'Donnell, "Joseph Brant," in ibid., 21–40; Isabel Thompson Kelsay, *Joseph Brant, 1743–1807: Man of Two Worlds* (Syracuse, 1984). Gary Nash has also noted the significance of these two men. See Nash, "The Forgotten Experience," in Fowler and Coyle, eds., *The American Revolution*, 29–46.

28. Green, "McGillivray," in Edmunds, ed., *Indian Leaders*, 48.

29. O'Donnell, "Brant," in ibid., 34.

30. Green, "McGillivray," in ibid., 48–53, 57–60.

31. Quoted in Downes, *Council Fires*, 300.

32. For example, see Wright, *Britain and the American Frontier*, 12, 41, 80–81, 93; Tanner, "Pipesmoke and Muskets," in Proctor, ed., *Eighteenth-Century Florida*, 33–34.

33. Quoted in Wright, *Britain and the American Frontier*, 80.

34. Green, "McGillivray," in Edmunds, ed., *Indian Leaders*, 52–53; Tanner, "Pipesmoke and Muskets," in Proctor, ed., *Eighteenth-Century Florida*, 34; Cotterill, *Southern Indians*, 70–74, 76; Downes, *Council Fires*, chap. 13; Wilcomb Washburn, *The Indian in America* (New York, 1975), 162.

35. Jones, *License for Empire*, 150–52.

36. Quoted in Horsman, *Expansion and Indian Policy*, 41–42, 37. Knox's reports are recounted in ibid., 34–39.

37. Quoted in Downes, *Council Fires*, 323. For the return to Indian customs, see Tanner, "Pipesmoke and Muskets," in Proctor, ed., *Eighteenth-Century Florida*, 36, 38.

38. Quoted in Jones, *License for Empire*, 179. On retrocessions, see ibid., 177–79, and Cotterill, *Southern Indians*, 85–86.

39. Downes, *Council Fires*, 309; Horsman, *Expansion and Indian Policy*, 60, 61.

40. Quoted in McLoughlin, *Cherokees and Missionaries*, 34.

41. See Horsman, *Expansion and Indian Policy*, chap. 4; Sheehan, *Seeds of Extinction*, chap. 5; Robert F. Berkhofer, Jr., *The White Man's Indian: Images of the American Indian from Columbus to the Present* (New York, 1978), 134–45. The irony of terming this policy "Americanization" is obvious, but the alternatives—"civilization" or "acculturation"—present problems of their own. "Americanization" at least captures the new nation's effort to define what it was to be "an American" and to bring the Indian to conform to that definition. See Berkhofer, *White Man's Indian*, 135–36.

42. Edmund S. Morgan, *American Slavery, American Freedom: The Ordeal of Colonial Virginia* (New York, 1975), chap. 1; Pearce, *Savages of America*, part I.

43. Prucha, *American Indian Policy*, 214; Charles Coleman Sellers, *Charles Willson Peale* (New York, 1969), 195; Richard B. Morris, *The Peacemakers: The Great Powers and American Independence* (New York, 1965), 449; Barsh, "Loyalists and Patriots," *Ind. Historian*, X (1977), 12; Sheehan, *Seeds of Extinction*, 175.

44. Quoted in O'Donnell, *Southern Indians in the Revolution*, 128.

45. Quoted in Horsman, *Race and Manifest Destiny*, 107, and Horsman, *Expansion and Indian Policy*, 64.

46. Horsman, *Race and Manifest Destiny*, chap. 5.

47. Quoted in ibid., 107. See also Sheehan, *Seeds of Extinction*, 124–25. The philosophy is summarized in Sheehan, *Seeds of Extinction*, part I, and Berkhofer, *White Man's Indian*, 38–49.

48. Quoted in William G. McLoughlin, "Cherokee Anomie, 1794–1809: New Roles for Red Men, Red Women, and Black Slaves," in Richard L. Bushman, et al., eds., *Uprooted Americans: Essays in Honor of Oscar Handlin* (Boston, 1979), 143.

49. For Wayne's victory, see Downes, *Council Fires*, 324–38. For the Cherokees, see McLoughlin, *Cherokees and Missionaries*, 6; Horsman, *Expansion and Indian Policy*, 77–78. Cherokee losses are summarized in McLoughlin, "Cherokee Anomie," in Bushman, et al., eds., *Uprooted Americans*, 130–31, and McLoughlin, *Cherokees and Missionaries*, 13–14. For the Iroquois, see Wallace, *Death and Rebirth of the Senaca*, 179–83, 196.

50. For hiring out, see Merrell, "Natives in a New World," 604–05; McQuaid, "William Apes," *NEQ*, L (1977), 607–11. For "Wild West" shows, see Merrell, "Natives in a New World," 603–4; McLoughlin, *Cherokees and Missionaries*, 131. For horsestealing see McLoughlin, "Cherokee Anomie," in Bushman et al., eds., *Uprooted Americans*, 150–55. The fall in hunting and warfare may be traced in McLoughlin, *Cherokees and Missionaries*, 14–15, and Merrell, "Natives in a New World," 596, 600–03.

51. McLouglin, "Cherokee Anomie," in Bushman, et al., eds., *Uprooted Americans*, 132–35.

52. Wallace, *Death and Rebirth of the Seneca*, 193–94, 199–201; Edmunds, *Shawnee Prophet*, 5–6, 23–25; McLoughlin, "Cherokee Anomie," in Bushman, et al., eds., *Uprooted Americans*, 150; Merrell, "Natives in a New World," 598–99.

53. Downes, *Council Fires*, 186–87; Wallace, *Death and Rebirth of the Seneca*, 168–72, 202–04; Edmunds, *Shawnee Prophet*, 16–20; McLoughlin, *Cherokees and Missionaries*, 45–46, and passim; idem, "James Vann: Intemperate Patriot, 1768–1809," in McLoughlin, *The Cherokee Ghost Dance: Essays on the Southeastern Indians, 1789–1861* (Macon, Ga., 1984), 39–72; Merrell, "Natives in a New World," 619–21; Ronda and Ronda, "As They Were Faithful," *Am. Ind. Culture and Res. Jnl.*, III (1979), 43–55. The quotation is by a Cherokee, in William McLoughlin, "Thomas Jefferson and the Beginning of Cherokee Nationalism, 1806 to 1809," *William and Mary Quarterly*, 3rd ser., XXXII (1975), 554.

54. For the policies, see Prucha, *American Indian Policy*. For the persistence, see Sheehan,

Seeds of Extinction, 3–8, 11. For the missionaries, see McLoughlin, *Cherokees and Missionaries*, and Robert F. Berkhofer, Jr., *Salvation and the Savage: An Analysis of Protestant Missions and American Indian Response, 1787–1862* (Lexington, Ky., 1965).

55. For an example, see Sheehan, *Seeds of Extinction*, 191–92.

56. Quoted in McLoughlin, *Cherokees and Missionaries*, 112.

57. Prucha, *America Indian Policy*, 149–50.

58. Quoted in Horsman, *Race and Manifest Destiny*, 111. See Woodward, *The Cherokees*, 103–04, and Rogin, *Fathers and Children*, 135; Craig Symonds, "The Failure of America's Indian Policy on the Southwestern Frontier, 1785–1793," *Tennessee Historical Quarterly*, XXXV (1976), 29–45; Cotterill, *Southern Indians*, 80, 109–10.

59. Symonds, "Failure of Indian Policy," *Tenn. Hist. Qtrly.*, XXXV (1976), 30–31; Prucha, *American Indian Policy*, 143. For their complaints, see Horsman, *Expansion and Indian Policy*, 29–30, 71, and Prucha, *American Indian Policy*, 151–53. For another example of contention between federal officials and representatives of a state, see Clyde R. Ferguson, "Confrontation at Coleraine: Creeks, Georgians, and Federalist Indian Policy," *South Atlantic Quarterly*, LXXVIII (1979), 224–43. The growing corruption of Creek Indian agents may be followed in Green, *Politics of Removal*, chap. 3.

60. See Vaughan, "From White Man to Redskin," *AHR*, LXXXVII (1982), 917–53. Pearce (*Savages of America*, 4, 41–42, 48–49) sees a similar shift prior to the Revolution. Horsman (*Race and Manifest Destiny*) is more convinced of the new nation's enthusiasm for assimilation, but he, too, finds a change shortly after 1800. For the ambivalence expressed by many of the Founding Fathers, see Ernest L. Schusky, "Thoughts and Deeds of the Founding Fathers: The Beginning of United States and Indian Relations," in Ernest L. Schusky, ed., *Political Organization of Native Americans* (Washington, D.C., 1980), 24–33.

61. Quoted in Sheehan, *Seeds of Extinction*, 269. For the enforcement, see Prucha, *American Indian Policy*; Berkhofer, *White Man's Indian*, 146–48.

62. For the view of the land, see Berkhofer, *White Man's Indian*, 137–41. For promises and coercion, see Horsman, *Expansion and Indian Policy*, chaps. 8–9 (quotation on 125). The Choctaw experience is recounted in Arthur H. DeRosier, Jr., "Myths and Realities in Indian Westward Removal: The Choctaw Example," in Hudson, ed., *Southern Indians*, 86.

63. The idea was Jefferson's. See Prucha, *American Indian Policy*, chap. 5; Horsman, *Expansion and Indian Policy*, 145.

64. Berkhofer, *White Man's Indian*, 149; Edmunds, *Shawnee Prophet*, 17–19; McLoughlin, "Cherokee Anomie," in Bushman, et al., eds., *Uprooted Americans*, 136; McLoughlin, *Cherokees and Missionaries*, 16; Horsman, *Expansion and Indian Policy*, 83; Wallace, *Death and Rebirth of the Seneca*, 219–20; Sheehan, *Seeds of Extinction*, 121–23.

65. This point is also made, though never thoroughly explored, in Berkhofer, *White Man's Indian*, 114; Horsman, *Expansion and Indian Policy*, 172–73.

66. Quoted in Ronda and Ronda, "As They Were Faithful," *Am. Ind. Culture and Res. Jnl.*, III (1979), 46; Wallace, *Death and Rebirth of the Seneca*, 206; McLoughlin, *Cherokees and Missionaries*, 13 (emphasis added).

67. Merrell, "Natives in a New World," 618, 579.

68. Theron A. Nunez, Jr., "Creek Nativism and the Creek War of 1813–1814," *Ethnohistory*, V (1958), 8–9; Edmunds, *Shawnee Prophet*, 28–32; Wallace, *Death and Rebirth of the Seneca*, 228–30.

69. Quoted in Nunez, "Creek Nativism," *Ethnohistory*, V (1958), 148.

70. Anthony F. C. Wallace, "Revitalization Movements," *American Anthropologist*, n.s., LVIII (1956), 264–81.

71. Sheehan, *Seeds of Extinction*, 216.

72. Edmunds, *Shawnee Prophet*, chap. 2; Wallace, *Death and Rebirth of the Seneca*, 249–54, chaps. 9–10.

73. Edmunds, *Shawnee Prophet*, 32–39, quotations on 38 and 39. For the Creeks, see Nunez, "Creek Nativism," *Ethnohistory*, V (1958), 14, 143–52; Green, *Politics of Removal*, 40–42.

74. R. David Edmunds, *Tecumseh and the Quest for Indian Leadership* (Boston, 1984); idem, *Shawnee Prophet*, chaps. 5–9.

75. Green, *Politics of Removal*, 42–43; Nunez, "Creek Nativism," *Ethnohistory*, V (1958), 10, 12, 14, 168–73; Rogin, *Fathers and Children*, 145–59.

76. For the Cherokee revival, see McLoughlin, *Cherokees and Missionaries*, chap. 4. For the Iroquois, see Wallace, *Death and Rebirth of the Seneca*, chaps. 8–10, esp. 249–54, 277–85, 303–18.

77. Quoted in McLoughlin, *Cherokees and Missionaries*, 124.

78. Ibid., 125.

79. Quoted in ibid., 131. For Cherokee developments, see ibid., 75, 124–28, 181–82, 215–19.

80. William G. McLoughlin, "Experiment in Cherokee Citizenship, 1817–1829," *American Quarterly*, XXIII (1981), 3–7.

81. McLoughlin, *Cherokees and Missionaries*, 219–32; Sheehan, *Seeds of Extinction*, 258–59.

82. McLoughlin, *Cherokees and Missionaries*, 186; McLoughlin, "Experiment in Citizenship," *Am. Qtrly.*, XXIII (1981), 8–25; Reginald Horsman, *The Origins of Indian Removal, 1815–1824* (East Lansing, Mich., 1970), 10–18.

83. Quoted in Green, *Politics of Removal*, 46; McLoughlin, *Cherokees and Missionaries*, 119; Horsman, *Race and Manifest Destiny*, 198.

84. Sheehan, *Seeds of Extinction*, 8.

85. Horsman, *Race and Manifest Destiny*, chaps. 3, 7–8, 10; Berkhofer, *White Man's Indian*, 55–61.

86. Rogin, *Fathers and Children*.

87. Ibid., 190–93.

88. Quoted in Prucha, *American Indian Policy*, 236–37.

89. Berkhofer, *White Man's Indian*, 145–53.

90. Rogin, *Fathers and Children*, 4.

91. Drinnon, *Facing West*, 74; Douglas Southall Freeman, *George Washington: A Biography*, vols. 1 and 2 (New York, 1948).

92. E. McClung Fleming, "The American Image as Indian Princess, 1765–1783," *Winterthur Portfolio*, II (1965), 65–81, and Fleming, "From Indian Princess to Greek Goddess: The American Image, 1783–1815," ibid., III (1967), 37–66.

93. McQuaid, "William Apes," *NEQ*, L (1977), 617.

CHAPTER 12

Self-Interest Conquers Patriotism: Republicans, Liberals, and Indians Reshape the Nation

John M. Murrin

If the word *critic* implies severe censure, a commentator on these two excellent chapters will have little to say. But we can ask what happens if we try to put them together. Obviously, both explain to us the significance of the West in the early republic—what it meant to the settlers who grabbed it and to the Indians who lost it. Peter S. Onuf has dissected for us an intense three-year debate in and around Congress about the disposition of Western lands. His is no narrow analysis of the emergence of a specific policy. Rather, he uses this material to make a sweeping statement about the entire political economy of the new nation.

James H. Merrell also thinks on a gigantic scale. He describes with greater economy, elegance, and precision than I have seen anywhere else the conflict of cultures between settlers and Native Americans between the Revolution and the age of Jackson. For half a century, the major tribes east of the Mississippi resisted the efforts of settlers to crush them or to transform them into something else, to "Americanize" them. They began the period outnumbered almost twenty to one and divided into far more units than the thirteen colonies that created the American union. By Jackson's administration, the Indians had absorbed appalling losses, while white settlers had multiplied fourfold to more than ten million. In the process of resisting encroachment, the Indians experimented creatively with nearly every social permutation available to them, from revitalization movements that rejected nearly everything European, to the replication of basic European institutions as a way of getting the settlers off their backs and out of their lands. They lost, no matter what they tried. But along the way they endured hardships and accepted fatalities on a scale that, for example, made American losses against the British in the Revolution seem almost trivial, even though the Revolution was in per capita terms the second bloodiest war this nation has ever fought.

If patriotism was the subordination of private interests to the common good, the most heroic patriots of the period were Indian warriors—and also Indian women, who became targets of military campaigns in a way that seldom happened to settler women. The myth of the noble savage—a European invention, of course—acquired enduring power, I suspect, because it reminded the settlers of what they professed to be but never were. Americans claimed to be more virtuous and patriotic than Europeans, whose societies were, according to this vocabulary, thoroughly corrupt. Indians really were more selfless and courageous than the settlers. In military terms, one Indian was indeed worth several settlers. But when the odds became a hundred to one by the 1830s, resistance was hopeless.

In a strange way, this reflection brings me back to Onuf's chapter, which jumps into the middle of what I see as the most important controversy taking shape in recent years about early American history. We might call it the Great Transition debate. Did North America experience a transition from a premodern to a modern social order? This dispute is creating very odd academic alignments. It now pits historians of ideas (especially the "republican" or "civic humanist" school) and Marxists against traditional liberals and neoclassicists, most of whom are professed conservatives. In a sane world, Marxists denounce the history of ideas as a waste of time, and liberals duel happily with conservatives. But that is not what is happening on early American turf these days.

Students of civic humanism (John Pocock, Bernard Bailyn, Gordon Wood, Lance Banning) agree with Marxists (such as Michael Merrill or Sean Wilentz) that a huge gulf separates the premodern from the modern world. On the plane of ideas, the contrast lies between civic humanism (or republicanism) on the one hand and liberalism on the other. For civic humanists, virtue was a masculine quality, something that only men could exercise, and then only in the public sphere when they voluntarily subordinated their self-interest to the common good. For liberals, the public good was best served by individuals pursuing their self-interest. To get from one realm to the other required a major shift in sensibilities—a transition. To a

Marxist, this dichotomy closely parallels the shift from premodern to modern economies, from a premodern society in which most producers owned the means of production, to a modern one in which capitalists own those means and employ workers who use them to produce wealth.

Arrayed on the other side of the debate are such liberals as Joyce Appleby and John P. Diggins who think that America was almost born modern—that civic humanism was never much more than an aberrant blip on a liberal graph. Neoclassicists, such as Winifred Rothenberg, believe that no transition ever occurred or was necessary. They argue their point by demonstrating that virtually every settler in America, as far back as records and meaningful statistics will carry us, was part of a market economy—and therefore already modern.

The debate has been clouded by one misconception. Diggins, for example, seems to think that historians of eighteenth-century ideology doubt that America has ever been a liberal society, and he has written a long book to prove that liberals did exist. To my knowledge, no one associated with the ideological interpretation has ever said otherwise. Bailyn's book culminates in a transformation and a contagion of liberty. Wood leaves us with the death of classical politics around 1788. Banning, echoed by Pocock and myself, insists that if classical politics did suffer from rigor mortis by 1790, it was either a mild case, or we need to invoke a splendid resurrection to explain what happened in the 1790s. Maybe that argument is the source of the confusion. But all of us have insisted, and still do insist, that there was a transition, a before and after. We do not believe that America was born modern. We tend to locate Jefferson on the premodern side of the divide. We probably do agree that the shift to modernity was virtually complete by the 1820s, but no doubt we can still quarrel about how it happened, among whom, and why.

I shall leave the Marxists to explain their transition in their terms. Let me concentrate on the world of ideology, or at least sensibility. Around 1770, most patriots drew a sharp distinction between private interest and the public good. Virtue was an intensely masculine term, a quality that patriots—citizen warriors, if you like—exercised in the public sphere. The supreme act of patriotism remained death—to die willingly for one's country, the fullest way imaginable to sacrifice all personal interests for the common good. Only autonomous men—those with enough property to remain independent of the wills of other men—could be truly virtuous.

Only they were capable of *choosing* to subordinate personal interest to the public welfare. Much could go wrong with these expectations, of course, and in the histories of earlier republics, it always had. Republics died of corruption, the subordination of the public good to private interest (with faction as the principal example), or the surrender of the wills of some (usually most) citizens to those of a few others.

By 1830 all of these terms remained visible on the American scene, but their mutual relationships had changed. Virtue was well on its way to becoming a feminine quality, something that women guarded within the household, something that they protected against lustful males. It was moving from the public to the private sphere. Interest, by contrast, remained explicitly male, but it was moving from the private circle to the public arena. It was something that men now pursued, frankly and openly, in their public relations with one another. A liberal society was one comfortable with this arrangement. Women, by the way, could not be liberals any more than they could be patriots a generation earlier. They were still asked to subordinate their self-interest to the welfare of their husbands and children. Except in their role as consumers, wives became insulated from the market to a degree that we now recognize as quite extraordinary in the larger pattern of modern history. This shift may even explain why in the mind of reformers prostitution suddenly emerged as an immense social problem. It marked the perversion of spheres as women sold sex on the open market.

Nevertheless, the age of Jackson remained as obsessed with corruption as the revolutionary generation had been. The pursuit of self-interest in public—in the market—was legitimate. To carry that pursuit from the market into government was corrupt. To use legislation or other levers of public power for one's personal aggrandizement became a perversion, not just of the polity, but of the market itself on which all other men had to rely. Jacksonians believed that any central bank had to be corrupt. It distorted the market. It redistributed economic benefits in unfair ways. Radical Jacksonians levelled the same charge against all banks. Whigs denied the equation. They insisted that banks and other corporations merely provided the economic superstructure within which all men could pursue their interests to maximum personal and public advantage. In subtle ways, the meaning of corruption was itself shifting, from the use of public favors to undermine the virtue of the autonomous citizen and legislator, to the use of governmental power to distort the market in favor of one's own special interest.

One of John Pocock's most important contributions to this debate has been to place economic man and political man in the same arena as part of the same construct. For Bernard Bailyn, the discussion of virtue had almost no economic content. For Pocock it did, because his country ideologues could not easily understand the fiscal and commercial forces that were already transforming the Anglo-American world by the late seventeenth century. Pocock located advocacy of economic development with the court, and resistance to that process with the country. The American counterpart of this conflict, as Lance Banning has insisted, came in the 1790s. Like English court spokesmen, Alexander Hamilton was a social conservative and an economic modernizer. Thomas Jefferson was a social radical but an economic traditionalist. Hamilton equated social hierarchy and government power with economic development, or industrialization. He hoped that America by 1900 would be a dramatically different place from what it was in 1800. Jefferson, by contrast, wanted the economy of the United States in 1900 to look pretty much the same as it did in 1800, except that it would accommodate vastly more people over a much greater space. He always understood, as Drew McCoy has shown, that to achieve that goal, he had to make commercial agriculture possible throughout the republic. He had to favor internal improvements to settle the continent at all, as Onuf shows. The United States could avoid Hamiltonian development only through Jeffersonian expansion—the spread, that is, of commercial farming. Jefferson, in short, supported a number of liberal measures to achieve a civic humanist result. To see him as a pure liberal misreads his career. It is quite another matter, however, to look for America's first liberals among his followers. That effort makes excellent sense, and that is part of what Onuf is doing for us today.

My only quarrel with Onuf is to urge him to be more cautious in his use of the word "developmental." He employs it to mean something quite specific. Unless Western farmers could be brought inside the market already enjoyed by Eastern settlers, the American union could not survive. Jefferson's goal always assumed that farmers would be commercial, and it required a major commitment to internal improvements, even at public expense. It did not mean the endorsement of industrialization, nor did it yet imply a full understanding of and commitment to intensive growth, or what economists usually mean by "development"—the steady and measurable increase of per capita wealth.

The imperative upon expansion had to mean inevitable conflict with the Indians, and it led under Andrew Jackson to their massive expulsion from the eastern United States. Let us not deny what was happening. The Indians were, I repeat, the truest patriots of the era. Their men were warriors. They were far less vulnerable to economic temptations largely because their society structured gender relations very differently. Women, not men, were the principal property holders, and they desired no more goods than they could conveniently haul from place to place in their frequent tribal moves. Warriors, unlike settlers, seldom let their wills be cowed by anyone else, and they were far more willing than the settlers to sacrifice everything for the good of the whole.

Jeffersonians needed Indians to illustrate what a serious alternative to commercial farming looked like. Indians constantly reminded Jeffersonians of *progress*, of the development of mankind from savagery to civilization. By stressing this dichotomy, Jeffersonians proved largely immune to the bad conscience that Indians ought to have inflicted upon them. Only with the rise of modern anthropology can we put all of these competing groups in a common perspective as part of a total system. With its aid, we can see how these chapters enrich each other and what it means to insist that the early republic was a triracial society. Indians stood to Jeffersonians as Jeffersonians stood to Hamiltonians. If we line them up from left to right, each said to the group to its right: Thus far you may change our way of life, and no farther. They were wrong. They lost. No doubt much is still living in the thought of Thomas Jefferson, but Jeffersonian America is as dead as the Indian world it deliberately destroyed.

CHAPTER 13

Liberty, Equality, and Slavery: The Paradox of the American Revolution

Sylvia R. Frey

We hold these truths to be self-evident, that all men are created equal, that they are endowed by their Creator with certain unalienable Rights, that among these are Life, Liberty, and the pursuit of Happiness. That to secure these rights, Governments are instituted among Men, deriving their just powers from the consent of the governed.

In 1776, from his home in exile, Thomas Hutchinson, former royal governor of Massachusetts, read the Declaration of Independence with astonishment and disbelief. Determined to expose the "false hypotheses" of that soon-to-be famous document, Hutchinson published what was neither the first nor the last challenge to the legitimacy of its premises.

". . . In what sense," he demanded to know, are all men created equal, and "how far life, liberty, and the *pursuit of happiness* may be said to be unalienable. . . ." Addressing himself directly to the representatives of the slave states in the Continental Congress, Hutchinson squarely posed the great question that vexed the Revolutionary generation and has confused generations of scholars after them. How, he asked, do the delegates of Maryland, Virginia, and the Carolinas and their constituents ". . . justify the depriving more than an hundred thousand Africans of their rights to liberty, and the *pursuit of happiness,* and in some degree to their lives, if these rights are so absolutely unalienable."[1]

The great disparity between democratic theory and the perquisites of practice has stimulated considerable scholarly debate on the subject of the legitimacy of slavery in a republic. Historians writing in the Civil War era, reflecting the interest of contemporaries in trying to explain the great upheaval, viewed the Revolutionary period as one of profound opposition to the institution of slavery. Predictably, the consensus of Northern writers was that at the adoption of the Constitution and during the early years of the Republic, there was no sectional disagreement. In this view both the North and the South looked on slavery as a social, political, and moral evil, evidenced by the original draft of the Declaration of Independence, which denounced the slave traffic; the Virginia law of 1777, which prohibited the slave traffic; the prohibition of slavery in the old Northwest by the Northwest Ordinance; the Constitutional abolition of the international slave trade in 1808; and the words and deeds of the Founding Fathers. The cumulative effect of this argument was to demonstrate that Southerners of the Civil War generation had deviated from the classical republican ideology of their Revolutionary forebears.[2]

A reassessment of the subject in the 1930s led scholars to the conclusion that although republican ideology contributed to the growth of the antislavery movement in the northern and middle states, its impact in the South was limited to a handful of leaders, whose commitment to principle was insignificant compared to the massive moral indifference of their contemporaries.[3] The civil rights movement of the 1960s led to a new burst of interest and a fresh analysis of the problem. Most of the excellent regional and local studies that issued from that period generally agreed that Southern antislavery leaders were atypical, although historians have sometimes taken the views of such leaders as evidence of general antislavery sentiment in the post–Revolutionary-War South.[4]

Heightened interest within the last twenty years in republicanism itself has extended much farther the lines of enquiry. Bernard Bailyn's *Ideological Origins of the American Revolution* and *The Origins of American Politics* represent the first systematic analysis of the subject. Taking the broad view, Bailyn concluded that Americans shared a common set of political and social attitudes, which inspired them in their struggle for independence and guided them through the difficult efforts to build new social and political structures in the post-Revolutionary period. The Bailyn paradigm of a single political and constitutional ideology producing a single, unified response from a substantially homogeneous colonial population was carried forward by a number of adherents. By the early 1970s, however, the consensus theory had come under heavy attack from a number of scholars, whose studies of local situations uncovered evidence of great diversity among Americans. In place of the picture of a relatively homogeneous society animated by a commonly held set of political ideas, a collage of increasingly heterogeneous communities strained by deepening social and economic cleavages and sharp ideological differences began to emerge.[5]

Literally dozens of local and regional studies have appeared over the last two decades, providing detailed pictures of the socioeconomic development of New England, the Middle Colonies, and the Chesapeake. Collectively they tell us that over the course of the eighteenth century, all thirteen of the British mainland colonies were moving toward the development of commercialized economies, but that the character and pace of change varied markedly from one region to the other. Although the proportion of slaves fluctuated according to labor needs and economic conditions, the urban, mercantile centers of New England, the staple-producing economies of the South, the commercial farm and livestock-raising centers of the Middle Colonies, were all to some degree dependent on black slave labor. Sanctioned in law, countenanced by every colonial government, condoned by every major church, slavery was everywhere an established institution that, except for the solitary protests of the Quakers, enjoyed almost universal acceptance.[6]

Inhibited somewhat by a cold climate, rocky soil, low crop yields, a finite supply of land, and the powerful traditions of a Christian commonwealth, New England's economic activity slowly changed from household production to a commercialized economy based on manufacturing and processed foods for market.[7] Although slavery existed, it was a marginal interest, central to neither the economic nor social life of the community. As a result of Puritan reliance on the Mosaic laws of bondage, which regarded slavery as a mark of personal misfortune, not as evidence of inherent inferiority, and the high premium that Puritans placed on education, blacks enjoyed a unique legal position and educational opportunities in New England not accorded them in other colonies. Moreover, because most of New England's small black population, which never exceeded 16,000, was native-born, they spoke English and shared certain white values, making their potential integration into white society possible.[8]

Lacking the geographic and religious constraints that delayed the development of a capitalist economy in New England, the Southern mainland colonies rapidly made the transition from subsistence to commercial agriculture. Beset by a high sex ratio and extraordinary morbidity in the early decades, the Chesapeake after 1720 moved rapidly to develop a staple economy, whose growth and expansion were closely tied to the procurement and maintenance of an unfree labor force based upon African imports until about 1720 and upon natural increase of the slave population thereafter.[9] In the quarter century after 1695, the frontier colony of South Carolina evolved from a mixed economy to a staple-producing economy that was increasingly dependent upon African slave imports.[10] Despite the Georgia Trustee's efforts to avoid the agricultural capitalism that had emerged in neighboring South Carolina, by the 1750s and 1760s Georgians had likewise succeeded in creating a plantation economy based upon African slave labor that closely resembled that of South Carolina.[11] Heavily concentrated in the tidewater counties of Virginia and in the lowland parishes of South Carolina and Georgia, black slaves played a crucial role in the prosperous plantation economies of the Southern colonies.

Occupying an intermediate geographic position, the Middle Colonies reproduced some of the same social patterns that existed in New England and in the South. Blessed by good soil quality, a long growing season, access to water transportation and to markets, the Middle Colonies moved more rapidly to develop a varied economic life based upon the production of naval stores, lumber, wheat, flour, and livestock in New York, and on the cultivation of grain crops, iron production, shipbuilding, and the processing of raw materials in Pennsylvania. Characterized by ethnic and religious diversity, the economy of the region relied upon a mix of white labor, including apprentices, servants, and wage workers, and unfree slave labor.[12] In parts of New York and in eastern New Jersey, where the plantation system existed on a small scale, blacks constituted up to fourteen percent of the total population and slavery was well entrenched. In Pennsylvania, where blacks accounted for only 2.5 percent of the population, slavery was, as in New England, only a marginal interest. As a result of the efforts of the Society for the Propagation of the Gospel and the Quakers in parts of New York and in Pennsylvania, blacks also enjoyed the benefits of education and of church membership. A fractional minority of the total population, they were less able to resist assimilation into white social and cultural structures.[13]

The diversely developing economic systems were attended by corresponding shifts in the patterns of social development. In New England the moderate pace of economic change produced no significant structural transformation prior to 1800. Expanding markets for manufactures and processed foods contributed to a generally rising standard of living and, in the aggregate, to stability in the distribution of wealth.[14] New England remained therefore a relatively egalitarian society, ideally suited for republican ideology, which favored a society composed of relatively homogeneous, egalitarian communities made up of free and independent individuals who shared similar physical and cultural characteristics. A similar pattern of social development evolved in the rural hinterlands of the Mid-Atlantic, although everywhere in the North a concomitant of economic change was the growth of inequality in urban areas, owing principally to the series of international wars that created opportunities for the accumulation of great wealth, and to demographic factors, including the age structure of the urban population, and the concentration in urban centers of what one scholar has called "the mobile poor."[15] By contrast, in the South the rapid development of commercial agriculture based upon slave labor led to a highly stratified social structure, pyramidal in shape, the apex formed by planters of great wealth, the descending face made up of yeoman farmers and an expanding body of tenant farmers, the broad supporting base resting on exploited slave labor.[16]

These socioeconomic differences contributed to the development of distinctive ideological constructs as peculiar to each region, or even subregion, as were the social and economic systems briefly described herein. In New England the social trauma of change had helped produce the period of evangelical revivalism known as the Great Awakening, which swept the region in the second quarter of the century. Although the spreading movement did not immediately yield broad theological or metaphysical arguments, its radical democratic critique of social institutions contributed to the growth of social and political consciousness and paved the way for Whig antislavery arguments.[17] In the Middle Colonies evangelical revivalism reinvigorated the Quaker antislavery tradition and led to the adoption of a tough new antislavery policy by the 1758 yearly Meeting.[18]

The religious frenzy of revivalism was also experienced in the South beginning in the 1740s, but its geographic strength was concentrated in a tier of counties in Virginia's Piedmont and in the upper Tidewater. Official hostility and popular preoccupation with matters of political concern caused the movement to falter, beginning in the 1770s. Enthusiasm among clergy and laity for the American Revolution drained off much of the energy needed for growth and the movement stalled during the war years. A disordered economy, the unsettled state of politics, and the excitement of westward migration in the postwar period, combined to delay the development of a general religious revival such as had occurred in the North. As a result, Southern republicanism in general and the antislavery movement in particular lacked the moralistic fervor that inspired it in New England and in parts of the Mid-Atlantic. By the time the religious fires of revivalism began to spread again across the South beginning in 1800, Southern society was nearly united on the issue of slavery.[19] To further evangelicalism Baptists and Methodists had to accommodate their radical racial attitudes to that reality. In place of emancipation they began to preach amelioration. Instead of condemning Southern society, they gradually came to defend it. Only the Quakers, few in numbers but united in their hostility to slavery, remained firm champions of emancipation.[20]

During the decade of public debate over America's status within the Empire, many of these religious ideas were channeled into the mainstream of American political thought, from which they emerged in the fresh, secular language of intellectual discourse.[21] In their resistance to Britain, American revolutionaries had used the guiding values of republican ideology—liberty, equality, and property—to justify resistance to colonial rule; to claim equality of American citizens with the inhabitants of Britain; to argue for self-government within the Empire.[22] Inevitably, their discussions raised questions about the legitimacy of slavery in a republic. Although the concerns of theory demanded unequivocal answers, the constraints of practice produced ambiguous replies.

Despite the resounding phrase in the Declaration of Independence that proclaimed "All men are by nature equally free and independent," and similar phrases that resonated through the bills of rights of several state constitutions, only the Vermont constitution carried the liberty clause to its logical conclusion and abolished slavery,[23] although most of the Northern states gradually moved toward, if not beyond emancipation. Generally speaking, states with small, assimilable slave populations whose labor was not central to the social or economic life of the community, with a pre-Revolutionary history of religious opposition to slavery, and with early and widespread enthusiasm for republican ideology were the first to confront the problem of bondage in a free society.[24]

Building upon a persistent religious tradition hostile to slavery and buttressed by republican ideology, during the Revolutionary War years all of the Northern states but New York and New Jersey took steps to eradicate slavery: by judicial, legislative, or constitutional action in Massachusetts and New Hampshire, by a process of gradual abolition in Pennsylvania, Rhode Island, and Connecticut. In New York and New Jersey, where slavery was more deeply entrenched socially and economically, where the tradition of religious antislavery was weaker, proslavery forces beat back abolitionist efforts until 1799, when a gradual emancipation bill was adopted in New York, and 1804, when the New Jersey legislature approved a similar measure. In both states the acceptance of gradual emancipation was contingent upon the inclusion of abandonment clauses, called by Arthur Zilversmit "thinly disguised schemes for compensated emancipation."[25]

If the philosophy of natural rights had different meanings to different societies, it had also, in the words of Duncan MacLeod, "racical limits."[26] Although most Northern states decided that the liberty clause of the Declaration was universally applicable, they refused to concede that the equality principle was extendible to blacks. Both in theory and in practice, the postulate of equality was, from its inception, limited in scope.[27] As part of the concept of the social contract formulated by the English Whigs, it was incorporated into English constitutional theory. Whether or not, as James Kettner has recently argued, the Lockean argument that political society originated in the consent of free and equal individuals logically implied the obliteration of the formal laws that set up separate legal categories of citizenship and created invidious distinctions in political rights among them, Whig theory, as it had developed prior to the Revolution, emphatically did not call for the abolition of such distinctions. On the contrary, they remained largely unquestioned until some Americans of the Revolutionary generation began to extend Lockean contractural theory in such a way that implied the elimination of such distinctions and the establishment of political equality.[28]

Impelled by practical circumstances in the New World and by the imperial crisis of the 1760s, Americans logically deduced that since government originated in the consent of free and autonomous individuals, it necessarily followed that those same individuals should share the same political status and rights. In place of the English notion of second-class citizenship, they therefore substituted the idea of political equality, which was implicit in the Lockean theory of the contractual basis of all political obligation.[29] By and large the new republican governments that assumed responsibility for determining who was capable of membership in a republican society shared certain common assumptions about the qualifications for citizenship, among them being the conviction that only freemen possessed of a clear and conscious attachment to republican principles should be eligible to partake of the rights, privileges, and immunities of the body politic. Women, minors, aliens, Catholics, and Jews, whose natural or cultural disabilities or status as dependent persons made them incapable of independent political action, Indians, whose membership in the tribe claimed their allegiance, and blacks, whose inferior rank in the scale of nature disqualified them, were all unfit for membership in the political community.[30] Accordingly, although Northern state constitutions granted blacks legal protections they continued to deny them full political and social equality. Because neither equal political rights nor economic independence could alter the dependent and degraded status of blacks, many Northerners turned to colonization as the most pragmatic solution to the problem raised by the presence of an inferior race in a homogeneous nation of freemen.[31] By rejecting birth and legal privilege as the proper criteria for differentiating among citizens, the Revolutionary generation had succeeded in expanding the meaning of the equality principle. It would remain for later generations to enlarge its meaning further by adding race and gender to the proscribed list.[32]

Despite the limits of emancipation in the North, slavery had ceased to exist as a national institution. At the same time, however, it had become a deeply entrenched sectional institution. By the era of the American Revolution Southerners had succeeded in building a free political community that rested upon a slave economy. Although the ruthless pursuit of profit and privilege by the planter class had caused acute economic and social distress and contributed to the growth of class-consciousness among the first generations of Virginians, the development of tobacco culture and the establishment of slavery and racism led ultimately to the emergence of a political system that, on the issue of slavery, united the interests of large landowners and yeoman farmers.[33] Although the spread of the evangelical movement produced severe strains,[34] the white consensus on the issue of race was maintained and even reinforced by the experience of the American Revolution.

The war's crippling effect on the Southern economy and the heavy wartime losses in slaves convinced white planters that the full recovery of Southern prosperity and the Southern way of life was inseparably linked to the restoration of the slave labor system.[35] The pent-up demand led to the massive importation into Georgia and South Carolina of slaves from Africa and for a temporary period from neighboring states and from the Chesapeake.[36] Left by the transition from tobacco to wheat with a large surplus of slaves, planters in the Chesapeake resorted to the marketing of slaves in developing regions and to renting slaves to the growing numbers of tenants and small farmers and owners of local industries. The effect was to entrench slavery in the Lowcountry and the Tidewater, to extend it into the backcountry everywhere but in Maryland, and to disperse support for it throughout Southern society.[37]

Although it was a Virginian who formulated and articulated republican ideas on liberty in the most sublime form in the Declaration of Independence and the state of Virginia that produced in the Declaration of Rights the model for other states to follow, no genuine spirit of emancipation existed in Virginia or anywhere else in the South, except briefly during the 1780s when the Methodists and Quakers were officially pledged to end slavery,[38] and Maryland and Delaware briefly debated gradual abolition. Beginning in 1792 David Rice led a short-lived Presbyterian antislavery movement in Kentucky, and a Baptist emancipationist movement led by David Barrow also flourished briefly there. In the face of powerful opposition, however, religious antislavery faltered, forced by the pressures for survival to retreat or compromise.[39] It was fear of slave insurrections, not concern over the iniquities of the slave trade, that led Virginia in 1778 and Maryland in 1783 to prohibit slave importations.[40] Not until the frenzied pace of slave imports threatened to produce economic havoc in South Carolina did the General Assembly in 1787 temporarily suspend the slave trade. Georgia waited until 1798, after the pent-up demand for slave labor had been satisfied, before prohibiting the trade.[41] Virginia's revision of the slave code in 1782 to permit individual manumissions resulted in the freeing of some 10,000 slaves, most of them by Quakers and Methodists, but the proportion of freedmen remained small in comparison to the size of the slave population, which continued to grow numerically and expand spatially.[42]

To be sure, some Southern political leaders were troubled by the obvious contradiction between their professed belief in all men's natural and unalienable right to liberty and the existence of chattel slavery. But antislavery leaders like Thomas Jefferson, George Washington, and James Madison of Virginia, and the Laurenses and David Ramsay of South Carolina were exceptional rather than representative. In most cases, they were forced to conform or pay the political consequences[43] because the majority of Southerners came out of the war convinced that the promises of the Declaration of Independence could only be secured to them by the continuation of slavery.

Although unsuccessful, antislavery assaults on the validity and justice of slavery led to the development of the first conscious proslavery theorizing. Following in the slipstream of classical authorities and later philosophers such as Thomas Hobbes and John Locke, Southerners, in popular petitions and proslavery writings and in political debates in state assemblies and the national Congress, laid the theoretical foundations for proslavery thought. The ideas they formulated would later be utilized more systematically by another generation of Southerners.[44] It was in response to attacks by religious emancipationists, whose opposition to slavery was based principally on religious and moral grounds, that proslavery writers first began publicly to defend slavery as a moral institution. In so doing they had, as David Brion Davis has observed, "a long tradition of justifying human bondage to draw upon."[45] The first and most comprehensive religious justifications for slavery were written by non-Southerners: Richard Nisbet, a native of the West Indies whose proslavery tracts were, however, published in Philadelphia; Bernard Romans, a native of Holland who served as a Crown official in East Florida; and William Graham, a native of Paxton, Pennsylvania, who served as rector and principal instructor of Liberty Hall Academy in Lexington, Virginia.[46]

Slavery, these writers insisted, was already a part of the civil constitution of most countries when Christianity appeared. Instead of trying to alter the political or civil state of human relations it found, early Christianity accepted slavery as part of God's design. As the inspired word of God, the Bible offered proof for the theory of the divine ordination of slavery: as a punishment for crimes and as a consequence of war, custom, consent or birth. Just as Noah in Genesis, chapter 9, verses 25 and 27, condemned Ham, his son, to slavery for the crime he committed, so too slaves, as descendants of Ham, were visited with the crimes of their fathers. The enslavement of captives taken in war received divine approval in Joshua, chapter 9, verse 23, while Exodus, chapter 21, verse 7, and Matthew, chapter 18, verse 25, confirmed divine sanction for the parental sale of children. In vindication of the perpetuity of slavery, which distinguished black slavery in the South from ancient slave systems, proslavery writers invariably invoked Leviticus, chapter 25, verses 39–47: "Both thy Bond Men and Bond Maids, which thou shalt have, shall be the Heathen that are round about you; of them shall ye buy Bond Men and Bond Maids. Moreover, of the Children of the Strangers that do sojourn among you, of them shall ye buy, and of their Families that are with you, which they beget in your Land, and they shall be your Possession, and ye shall take them as an Inheritance, for your Children after you, to inherit them for a Possession; they shall be your Bond-men forever." Rather than offering a mode of emancipation, or even suggesting the propriety of it, the Holy Word, these defenders suggested, ". . . only directs [slaves] diligently and faithfully to perform the duties of their station as doing the Lord's service and therefore performing his will."[47]

The resolution of religious uncertainties provided proslavery spokesmen with a moral framework in which to construct their defense of slavery. When James Jackson of Georgia rose in Congress in 1790 to dispute the arguments for emancipation offered in Benjamin Franklin's memorial to Congress, he invoked scriptural sanctions "from Genesis to Revelations."[48] William Smith of South Carolina read quotations from Greek and Roman history to prove that slavery existed "at the time Christianity first dawned on society," and that it "was not disapproved of by the Apostles when they went about diffusing the principles of Christianity."[49] By degrees the presumption of divine ordination assumed the character of an axiomatic truth. Despite William Smith's efforts to prove the religious justification for slavery, some vagrant doubts appear to survive in his admission that ". . . if [slavery] be a moral evil, it is like many others which exist in all civilized countries and which the world quietly submit to."[50] No such doubt remains in Georgia congressman Peter Early's candid confession to his colleagues sixteen years later that "A large majority of the people in the Southern States do not consider slavery as a crime. They do not believe it immoral to hold human flesh in bondage. Many deprecate slavery as an evil; as a political evil . . ." but "few, very few, consider it as a crime."[51]

With the development in the decade before the Revolution of secular antislavery, with its emphasis on natural rights arguments, proslavery forces turned increasingly to republican ideology and forged out of the ambivalence inherent in it weapons that later were to become the mainstay of Southern proslavery arguments. Republican ideology in its inception rested upon a diverse array of doctrines which lent themselves easily to semantic confusion. Conventional Whig wisdom from James Harrington and John Locke to Richard Price had proclaimed property to be a "natural" right associated with each individual's right to life. Whatever the Whig philosopher's intention in claiming the status of natural right for all kinds of property, proslavery spokesmen fastened on the idea that the right of private property was fundamental.[52]

Above all, property in the South meant slaves. Defined by law as a capital asset,[53] slaves accounted for almost half of the total physical wealth of the region. Although half of the total wealth was owned by the richest tenth of the householders,[54] small farmers and even tenants were heavily dependent upon the labor of slaves. A half century after abandoning white contract labor in favor of black slave labor, Chesapeake planters were more than ever convinced that "it is impossible to grow tobacco without slaves."[55] Mindful of the connection between the commercial development of rice and the introduction of slaves from the rice-producing areas of West Africa, South Carolina planters had likewise concluded that the great export commodity could "only be cultivated by slaves; the climate, the nature of the soil, ancient habits, forbid the whites from performing the labor. . . . Remove the cultivators of the soil, and the whole of the low country, all fertile rice and indigo swamps will be deserted, and become a wilderness."[56] So inextricably linked was slave labor to agriculture, it was assumed that without slaves the Southern economy was doomed.[57]

The Southern defense of the primacy of property rights was not, however, merely a tactical or instrumental requirement but related to their fundamental understanding of republicanism. A paean to human liberty, Locke's celebrated *Treatises* nevertheless justified the holding of foreign captives as slave property. Jefferson had amended the classic Lockean triad of "life, liberty and estate," to "Life, Liberty, and the pursuit of Happiness," perhaps because he personally questioned the moral basis of some forms of property.[58] Southern proslavery spokesmen did not abjure the basic premises of the Declaration; what they did instead was to adhere to them as inherited dogma. Like most Americans, Southerners believed that the Revolutionary War had been a crusade to secure liberty against Britain's surreptitious assaults. By a kind of ironic paradox, however, they equated property with "liberty" and translated "liberty" as the freedom to own human beings. In their petition to the Virginia assembly for repeal of the private emancipation act of 1782, and for the rejection of Methodist emancipation proposals, citizens of eight Virginia counties emphasized that they had ". . . waded thro' Deluges of civil Blood to that unequivocal Liberty, which alone characterises the free independent Citizen . . . ."

Through the agonies of war, they had ". . . seald with our Blood, a Title to the full, free, and absolute Enjoyment of every Species of our Property, whensoever, or howsoever legally acquired. . . ."[59] The same theme resonates through James Jackson's bitter denunciation of a Quaker emancipation petition in 1790. Georgia slaveowners had fought in the Revolutionary War while Quakers had opposed it: "Why, then on their application should we injure men Who, at the risk of their lives and fortunes, secured to the community their liberty and property."[60]

The explicit association of the right of property with liberty had another component, safety and happiness, which like property was an element of the inalienable legacy. Arguing from the Lockean premise that the right of property derives from each person's right to life, Americans of the Revolutionary generation proclaimed property the necessary foundation of happiness, without which no individual could enjoy independence or free will, the most essential component of liberty.[61] State constitutions written during the Revolutionary period invariably link the three words, liberty, property, and happiness, as though each implied the other.[62] In their defense of slavery, proslavery spokesmen used without change that political frame of reference. When, for example, William Smith of South Carolina spoke against the Quaker emancipation petitions he maintained that ". . . slavery was so ingrafted into the policy of the Southern States, that it could not be eradicated without tearing up the roots of their happiness, tranquility, and prosperity."[63] Speaking of "the almost insurmountable difficulties" surrounding the question of slavery, Henry Laurens singled out the "great task effectually to persuade Rich Men to part willingly with the very source of their wealth &, as they suppose, tranquility."[64] Whatever other meanings it might have had, to the Southerner tranquility meant the right to live free of the fear of slave insurrections.

More than merely the source of Southern wealth and prosperity, slavery was, in the words of William Smith, "the palladium of the property of our country."[65] Smith's homologue of the statue of Pallas Athena, the preservation of which was believed to ensure the safety of Troy, and the institution of slavery was singularly appropriate. As Edmund Morgan has brilliantly demonstrated, the existence of slavery had made possible the freedom espoused by republican ideology. Like Greece and Rome, Southern slave society had produced "industry crowned with affluence, hospitality, liberality of manners . . . ," the "noblest sentiments of freedom and independence,"[66] a land, as Morgan writes, "to fit the picture of republican textbooks."[67] Although slaves were admittedly useful members of that society, they were also ". . . savages whose dispositions prompt[ed] them to act as savages in opposition to every principle of humanity and such persons cannot be fit for civil liberty . . . ," nor for that matter "would it be safe to trust them with it."[68]

Heightened slave rebelliousness during the era of the Revolutionary War had revived latent white fears of slave risings.[69] Acutely conscious of their own vulnerability, Southerners drew peculiar comfort and a certain specious support from another element of republican ideology, the right of self-preservation. Emancipation, they argued, would be attended with the most dire consequences, for slaves and their owners. Insisting upon the amiable fiction that slaves were more humanely treated than were the lower classes of whites in many countries,[70] most proslavery writers argued that emancipation would "tend to make slaves wretched in the highest degree."[71] Should they be "thrown upon the world void of property and connections," they would, as the Maryland experience had already shown, "turn out common pickpockets, petty larceny villains."[72] Worse than that, emancipation would destroy Southern society by producing "one or other of these consequences: either that a mixture of the races would degenerate the whites, without improving the blacks, or that it would create two separate classes of people in the community involved in inveterate hostility, which would terminate in the massacre and extirpation of one or the other. . . ."[73] In the catalog of emancipation horrors were "Want, Poverty, Distress, and Ruin to the Free Citizen; Neglect, Famine and Death to the black Infant and superannuate Parent; The Horrors of all the Rapes, Murders, and Outrages, which a vast Multitude of Unprincipled, unpropertied, revengeful, and remorseless Banditti are capable of perpetrating. . . ."[74] Preoccupied to an almost obsessive degree by fear, proslavery spokesmen concluded that emancipation was impossible because "the first law of self-preservation forbid it."[75]

Despite certain elements of logical incompatibility, proslavery spokesmen had thus achieved an apparent reconciliation of slavery with the moral precepts of republican ideology. The next step was to secure the existence of slavery, which they temporarily accomplished, by relying upon constitutional guarantees. In their petition to the Virginia assembly for repeal of the manumission act of 1782, the citizens of Lunenberg County appealed to the Virginia Declaration of Rights, claiming that by it their property rights were "so clearly defined; so fully acknowledged; and so solemnly ratified and confirmed . . . as not to admit of an equivocal Construction, nor of the smallest Alteration or Diminution, by any Power, but that which originally authorised its Establishment."[76]

Southern representatives in Congress did not yet interpret the Constitution as an expressly proslavery document. Instead, they argued that it clearly limited the national government in the scope of its powers and in that way served as a vessel to protect slavery. They supported their position with a reliance upon contract theory and strict construction of the Constitution. In one of the seminal assertions of the doctrine of strict construction, William Smith argued that slavery was present when the union was formed: ". . . for better or for worse," he contended, "the Northern States adopted us with our slaves, and we adopted them with their Quakers. There was then an implied compact between the Northern and Southern people, that no step should be taken to injure the property of the latter, or to disturb their tranquillity." As the original contractors to the formation of the union the "State Governments clearly retained all the rights of sovereignty which they had before the establishment of the Constitution, unless they were exclusively delegated to the United States. . . ."[77] The bounds thus drawn around the powers of Congress clearly protected slavery from any change by action of the national government.

The first test of that theory came in 1797 when a group of manumitted slaves from North Carolina attempted to petition Congress to review their situation. Manumitted by their Quaker owners in apparent violation of a state law prohibiting the freeing of any slaves except for "meritorious services, acknowledged by a license of the court," some 134 former slaves were apprehended under the federal fugitive slave law of 1793 and were subsequently returned to slavery. Antislavery spokesmen, who supported their petition, argued that as freedmen they were not subject to the federal fugitive slave act and were moreover entitled to claim the protection of the House. Proslavery spokesmen on the other hand insisted that under the state law the petitioners were slaves and were accordingly subject only to state authority: "This is a kind of property on which the House has no power to legislate," not even to receive the slaves' petition. Referred to a select committee, the committee decided that the matter was "exclusively of judicial cognizance" and recommended that the petition be withdrawn. Although they had not expounded their principles in a comprehensive philosophical treatise, proslavery spokesmen had made it clear that slave property enjoyed so privileged a position under the Constitution that should human claims be advanced against it, the rights of property must prevail.[78]

Poles apart in moral intent and purpose, proslavery and antislavery spokesmen nevertheless drew from the same wellspring. Republican ideology, as William Freehling has observed, articulated concern for both liberty and property. For reasons peculiar to the cultural and social context from which most of them issued, antislavery spokesmen identified with the root postulate of liberty and accorded to property an instrumental or secondary character. For hard practical reasons, proslavery spokesmen presumed that the right of property was fundamental, standing as it were on an equal plane with liberty. In the beginning antislavery forces conceded, in part because as property-conscious republicans themselves, they too believed that property was *a* fundamental right, if not *the* fundamental right; in part because as Freehling has also noted, they had a passion for creating and preserving the Union, which led them to accept "endless compromises."[79]

In the end, the apocryphal logic employed by proslavery spokesmen could not be maintained against the moral drive and power of the antislavery forces. Challenged by the inspired humanitarianism of the Quakers, proslavery spokesmen fashioned a justification for slavery from arguments that had flowed without break from ancient slave societies and had been given enhanced force by the logic of republican ideology. Refracted through the lens of radical religion, however, republican ideology became a transformed and a transforming creed. Expropriated by the incipient abolitionists, as David Brion Davis has called them, over the next fifty years the inconsistencies inherent in it were gradually dissolved while the cluster of ideas and values were distilled into the deathless truths that have since functioned as the conscience of society.

NOTES

1. Thomas Hutchinson, *Strictures Upon the Declaration of the Congress at Philadelphia* (London, 1776), 9–10.

2. William Goodell, *Slavery and Anti-Slavery; A History of the Great Struggle in Both Hemispheres; With a View of The Slavery Question in the United States* (New York, 1852); George Livermore, *An Historical Research Respecting the Opinions of the Founding Fathers of the Republic on Negroes as Slaves, as Citizens and as Soldiers* (Boston, 1863).

3. Matthew T. Mellon, *Early American Views on Negro Slavery: From the Letters and Papers*

of the Founders of the Republic (New York, 1969); William Sumner Jenkins, *Pro-Slavery Thought in the Old South* (Chapel Hill, N.C., 1935); James Hugh Johnston, *Race Relations in Virginia and Miscegenation in the South 1776–1860* (Amherst, 1937).

4. Leon Litwack, *North of Slavery: The Negro in the Free States, 1790–1860* (Chicago, 1961); Robert McColley, *Slavery and Jeffersonian Virginia* (Urbana, Ill., 1973); Donald L. Robinson, *Slavery in the Structure of American Politics* (New York, 1971); Duncan J. MacLeod, *Slavery, Race and the American Revolution* (Cambridge, Mass., 1974); Charles Duncan Rice, *The Rise and Fall of Black Slavery* (London, 1975); Harry P. Owens, ed., *Perspective and Irony in American Slavery* (Jackson, Miss., 1976).

5. Bernard Bailyn, *The Ideological Origins of the American Revolution* (Cambridge, Mass., 1967), and *The Origins of American Politics* (New York, 1967); Gordon Wood, *The Creation of the American Republic, 1776–1787* (Chapel Hill, N.C., 1969); J.G.A. Pocock, *The Machiavellian Moment: Florentine Political Thought and the Atlantic Republican Tradition* (Princeton, 1975); see also Caroline Robbins, *The Eighteenth-Century Commonwealthman: Studies in the Transmission, Development and Circumstance of English Liberal Thought from the Restoration of Charles II until the War with the Thirteen Colonies* (Cambridge, Mass., 1959). For a very thorough review of the literature on republicanism see Robert C. Shalhope, "Toward a Republican Synthesis: The Emergence of an Understanding of Republicanism in American Historiography," *William and Mary Quarterly*, 3rd ser., 29 (1972), 49–80; idem, "Republicanism and Early American Historiography," ibid., 3rd ser., 39 (1982), 334–56.

6. David Brion Davis, *Slavery and Human Progress* (New York, 1984), contends that proslavery arguments had been almost universally accepted for centuries and that no systematic body of argument against it existed; see especially 80, 81, 107–08.

7. See for example Bruce C. Daniels, "Economic Development in Colonial and Revolutionary Connecticut: An Overview," *William and Mary Quarterly*, 3rd ser., 37 (1980), 429–50; James F. Shepard and Gary M. Walton, *Shipping, Maritime Trade, and the Economic Development of Colonial North America* (Cambridge, Mass., 1972); Darrett B. Rutman, "Governor Winthrop's Garden Crop: The Significance of Agriculture in the Early Commerce of Massachusetts Bay," *William and Mary Quarterly*, 3rd ser., 20 (1963), 396–415; Bernard Bailyn, *The New England Merchants in the Seventeenth Century* (New York, 1955); Howard S. Russell, *A Long, Deep Furrow: Three Centuries of Farming in New England* (Hanover, N.H., 1976).

8. Arthur Zilversmit, *The First Emancipation: The Abolition of Slavery in the North* (Chicago, 1967), 4–5.

9. For economic developments see Jacob M. Price, *France and the Chesapeake: A History of the French Tobacco Monopoly, 1674–1791, and of Its Relationship to the British and American Tobacco Trades*, 2 vols. (Ann Arbor, Mich., 1973); Carville V. Earle, *The Evolution of a Tidewater Settlement System: All Hallow's Parish, Maryland, 1650–1783* (Chicago, 1975); Paul G.E. Clemens, *The Atlantic Economy and Colonial Maryland's Eastern Shore: From Tobacco to Grain* (Ithaca, 1980); for the growth of slavery see Edmund Morgan, *American Slavery, American Freedom: The Ordeal of Colonial Virginia* (New York, 1975); Russell R. Menard, "From Servants to Slaves: The Transformation of the Chesapeake Labor System," *Southern Studies*, 16 (1977), 355–90; Allan Kulikoff, "A 'Prolifick' People: Black Population Growth in the Chesapeake Colonies, 1700–1790," *Southern Studies*, XVI (1977), 392–414; Russell R. Menard, "The Maryland Slave Population, 1658 to 1730: A Demographic Profile of Blacks in Four Counties," *William and Mary Quarterly*, 3rd ser., 32 (1975), 29–54.

10. Peter H. Wood, *Black Majority: Negroes in Colonial South Carolina from 1670 through the*

Stono Rebellion (New York, 1975); see also Daniel Littlefield, *Rice and Slaves: Ethnicity and the Slave Trade in Colonial South Carolina* (Baton Rouge, La., 1981).

11. Betty Wood, *Slavery in Colonial Georgia* (Athens, Ga., 1984).

12. Thomas Elliot Norton, *The Fur Trade in Colonial New York, 1686–1776* (Madison, Wisc., 1974); Sung Bok Kim, *Landlord and Tenant in Colonial New York: Manorial Society 1664–1775* (Chapel Hill, N.C., 1978); Michael Kammen, *Colonial New York: A History* (New York, 1975); James T. Lemon, *The Best Poor Man's Country: A Geographical Study of Early Southeastern Pennsylvania* (Baltimore, 1972); Duane E. Ball and Gary M. Walton, "Agricultural Productivity Change in Eighteenth-Century Pennsylvania," *Journal of Economic History*, 36 (1976), 102–17.

13. Zilversmit, *First Emancipation*, 5, 6, 26–27.

14. James Henretta, "Economic and Social Structure in Colonial Boston," *William and Mary Quarterly*, 3rd ser., 22 (1965), 75–92; Gloria L. Main, "Inequality in Early America: The Evidence from Probate Records in Massachusetts and Maryland," *Journal of Interdisciplinary History*, VII (1977), 559–81, says that although gross inequality became a permanent feature of Southern life in the late seventeenth century, the same thing did not occur in Massachusetts until the early nineteenth century. G.B. Warden, "Inequality and Instability in Eighteenth Century Boston," *Journal of Interdisciplinary History*, VI (1976), 49–84, maintains that the distribution of wealth did not change between 1687 and 1772.

15. Kim, *Landlord and Tenant;* Edward Countryman, *A People in Revolution: The American Revolution and Political Society in New York, 1760–1790* (Baltimore, 1981); Lemon, *Best Poor Man's Country;* Stephanie Grauman Wolf, *Urban Village: Population, Community, and Family Structure in Germantown, Pennsylvania, 1683–1800* (Princeton, 1976); Gary B. Nash, *Urban Crucible: Social Change, Political Consciousness, and the Origins of the American Revolution* (Cambridge, Mass., 1979), 54–75; Duane E. Ball, "Dynamics of Population and Wealth in Eighteenth-Century Chester County, Pennsylvania," *Journal of Interdisciplinary History*, VI (1976), 621–44.

16. Aubrey C. Land, "Economic Base and Social Structure: The Northern Chesapeake in the Eighteenth Century," *Journal of Economic History*, 25 (1965), 639–54; Gerald W. Mullin, *Flight and Rebellion: Slave Resistance in Eighteenth-Century Virginia* (New York, 1972); Rhys Isaac, *The Transformation of Virginia, 1740–1790: Community, Religion, and Authority* (Chapel Hill, N.C., 1982). Some recent studies, including Isaac's *Transformation of Virginia*, emphasize the rise of tensions in society. See, for example, Marvin L. Michael Kay, "The North Carolina Regulation, 1766–1776: A Class Conflict," in *The American Revolution: Explorations in the History of American Radicalism*, Alfred F. Young, ed. (De Kalb, Ill., 1976), 71–123; Ronald Hoffman, *A Spirit of Dissension: Economics, Politics, and the Revolution in Maryland* (Baltimore, 1973); A. Roger Ekirch, *"Poor Carolina": Politics and Society in Colonial North Carolina, 1729–1776* (Chapel Hill, N.C., 1981); Richard R. Beeman, "Social Change and Cultural Conflict in Virginia: Lunenburg County, 1746 to 1774," *William and Mary Quarterly*, 3rd ser., 35 (1978), 455–76. For the growth of tenancy see Willard F. Bliss, "The Rise of Tenancy in Virginia," *Virginia Magazine of History and Biography*, 59 (1950), 427–41.

17. Richard L. Bushman, *From Puritan to Yankee: Character and the Social Order in Connecticut, 1690–1765* (New York, 1967), 113–95; Alan Heimert, *Religion and the American Mind: From the Great Awakening to the Revolution* (Cambridge, Mass., 1966), sees the Great Awakening as the intellectual force that propelled the colonies toward revolution. His work focuses principally on New England. John M. Murrin, "No Awakening, No Revolution? More Counterfactual Speculations," *Reviews in American History*, 11 (1983), 161–71, argues that although the Great Awakening did not create the Revolution, it

contributed to its success. Nathan Hatch, "The Christian Movement and the Demand for a Theology of the People," *Journal of American History*, 67 (1980–81), 545–67, stresses the liberating impact of the Revolution on religion.

18. Zilversmit, *The First Emancipation*, 71–74.

19. Wesley M. Gewehr, *The Great Awakening in Virginia, 1740–1790* (Chapel Hill, N.C., 1930), described the Great Awakening in Virginia as having three distinct phases; the last, the Methodist revival, was cut short by the Revolution. John B. Boles, "Evangelical Protestantism in the Old South: From Religious Dissent to Cultural Dominance," in Charles Reagan Wilson, ed., *Religion in the South* (Jackson, Miss., 1985), argues that although the South experienced a series of localized revivals, it was not until 1800–1805 that general revivalism swept the area. William Parks, "Religion and the Revolution in Virginia," in Richard A. Rutyna and Peter C. Stewart, eds., *Virginia in the American Revolution: A Collection of Essays* (Norfolk, Va., 1977), 38–56, demonstrates the geographic concentration of the movement, as does J. Stephen Kroll-Smith, "Transmitting a Revival Culture: The Organizational Dynamics of the Baptist Movement in Colonial Virginia, 1760–1777," *Journal of Southern History*, L (1984), 551–68; for postwar developments see John B. Boles, *The Great Revival in the South, 1787–1805: Origins of the Southern Evangelical Mind* (Lexington, 1972). Evidence for the proslavery consensus is extensive. See, for example, Thomas Coke, *Extracts of the Journals of the Reverend Dr. Coke's Five Visits to America* (London, 1793), 33, 37; Jesse Lee, *A Short History of the Methodists, in the United States of America; Beginning in 1766, And Continued till 1809* (Baltimore, 1810), 120; Jesse Lee, *A Short Account of the Life and Death of the Reverend John Lee, A Methodist Minister in the United States of America* (Baltimore, 1805), 126. See also Arthur H. Shaffer, "Between Two Worlds: David Ramsay and the Politics of Slavery,": *Journal of Southern History*, L (no. 2, 1984), 175–196; Larry Tise, "Proslavery Ideology: A Social and Intellectual History of the Defense of Slavery in America, 1790–1840," (Ph.D. diss., University of North Carolina, 1975), xxv.

20. McColley, *Slavery and Jeffersonian Virginia*, 154.

21. Murrin, "No Awakening, No Revolution," 161–71; Hatch, "The Christian Movement," 545–67.

22. Willi Paul Adams, *The First American Constitutions: Republican Ideology and the Making of the State Constitutions in the Revolutionary Era* (Chapel Hill, N.C., 1980), 165, 166, 169.

23. Ibid., 156–58.

24. This is the general argument made by Zilversmit, *The First Emancipation;* see also Litwack, *North of Slavery*, 4–23, which is in general agreement.

25. Zilversmit, *The First Emancipation*, 199. The gradual emancipation bill passed by New York in 1799 freed Negro children born after July 4, 1799, but required them to serve the masters of their mothers until they were twenty-eight (males) or twenty-five (females). The bill, however, permitted owners to abandon the children a year after their birth, after which time they were considered paupers and would be bound out to service by the overseers of the poor. The state would reimburse the towns for the support of abandoned children. Since the law did not prohibit overseers from binding out children to the same masters who abandoned them, masters could receive a lucrative income.

26. MacLeod, *Slavery, Race and the American Revolution*, 47.

27. J.R. Pole, *The Pursuit of Equality in American History* (Berkeley, 1978); chaps. 6, 7, and 8 deal with equality as it bears on race.

28. James H. Kettner, *The Development of American Citizenship, 1608–1870* (Chicago, c. 1978), 53–4; Adams, *First American Constitutions*, 165. For a different reading of

eighteenth-century insights on equality see Garry Wills, *Inventing America: Jefferson's Declaration of Independence* (Garden City, N.Y., 1978), 207–28, which argues for the influence in America of the moral-sense school represented by the Scottish Enlightenment. In recognizing the moral sense as man's highest faculty, Scottish philosophers such as Frances Hutcheson advanced the notion of a literal equality of men, which Wills believes was the formative influence on Jeffersonian thought.

29. Kettner, *Development of American Citizenship*, 213–47.

30. Jack P. Greene, *All Men Are Created Equal: Some Reflections on the Character of the American Revolution* (Oxford, 1976), 12, 15, 18, 23, 26. The classic study of the history of racism is Winthrop Jordan, *White Over Black: American Attitudes Toward the Negro, 1550–1812* (Chapel Hill, N.C., 1968); see also George M. Fredrickson, *The Black Image in the White Mind: The Debate on Afro-American Character and Destiny, 1817–1914* (New York, 1971).

31. Litwack, *North of Slavery*, 15, 16, 17, 22, 28; Adams, *First American Constitutions*, 184–85; David M. Streifford, "The American Colonization Society: An Application of Republican Ideology to Early Antebellum Reform," *Journal of Southern History*, XLV (1979), 201–20; Betty L. Fladeland, "Compensated Emancipation: A Rejected Alternative," *Journal of Southern History*, XLII (1976), 169–86.

32. Rowland Berthoff and John M. Murrin, "Feudalism, Communalism, and the Yeoman Freeholder: The American Revolution Considered as a Social Accident," in Stephen G. Kurtz and James H. Hutson, eds., *Essays on the American Revolution* (Chapel Hill, N.C., 1973), 282.

33. Morgan, in *American Slavery, American Freedom*, argues for a white political consensus based at least in part on the issue of slavery.

34. Issac, in *Transformation of Virginia*, stresses the strains on Virginia society caused by the rise of religious revivalism. My own research suggests that on the issue of slavery the consensus held firm and was in fact reinforced by the Revolutionary War experience.

35. Joseph Clay to James Jackson, February 16, 1784, in Letters of Joseph Clay, Georgia Historical Society, *Collections*, VIII, 194–95; from Ralph Izard, June 10, 1785 (Enclosure 2), in Julian P. Boyd, ed., *The Papers of Thomas Jefferson* (Princeton, 1950–) VIII, 199. See also Darold D. Wax, " 'New Negroes Are Always in Demand': The Slave Trade in Eighteenth-Century Georgia," *Georgia Historical Quarterly*, LXVIII (1984), 193.

36. Joseph Clay to Messrs. Scott Dover Taylor and Bell, April 15, 1783; and Clay to James Jackson, February 16, 1783, Letters of Joseph Clay, Georgia Historical Society, *Collections*, VIII, 187, 194–95; Philip D. Morgan, "Black Society in the Lowcountry, 1760–1810," in Ira Berlin and Ronald Hoffman, eds., *Slavery and Freedom in the Age of the American Revolution* (Charlottesville, Va., 1983), 83–141; Patrick S. Brady, "The Slave Trade and Sectionalism in South Carolina, 1787–1808," *Journal of Southern History*, XXXVIII (1972), 601–20.

37. Richard S. Dunn, "Black Society in the Chesapeake, 1776–1810," in Berlin and Hoffman, eds., *Slavery and Freedom*, 49–82; see also Allan Kulikoff, "Uprooted Peoples: Black Migrants in the Age of the American Revolution, 1790–1820," in ibid., 143–71; Sarah S. Hughes, "Slaves for Hire: The Allocation of Black Labor in Elizabeth City County, Virginia, 1782 to 1810," *William and Mary Quarterly*, 3rd ser., 35 (1978), 260–86.

38. McColley, *Slavery and Jeffersonian Virginia*, 148. The emancipation rule was suspended in 1785, ibid., 152.

39. Zilversmit, *First Emancipation*, 155. For the antislavery movement in Kentucky see John

B. Boles, *Religion in Antebellum Kentucky* (Lexington, Ky., 1976), 101–22; Jeffrey Brooke Allen, "Were Southern White Critics of Slavery Racists? Kentucky and the Upper South, 1791–1824," *Journal of Southern History*, XLIV (1978), 169–90. Professor Eugene D. Genovese has called to my attention the fact that in 1836 the Kentucky Presbyterian Synod published an antislavery manifesto. See Committee of the Synod of Kentucky, *An Address to the Presbyterians of Kentucky, Proposing a Plan for the Instruction and Emancipation of their Slaves* (Newburyport, Ky., 1836), cited in Genovese, " '*Slavery Ordained of God': The Southern Slaveholders' View of Biblical History and Modern Politics*," 24th Annual Robert Fortenbaugh Memorial Lecture, Gettysburg College, 1985, n. 14, 26.

40. McColley, *Slavery and Jeffersonian Virginia*, 117.
41. Brady, "The Slave Trade and Sectionalism," 602, n. 2.
42. Dunn, "Black Society in the Chesapeake," 49–82.
43. McColley, *Slavery and Jeffersonian Virginia*, 114–18; Arthur H. Shaffer, "Between Two Worlds: David Ramsay and the Politics of Slavery," *Journal of Southern History*, L (1984), 175–96. Some Southerners led an effort to defeat Jefferson's bid for the presidency in 1796 because of his antislavery views. See William Loughton Smith, *The Pretensions of Thomas Jefferson to the Presidency Examined*, (n.p., 1796). There is some evidence to suggest that it was not safe to publicly oppose slavery. See Albert Matthews, "Notes on the Proposed Abolition of Slavery in Virginia in 1785," Colonial Society of Massachusetts, *Publications*, VI (1904), 373, which describes the harrassment of Thomas Coke during a tour of Virginia. See also James Jackson's response to a comment made by a colleague during the Congressional debate over slavery in 1790 to the effect that "if he was a federal judge he does not know to what length he would go in emancipating these people;" but Jackson warned, "I believe his judgment would be of short duration in Georgia, perhaps even the existence of such a judge might be in danger," *Abridgment of the Debates of Congress* (February, 1790), I, 209.
44. Jordan, in *White Over Black*, 310–11, sees the Revolution as "a critical turning point," because for the first time Americans became conscious of the pervasiveness of slavery, which "mocked the ideals upon which the new republic was founded." Fredrickson, in *Black Image in the White Mind*, 3, contends that because antislavery forces were so weak in the South and because slavery had never been seriously threatened, "slavery in the South had survived the Revolutionary era and the rise of the natural rights philosophy without an elaborated racial defense—without, indeed, much of an intellectual defense of any kind." Tise, in "Proslavery Ideology," 94, sees the American Revolution as "the first great crisis which challenged the social and moral values of a slave society." Although I generally agree with Tise, his emphasis is on the tension between proslavery thought and the ideology of the Revolution. Although I recognize the tension, I emphasize the reliance of Southerners upon Revolutionary ideology to defend the institution of slavery; their rejection of the natural rights arguments occurred after 1800, as Tise's evidence clearly shows.
45. David Brion Davis, *The Problem of Slavery in the Age of Revolution* (Ithaca, 1975), 165 and especially chap. 34.
46. [Richard Nisbet], *Slavery Not Forbidden by Scripture* (Philadelphia, 1773); Bernard Romans, *A Concise Natural History of East and West Florida* (New York, 1775, reprint ed., 1961); David W. Robson, ed., " 'An important Question Answered': William Graham's Defense of Slavery in Post-Revolutionary Virginia," *William and Mary Quarterly*, 3rd ser., 37 (1980), 644–52.

47. [Nisbet], *Slavery Not Forbidden*, 3, 4; Romans, *A Concise Natural History*, 76–78; "Graham's Defense of Slavery," 650–51. The frequency with which proslavery figures invoked religious sanctions can also be inferred from antislavery writings. See, for example, John Woolman, *Some Considerations on the Keeping of Negroes* (Philadelphia, 1754).

48. *Abridgment of the Debates of Congress* (February, 1790), I, 209.

49. *Annals of Congress*, 1 Cong., 2 Sess., 1506 (March 17, 1790); see also "Early Proslavery Petitions in Virginia," Fredrika Teute Schmidt and Barbara Ripel Wilhelm, eds., *William and Mary Quarterly*, 3rd ser., 30 (1973), 139, 143, 149.

50. *Annals of Congress*, 1 Cong., 2 Sess., 1510 (March 17, 1790).

51. *Abridgment of the Debates of Congress* (December, 1806), III, 501.

52. William B. Scott, *In Pursuit of Happiness: American Conceptions of Property from the Seventeenth to the Twentieth Century* (Bloomington, Ind., 1977), 24–35.

53. For the history of colonial efforts to establish a statutory law of slavery, see A. Leon Higginbotham, Jr., *In the Matter of Color: Race and the American Legal Process: The Colonial Period* (New York, 1978); Whittington B. Johnson, "The Origin and Nature of African Slavery in Seventeenth Century Maryland," *Maryland Historical Magazine*, 73 (1978), 236–45; M. Eugene Sirmans, "The Legal Status of the Slave in South Carolina, 1670–1740," *Journal of Southern History*, 28 (1962), 462–73; William M. Wiecek, "The Statutory Law of Slavery and Race in the Thirteen Mainland Colonies of British America," *William and Mary Quarterly*, 3rd ser., 34 (1977), 258–80.

54. Alice Hanson Jones, ed., *American Colonial Wealth: Documents and Methods*, 3 vols. (New York, 1978), III, 1940, 1947.

55. Jacques-Pierre Brissot de Warville, *New Travels in the United States of America* (Cambridge, Mass., 1964), 231.

56. *Annals of Congress*, 1 Cong., 2 Sess., 1510, 1513 (March 17, 1790).

57. *Abridgment of the Debates of Congress* (February, 1790), I, 210. See also Romans, *A Concise Natural History*, 71.

58. Most Jefferson scholars agree that although Jefferson clearly believed that slavery was a moral evil, he also believed that the Negro was probably inferior. Jordan, *White Over Black*, 481, concludes that Jefferson's derogation of the Negro ". . . constituted, for all its qualifications, the most intense, extensive, and extreme formulation of anti-Negro 'thought' offered by any American in the thirty years after the Revolution." Proslavery forces in fact used Jefferson's *Notes on Virginia* to argue for Negro inferiority. See, for example, *Annals of Congress*, 1 Cong., 2 Sess., 1506 (March 17, 1790).

59. "Early Proslavery Petitions," 140, 141. Even Southerners who opposed slavery implicitly recognized that owners had a legally vested right of property in their slaves. See McColley, *Slavery and Jeffersonian Virginia*, 158, 186; Louis Morton, *Robert Carter of Nomini Hall: A Virginia Tobacco Planter of the Eighteenth Century* (Williamsburg, Va., 1941), 60–61; Arthur Lee, *An Essay in Vindication of the Continental Colonies of America: From A Censure of Mr. Adam Smith in his Theory of Moral Sentiments* (London, 1764). Although he opposed slavery, Lee defended the legality of it, which he contended derived from the legislative power in each society, 32. For a different view of Jefferson's omission of property from the list of "inalienable rights" see Willis, *Inventing America*, 207–39, 293–306, which argues that Jefferson's view of natural rights was more in accord with Scottish Enlightenment thought than with Lockean political principles.

60. *Annals of Congress*, 1 Cong., 1 Sess., 1229 (February 11, 1790).

61. Greene, *All Men Are Created Equal*, 18.

62. Adams, *The First American Constitutions*, especially chaps. 7, 8, and 9, which treat the three postulates separately.

63. *Annals of Congress*, 1 Cong., 2 Sess., 1508 (March 17, 1790). See also Rutland, ed., *Papers of George Mason*, III, 1065–66; "Early Proslavery Petitions," 140, 142, 145.

64. Henry Laurens to John Laurens, September 21, 1779, "Correspondence Between Hon. Henry Laurens and His Son, John, 1778–1780," *South Carolina Historical and Genealogical Magazine*, VI (1905), 150.

65. *Abridgment of the Debates of Congress* (February, 1790), I, 210.

66. *Annals of Congress*, 1 Cong., 2 Sess., 1511–12 (March 17, 1790).

67. Morgan, *American Slavery, American Freedom*, 377–78. I am indebted to Eugene D. Genovese for pointing out that Moses I. Finley, *Slavery in Classical Antiquity: Views and Controversies* (Cambridge, Mass., 1969), 52–72, first noted the historic relation of slavery to freedom.

68. "Graham's Defense of Slavery," 651.

69. Jeffrey J. Crow, "Slave Rebelliousness and Social Conflict in North Carolina, 1775 to 1802," *William and Mary Quarterly*, 3rd ser., 37 (1980), 79–102; Sylvia R. Frey, "Between Slavery and Freedom: Virginia Blacks in the American Revolution," *Journal of Southern History*, 49 (1983), 375–98.

70. *Abridgment of the Debates of Congress* (May, 1789), I, 74; *Annals of Congress*, 1 Cong., 2 Sess., 1502 (March 17, 1790), 1513 (March 19, 1790).

71. *Annals of Congress*, 1 Cong., 2 Sess., 1502 (March 17, 1790).

72. *Abridgment of the Debates of Congress* (May, 1789), I, 74.

73. *Annals of Congress*, 1 Cong., 2 Sess., 1508 (March 17, 1790).

74. "Early Proslavery Petitions," 141, 146.

75. *Abridgment of the Debates of Congress* (December, 1806), III, 498.

76. "Early Proslavery Petitions," 142.

77. *Annals of Congress*, 1 Cong., 2 Sess., 1504, 1508 (March 17, 1790). For other assertions of constitutional guarantees see *Abridgment of the Debates of Congress* (February, 1790), I, 209, 210; Smith, *The Pretensions of Thomas Jefferson*, 10.

78. *Annals of Congress*, 4 Cong., 2 Sess., 2015–24 (January 30, 1797); 5 Cong., 1 Sess., 658–70 (November, 1797); 1032–33 (February, 1798).

79. William W. Freehling, "The Founding Fathers and Slavery," *American Historical Review*, 77 (1972), 81–93.

CHAPTER 14

Dependence in the Era of Independence:
The Role of Women in a Republican Society

Elaine F. Crane

> Dependence, surely, is one of the capital evils,
> inflicted on the human species.
> > —Maria Armistead to Jane Armistead,
> > > April 9, 1789

> I am not for quite so much independence.
> > —Elizabeth Drinker,
> > > Diary, April 22, 1796

Only latently were women part of the unfinished agenda of the American Revolution. This is nowhere more evident than in the terminology employed in the title of the chapters in this volume. While several titles include appropriately active words such as *search, quest, pursuit,* or *creating,* as they apply to a particular topic, the relatively more passive word *role* seems more suitable for the chapter on women. This contrast reflects a broad agreement among Revolutionary leaders (and modern historians) about the significance of certain issues confronting the new nation. Some questions, such as the structure of government or Loyalist reintegration, required immediate attention. Others, the future of slavery or the disestablishment of the churches, could be postponed temporarily but not avoided for long. Still others, more theoretical long-range issues of education and even capital punishment, would never be fully resolved and so became part of a never-ending dialogue within American society.

The role of women did not fall into any of these three categories. Because it affected their place in the family, the nature of women's education received some consideration, but beyond that subject few contemporaries seemed to recognize that any special problems applied to women qua women. Thus, in 1764, when James Otis probed the constitutional relationship of women to the body politic, he asked only whether the nature of the governmental compact gave women a right to be consulted in the decision-making process but did not connect consent or suffrage to any specific female-related questions such as their disabilities under the common law. In short, most of the issues raised by later generations of feminists about the status of women never came under serious public discussion during the Revolutionary era. It is therefore scarcely surprising that Revolutionary leaders saw no need to respond to problems that, at least in the public realm, had not yet even been widely perceived, much less defined. As a result, those problems could hardly have been resolved.[1]

Among Revolutionary leaders, only Thomas Paine showed any comprehension of the problems inherent in the position of women on the eve of independence. In his "Occasional Letter on the Female Sex," Paine took a brief look at women around the world and noted that "even in the countries where they may be esteemed most happy [they are] constrained in their desires in the disposal of their goods, robbed of freedom of will by the laws, [are] the slaves of opinion . . . [, and are] surrounded on all sides by judges, who are at once [their] tyrants and their seducers." Although equally applicable to black and white women, Paine's comments referred only to the latter, as did the words of most of his contemporaries. Perhaps more important, even though Paine freely admitted that women and men were equal intellectually, he could not rise above other prejudices of the early modern era concerning women, and those prejudices prevented him from ever advocating equality of status for women. Rather, he insisted both that beauty was "the most essential characteristic" of the female sex and that women were tender, feeble, and the primary instruments for civilizing men whose duties as wives and mothers were "of no less consequence to society" than the functions usually performed by men. But he still relegated women to a separate sphere and never suggested that, even if man, "in all climates, and in all ages," had "been either an insensible husband or an oppressor," the new republic should add those inequities to its agenda of wrongs to be righted. Abigail Adams's famous letter to her husband John indicates that she had read and was convinced by Paine's arguments. How many other women were equally affected by his logic remains to be discovered.[2]

Most other founding fathers proved even less sensitive to women's issues than Paine. Alexander Hamilton, for instance, seems to have thought about the status of women only insofar as they constituted a potentially useful reservoir of labor for the new nation. As the advocate of a future based on manufacturing, Hamilton extolled the benefits of female employment. Farmers, he predicted, would reap additional profits from the increased industry of their wives and daughters, while women in general would be "rendered most useful" and saved from idleness "by manufacturing establishments." The economic writer Tench Coxe warmly supported Hamilton's proposals, adding, with the condescension characteristic of his age, that long hours of employment left few opportunities for vice.[3]

Such schemes held little appeal for Thomas Jefferson. His vision of a society based on agricultural pursuits left little room for an industrial nation, much less one that relied on the labor of women. His philosophy about the role of women in American society was clear, unshakeable, and inegalitarian, and his words seem to have reflected a strong current of national sentiment. Women, according to Jefferson, belonged at home, where they could be protected from and relieved of the burden of heavy labor. "In a civilised country," he declared, "men . . . never expose their wives and children to labour above their force or sex, as long as their own labour can protect them from it." To Jefferson, women were "objects of our pleasure" who were "formed by nature for attentions." Insisting that American women should never meddle in politics as did French women, Jefferson would have totally banished women from the public sphere.[4]

But, although Jefferson believed that it was most appropriate for women to confine themselves to needlework, the society of their husbands, the care of their children, and the arrangements of home and garden, he did recognize that a number of women would be forced to earn incomes outside the home. These unfortunates were best suited to "offices proper for . . . women," such as the needle and food trades or occupations as "housekeepers, housecleaners, and bedmakers." One of his fondest hopes was to domesticate the industrial revolution with small machines for the individual family. On his own estate he provided wheels and looms whereby female servants could supply all domestic textile needs. Because Jefferson was convinced that American women were content with their role, he did not raise questions about their status in American society.[5]

The only male literary figure who seems to have addressed the role of women in a republican society with any sensitivity to the possibility that the status of women might leave something to be desired was the novelist Charles Brockden Brown. Brown's first novel, *Alcuin,* was the most penetrating dialogue in America on women's rights up to that time. Through fictional conversation, Brown explored prevailing attitudes and their effects on women. Through his characters, he lamented not only women's lack of education but also the potentially stifling effects of matrimony. Although the gentleman visiting "Mrs. Carter" engaged in a spirited defense of the status quo, Brown clearly recognized that the institution of marriage enforced submission to husbands and often left women destitute of independent property. As far as the public sphere was concerned, Brown argued through his protagonist that the denial of the vote to women violated "pretensions to equality and liberty" and that it was a "gross abuse" for women to be thus foreclosed from a political voice. The earnest young man in *Alcuin* desired no alteration in the system so long as power was "equitably exercised." For him, it was enough that the happiness of women was "amply consulted" by those who were already in the political arena. Whether Brown's own position was closer to Mrs. Carter's or to that of her companion is difficult to say. Nevertheless, he raised the interrelated issues of justice, equity, and women—in a manner that was unparalleled among his peers.[6]

Women themselves showed little inclination to raise issues affecting their well being. Except for the well-known letter from Abigail Adams to John, female assertiveness seems to have been extremely limited. Ann Willing Bingham, wife of William Bingham (a diplomat and a founder of the Bank of North America), politely but firmly refuted Jefferson's arguments in letters to him, and the essayist and playwright Judith Sargent Murray was outspoken in condemnation of traditional attitudes toward women. But Murray's focus was on educational advancement for women, and she readily conceded that each sex should have its own separate sphere. She left women in charge of "domestick duties" but advocated no expansion of their economic roles outside the household. Murray's most important contribution was in her recognition of the "mortifying consciousness of inferiority" among women, a phenomenon that was visible in many diaries and letters of late eighteenth-century American women. Even Mercy Otis Warren failed to question conventional wisdom about the cult of domesticity.[7]

That there were so few female spokespeople—on women's issues, political issues, or any other contemporary topics for that matter—at a time when men had so much to say on so many different questions is striking. This situation was in sharp contrast to that in contemporary Europe. There were no Olympe de Gouges, Catharine Macaulays, Hannah Mores, or Mary Wollstonecrafts in America. Seventeenth-century America had had its Ann Hutchinson and Anne Bradstreet, but the sharp quills and even sharper wits that were so evident then and would be so again in the early nineteenth century were absent during the Revolutionary era.

There were at least two reasons why scant attention was paid—by either men or women—to the role or status of American women. Although the law recognized women as a monolithic group, they were, in fact, divided by an intellectual and economic class structure that precluded a common bond on the basis of gender alone. Similarly, ethnic and geographic divisions created schisms between blacks and whites, Northerners and Southerners, just as they did for men. Beyond the disabilities imposed by the legal system, there were few issues around which women might have rallied as women. Individual women who lived in both middle-class and upper-class conditions could define their republican roles quite differently, one from another, and they were in turn separated by an insurmountable wall from their female servants or slaves. Quite simply, there is no evidence that most women shared much sense of consciousness of common problems as women, and those who did were foreclosed from action by the broadly shared agreement about the position of women within late eighteenth-century American society.

Second, the Revolution had little meaning for women as women, albeit this is not to say that their role was indistinguishable from that of men. Men were far more likely to engage in actual combat, while women stayed home to mind farms, households, and businesses. But insofar as women participated in the Revolution, they did so not on behalf of themselves as women but on behalf of the families, communities, and societies of which they were a part. There is thus little plausibility to any conception of the Revolution as a watershed for women. Indeed, it can be argued that the whole process by which we have come to understand the Revolution was actually reversed for women. As the new American nation moved toward independence from Great Britain, women remained in a state of submissive dependence. The revolutionary concept of equality and the application of democratic principles as espoused by Thomas Jefferson and others turned out to have far less immediate relevance for women as a group than ιor blacks. During the French Revolution, many people raised and debated questions about women's political role under the banner of *égalité*. Not so in America, where some natural laws were obviously not nearly so universal as they have sometimes been said to be.

The fact is that the status of women in British America had deteriorated considerably over the previous century and a half, and herein lies the most important explanation for their passivity in the Revolutionary era and early republic. The role women would play in the new nation had already been determined by changes in custom, law, economy, and religion between 1607 and 1783. The Revolution only heightened and enhanced the power of conditions that had been long in the making. Far from being the independent people that the revolutionaries extolled, women following the Revolution were as dependent as ever. Their role in the new nation had already been determined by their declining position in colonial society. Hence, an appreciation of their status in the new republican order can only be obtained by examining the changes they had experienced in the earlier era.

For instance, the controversy over the economic character of the new nation in the 1790s had little to do with white women, whose economic position seems to have declined considerably over the colonial period. In particular, the changing demography of colonial America was directly related to the material well-being of many women. In the early seventeenth century, the sex ratio virtually guaranteed a husband for any woman who wanted one. In economic terms, this meant that most women could rely on male income to provide the necessities of life. At the same time, the abundance of land assured real property ownership for most free families, while a scarcity of labor and commodities often made it possible for both married and single women to earn at least a modest income of their own. Over time, however, the sex ratio shifted, and as it did single women grew in number, particularly along the Eastern seaboard and in Bermuda and Barbados.[8]

Concurrently, a declining land supply in older settled areas may have jeopardized the well-being of both men and women. Not only did wives stand to lose if their husbands could not find land or some other means of income, but single women, who stood last in line to receive a share of a finite supply of land, were also threatened. Probate records for Essex County,

Massachusetts, show that the proportion of women owning real property declined during the seventeenth century. Without real property (either left to them by parents or husbands, or purchased on their own), women could not collect rent—an important source of income for people who had few skills that could be translated into cash. Moreover, personal property, which under more expansive economic conditions might have been left to women as a substitute for real property, also ended up in the possession of males—leaving women with still less. The colonial era began and ended with 9 to 10 percent of the total wealth of Essex County being held by women, even though the pool of single women who legally might have held property in their own right increased dramatically. This pattern strongly suggests that women as a group were losing ground economically.[9]

Though more susceptible to misinterpretation than probate documents, tax assessments tell a similar story. Proportionately speaking, men and women paid almost equal shares of the 1687 Boston assessment. That is, 7.8 percent of those assessed were women, and they paid 7.1 percent of total taxes. By contrast, the 1771 tax assessment for Boston suggests that this near equity of assessed wealth had dissipated in the intervening eighty-four years. The percentage of women assessed had dipped only slightly to 7.3 percent, but the proportion of taxable wealth they owned had dropped to 5.7 percent of the total value of assessed property, and they averaged a far smaller contribution than their male counterparts.[10]

Alice Hanson Jones's analysis of the wealth structure of the colonies in 1774 makes clear the economic disparity between women and men on the eve of the Revolution. "On average," she reports, "women wealth holders held distinctly less wealth than men." This was true for all regions and was most strikingly obvious in New England, where the sex ratio had changed most dramatically over the years in favor of women. In the Southern colonies, women held a somewhat greater share of total wealth than did their counterparts in either the middle colonies or New England. Still, their probated wealth was only half that of men. Clearly, the economic status of women all but eliminated any possibility for economic independence for most women. Women's upward mobility—sometimes even their survival—depended largely on marriage. As the Philadelphia Quaker Elizabeth Drinker noted in her long and perceptive diary, "she married . . . to keep her and her children from starving."[11]

Poorhouse records indicate that the Revolutionary years saw an increase in the number of women unable to provide for themselves. While women always outnumbered men as public charges, their proportionate numbers soared as hostilities drew men away from their homes and families. Not all women were placed in economic jeopardy, of course. Some took over farms and businesses and helped turn a potentially adverse situation into a profitable one. Nevertheless, as commerce dwindled, as communities were occupied, as travel was disrupted and property destroyed, many women found their resources greatly strained. By the end of the war, nearly every community must have counted more widows than ever before. Moreover, the one major economic issue related to the era—pension rights for Revolutionary War widows—was never equitably settled.[12]

The seventeenth century may not have been a golden age for white women in the colonies, but it appears to have offered them more economic opportunity than the eighteenth. For much of the eighteenth century, the vast majority of free colonists seem to have enjoyed a rising prosperity, but women shared in this growing affluence largely only as wives of economically successful men and not as independent people. Much later, the British traveler Harriet Martineau noted this paradox in 1837 when she observed that "the prosperity of America is a circumstance unfavourable to women."[13]

The conditions that created this unfavorable situation seem to have been related to the growing sophistication of the American economy. In particular, the proliferation of the wage system may have had particularly detrimental effects. The English and earlier colonial tradition, which coupled labor with room and board, seems to have been more favorable to women than one in which compensation was made solely in wages. Often, wages could not buy the same standard of food and living accommodations that were enjoyed by live-in servants. In addition, as the putting-out system expanded in places like New England, entrepreneurs more and more tended to pay women by the piece rather than for the time expended, an arrangement which in turn limited the amount women could earn. At the same time, an expanding economy created opportunities for investment that required capital and credit. But contractual disabilities under common law rendered credit unavailable to married women, while single women were probably at as much of a disadvantage in borrowing funds as they have been in the twentieth century.

Another reason for the decreasing economic status of women, particularly widows, was that they were less likely to manage estates or control property as the eighteenth century advanced. According to Daniel Scott

Smith's study of Hingham, Massachusetts, before 1720, 27 percent of colonial wives with adult sons were named by their husbands to be sole executrixes of their husband's property. Between 1761 and 1800, only 6 percent were so named. Enough studies of the situation elsewhere have now been completed to show that this development was not atypical. Thus, Joan Gundersen and Gwen Gampel in a study of Virginia have found that after 1750 there was both an increase in the proportion of wills that gave wives no interest in land and that the legacies men left their wives "changed from unencumbered ownership to life interests." Along with "the more frequent use of limitation of property to widowhood," this shift obviously "had great consequence for the freedom of widows to manage their affairs." In short, it discouraged female independence, as did a tendency, manifest in New York after 1750, to reduce the household space a widow could occupy.[14]

The most recent research by Lois Green Carr, David Narrett, Carole Shammas, and Marylynn Salmon suggests two additional trends in the late eighteenth and early nineteenth centuries that prevented more than a handful of women from achieving personal independence. First, children seem to have benefited from a relatively larger share of the estate than they had previously, so that widows became more dependent on their children for support. Second, while daughters as well as sons shared in the distribution of an estate, female children were more likely than their brothers to receive their portions in the form of personal property. This trend seems to have accelerated as the economy of the United States became increasingly commercial and industrial with an ever greater emphasis on liquid—rather than landed—wealth.[15]

This situation worked to the disadvantage of women, because under Anglo-American law husbands obtained total control of personal property, whereas real property brought to marriage was preserved for children. Thus, while the abolition of primogeniture and double shares for eldest sons gave way to equality of distribution among children, young women stood to gain from this egalitarian trend only as femes soles. Eventually, in the middle of the nineteenth century, these inequities would be addressed in the various married women's property acts. But in the immediate post-Revolution decades the economic independence of women suffered a decline. Business and retail trades offered fewer opportunities for women than they had previously, and, according to Gerda Lerner, there were proportionately fewer female storekeepers and businesswomen in the

1830s than there had been earlier. Simultaneously, one task after another began to be performed in the factory rather than in the house, with the result that women had less and less scope to contribute economically to their families. Just as in the earlier period, law and medicine continued to exclude women altogether. As Alice Hanson Jones concludes, "a case could be made that, in the nineteenth century, American women lost rather than gained in such economic control and management of wealth as they possessed in the eighteenth century."[16]

The law did not serve women any better than did the economy in the years following independence. There were no alterations in laws affecting single women. Nor, as Marylynn Salmon has pointed out, were there any "radical changes" in "the basic position of dependency occupied by married women." Despite the fiction of marital unity so eloquently expressed by Sir William Blackstone, American colonial women had long had the right in equity to separate estates. Equity courts (or courts with equity power) were never enthusiastic about this practice. But they did uphold the right of women to marriage settlements that kept their separate property out of the hands of their husbands, not to mention their husband's creditors. For the vast majority of American women, however, the importance of marriage settlements was minimal. If South Carolina is typical, no more than "1–2% of marrying couples created separate estates." Of these, couples from the wealthiest social strata were disproportionately represented. Some colonies, such as Massachusetts, had no equity courts and did not even recognize marriage settlements, and Massachusetts appears to have extended its conservative attitude even after it had granted the common law courts equity jurisdiction in 1818. Similarly, very few marriage settlements were recorded in either Connecticut or Rhode Island.[17]

Those marriage settlements that survive provide yet further evidence of the deteriorating position of women over the years. According to Salmon's careful study, not only was there "a small but steady decline" in the number of women who retained sole management of their own estates between 1730 and 1830, but also women were less likely to secure power to write a will. Between 1730 and 1750, Salmon finds, 62 percent of women who signed marriage settlements declared their ability to write wills. After 1800, however, "fewer than one-third of all femes covert could write wills under the stated terms of their settlements." Both these trends described by Salmon suggest a loss of power. Even if, as Salmon argues, South

Carolina courts consistently upheld the validity of marriage settlements after the Revolution, the balance sheet is still negative: settlements were too few to have much impact, and their provisions were less favorable to women than they had been one hundred years earlier. In addition, because equity itself suffered a decline during the first half of the nineteenth century and access to equity courts thus became more limited, it is possible that marriage settlements became even more rare in the decades following independence than they had been earlier.[18]

The right to a separate estate paralleled the recognition of what was known legally as a separate examination. Of all the legal safeguards available to women, the right to a separate examination by a judge to ensure the willingness of a married woman to part with real property was, at least theoretically, a development in her favor. Of course, the actual benefits of this safeguard may have been slight because, no matter what she said in private to the judge, she subsequently had to return home to face her husband. Moreover, what the law gave with the right hand it took away with the left, and while state legislatures and judges were making the right to a separate estate an accepted feature of equity law, judges increasingly questioned the ability of women to resist pressure from husbands who coveted their wives' property and actually twisted this uncertainty into an excuse for suppressing the small gains that women had made under equity. Thus, Oliver Ellsworth of Connecticut thought that because married women were susceptible "to coercions imperceptible to others" they should not be permitted to make wills at all. Similarly, Chancellor James Kent of New York argued in 1827 that, as married women gained more control over their property, they actually had less and less protection in their property from "that powerful marital influence." If the leading jurists of the new republic continued to assume that women were incapable of independent judgment, that they could not resist coercion from their husbands, and that they needed protection, it is scarcely accurate to suggest that "the [legal] props of patriarchical power were gradually crumbling" in the North.[19]

Dower rights, too, underwent scrutiny from judges and legislators and legal change in the aftermath of independence. As Linda Kerber has pointed out, "the erosion of dower rights was the most important legal development directly affecting the women of the early Republic." Although women in South Carolina *may* have benefited from the exchange of their traditional dower rights for a direct cash payment, and it is true that the absolute right of ownership granted by that state in 1777 offered greater advantages than the limited rights enjoyed previously, nevertheless, dower rights in general seem, as Kerber shows, to have suffered a blow in the new nation that outweighed the few favorable developments. Thus, in the name of equality, the North Carolina legislature abolished entail and simplified the law of property descent in 1784, but, in doing so, it forced widows with more than two children to share equally in any inheritance and thus diminished her traditional right to a one-third allotment. Within a decade, this chink in the wall guarding widows' rights permitted a North Carolina judge to argue that "dower at the common law is abolished."[20]

While judges in other states upheld the concept of dower, the protection it had once afforded married women was chipped away little by little. In some states after the war, widows were denied dower in unimproved lands, and in at least two states the courts ruled that widows could not realize gains on land prices or on the improvement of land. Even in South Carolina where, to some extent, dower provisions had been liberalized in 1777, the demands of creditors took precedence over what had once been the sacred right to thirds. Because of the expansion of commerce and an increasing emphasis upon liquidity, moreover, judges often upheld the claims of creditors against those of widows. According to one study, "widows were effectively denied traditional dower rights in all cases involving creditors."[21]

Divorce laws, likewise, did not automatically improve the status of women. Although some states passed more liberal divorce laws, the number of divorces was still very small during the early years of the republic. Even if women were more likely to sue for divorce during and after the Revolutionary era, the number of women affected by a successful action was so small as to have no effect upon American society as a whole. Women could get divorces in early nineteenth-century New England, but the process was actually longer and more expensive than it had been earlier. Although Pennsylvania liberalized its divorce law as part of the republican experiment in 1785, most other states permitted divorce only by application to the legislature. After the Revolution as before, women thus continued to be dependent upon the gracious acquiescence of male legislators. Although divorce was nearly as difficult in the postwar years as it had been previously, women were not altogether without recourse. Research by Norma Basch suggests that women may have simply walked away from unsuccessful marriages more frequently than they had in the past. If that is true, perhaps a few founding mothers had indeed translated the word "freedom" into something more than the founding fathers had intended for them. But, at the same time, the feasibility of setting up a separate household remained limited by the resources a woman could command, and for many women the only realistic alternatives to an unhappy marriage were poverty, adultery, or bigamy.

If the common law and colonial statutes gave women but small measure of independence in terms of property rights, they placed those women without any claims to property in an especially dependent situation. As colonial population grew and many older communities were faced with growing demands on the public purse, local authorities had to devise policies to combat the rising problem of poverty. They responded with increasingly paternalistic solutions that affected more women than men for the simple reason that there were more poor women than poor men—at least in the North. In the early years of the colonies—indeed, throughout the seventeenth century in most New England communities—the poor were boarded with families who received public stipends for this service. As the number of poor increased during the eighteenth century, however, this arrangement drained the resources of the community. In one community after another, officials decided to house the poor in a central location as a way of cutting costs. Boston opened British America's first almshouse in 1644, and New York had one by 1700. In 1722, the selectmen of Portsmouth, New Hampshire, "voted that all persons that have any Dependence on the Town shall be put into the Almshouse," while in 1749 the freeholders of Salem directed the local overseers of the workhouse "to move all persons there who are wholly maintained by the Town."[22]

Of course, the poor had no more say about whether or not they went into an almshouse than they had about the legislation that, at one stroke of the quill, stripped them of their decision-making power and placed them under the direct control of overseers. Instead of being given money to live independently, they were institutionalized and not permitted to make decisions concerning their own well-being. For poor women, who by custom and tradition were assumed to be dependent on a male provider, the laws governing the poor simply reinforced this assumption by replacing an absent husband with local officials.

Other laws relating to the poor were no more helpful to women.

Husbands who were shown to be less than adequate providers (even when "bred to some good trade") could be placed in the workhouse and given employment suitable to their skills and an account kept of earnings and maintenance costs deducted with any surplus being "applied to the support of their Family in such ways and methods as the Overseers or their Committee shall direct." In short, the overseers had authority to decide how the wife and children should live. Moreover, those people (mostly women) who were institutionalized in Boston remained in the almshouse or workhouse until dismissed by vote of a majority of the overseers. But, once dismissed, the women, more frequently than men, proved to be unable to support their children and left them at the almshouse. By so doing they risked losing their children altogether, because the overseers had authority to bind them out without permission of the parents. Laws governing bastard children also placed women at a greater disadvantage relative to men over the course of the eighteenth century. Earlier, the putative father of a bastard child paid the mother directly for its support. With the establishment of overseers of the poor, however, money was channeled through them to the mother, an arrangement that gave the committee, not the mother, discretionary power over the funds involved.[23]

The legislators of the new nation recognized their obligation to the less fortunate members of American society, including an ever-growing number of women, many of whom had been widowed during the Revolution. But they did not even question, much less repudiate, the assumptions of female dependence, which in turn played no small part in the feminization of poverty described above.

Historians have increasingly taken notice of the concept of the republican mother, first described and most creatively analyzed by Linda Kerber. The role of women as mothers was the one issue relating to gender that was publicly debated in the years following independence. The consequence of this debate was to assign mothers a political role—albeit a narrow and private one—as transmitters of republican values to each succeeding generation. Kerber emphasizes the paradox implicit in the concept of republican motherhood: it legitimized political participation but confined women to a separate sphere; it encouraged female deference at a time when men were shedding their deferential attitudes. In short, as Kerber points out, this new role devised for and accepted and internalized by women tended to reinforce traditional female dependence at the same time that it assigned women a limited political role.[24]

More recently, however, other historians have stressed the extent to which the idea of republican motherhood actually contributed to raise the status of women in the post-Revolutionary era. Some of the new scholarship suggests that this concept represented an advance for women by providing them with an "avenue of power." Even though these historians concede that the concept of republican motherhood contained confining—even stultifying—tendencies, this view is troubling because it pays little attention to anything more than contemporary rhetoric. In particular, it does not consider exactly what a republican mother could do that a colonial mother could not. With a falling birthrate in many areas of the country, more women were probably able to spend more time with each child. But as late as 1830 women could still expect to have six to seven children, so that they were still closely tied to the cycle of birth, nursing, weaning, and pregnancy. Although household chores were elevated to the status of heavenly delights by the eloquence of some (mostly male) pamphleteers, those chores were no less demanding, time-consuming, and burdensome than before. Clearly, the writers of these tracts had never tried simultaneously to cook a meal, sweep a floor, stop a five-year-old from biting her brother, and change a diaper by candlelight.[25]

The fundamental role of the republican mother was to instill a sense of virtue in her republican children, private virtue in both sexes and, most importantly, civic virtue—a desire to promote the common good in the public realm—in her sons. But precisely how this task was accomplished was not made entirely clear by its proponents. Was it to be by constant lectures? A word here and there? And how did these words differ from what a colonial—a pre-republican—mother might have said to her children? Was the desirability of virtue not part of the colonial mother's prescriptions to her children? One might even propose the opposite argument: that the colonial mother had more influence over and more responsibility for shaping her children's morality because she was less likely to share her youngsters with a formal schoolteacher.

If the republican mother was supposed to sacrifice herself to her family, she was in fact doing no more than the colonial mother had done without the lofty ideology of republican motherhood. That in the seventeenth and eighteenth centuries no one asked women to bear moral responsibility for the family does not mean that women did not to a great extent do so.

Female communicants and congregants heavily outnumbered males after 1650, and it is entirely possible that the "primary responsibility for teaching religion gradually shifted to the mother" in the years thereafter and that her supposedly "new" role as guardian of virtue in the 1780s and 1790s simply represented an articulation and codification of what she had been doing for at least a century before. Moral perspectives might have changed somewhat in the intervening years, but it is hard to imagine that colonial women played a smaller role in the moral and spiritual development of their children than did their post-Revolutionary successors.[26]

In all probability, the most important contribution of the ideology of the post-Revolutionary years was to reinforce and justify the idea of separate spheres for women and men, which is tantamount to saying that ideology was beginning to reflect reality. There can be no doubt that this idea was appealing to some women who saw this "new" role as a means of exorcising their own inferiority. But its long-range implications did little to undermine the traditional assumptions that had long sustained and justified female dependence. Rather, it simply made female identity dependent upon a single role that was inextricably linked to gender. As republican fathers became more nearly equal with one another, republican mothers became less nearly equal with the fathers—a situation that became ever more self-perpetuating as time went by. Historians who have seen the articulation of the concept of republican motherhood as a first step toward a fuller political role for women have perhaps misjudged the intentions of its authors. For, considering the publicity accorded to the political activities of women during the French Revolution, the political potential of women was hardly unknown in America, and it is not impossible that at least some exponents extolled republican motherhood as a means of deflecting or containing the ambitions of women for a political role. Certainly, republican motherhood brought suffrage to American women no sooner than its absence enfranchised British women.

Developments in education and religion also affected the lives of women in the new republic. To some extent, widening educational opportunity for women during the early nineteenth century encouraged female independence. Well before the Civil War, the literacy gap between men and women had closed, and women were becoming teachers and writers in far greater numbers than ever before. Nevertheless, the educational system also reinforced the idea of separate spheres, and in so doing confined the use of female intellectual achievements to a few prescribed areas. As Kerber notes, women as educated people able to use that education to think and act independently were threats, rather than assets, to the nation. In the end, of course, education led to female activism and thus to the women's movement. But this was neither the vision of those early nationalists who advocated more and better education for women nor any part of the contemporary agenda for the American Revolution.[27]

The interrelationship among women, religion, and revolution presents much the same picture. By virtue of their disproportionate representation in the churches, women were the most likely conduits through which ministerial exhortations reached those who did not attend regular church services. In the Revolutionary era, the message from much of the rebel pulpit was that a licentious America, brimming with sin, had lost its virtue and that Americans should give up their sinful ways before God abandoned the New Eden forever. To the extent that they carried this message both faithfully and convincingly, American women deserve at least partial credit for persuading their fellow Americans that separation from Britain was in their best interests. Indeed, it is far from ludicrous to suggest that the revolutionary ardor for behavioral reform, to some extent inspired by women, helped to pave the way for the Second Great Awakening and thus contributed to the evangelical fervor of the early nineteenth century and even to the proliferation of female prayer meetings.[28]

If one accepts this line of reasoning, one can then posit a clear and direct relationship among the Revolution, a civil religion expostulated by women, and a heightened concern for morality. Although this sequence of developments may have contributed to increased sensitivity about the moral problems inherent in slavery and poverty, it certainly did not contribute to any significant mitigation of traditional female dependence or provide them with an expanded role in the church. Women remained unable to preach in most churches or in front of mixed audiences. St. Paul's words, that "the women should keep silent in the churches" (1 Cor. 14:34), continued to resound more loudly than the timid voices of those who hesitantly called for some formal decision-making power for women within the church. Followers of Mother Ann Lee, Jemima Wilkinson, and several other radical sects were small in number and hardly a threat to the established churches. Like republican motherhood, the increasing religiosity of women and feminization of the churches served to reinforce the notion of separate spheres and the cult of true womanhood.

The connection between church and state—by all standards an issue raised but not resolved by the Revolution—affected the role of women, albeit indirectly. Mary Beth Norton correctly points out that disestablishment was one of the most important developments in the lives of nineteenth-century American women. Deprived of state funds, churches had to seek other sources of revenue to meet their expenses, not the smallest part of which was occasioned by the need to support indigent women. Churches were only one among many female voluntary organizations that proliferated in the years between the Revolution and the Civil War and provided women with organizational experiences that had not been available to them earlier. Of course, there were negative aspects to volunteerism: by reinforcing the idea that what women do is not worthy of monetary rewards, working without pay contributed little to the upward mobility of women, and the women who worked on behalf of these organizations were, as they have always been, supplicants, who could cajole, preach, reason, and petition, but who had no authority by which they could enforce their wills. Clearly defined, their female roles demanded passivity, and they were almost always dependent upon male acquiescence for the achievement of specific goals. Still, if America's story could be rewritten from the perspective of women's history, surely these efforts of women to achieve through voluntary organizations a more civilized society would stand among women's most important contributions.[29]

Ironically, given the awkwardness of slavery in the era of independence, black women may well have achieved more than white women during these years. Having been more deprived, they of course had more to gain, and by their behavior they emphatically raised the basic question of their own personal liberty. At the same time that gradual emancipation laws provided some slave women a promise of eventual freedom, others fled their slave situations both as individuals and as parts of family groups. Small as was the proportion of these women among the total population of slave women, their success in securing personal autonomy for themselves was nonetheless far more impressive than anything achieved by white women as a result of revolutionary stirrings. Between 1790 and 1810, the number of free blacks in the United States tripled, and a significant proportion were women.[30]

Though black women willingly paid the price of freedom, it may have been a very high price indeed in terms of material comforts, especially if the growing prosperity of the plantation economy had any spillover effects that reached slave cabins. Even if slaves shared only to a small extent in the profits of the Southern staple economy, their value as laborers probably assured them of a minimum allotment of food and clothing. Thus, while no modern analysts will debate the relative merits of freedom and slavery, the economic insecurity of freedom may have created severe problems for many black women. Sharon Harley has described the job discrimination suffered by blacks in the early republic. While free black men had difficulty finding any jobs at all, free black women were probably relegated to work either as domestic servants or washerwomen, and the free black family must have lived barely above the subsistence level.[31]

But the lives of free black women is an area about which we have little concrete information. Whether the cult of republican motherhood had any affect upon the lives of black women; how they supported themselves economically; whether they were assigned only gender-identified jobs; how laws affecting property rights applied to them; whether they had enough property even to make those laws applicable; whether the disestablishment of the churches also fostered voluntary organizations among black women; whether women were as disproportionately represented among church members in black churches as in white; how and to what extent black women educated their children; what kinds of networks developed among free black women to replace the extended families on plantations; how competition for jobs between black and white women affected racial tensions; whether recent findings about the high rate of women heading free black households in Petersburg, Virginia, was common elsewhere—these are all questions that call for further research.[32]

The Revolutionary generation raised few questions concerning the role of women in American society and none at all that addressed the most fundamental conditions affecting their lives. Given prevailing assumptions about the place of women in society, this is scarcely surprising. John Adams expressed the predominant point of view in May 1776 when he linked civil rights with the possession of the property, which presumably conferred independent judgment upon the holder. Although Adams conceded that women were capable of "good judgments" and "independent minds," he did not advocate giving married women the vote because they were not independent people but dependent upon (and presumably swayed by) their husbands in much the same way as were propertyless men upon their employers. But Adams's denial of the vote to single women who did have sufficient property to make them economically independent strongly suggests that Adams, like most other members of his generation, perceived women as unequal for other reasons, primarily because, like children, they were, despite a lot of evidence to the contrary, widely presumed to lack the capacity for competence and independent judgment.[33]

In 1790, an essay in a Boston newspaper perceptively explored the connection between the economic advancement of the nation and the liberty and personal independence of its people. As "the lower class of people" became more financially independent, the author argued, they would "exert *those sentiments of liberty* which are natural to the mind of man." As people needed fewer favors, he suggested, they would not only seek less patronage but also develop "those talents which are useful in the exercise of their employments." As a consequence, he predicted, "the impressions which they received in their former state of dependence [would be] gradually obliterated." The presumption, so succinctly stated by this essayist, that economic development of the new nation would enable lower-class males to begin to shed their deferential habits, obviously did not apply to women. Precisely because their "circumstances" during and after the Revolution demanded that they remain in a subordinate and deferential position to the independent males who presided over American society, they would for many decades remain in a dependent condition within an independent American world.[34]

The phrase "all men are created equal" in the Declaration of Independence at least suggested the possibility of a more equal status for women, and this suggestion was actually taken up by a few articulate women such as Abigail Adams. Ultimately, however, what is most impressive about the American Revolution in regard to women is that so few people of either sex pursued these implications to their ultimate conclusions, that they fought a war in the name of independence without generating any palpable demand for the independence of the more than half the population who remained— by virtue of their gender—so thoroughly dependent upon the male segment of the population.

NOTES

1. James Otis, *The Rights of the British Colonies Asserted and Proved* (Boston, 1764), in Bernard Bailyn, ed., *Pamphlets of the American Revolution 1750–1776* (Cambridge, Mass., 1965), I, 419–22.

2. Presumably they were most happy in the United States. Thomas Paine, "An Occasional Letter on the Female Sex," in Daniel E. Wheeler, ed., *Life and Writings of Thomas Paine* (New York, 1908), II, 187, 190, 192; see Abigail Adams to John Adams, March 31, 1776, in L.H. Butterfield, Marc Friedlaender, and Mary-Jo Kline, eds., *The Book of Abigail and John: Selected Letters of the Adams Family 1762–1784* (Cambridge, Mass., 1975), 121. Paine's essay was originally published in the *Pennsylvania Magazine* in August 1775.

3. Alexander Hamilton, "Report on the Subject of Manufactures," in *Works of Alexander Hamilton* (New York, 1810), 176–177; Samuel Rezneck, "The Rise and Early Development of Industrial Consciousness in the United States 1760–1830," *Journal of Economic and Business History*, 4 (August 1932), 792, 799.

4. "Notes of a Tour into the Southern Parts of France" [March 3, 1787], Thomas Jefferson, in Julian Boyd, ed., *The Papers of Thomas Jefferson* (Princeton, 1950–71), XI, 415; "Notes of a Tour through Holland and the Rhine Valley" [April 19, 1788], Jefferson, *Papers*, XIII, 27.

5. Thomas Jefferson to Anne Willing Bingham, Feb. 7, 1787, in Jefferson, *Papers*, XI, 122–23; "Notes of a Tour into the Southern Parts of France" [May 15, 1787], Jefferson, *Papers*, XI, 446–47; Rezneck, "The Rise . . . of Industrial Consciousness . . . ," 799.

6. Charles Brockden Brown, *Alcuin: A Dialogue* (New York, 1798; New Haven, 1935), 57, 66.

7. Ann Willing Bingham to Thomas Jefferson, June 1, 1787, Jefferson, *Papers*, XI, 392; Judith Sargent Murray, "On the Equality of the Sexes," in *The Massachusetts Magazine* (March 1790), 132–135, (April 1790), 223–226.

8. Even in Virginia where, in the seventeenth century, the sex ratio had been so heavily in favor of men, by 1790, thirteen counties had a surplus of free white women. U.S. Bureau of the Census, *Heads of Families at the First Census of the United States Taken in 1790: Records of the State Enumerations 1782 to 1785, Virginia* (Washington, D.C., 1908).

9. *Probate Records of Essex County, Massachusetts, 1635–1681* (Salem, Mass., 1916–1920), 3 vols., passim; Alice Hanson Jones, *Wealth of a Nation to Be* (New York, 1980), 323.

10. The 1687 assessment is reprinted in *First Report of the Records Commissioners of the City of Boston* (Boston, 1876), 91–133; Bettye H. Pruitt, ed., *The Massachusetts Tax Valuation List of 1771* (Boston, 1978), 2–46.

11. Jones, *Wealth of a Nation to Be*, 323, and Table 7.5, 224; The Diary of Elizabeth Drinker, May 29, 1806, located in manuscript at the Historical Society of Pennsylvania.

12. See, for example, the poorhouse list for Salem, Massachusetts, June 8, 1775, in Public Welfare Dept., vol. 14, 1749–1798, Essex Institute, Salem, Massachusetts; Linda Kerber, *Women of the Republic: Intellect and Ideology in Revolutionary America* (Chapel Hill, N.C., 1980), 92, 287.

13. Harriet Martineau, *Society in America* (London, 1837). Extracts reprinted in Alice S. Rossi, ed., *The Feminist Papers* (New York, 1973), 129.

14. Daniel Scott Smith, "Inheritance and the Position and Orientation of Colonial Women," paper delivered at the Second Berkshire Conference on the History of Women, Oct. 27, 1974, 6, 10, 11, 13, and cited in Joan Hoff Wilson, "The Illusion of Change: Women and the American Revolution," in Alfred F. Young, ed., *The American Revolution* (DeKalb, Ill., 1976), 417; Joan R. Gundersen and Gwen Victor Gampel, "Married Women's Legal Status in Eighteenth-Century New York and Virginia," *William and Mary Quarterly*, 3rd ser., 39 (January 1982), 121, 122, 123.

15. Lois Green Carr, "Women and Inheritance in the Colonial Chesapeake," David E. Narrett, "Patterns of Inheritance, the Status of Women, and Family Life in Colonial

New York," Carole Shammas, "Early American Women and Control Over Capital," Marylynn Salmon, "Republican Sentiment and the Rights of Women in American Law, 1780–1820," papers presented at the United States Capitol Historical Society Conference, March 27–28, 1985: *Women in the Age of the American Revolution.*

16. Gerda Lerner, "The Lady and the Mill Girl: Changes in the Status of Women in the Age of Jackson, 1800–1840," in Nancy F. Cott and Elizabeth F. Pleck, eds., *A Heritage of Her Own* (New York, 1979), 188. For a slight modification of Lerner's thesis see Claudia Goldin, "The Economic Status of Women in the Early Republic: Quantitative Evidence," *Journal of Interdisciplinary History,* 16 (Winter 1986), 375–404; Jones, *Wealth of a Nation to Be,* 325.

17. Marylynn Salmon, "Life, Liberty, and Dower: The Legal Status of Women After the American Revolution," in Carol R. Berkin and Clara M. Lovett, eds., *Women, War, and Revolution* (New York, 1980), 85; Marylynn Salmon, "Women and Property in South Carolina: The Evidence from Marriage Settlements, 1730–1830," *William and Mary Quarterly,* 3rd ser., 39 (Oct. 1982), 663, 664; Marylynn Salmon, paper delivered at the Columbia Seminar on Early American History and Culture, May 10, 1983.

In her study of Petersburg, Virginia, Suzanne Lebsock argues that separate estates were sufficiently numerous to advance the condition of women overall and that their development suggests that overt feminism was unnecessary to improve the status of women. From her own evidence, however, these claims would seem highly problematic. Before 1810, separate estates were almost unheard of in Petersburg. Prior to 1820, there were only thirty-three altogether. The rise in usage thereafter corresponds closely to the rise of feminism in America, and it is not unreasonable to posit the existence of a causal relationship between these two developments. Suzanne Lebsock, *The Free Women of Petersburg: Status and Culture in a Southern Town, 1784–1860* (New York, 1984), 58, 60, 274 n.9.

18. Salmon, "Women and Property," 669, 677.

19. These cases are discussed in Kerber, *Women of the Republic,* 143–44. Mary Beth Norton, "The Evolution of White Women's Experience in Early America," *American Historical Review,* 89(1984), 613.

20. Kerber, *Women of the Republic,* 147.

21. Salmon, "Life, Liberty, and Dower," 93.

22. David Rothman, *The Discovery of the Asylum: Social Order and Disorder in the New Republic* (Boston, 1971), 36, 39. Records of the Town of Portsmouth (N.H.), vol. 2, part 1, 1695–1779, May 28, 1722, FO 59-F-A; March 25, 1751, p. 125A, Portsmouth Public Library, Portsmouth, N.H.; November 17, 1749, Selectmen's Records, Salem, Mass., box 4, p. 53, Essex Institute.

23. "Rules and Orders for the Management of the Workhouse in Salem, Mass.," p. 3, Public Welfare Dept., vol. 14, Essex Institute; Accounts of people who supplied the workhouse in Salem, Mass., 1772–84, Public Welfare Dept., vol. 14; Selectmen's Records, Salem, Mass., passim, Essex Institute; "An Act for Employing and Providing for the Poor of the Town of Boston, May 28, 1735," Overseers of the Poor, box 13, folder 1, Massachusetts Historical Society; Overseers of the Poor, Admissions Book to Almshouse, 1763–1771, box 9, folder 2, Massachusetts Historical Society. Salem, Massachusetts court records, June 26, 1711, vol. marked sessions Dec. 1709 to July 1726; court records March 27, 1694, vol. marked sessions July 1692 to Sept. 1709; court records, Dec. 25, 1744, vol. marked sessions July 1744 to Sept. 1761, Essex Institute, Salem, Mass.

24. Kerber, *Women of the Republic,* 284–285.

25. Nancy Cott, *The Bonds of Womanhood: "Woman's Sphere" in New England, 1780–1835*

(New Haven, 1977), 200; Nancy Woloch, *Women and the American Experience* (New York, 1984), 84–85; Daniel Scott Smith, "Family Limitation, Sexual Control, and Domestic Feminism in Victorian America," in Cott and Pleck, *A Heritage of Her Own*, 223, 231.

26. Gerald F. Moran and Maris A. Vinovskis, "The Puritan Family and Religion: A Critical Reappraisal," in *William and Mary Quarterly*, 3rd ser., 39 (Jan. 1982), 49.

27. Kerber, *Women of the Republic*, 285.

28. On these topics see Rosemary Skinner Keller, "Women, Civil Religion, and the American Revolution," in Rosemary Radford Ruether and Rosemary Skinner Keller, eds., *Women and Religion in America* (San Francisco, 1983), II, 368–80; Martha Tomhave Blauvelt, "Women and Revivalism," in Reuther and Keller, II, 1–9; Robert Bellah, "The Revolution and the Civil Religion," in Jerald C. Brauer, ed., *Religion and the American Revolution* (Philadelphia, 1976), 55–73; Stephen Marini, *Radical Sects of Revolutionary New England* (Cambridge, 1982).

29. Mary Beth Norton, "The Evolution of White Women's Experience," 616; Anne M. Boylan, "Women in Groups: An Analysis of Women's Benevolent Organizations in New York and Boston, 1797–1840," *Journal of American History*, 71(Dec. 1984), 497–523.

30. *Population of the United States in 1860* (Washington, D.C., 1864), 600–01.

31. Sharon Harley, "Northern Black Female Workers: Jacksonian Era," in Sharon Harley and Rosalyn Terborg-Penn, eds., *The Afro-American Woman: Struggles and Images* (Port Washington, N.Y., 1978), 7, 10; Lebsock, *The Free Women of Petersburg*, 97–99, 100–101, 102.

32. Philip D. Morgan, "Black Society in the Low Country, 1760–1810," in Ira Berlin and Ronald Hoffman, eds., *Slavery and Freedom in the Age of the American Revolution* (Charlottesville, Va., 1983), 97; Lebsock, *The Free Women of Petersburg*, 89, 100; "An Account of the Number of Families and Inhabitants of the Town of Newport, 1774," Rhode Island State Archives, Providence, R.I.; Gary Nash, "Forging Freedom: The Emancipation Experience in the Northern Seaport Cities, 1775–1820," in Berlin and Hoffman, *Slavery and Freedom*, 34–35.

33. John Adams to James Sullivan, May 26, 1776, in Robert J. Taylor, ed., *The Papers of John Adams* (Cambridge, Mass., 1979), IV, 211.

34. [Boston] *Independent Chronicle and Universal Advertiser*, Jan. 7, 1790.

CHAPTER 15

On the Bracketing of Blacks and Women in the Same Agenda

Winthrop D. Jordan

Both these chapters, by Sylvia R. Frey on blacks and by Elaine F. Crane on women, agree that the logic of the American Revolution placed these two groups on the agenda for change. Very baldly summarized, they argue that little change took place during or in the immediate wake of that upheaval. This contention strongly implies that the Revolution itself was far from being a complete "success," especially in light of its own ideology.

In the case of blacks, Professor Frey stresses that an important aspect of Revolutionary ideology worked against a change in the status of most blacks. In making this case, she relies on proslavery pronouncements in the South, especially from the 1790s, and their apotheoses of the natural right of property. She suggests quite rightly that Revolutionary ideology provided an ambiguous, perhaps even a dual, legacy for both slaveholders and black Americans.

The controversy with Great Britain had indeed turned on the question whether the government could deprive the people of their property without their consent—taxation without representation. To the extent that slaves were property, slave ownership was a natural right. To the extent that they were also human beings, however, holding blacks as slaves meant violating the equally self-evident natural rights of liberty and even of life. In both law and practice slaves partook of a dual character: they were both persons and property. They could be bought and sold like cattle; but they could also be prosecuted for murder, unlike a horse that kicked someone in the head. This crucial duality found ironically direct recognition in the three-fifths compromise and James Madison's defense of it in *Federalist* No. 54.

Professor Crane's chapter deals much less with ideology, but by implication suggests its failure to alter the status of women. By looking especially at occupational and legal arrangements, she finds that the Revolutionary era saw an actual decline in the position of women, at least of white women. In doing so she comes down hard on one side of a current, ongoing debate about the timing of the rise or fall of women's condition in American history. This debate keeps rearranging peaks and valleys on the landscape of our past. Craine finds declension during the Revolutionary era, a decline that went unchecked by the winds of ideological change. Other historians have found these atmospheric changes to be of central importance. In my opinion, we may have something of a false issue here, one rather like the slightly older debate about the "decline" of Puritanism in the seventeenth century. Perhaps we will have a better picture of the situation if we abandon verticality as an organizing principle and perceptual framework. It is indeed quite possible that the condition of women actually changed without necessarily going up or down on some sort of roller coaster or elevator of twentieth-century creation.

Both chapters raise interesting questions about the relationship between formalized ideology and social change. In the case of blacks, the case is clearer than it is with women, largely because the social condition of being a chattel slave was pretty much an either/or matter, at least at law. The fact of being female was clear enough, but its social implications were a great deal more fuzzy. In gross terms, it is obvious that the Revolution resulted in a momentous alteration in the institution of slavery. It was put on the road to extinction in some states and not in others. This development split the states geographically along a line that was most fundamentally demographic.

The split was not as clear-cut at the time as it appears in retrospect. At the Philadelphia Convention, the Founding Fathers spoke consistently of eight Northern and five Southern states, more often using the terms "commercial" and "plantation." They expected that Delaware, with its historical connections with Pennsylvania, would soon join the ranks of the free states. Events proved them wrong. A more interesting matter remains largely unexplored—that the last holdouts among the slaveholding class in the Northern states were people of Dutch descent. It was their opposition that largely explains why New York and New Jersey lagged some twenty years behind the other Northern states in passing gradual emancipation acts.[1]

Both chapters were originally presented at the same panel, a practice so common that it has become almost customary. The commentator is implicitly enjoined to find some connection between the two. What especially concerns me about this injunction is that it is so commonly issued or self-imposed without adequate assessment of the underlying rationale for lumping blacks and women together in the same admittedly badly leaking boat.

One might ask, then, why these two particular groups are so frequently perceived as occupying an equivalent or at least essentially similar position in American society. Both groups have clearly been "excluded" or "disadvantaged." They also share the common qualities of being relatively discrete and easily identifiable, more so than such groups as the "poor," the "powerless," and the "inarticulate." The latter are certainly real enough, of course, but as human groups they have at least in this country lacked strong conscious cohesion. Indeed, they seem much more like human categories than human groups, deriving what little cohesion they have from the definitions imposed by people who are not themselves members. Blacks and women, as groups, do indeed share, by reason of the clarity of their boundaries, a common ground of relatively easy self-definition.

Yet we should be aware that this commonality between blacks and women is itself an artifact of American culture. In most, or perhaps all, societies, women and men are easily identifiable as members of two distinct groups. In many of the former plantation slave societies of the New World, however, the distinction between whites and blacks was and is not nearly so clear. Indeed we now realize that the United States is unusual in its reliance on a bipolar system of racial classification. The phenomenon of "passing" testifies to the rigidity rather than the fluidity of this system. This mode of classification has meant that white Americans have never been able to consider extending politically formalized rights to some Afro-Americans on the basis of their degree of intermixture with whites. Expansion of rights to blacks has been, just as with women, an all-or-nothing proposition. In this sense, blacks and women have been more alike one another in this country than in most others.

The connections between a racial group and one defined by gender have always been muddied by the fact that the two groups overlap. Professor Crane's chapter takes this overlapping into account, while Professor Frey's does not. This difference between the two seems not to result from divergence in approach. Rather, it reflects certain felt differences between the two groups being considered. American historians reflect these differences in interesting and often unconscious ways. We reveal a very profound discrimination, very possibly an invidious one, when we employ a possessive apostrophe with one group and not the other, when we say "women's" history but not "blacks' " history. We refer to the "women's rights movement," but to the "abolition movement" and the "civil rights movement" *for* (not *of*) Afro-Americans.

This apostrophic treatment of women's history reveals a powerful feeling of possession, a deep-seated sense that the history of women somehow belongs to her, that it is deeply her own. The history of blacks in this country ascribes no such possessiveness, as if the history of black people is somehow, but importantly, not really theirs.

There is another fundamental difference between these two discrete groups, one so obvious that it is easy to overlook. In aggregate, in terms of socialization and daily contact, women in the United States have always interacted face-to-face with men far more frequently and continuously than blacks with whites. Not only this, but the affective content of this interaction has been fundamentally different. No matter how closely intertwined sex and race have been in American culture, the emotional freight involved in the interaction of sexes is not the same as between the two racial groups. There are a host of problems here. They are generic to American history and indeed to interethnic contact throughout the world. They are also pertinent to the American Revolution. The primarily *political* orientation of Revolutionary thought has tended to obscure important distinctions between the two disadvantaged groups. In all of American history, women have never been hyphenated like Afro-Americans or German-Americans, as passengers lodged at some way station along the road to cultural amalgamation. Women are not treated as a descent group. Blacks are.

Just as blacks and women share the quality of being readily identifiable groups, they have long shared many common elements of social, civil, and political disability, even to the point of near helplessness. They have been denied economic power and effectively suppressed into the lower reaches of the occupational scale. By somewhat differing means they have both been deprived of the kind of full control over their private property that has been accorded white adult males. Yet even this control has been marked by an important distinction between the two groups, for blacks never legally owned white women, a fact that should in itself militate against any too-rapid equation of the two disadvantaged groups.

Of course, we have had a great deal of sexual exploitation of both women and blacks. On this matter, the overlapping of the two groups most readily breaks down to create three primary sets of victims: white women, black women, and black men. Here we are often careless when we say that black women have been doubly exploited, for to say that female blacks have been exploited in the two modes of gender and race should not be taken as equivalent to saying that they have been twice as badly exploited. The relationship between the two kinds of exploitation is too complex to be measured by a process of simple addition or multiplication. On this matter one has only to ask which gender of the black population became the primary target of lynch mobs.[2]

All this may seem to take us rather far from the agenda of the American Revolution. Yet the republican ideology of that Revolution had obvious implications for the condition of all Americans, implications that proved to have enormous reverberative power. At the time, two very large social groups were in large measure left out, though today historians seem more certain about how blacks fared than women did.

In the 1830s, two generations after the Revolution, there was a rapid rise in consciousness that these two groups had in fact been excluded from full participation in the republican experiment. This rise and broadening of recognition and consciousness, which was acute in individuals more than it was endemic to the society as a whole, took place at exactly the time that Americans began assuming that their national union was no longer an experiment but a permanent monument to the essence of the progress of self-government in the world. In my opinion, this temporal conjunction of abolition, women's rights, and sense of permanent democratic nationhood was no accident. Furthermore, so far as I can see the matter, these feelings, which were at the same time "issues," lay closer to the heart of Jacksonian America than economic affairs such as the Bank, the Panic, and the Depression. The same cannot be said of the 1890s or 1930s. Yet a similar questioning about the very nature of society, quite apart from its economic arrangements, took place in the 1960s. During that decade, the congruence of the sequence from the rights of blacks to the rights of women with the much earlier one of the 1830s is downright stunning. But as legatees of the Revolutionary inheritance, we are still bound by its ironies, by the fact that it lay uneasily on a cusp concerning political rights. The Revolution rested on a bedrock assumption of majoritarianism. That cusp may in fact have been a part of a long-term modern shift in Western culture from corporate to individual political identity. In our present case, that shift—and one if its peculiarly American forms—may lie half-hidden in the common introductory phrase: ". . . blacks, women, and other minority groups—oh, of course, women aren't actually a minority group, but. . . ." This, in a nation "of, by, and for" "we the people." But of course the ambiguity of this phrase testifies less to the weakness of the Revolutionary agenda than to its sweeping power in the face of social realities.

NOTES

1. It was the case, however, that New York and New Jersey had the highest proportion of blacks of all the Northern states, slightly over 7½ percent of their total populations. Their gradual emancipation acts were passed in 1799 and 1804. Yet Rhode Island, with 6½ percent, had passed its own act in 1784. By the end of that year all other Northern states except New York and New Jersey had (with the possible, mystifying exception of New Hampshire) taken steps to end slavery. Delaware's population was nearly 22 percent black, but two-thirds of them were free at the time of the Convention. Slavery was ended in Delaware by the Thirteenth Amendment, even though the Delaware legislature refused to ratify it.

2. At the conference, several people in the audience objected very strenuously to this disparaging remark about the idea of "double" exploitation. My response was that assessment of human oppression should not become a matter of moral calculus, that exploitation of human beings is and always has been a reality too complex (and far too serious and tragic) for measurement with a pocket calculator.

CHAPTER 16

Creating a Republican Citizenry

Melvin Yazawa

Benjamin Rush virtually gushed with excitement in his letter to his "dear friend" Ebenezer Hazard in 1768. He had visited the houses of Parliament, and his tour of the House of Lords was clearly the emotional highlight of his experiences abroad. The young Pennsylvanian, not quite twenty-three years old, had earlier described his two years of medical study in Edinburgh as the "happiest period of my life," "my halcyon days," but no episode there could rival the intensity of the emotions evoked during his Parliamentary visit. Upon entering the House of Lords, Rush confessed, "I felt as if I walked on sacred ground." The sight of the royal throne in particular left him dumbfounded at first. As he gazed in wonderment he was overcome "with emotions that I cannot describe." "Some time" later the young physician felt compelled to ask the "guide if it was common for strangers to set down upon it." The guide said no, but Rush persisted. Finally, after "importuning him a good deal I prevailed upon him to allow me the liberty. I accordingly advanced towards it and set in it for a considerable time." The experience proved altogether too heady. "When I first got into it, I was seized with a kind of horror which for some time interrupted my ordinary train of thinking." And though he struggled mightily to regain control of his thoughts, the effort was futile: "such a crowd of ideas poured in upon my mind that I can scarcely recollect one of them." The enchantment was complete.

More than three decades and a Revolution separated this incident from the summer of 1800, when Rush began to compose his autobiographical *Travels Through Life*. No longer a young man, but still perhaps every bit as excitable, Rush's account of his experiences abroad in the late 1760s contained a new highlight. Now the incident that ranked above all others was his chance encounter with a fellow medical student at Edinburgh, John Bostock. "In the course of our acquaintance," Bostock "opened his mind fully to me, and declared himself to be an advocate for republican principles." He spoke in "raptures of the character of [Algernon] Sidney," the martyred seventeenth-century English commonwealthman. "Never before had I heard the authority of Kings called in question," Rush declared. "I had been taught to consider them nearly as essential to political order as the Sun is to the order of our solar System." The impact of Bostock's revelation was far-reaching. "For the first moment in my life I now exercised my reason upon the subject of government. I renounced the prejudices of my education upon it." Rush was converted to the belief that "no form of government can be rational but that which is derived from the Suffrages of the people." The effects of this republican conversion were not confined to the arena of politics. Republicanism was an "active truth"; it became a "ferment in my mind." From that moment on, Rush proclaimed, "I . . . suspected error in every thing I had been taught, or believed, and as far as I was able began to try the foundations of my opinions upon many other subjects." Rush's boyish reverence for the "sacred ground" of the House of Lords was of course out of place in this republican reminiscence and, not surprisingly, received no mention. The sacred ground of the *Travels Through Life* was the forest surrounding "Sidney's country house." In these woods, Rush reported reverentially, the great Sidney was "accustomed to meditate when he composed his famous treatise upon government." Much had changed since the 1760s, for Rush as well as for the American public, and a selective memory was of no small benefit in easing the transition.[1]

Rush's experience is valuable for the light it sheds on the problem of civic education in the new republic. Rush was not alone in renouncing the "prejudices" of past education. Indeed, widespread declarations to that effect on the part of the Revolutionaries have led some twentieth-century observers to focus on what they see as an inconsistency in the educational history of the period. Revolutionary expressions of concern seem not to have been accompanied by immediate changes in the institutional fabric of the nation. Thus the statements of the Revolutionaries are dismissed as rhetorical bombast. Real commitment to education, we are led to believe, came only in the course of the nineteenth century, as evidenced in the growth of the public school system in America, and this commitment was due primarily, if not entirely, to the anxiety attendant upon the social changes that characterized the Jacksonian era.

It would be incorrect, however, to dismiss the pronouncements of the Revolutionaries as so much empty rhetoric. After all, there were institutional changes initiated in the wake of independence. Provisions for the creation of new schools, along with reforms in the governance, goals, and curricula of existing establishments, have been detailed in a number of studies.[2] A more revealing shortcoming of the modern critique centers on the problem of perspective and definition. Twentieth-century observers are wont to equate education with schooling; hence they betray a fascination with the institutional manifestations of change. This propensity, firmly rooted in the nineteenth-century search for institutional remedies for societal problems—the "discovery of the asylum"—distorts our appreciation of the significance and impact of the educational commitment of the Revolutionary generation.[3]

We need to begin, then, as the Rush episode indicates, with a broad definition of education; one geared not to the mechanics of reading, writing, and arithmetic, but rather to the dynamics of socialization. Education in this sense is nothing less than the process by which the uninitiated are transformed into full participating members of a given society. Robert Coram, editor of the *Delaware Gazette,* provided as terse an eighteenth-century definition as there is: "Education . . . means the instruction of youth in certain rules of conduct by which they will be enabled to support themselves when they come to age and to know the obligations they are under to that society of which they constitute a part."[4]

By employing this perspective we are able to trace a shift in American education corresponding to the fundamental change in social perceptions that formed an essential part of the Revolution. Colonial education was best suited to an hierarchical society whose members were nevertheless prepared to engage in a great deal of face-to-face interaction. Ideally, the regulating principle underlying these encounters, and therefore the primary social virtue instilled by parents as educators of the first order, was "affection." Not only domestic peace, but also harmony in the larger public world, was dependent upon the dissemination of this basic social virtue. Just as the ligaments of the natural body held it together, the "bonds of affection," by holding the collective body of men together, were the proper ligaments of society. Without such bonds, civil society would amount to nothing more than a multitude of discrete parts.[5]

Two things must be understood before we can fully appreciate the social significance of affection. First, affection, in this eighteenth-century civic context, was a generic term comprising a whole spectrum of delicately balanced dispositions. By the early decades of the nineteenth century the scope of this social virtue had been reduced to sentimentalism and came to describe what Tocqueville identified as "colloquial equality." In pre-Revolutionary America, however, affection signified not merely intimacy, but also such mixed emotions as desire and hatred, hope and anger, joy and grief, and gratitude and pity. Colonial descriptions of the ideal familial order, which, as most writers were quick to point out, was the basis and model for the larger civil society, depended on a complex understanding of affection. The proper affection to be instilled in children was filial fear; that is, a *"loving-feare"* or, as Isaac Ambrose explained, a fear "mixt with *Love*." Dutiful children obeyed parental commands not because they feared the rod but because they feared to appear offensive and undeserving in the eyes of their parents. According to Benjamin Wadsworth, children "fear to offend, grieve, disobey, or displease" their fathers and mothers because such disregard bespoke a base ingratitude that was altogether unnatural. The child's fear could thus be distinguished from the servant's. Filial fear anticipated parental feelings, but servile fear was a response to the master's power to inflict punishment.[6]

Affections were at least as important in rulers as in the ruled. The second point to keep in mind, then, is that the bonds of affection were bonds of mutual dependence. In the familial commonwealth, good order could prevail only if superiors and subordinates alike acted in accordance with the prescriptions of affection. This meant that the social doctrine summarized in the Fifth Commandment was comprehensive. The same social lesson that taught children to treat all superiors as parents—whether in the family, school, church, or state—also taught superiors to consider themselves bound by parental obligations. "The fifth Commandment requireth," readers of the *New England Primer* learned, "preserving the Honour & performing the Duties belonging to every one in their several Places and Relations, as Superiours, Inferiours, or Equals." Under the terms of the Fifth Commandment, parents and children, magistrates and subjects, ministers and church members, rich and poor, well-descended and lowly, talented and not-so-talented, all must recognize that "there are reciprocal Duties incumbent on them," Samuel Willard declared.[7]

If subordinates were obliged to respond with filial fear, superiors were obligated to discharge their responsibilities with parental faithfulness. Good rulers must treat their people "with a fatherly Affection and Tenderness," William Balch asserted. They must be willing to hazard their own interests and welfare for the care and protection of the people. Through such faithfulness, good rulers succeeded in gaining compliance to their commands without the least bit of "murmuring." Disaffected rulers, on the other hand, rulers unable to temper their power with "Humility & Modesty, Sincerity & Self-denial, Diligence & Watchfulness, Justice & Benevolence, Prudence & Constancy" found it impossible to gain the "Hearts" of the people. Afflicted with a "churlish and imperious Manner," these rulers could only hope to perpetuate a servile rather than a filial relationship with their charges.[8]

The bonds of affection were thus as fragile as they were essential to social peace. If affectionate restraints ensured that, as Daniel Lewis asserted, "Rulers will not grasp after *more* Power than properly belongs to them, nor the People be under a Temptation to wish it *less* than it is," then the apparent absence of such restraints must inevitably give rise to constant, acrimonious confrontations. So essential was the affectionate bond that without it the familial commonwealth degenerated into a tyrannical domain. Disaffected superiors, Lewis said, may be properly "look'd upon rather as *Tyrants* than *Fathers*."[9]

All of this suggests that the colonists' education instilled in them a predisposition to interpret filial obedience as a conditional obligation. It was due ultimately, Elnathan Whitman observed, only to superiors who "faithfully discharge the duties of their Places." The bonds of affection being mutual, the "People have their Rights as well as Rulers," Stephen White declared. Thus the divine precept calling for obedience to the commands of an affectionate father was manifestly not the same thing as the "absurd" doctrine demanding unlimited submission to the dictates of an abusive tyrant. Subordinates were bound to submit only to superiors "acting in Character. I say, acting in Character with special Emphasis."[10]

Lessons on familial affection and authority shaped colonial protests against perceived violations of the imperial order in the decade after 1763. As Richard Bland explained in the aftermath of the Stamp Act crisis, it was useless "to search the civil Constitution of *England* for Directions in fixing the proper Connexion between the Colonies and the Mother Kingdom" because the civil constitution alone did not comprehend "what their reciprocal Duties to each other are, and what Obedience is due from the Children to the general Parent." Instead, the Fifth Commandment might be a more appropriate guideline, for, as Oxenbridge Thacher pointed out, "filial" and "parental affections" constituted the bond between England and her American colonies, and these affections determined the extent of their reciprocal duties as well as the nature of colonial obedience. The imperial union must be understood, Joseph Reed concluded, as a "grand FAMILY COMPACT, which must be cemented by every tie of duty, loyalty and affection from the Provinces, and every mark of kind protecting tenderness from the mother country."[11]

The expectations and obligations inherent in the familial paradigm—the familial model of the ideal polity—affected the Revolutionary movement in seemingly contradictory ways. Initially, it magnified the difficulty of desacralizing British moral authority. If, as the paradigm implied, the colonies were in a state of infantile incompetence, then separation might prove fatal. "In the political as well as the natural body," Henry Barry reminded the colonists as late as 1775, the "progressions to independence are gradual and imperceptible, and all uncommon attempts to force either, are usually destructive to their end." Concerns over self-preservation seemed to necessitate the American union with England. But there was more involved, for England had not been merely a protector, she had been a true "nursing mother of her Colonies." The arts and sciences, agriculture and commerce, had been "planted, cherished and encouraged" by this affectionate parent. And because England had acted as "an indulgent and kind mother," Americans felt compelled to respect and obey her with filial fear. During the crises of the 1760s and less frequently during the 1770s, colonial spokesmen continued to allude to the familial pattern of affectionate obligations. "Far be it from the heart of a child essentially to injure a parent," Richard Wells advised.[12]

While the parent-child understanding of the empire retarded the movement toward independence, it eventually enhanced the explanatory power of the "country" ideology which, in turn, increased the moral indignation of the colonists and helped to make separation a categorical imperative. The country ideology was founded on the belief that man, an imperfect being likely to succumb to temptations, existed in a world in which he was constantly tempted by the forces of vice and corruption. In the realm of politics, where some men were necessarily entrusted with public authority, there was a continuing danger that they would attempt to enlarge their powers at the expense of public liberty. The people out of office, therefore, had to ensure that the powers delegated were not abused, and this depended first upon their vigilance in resisting the snares of luxury and indolence, and second upon their ability to detect early signs of corruption in public officers.[13]

For men schooled in this tradition, wary of any deviation from the norm, what could be a surer sign of corruption than the repeated attempts of the mother country to "murder and butcher" its "children . . . that have been so obedient, useful and affectionate"? What could be more alarming than "unnatural Encroachments, from a haughty Parent Country, that should treat them affectionately, even with a tender Guardian Friendship"? Samuel Langdon concluded that the imperial mother must have been impelled by her public vices "to wage a cruel war with its own children in these colonies, only to gratify the lust of power, and the demands of extravagance!" To be sure, added Stephen Hopkins, "natural parents, thro' human frailty, and mistakes about facts and circumstances, sometimes provoke their children to wrath, tho' they tenderly love them, and sincerely desire their good." But repeated encroachments, regardless of their causes, indicated that the moral order of the family was "unhappily changing." The colonists' distress could only be attributed, explained an anonymous writer, to "our Mother's slumbering Delusions" or to her desire to "gratify imperious Lust very wantonly, impoliticly, and even very unnaturally in her advanced years, at the Expence or Ruin of her legitimate Offspring, and hitherto dutiful Children." The colonists had hoped that the grievious imperial situation was caused by the former, but they came increasingly to fear that it proceeded from the latter.[14]

The familial paradigm of the imperial union made it a very special relationship founded on mutual affection. It was a relationship that ought not to be confused with other forms of authority and subordination. Parents were "not *tyrants,* or even *masters,*" Jonathan Mayhew explained, and children were "not *slaves,* or even *servants.*" The colonists, therefore, were to be "humble and respectful, tho' not abject and servile." Imperial policies seemed to be ignoring this crucial distinction and were straining the colonists' assumption that England was attached to them "by the natural ties of a mother country." The irregular restraints placed upon them would inevitably reduce the colonists to slavery, Maurice Moore said, and this was a "situation in which, it is very unnatural to think, a Mother can take pleasure in viewing her Children."[15]

Allegiance and protection, filial fear and parental faithfulness, were largely reciprocal obligations. Once the colonists were convinced that England was purposefully rather than unintentionally violating the familial codes of union, they were encouraged to renounce their dependence and to opt for revolution. "But what do we mean by the American Revolution?" John Adams asked in his famous query to Hezekiah Niles in 1818. "Do we mean the American War?" Clearly not, for the "Revolution was effected before the War commenced. The Revolution was in the Minds and Hearts of the People." In answering his own query, Adams focused on the education and expectations of the colonists. "The People of America had been educated in an habitual Affection for England as their Mother-Country; and while they thought her a kind and tender Parent (erroneously enough, however, for she never was such a Mother), no Affection could be more sincere. But when they found her a cruel Beldam, willing, like Lady Macbeth, to 'dash their Brains out,' it is no Wonder if their filial Affections ceased and were changed into Indignation and horror. This radical Change in the Principles, Opinions, Sentiments and Affections of the People, was the real American Revolution."[16]

Although the process had been emotionally stressful, the Revolutionaries were singularly optimistic once the separation from England had been formalized. By the mid-eighteenth century most of the colonies had developed sufficient social and political competence for self-government. This experiential background, plus their work on the extralegal associations of resistance during the imperial crisis, contrasted sharply with the suggestion that the colonists were still incompetent dependents. If initially they had been compelled to seek independence in response to the actions of a demented imperial mother, Americans were soon convinced that the Revolution had actually restored the order of nature. England, certainly, had behaved unnaturally as a sort of cruel stepmother after the mid-1760s. But no less unnatural, the Revolutionaries were telling themselves after 1776, was their unnecessarily prolonged nursing period. "To know whether it be the interest of this continent to be independent," declared Thomas Paine, "we need only ask this easy simple question: Is it the interest of a man to be a boy all his life?" Americans had been such "dutiful children," filially adopting the prejudices of the parent they considered, as Joseph Buckminster said, "superior in every respect to all others on earth," that they had failed to notice their own accomplishments. That realization came with independence, and thus, David Ramsay noted, the "separation which the Colonists at first dreaded as an evil, they soon gloried in as a national blessing."[17]

It appeared as though the American genius had remained dormant until the bonds of affection with England were severed. Only after Americans had dissociated themselves from the imperial mother and the constraints of the familial paradigm were they able to perceive the latent promise of their condition. While in a state of filial dependence, Jefferson observed, "our minds were circumscribed within narrow limits, by an habitual belief that it was our duty to be subordinate to the mother country in all matters of government, to direct all our labors in subservience to her interests." Jefferson almost surely would have found congenial John Brooks's declaration that independence "awakened all the active powers of the human mind, and seemed to add fresh vigour to its native elasticity." It was clear that, according to David Daggett, a "nation, like an individual, while dependent, will forever be confined in its operations." Because they met with "no real incentives to great exertions," the colonists, like indolent children, had tended to "drag heavily along, contented with a state of mediocrity." Once their filial dependence was ended, Americans were able to change "their mode of thinking and acting."[18]

The most important manifestation of this change in their mode of thinking and acting was the Revolutionaries' commitment to republicanism. In making this commitment, Americans had, as Benjamin Rush's autobiographical account suggested, to renounce the prejudices of their education on the subject. The received wisdom of the eighteenth century cautioned against the adoption of a republican form of government. The Revolutionaries, however, treated conventional antirepublican arguments as potentially irrelevant. In the first place, whenever they contemplated the future of America they were enormously impressed by what they perceived to be the significance of their historical moment. "Experience proves," David Tappan said, "that political bodies, like the animal economy, have periods of infancy, youth, maturity, decay, and dissolution." The American body politic, only recently weaned from the imperial mother, was entering the promising stage of youth. During this time, said Tappan, people were "usually industrious and frugal, simple in their manners, just and kind in their intercourse, active and hardy, united and brave." These admirable, republican virtues were natural responses to the "feeble, exposed and necessitous condition" of the body politic.[19]

Other characteristics of youthful independence were equally encouraging. "Countries, like individuals, commonly enjoy most quiet when they are young," Charles Backus declared. Having freed themselves from the unyielding prejudices of a deteriorating mother country, there was little chance of Americans suffering from deep-seated tensions. Everything in the young body politic, Rush insisted, was in a "plastic-state." Whereas rigid habits confounded all attempts at reform and improvement in old states, such as those of Europe, the situation in America was quite different. Here, Rush said, "everything is new & yielding." America was presently in a "*forming* state."[20]

The Revolutionaries' ready acceptance of republican doctrine was further influenced by their belief in the conjunction of providential and historical currents in the new nation. Not only was the American polity in its forming stage, but it had entered that stage at an especially propitious moment. The disruption of the imperial family was, in this context, a fitting culmination to the advances made under special circumstances and a proper beginning of a new era in the history of mankind. In the newly invigorated Revolutionary imagination, American independence seemed to fall squarely in line with established patterns in the evolution of society and civilization. From time immemorial, Revolutionary spokesmen explained, the "progress of Liberty, of Science and of Empire has been . . . from east to west." The idea of such a transit of civilization was, of course, widely accepted in the eighteenth century, and nowhere more so than among independent Americans. There was welcomed reassurance in the thought that, as David Ramsay said, "true Religion, Literature, Arts, Empire and Riches" were about to settle in "their long and favorite abode in this new western world." The Revolutionaries found added encouragement in their belief that the "glory of empire has been progressive, the last constantly outshining those which were before." By this reckoning, the British empire was superior to its predecessors, and the developing American empire likely to surpass the British.[21]

Implicit in the celebration of the westward transit of civilization was the assumption that all knowledge was cumulative and, therefore, that current generations know more about themselves and universe around them than their forefathers knew. "This empire is commencing," Timothy Dwight observed, "at a period when every species of knowledge, natural and moral, is arrived at a state of perfection, which the world never before saw." Hence the theories and principles of past generations need no longer be humbly accepted. Rather, Americans were positioned freely to examine such ideas and to improve them by experiment or to expose them as absurdities.[22]

The assumed superiority of the American present, complemented by the idea of the plasticity of the body politic in its forming stage, inspired the Revolutionaries to contend that the historical record of past republican failures might be safely ignored because, as Noah Webster put it, no previous nation "was ever in a situation to make the experiment." Even the Greeks and Romans had been handicapped by their relatively crude knowledge of the essentials of republicanism, David Ramsay thought; thus the principles of republican government had "never yet been fairly tried." The advantages of the Americans would enable them to make a fair trial.[23]

Finally, social changes reinforced the Revolutionary commitment to republicanism. Recent studies have shown that by the middle decades of the eighteenth century American society had undergone some fundamental alterations. Demographic conditions, in particular, seemed to have diminished the social space occupied by the family and reduced the scope of paternal authority. Ideals, however, lagged behind this societal transformation. Thus an ever-widening gap between the way men were and the way they thought they ought to be produced anxieties and some tension. What was needed was a new mode of perceiving civil relationships, one not so dependent on the familial model. The republican paradigm constituted a compelling alternative. Indeed, a large part of the appeal of republicanism was that for the Revolutionaries it helped to explain their past experiences as well as to express their hopes for the future. Americans, as colonists, had never been at ease with their departure from the standards of familial harmony. But Americans, as independent Revolutionaries, came to view such departures as milestones in the progression toward republican perfection. The gap between the ideal and the real, which earlier had served as evidence of unfortunate behavior, was now taken as indicative of erroneous standards. The Revolution, as Benjamin Franklin observed, forced men to break the bonds of dependence and, consequently, to "comprehend the character they had assumed."[24]

The new republican character was no longer bound by the prescriptions of affection so central to the familial order. The familial commonwealth placed a premium on the intricacies of mutual dependence. A "Mutual good Affection" was the preferred basis of stability. The commitment to republicanism undermined the social significance of the bonds of affection. Citizens of a republic, by definition, ought to be autonomous in their personal bearing and independent in the exercise of their wills. Dependence of any kind supposedly rendered one susceptible to all sorts of temptations and impositions. Thus dependence was despised by republicans and dependent persons became objects of suspicion because they were easy targets of corruption.[25]

What Rush referred to as the "new complexion" assumed by the "business of education" reflected this change in social perceptions. The "form of government we have assumed," Rush said, "has created a new class of duties to every American." Unlike subjects, citizens had to be prepared for a life of active participation in the affairs of the state. If they ignored their civic duties, or if they participated haphazardly, then the republic was doomed to be a chaotic and temporary experiment.[26]

In 1786 Rush summarized the goals of a "Mode of Education Proper in a Republic":

Let our pupil be taught that he does not belong to himself, but that he is public property. Let him be taught to love his family, but let him be taught, at the same time, that he must forsake, even forget them, when the welfare of his country requires it. He must watch for the state, as if its liberties depended upon his vigilance alone. . . . He must love private life, but he must decline no station, however public or responsible it may be, when called to it by the suffrages of his fellow citizens. He must love popularity, but he must despise it when set in competition with the dictates of his judgment, or the real interest of his country. He must love character, and have a due sense of injuries, but he must be taught to appeal only to the laws of the state, to defend the one, and punish the other. He must love family honor, but he must be taught that neither the rank nor antiquity of his ancestors, can command respect, without personal merit. . . . He must be taught to amass wealth, but it must be only to encrease his power of contributing to the wants and demands of the state. . . . Above all he must love life, and endeavor to acquire as many of its conveniences as possible by industry and economy, but he must be taught that this life "is not his own," when the safety of his country requires it.[27]

In order for the republic to survive, ordinary men had to assume extraordinary responsibilities. Citizens must be attached not to each other, let alone to their selfish interests, but to the republic itself. "Our country includes family, friends and property, and should be preferred to them all," Rush declared. Furthermore, while sacrifices had to be made for the sake of the larger whole, the work was no longer communal. Each citizen learned that he was commissioned individually to fulfill his responsibilities. The virtuous republican had to look after the welfare of the state "as if its liberties depended upon his vigilance *alone*." Above all, he must be independent: loving popularity, but acting only in response to the "dictates of his judgement"; loving family honor, but commanding respect only through "personal merit."[28]

The actual disposition of many Americans in the 1780s made Rush's exegesis of republican education appear especially timely. David Ramsay had written to Rush in 1786 confessing that he was "ashamed" to have to admit that the "morals of the people are so depreciated that legal honesty is all that is aimed at by most people." Ramsay, who in 1778 had produced a euphoric "oration on the advantages of American independence," was now bemoaning the "declension of our public virtue." Other observers of the American scene agreed with Ramsay's assessment. At the very moment when the promise of independence should have been progressing toward full realization, it was in danger of being squandered away. The predicament was a matter of some astonishment: "Could anyone have conceived that a people who had given such signal displays of fortitude and patriotism" during the imperial crisis would "soon, very soon, so far forget their own dignity and interest, as to abuse their liberty, and prostitute it to the vile purposes of licentiousness?" asked John Brooks.[29]

These Revolutionaries, whose version of historical change recapitulated the cyclical imperatives of the organic model of society, knew that the vices of old age inevitably followed the virtues of maturity. Natural sequences of growth and development, sequences essentially beyond the control of man, tended toward decline. The most that one could hope to accomplish in this realm of long-term trends was to forestall the slide into corruption. The complaints voiced by Ramsay and others, however, were rooted in a more immediate apprehension. They feared that the American republic had made unnatural advances toward maturity, and hence that, as David Rittenhouse predicted, "in all probability our fall will be premature." The source of this corruption was to be found in the people themselves, attributable to personal failings rather than to organic processes.[30]

The Revolutionaries addressed this problem in two distinct but related ways. First, they envisioned an arrangement of the institutions of government that might prolong the life of the republic by encouraging the best instincts in the moral character of the people. James Madison presented the most coherent arguments in support of this position. According to Madison, the instability and oppression too often identified with republican governments could be traced back to two sources. The first and "more fatal" source involved the citizenry. Because the founding principle of a republic was that the "majority however composed" must "ultimately give the law," what would keep an impassioned majority from invading the "rights and interests of the minority, or of individuals?" Madison's answer is well known: minority and individual rights would be secured by the heterogeneity of interests encompassed in a large republic. The disarray of contending interests protected private rights because out of this multiplicity the formation of an unjust combination constituting a majority of the whole was highly improbable. Separate factions would lack either a common motive or a convenient opportunity to form a self-interested majority capable of subverting minority rights.[31]

Madison's second, and more frequent if less fatal, source of republican vices was not brought under control by the remedy offered for the first. Indeed, the operation of countervailing passions potentially intensified the absolutist impulses of the government. The variety that curbed the ill-effects of factions by making difficult any sort of concerted action by self-interested groups likewise diminished whatever influence the governed might have in relation to their governors. The people, after discovering the "impossibility of acting together," would realize also the "inefficacy of partial expressions of the public mind." Eventually, in despair, they would be tempted to succumb to a "universal silence and insensibility, leaving the whole government to that *self-directed course,* which, it must be owned, is the natural propensity of every government." Madison, in effect, subscribed to a version of the conventional argument that a large republic might be handicapped by its size. The "more extensive a country, the more insignificant is each individual in his own eyes—This may be unfavorable to liberty."[32]

Madison applied the idea of institutional checks and balances to the paradox of the extended republic: the possibility that the same variety of interests that controlled the effects of factions might also render all concerted action by the citizenry so difficult and the individual so insignificant as to threaten the foundations of liberty. In a "compound republic," such as America, the powers delegated by the sovereign people were not committed to a single level of jurisdiction; on the contrary, they were distributed among multiple levels of the extended state. The different levels jealously controlled one another, while their internal arrangements, subdivisions among "distinct and separate departments," forced them to control themselves. Security against the usurpations of power must, therefore, "increase with the increase of the parts into which the whole can be conveniently formed." The eventual end of these successive reductions was an enhancement of the role of the individual. Through local agencies of the compound republic, the will of an autonomous citizenry might still be ascertained. Rather than becoming silent and insensible, the "private interest of every individual may be a sentinel over the public rights."[33]

The concept of the individual as constitutional sentinel was an arresting one, ideally suited to a republic in which the people, undifferentiated, were sovereign. Requiring none of the higher orders of men to make it work, the system proportionately increased the burden of responsibilities to be assumed by ordinary citizens. Precisely because of this, however, the system promised to increase the civic trustworthiness of the citizen. If in a republic it was true that much was demanded of the individual, it was equally true that a proper institutional arrangement could engender the very qualities of public spiritedness that Montesquieu had identified as "virtue." Even John Adams, whose faith in the moral condition of the American people had waned precipitously in the years after Independence, believed in the efficacy of organizationally induced virtue. The "best republics will be virtuous, and have been so," Adams observed, "but we may hazard a conjecture, that the virtues have been the effect of the well-ordered constitution, rather than the cause." Adams's continued commitment to a republican form of government in the face of his disillusionment with the American character must be attributed at least in part to this belief. In a world where prejudices, passions, and selfish interests predominated, it appeared as though "neither religion . . . nor anything, but a well-ordered and well-balanced government" could encourage men to be just. In his *Defence of the Constitutions* Adams reiterated his conviction that a salutary arrangement of the institutions of government would "always produce" those treasured republican characteristics: patriotism, simplicity, reason, and tranquility. Indeed, Adams explained to Henry Marchant, the moral deterioration they both abhorred in Americans might accurately be attributed to the carelessly assembled constitutions under which the people lived.[34]

Structural improvements in the frame of government formed only one part of the Revolutionaries' response to the threat of the premature demise of the commonwealth. The assemblage of checks and balances included in the compound republic presupposed the possession of a certain amount of knowledge by its citizenry. As a minimum, the people must know enough to recognize their civic duties. Advances in statecraft had to be complemented by a system of education designed, as Benjamin Hichborn said, to render every citizen a *"Soldier, Politician* and *Patriot."*[35]

This political impulse behind the Revolutionary commitment to civic instruction established the priorities of public policy. First, political concerns ensured that republican education would be from its inception self-consciously patriotic. Montesquieu had popularized the argument that "a government is like every thing else: to preserve it we must love it." Monarchies survived over long periods of time and, unfortunately, even despotic governments were often long-lived, because kings and princes were exceedingly fond of the states over which they ruled. For a republic to be durable, the people, upon whose will the commonwealth revolved, had to be similarly disposed. They had to be infused with a "love of the laws and of . . . [their] country." Rush's description of the "new complexion" of education was founded on this notion of civic love. One of the first lessons to be taught to the children of the republic, Rush said, was a "SUPREME REGARD TO THEIR COUNTRY." Family, friends, and property were all dear, to be sure, but none took precedence over "our country." Republican education must aim for a broad diffusion of knowledge about the arts and sciences, Noah Webster agreed, but in the first years of independence it was perhaps even more important to inspire among the citizens an "inviolable attachment to their own country."[36]

That Americans had committed themselves to an historically ephemeral form of government, and that the people-at-large seemed to be evidencing an unsettling decline in moral character, only made the necessity of patriotic education more acute in the eyes of these writers. The effort to nurture a spirit of patriotism in Americans took on the aura of a "moral and religious duty." And well it should, Benjamin Rush declared, because patriotism was a "virtue . . . as necessary for the support of societies as natural affection is for the support of families." Jonathan Mason argued that "Patriotism is essential to the preservation and well being" of republican governments in particular because it encouraged the cultivation of every other social virtue and, in so doing, supported public liberty, security, and happiness. "Without some portion of this generous principle," Mason warned, the "jarring interests" of selfish individuals would lead directly to "anarchy and confusion" and bring about the "ruin and subversion of the state." In fact, the jealousy and discord that had become so alarmingly commonplace since the end of the war stemmed from a "want of true patriotism," Samuel Wales explained. "Some semblances and imitations" of national affection were evident, but "genuine patriotism" had somehow vanished. "Pretended patriots," William Wyche sadly concurred, were responsible for precipitating much of the factional squabbling that plagued public discussions in the 1780s.[37]

It is important to note, as these statements suggest, that the Revolutionaries viewed patriotism as an artificial affection. Unlike the affection that prevailed in the family, which was "natural" because, as John Locke explained, "God hath woven into the Principles of Humane Nature . . . a tenderness for their Off-spring," patriotism had to be inculcated, sometimes forcibly. Furthermore, unlike the familial commonwealth, which was local and personal, the new republic was extensive and impersonal; therefore, the scope of this national affection was vastly larger, temporally as well as geographically, than its earlier social counterpart. As Rush put it, patriotism "comprehends not only the love of our neighbors but of millions of our fellow creatures, not only of the present but of future generations."[38]

The desire to inculcate this intangible and artificial, but nevertheless essential, bond of national affection in the citizenry, strengthened the Revolutionaries' conviction that an "education in our own is to be preferred to an education in a foreign country." The "principle of patriotism," Rush declared, "stands in need of the reinforcement of *prejudice*, and it is well known that our strongest prejudices in favor of our country are formed in the first one and twenty years of our lives." In particular, an "early attachment . . . to the laws and constitution" of the republic would be formed, and the bonds of patriotism thereby tempered, by an American education. Noah Webster, whose efforts at "forming" the American mind were unsurpassed, proposed an educational exercise that was unabashedly patriotic. One of the first lessons in Webster's program of instruction was a kind of political catechism for the American child: "As soon as he opens his lips, he should rehearse the history of his own country; he should lisp the praise of liberty and of those illustrious heroes and statesmen who have wrought a revolution in her favor."[39]

This was, of course, a form of political indoctrination. In the Revolutionary perspective, however, with the fate of the republic resting in the balance, this emphasis on "Americanism" hardly needed to be justified. It was true, Rush acknowledged, that the argument had been made that children ought to be kept free of all prejudices so that "after they arrived at an age in which they are capable of judging for themselves," they might "choose their own principles." If it were possible to "preserve the mind in childhood and youth a perfect blank," then "this plan of education would have more to recommend it, but this we know to be impossible. The human mind runs as naturally into principles as it does after facts." The "young mind cannot be stationary," Simeon Doggett agreed. "As soon as the powers and capacities of the mind begin to unfold, the directing and fostering hand of education" must "turn the mind right"; otherwise, indulgence and bad examples will "turn it wrong."[40]

Thus it was because, in the words of David McClure, "youth is a susceptible age," that a republican catechism was necessary. The "HUMAN MIND bears a strong resemblance to the wild and unmanured garden of nature," declared a Yale commencement speaker in 1772, "which (tho' amidst an infinite profusion of weeds and briers) by diligence and culture becomes fertile, fair and flourishing." This proposition was by no means novel. In 1699 a student orator at the College of William and Mary had employed a similar comparison to support his contention that "Education helps Nature." As a "field w[hi]ch of it Selfe is Barren & brings forth nothing but Bryars & weeds by Manuring & Tillage may be made fertill[,] Soe a vitious disposition by discipline & good Literature may be made vertuous." The analogy of the mind and the garden remained popular with the Revolutionaries, perhaps because it conveyed the need for constant care and cultivation even more strongly than did the traditional simile that likened the mind to wax. "Youth are daily growing up to manhood," Jeremy Belknap cautioned, "and if good principles are not early implanted in their minds, bad ones will assume their place like noxious weeds in a neglected garden." The "active nature" of the child's mind necessitated the "most assiduous care with respect to its earliest stages, lest rank and poisonous weeds spontaneously shoot forth their baneful influence," warned an anonymous writer. "The human mind is like a rich field," Webster concluded, "which, without constant care, will ever be covered with a luxuriant growth of weeds."[41]

If, in other words, an American education did not inspire American youths with an affection for their country and its republican principles, then a foreign education would give rise, like weeds in a neglected garden, to an attachment to a foreign government or to principles foreign to America. George Washington, certainly, was troubled by this prospect. "It has always been a source of serious reflection and sincere regret with me," he confessed, "that the youth of the United States should be sent to foreign countries for the purpose of education. Although there are doubtless many, under these circumstances, who escape the danger of contracting principles unfavorable to republican government, yet we ought to deprecate the hazard attending ardent and susceptible minds, from being too strongly and too early prepossessed in favor of other political systems, before they are capable of appreciating their own." If youths were sent abroad "before their minds were formed," or before they had "imbibed any adequate ideas of the happiness" engendered by the republican form of government, Washington recorded in his will, they adopted "too frequently, not only habits of dissipation & extravagance, but principles unfriendly to Republican Governm[en]t . . . which, thereafter are rarely overcome."[42]

Noah Webster was even more direct in his pronouncement that "an attachment to a *foreign* government, or rather a want of attachment to our *own*, is the natural effect of a residence abroad during the period of youth." Nearly all, "ninety-nine persons of a hundred," who spend these formative years in a foreign country develop a preference for its people, manners, and laws, Webster declared. Moreover, because the impressions received during this critical period usually lasted a lifetime, it was a matter of "infinite importance that those who direct the councils of a nation should be educated in that nation." This did not mean that citizens must restrict their acquaintances to their own country. Such provincialism was contrary to the spirit of the Revolution. What it did mean, however, was that "their first ideas, attachments, and habits should be acquired in the country which they are to govern and defend."[43]

In a very real sense, this notion of patriotism, and of the prejudice needed to reinforce patriotic principles, were merely extensions of those unseemly and unrepublican passions, pride and selfishness. Individual vices, however, did not always translate into corresponding national vices. "There is indeed such a thing as a predilection for *one's own* country . . . which, although it savours of prejudice, is the basis of patriotism," assured one contributor to the *Columbian Magazine*. "This, so far from being reprehensible, is an exalted virtue." It was not prejudice proper, or a "preference . . . founded on real merit and superior excellence," but rather "*ill-founded* prejudice" that had to be eliminated. Benjamin Rush endorsed this distinction. "Prejudices are of two kinds, true and false," he argued, and "in a world where *false* prejudices do so much mischief, it would discover great weakness not to oppose them, by such as are *true*." A well-founded preference, one which promoted the public good and opposed error, was, Jonathan Mason observed, a "noble passion." So noble in fact was this patriotic zeal, Rush added, that "even our Savior himself gives a sanction to this virtue." After all, the Savior as a true patriot had "confined his miracles and gospel at first to his own country."[44]

If the Revolutionaries seemed preoccupied with the task of inculcating patriotism it was also because they believed that in the monarchical world of the eighteenth century, the rather solitary American republic had a special need for a patriotic citizenry. "While we are conversant with the people of other nations, and are visited by men who hold by inheritance, or by indefeasible grant, high offices, to which large emoluments are annexed, we are not to feel ourselves as inferior to them," advised James Sullivan. "There is a kind of republican pride, that must be cherished in our minds, if we mean to support a free government."[45]

The political significance of education in the republic affected national priorities in a second way. "Wisdom and knowledge, as well as virtue, diffused generally among the body of the people, being necessary for the preservation of their rights and liberties," declared the Massachusetts Constitution of 1780, it is the "duty of legislatures and magistrates" to extend the "opportunities and advantages of education in the various parts of the country." This theme, that it was a solemn civil duty of the state to supervise and expand the realm of education, was a favorite among the Revolutionaries. Circumstances not only justified, they dictated the "establishment of a system which shall place under a control, independent of and superior to parental authority, the education of children," Samuel Harrison Smith declared. The inculcation of knowledge was "so momentously important," with consequences directly related to the fate of the republic, that it "must not be left to the negligence of individuals." The commonwealth, Robert Coram asserted, could not afford to trust education to the "caprice or negligence of parents." Education, an anonymous essayist noted, must be made "wholly a public concern."[46]

In addition to the desire to minimize the possible ill-effects of parental negligence, this sentiment for making the student "public property" was supported by the Revolutionaries' understanding of the life of the mind. It was widely acknowledged, as Rush remarked, that "first impressions upon the mind are the most durable." Indeed, Smith exclaimed, "first impressions are almost omnipotent." This meant that the "first great object of a liberal system of education should be the admission into the young mind of such ideas only as are either absolutely true or in the highest degree probable; and the cautious exclusion of all error." It also meant, said Rush, that the moral character of men and the moral fiber of the republic were formed in nurseries, and by women because the "*first* impressions upon the minds of children are generally derived from the women." As Smith put it, the "virtue or the vice of an individual, the happiness or the misery of a family, the glory or the infamy of a nation, have had their sources in the cradle, over which the prejudices of a nurse or a mother have presided." "Mothers and school-masters plant the seeds of nearly all the good and evil which exist in our world," Rush emphasized. If, therefore, American mothers did not "concur in all our plans of education for young men . . . no laws will render them effectual."[47]

A partial solution to this predicament was obvious: because mothers played such a crucial role in forming the dispositions of children and were thus instrumental in "controlling the manners of a nation," women should be qualified for this purpose. Noah Webster, who believed that the "only way to make good citizens" was to "nourish them from infancy," argued that in constructing a truly effective system of education the "female sex" must "claim no inconsiderable share of our attention." Moreover, the "usual branches of female education" were no longer adequate. Music, drawing, dancing, and household economics had to be complemented with studies that would enable women to "implant in the tender mind such sentiments of virtue, propriety, and dignity as are suited to the freedom of our governments." Republican mothers must, Rush insisted, be qualified to a certain degree to instruct "their sons in the principles of liberty and government." In order for them to do this, some of the conventional subjects taught to women had to be supplanted by concentrations of "history, philosophy, poetry, and the numerous moral essays." This substitution, Rush thought, was suited to the state of American society. It was essential for a republican system of education to include a "Peculiar mode of education proper for WOMEN in a republic."[48]

But female education was not a sufficient guarantee against the introduction of error into the young mind. It was still the "duty" of the state to "coerce" the education of all children. Unless education was handled by public agencies, there would always be the danger that private vices would become "as hereditary as titles." "Error is never more dangerous than in the mouth of a parent," Samuel Harrison Smith explained, because children customarily accepted without question the opinions of their parents. Ill-founded prejudices become hereditary simply "by the mechanical adoption of parental error or vice." A publicly supervised system "remote from parental influence" was best because it would encourage the exercise and development of the mental faculties of children and remove them "from an *entire* dependence on . . . [their] parents." This argument alone was a powerful motive for republicans who distrusted all forms of dependence. "Above every other consideration," Smith said, the "spirit of independent reflection and conduct" which it inspired "must give an undeniable ascendancy to the public over the private plan" of education in the republic. Ultimately, the Revolutionaries reversed the earlier colonial priorities of familial and civil responsibilities. The colonists had viewed public intrusion into the realm of parental obligations in education as a matter of last resort; the Revolutionaries came to accept it as a matter of first resort.[49]

The very idea of an educational system independent of and superior to parental authority was new. Under the old familial paradigm such a prospect was unthinkable, if only because of the fusion of civil and domestic concerns. With the establishment of the republic, civil authority could no longer be viewed as parental authority writ large. As a result, the Revolutionaries had to posit conceptual distinctions that once were unnecessary. The republican commitment thus reflected and contributed to the diminution of the social space occupied by the family.[50]

The Revolution and Revolutionary conception of the requirements of republican citizenship thus had important consequences in the history of American education. If the expansion of the public school system in the nineteenth century was a response to social change, it was nevertheless an extension of the priorities established during the Revolutionary era. The emphasis on public resources that characterized the antebellum educational reform movement and the "garrulous patriotism" that Tocqueville found so prevalent and so wearisome among Jacksonian Americans were rooted in the political imperatives of republican theory.

NOTES

1. Rush to Ebenezer Hazard, October 22, 1768, in L.H. Butterfield, ed., *Letters of Benjamin Rush*, 2 vols. (Princeton, 1951), I, 68; George W. Corner, ed., *The Autobiography of Benjamin Rush: His 'Travels Through Life' together with His Commonplace Book, 1789–1813* (Princeton, 1948), 45–46.

2. See Lawrence Cremin, *American Education: The Colonial Experience, 1607–1783* (New York, 1970); Howard Miller, *The Revolutionary College: American Presbyterian Higher Education, 1707–1783* (New York, 1976); David C. Humphrey, *From King's College to Columbia, 1746–1800* (New York, 1976); David Wendall Robson, *Educating Republicans: The College in the Era of the American Revolution, 1750–1800* (Westport, Conn., 1985); Phyllis Vine Erenberg, "Change and Continuity: Values in American Higher Education, 1750–1800" (Ph.D. diss., University of Michigan, 1974); Francis L. Broderick, "Pulpit, Physics, and Politics: The Curriculum of the College of New Jersey, 1746–1794," *William and Mary Quarterly*, 3rd ser., 6 (1949), 42–68; Robert Polk Thomson, "The Reform of the College of William and Mary, 1763–1780," *Proceedings of the American Philosophical Society*, 115 (1971), 187–213; Steven J. Novak, *The Rights of Youth: American Colleges and Student Revolt, 1798–1815* (Cambridge, Mass., 1977); David F. Allmendinger, Jr., *Paupers and Scholars: The Transformation of Student Life in Nineteenth-Century New England* (New York, 1975); Robert Middlekauff, *Ancients and Axioms: Secondary Education in Eighteenth-Century New England* (New Haven, 1963).

3. David J. Rothman, *The Discovery of the Asylum: Social Order and Disorder in the New Republic* (Boston, 1971).

4. Robert Coram, *Political Inquiries: To Which is Added, a Plan for the General Establishment of Schools* (Wilmington, 1791), in Frederick Rudolph, ed., *Essays on Education in the Early Republic* (Cambridge, Mass., 1965), 82. Bernard Bailyn first suggested the broad approach to the history of education in *Education in the Forming of American Society* (Chapel Hill, N.C., 1960); see also Robert Dawidoff, *The Education of John Randolph* (New York, 1979), for an intriguing application.

5. For a more detailed discussion of these ideas see Melvin Yazawa, *From Colonies to Commonwealth: Familial Ideology and the Beginnings of the American Republic* (Baltimore, 1985), chaps. 1 and 2.

6. William Gouge, *Of Domesticall Duties* (1622; Amsterdam and Norwood, N.J., 1976), 428–30; Isaac Ambrose, *The Well-Ordered Family* (Boston, 1762), 23; Benjamin Wadsworth, *The Well-Ordered Family* (Boston, 1712), 55; Samuel Willard, *A Compleat Body of Divinity* (1726; New York, 1969), 607. Tocqueville's discussion of the "intimate" and affectionate "democratic family" appears in John Stuart Mill, ed., *Democracy in America*, 2 vols. (New York, 1961), II, 229–36. See also Yazawa, *From Colonies to Commonwealth*, chaps. 1 and 2.

7. John Cotton, *Spiritual Milk for Boston Babes* (1656), in Robert H. Bremner, et al., eds., *Children and Youth in America: A Documentary History*, 2 vols. (Cambridge, Mass., 1970), I, 32; "Shorter Catechism" in Paul Leicester Ford, ed., *The New England Primer* (New York, 1962); Willard, *Compleat Body of Divinity*, 600, 647–51.

8. William Balch, *A Publick Spirit . . . Recommended to Rulers* (Boston, 1749), 21; Daniel Lewis, *Good Rulers the Fathers of Their People* (Boston, 1748), 13, 15, 19, 21–22, 24; Nathaniel Chauncey, *The Faithful Ruler Described and Excited* (New London, Conn., 1734), 8, 9, 26; John Barnard, *A Call to Parents and Children, or, the Great Concern of Parents; and the Important Duty of Children* (Boston, 1737), 34.

9. Lewis, *Good Rulers the Fathers*, 14, 21, 23.

10. Elnathan Whitman, *The Character and Qualifications of Good Rulers* (New London, Conn., 1745), 29; Stephen White, *Civil Rulers Gods by Office, and the Duties of Such Considered* (New London, Conn., 1763), 21; Nathaniel Appleton, *The Great Blessing of Good Rulers* (Boston, 1742), 58.

11. Richard Bland, *An Inquiry into the Rights of the British Colonies* (Williamsburg, Va., 1766), 13; [Oxenbridge Thacher], *The Sentiments of a British American* (Boston, 1764), in Bernard Bailyn, ed., *Pamphlets of the American Revolution* (Cambridge, Mass., 1965), 497–98; [Joseph Reed], *Four Dissertations on the Reciprocal Advantages of a Perpetual Union Between Great-Britain and Her American Colonies* (Philadelphia, 1766), diss. 3, 98. John Morgan, Stephen Watts, and Francis Hopkinson composed the first, second, and fourth essays.

12. [Henry Barry], *The Advantages Which America Derives from Her Commerce, Connexion and Dependence on Britain* (Boston, 1775), 4, 8; [Reed], *Four Dissertations*, 99; Isaac Hunt, *The Political Family: Or a Discourse, Pointing Out the Reciprocal Advantages* (Philadelphia, 1775), 13; [Richard Wells], *A Few Political Reflections Submitted* (Philadelphia, 1774), 10. See also Edwin G. Burrows and Michael Wallace, "The American Revolution: The Ideology and Psychology of National Liberation," *Perspectives in American History*, VI (1972), 167–306.

13. On the "country" ideology, see J.G.A. Pocock, "Machiavelli, Harrington, and English Political Ideologies in the Eighteenth Century," and "Civic Humanism and Its Role in Anglo-American Thought," both in *Politics, Language and Time: Essays on Political Thought and History* (New York, 1971), 80–147.

14. John Carmichael, *A Self-Defensive War Lawful* (Lancaster, 1775), 24–25; [Anon.], *Some Observations of Consequence . . . Occasioned by the Stamp-Tax* (Philadelphia, 1768), 11, 44, 48; Samuel Langdon, *Government Corrupted By Vice, and Recovered by Righteousness* (Watertown, 1775), 19; Stephen Hopkins, *The Rights of Colonies Examined* (Providence, 1765), in Bernard Bailyn, ed., *Pamphlets of the American Revolution*, 512.

15. [Anon.], *Some Observations of Consequence*, 46; Jonathan Mayhew, *The Snare Broken* (Boston, 1766), 25; John Morgan, *Four Dissertations* (Philadelphia, 1766), 25–26; Maurice Moore, *The Justice and Polity of Taxing the American Colonies* (Wilmington, 1765), 16.

16. John Adams to Hezekiah Niles, February 13, 1818, ed. by L.H. Butterfield, in Daniel Boorstin, ed., *An American Primer* (Chicago, 1966), 229–30.

17. Thomas Paine, "The Crisis III," in Philip S. Foner, ed., *The Complete Writings of Thomas Paine*, 2 vols. (New York, 1945), I, 78–79; Joseph Buckminster, *A Discourse Delivered . . . After the Ratification of a Treaty of Peace* (Portsmouth, 1784), 7; David Ramsay, *The History of the American Revolution*, 2 vols. (London, 1793), I, 345.

18. Jefferson, "Autobiography," in Paul Leicester Ford, ed., *The Writings of Thomas Jefferson*, I (1892), 5; John Brooks, *An Oration, Delivered to the Society of Cincinnati* (Boston, 1787), 4; James Campbell, *An Oration, in Commemoration of . . . Independence* (Philadelphia, 1787), 12; David Daggett, *An Oration Pronounced . . . in the City of New-Haven* (New Haven, 1787), 8.

19. David Tappan, *A Discourse, Delivered . . . Brattle-Street* (Boston, 1798), 18–19; also Joseph Lathrop, *National Happiness, Illustrated in a Sermon* (Springfield, 1795), 7; Thomas Barnard, *A Sermon . . . of National Thanksgiving* (Salem, 1795), 21–23.

20. Charles Backus, *A Sermon Preached in Long-Meadow* (Springfield, 1788), 9; Rush to Charles Nisbet, December 5, 1783; Rush to John Howard, October 14, 1789, in Butter-

field, ed., *Letters of Rush,* I, 315–16, 528; Rush to William Peterkin, November 27, 1784, Butterfield, ed., "Further Letters of Benjamin Rush," *Pennsylvania Magazine of History and Biography,* LXXVIII (1954), 26, 27.

21. Samuel Stillman, *An Oration, Delivered . . . Anniversary of American Independence* (Boston, 1789), 29–30; Ramsay, *Oration on the Advantages of American Independence,* in Robert L. Brunhouse, ed., *David Ramsay, 1749–1815: Selections from His Writings,* American Philosophical Society *Transactions,* 55 (1965), 190; David McClure, *An Oration on the Advantages of an Early Education* (Exeter, 1783), 16; John Trumbull, *An Elegy of the Times,* 12; [Timothy Dwight], *A Valedictory Address* (New Haven, 1776), 13–14.

22. [Dwight], *Valedictory Address,* 12–13; also Backus, *Sermon Preached in Long-Meadow,* 12; William Pierce, *An Oration Delivered at Christ Church* (Savannah, 1788), 5–7; Joel Barlow, *An Oration Delivered . . . at the Meeting of the Cincinnati* (Hartford, 1787), 4; Noah Webster, *Sketches of American Policy,* Harry R. Warfel, ed. (New York, 1937), 23.

23. Ramsay, *Oration on the Advantages of American Independence,* 189; Webster, *Sketches of American Policy,* 11.

24. The most suggestive account of the possible links between the evolution of the family and the commitment to Revolutionary politics is in Philip J. Greven, *Four Generations: Population, Land, and Family in Colonial Andover, Massachusetts* (Ithaca, 1970), 222–58, 279–82. On the gap between ideals and reality, see Jack P. Greene, "Search for Identity: An Interpretation of the Meaning of Selected Patterns of Social Response in Eighteenth-Century America," *Journal of Social History,* III (1970), 189–220; Bernard Bailyn, "Political Experience and Enlightenment Ideas in Eighteenth-Century America," *American Historical Review,* LXVII (1962), 339–51.

25. See Pocock, "Machiavelli, Harrington and English Political Ideologies," and "Civic Humanism and Its Role in Anglo-American Thought."

26. Rush, *Thoughts Upon the Mode of Education Proper in a Republic* (Philadelphia, 1786), in Rudolph, ed., *Essays on Education,* 9.

27. Ibid., 14–15.

28. Ibid., 14–15. See Yazawa, *From Colonies to Commonwealth,* chap. 7 for an extended discussion of this idea.

29. Ramsay to Rush, August 6, 1786, in Brunhouse, ed., *Ramsay Selections,* 105; Brooks, *Oration Delivered to the Cincinnati,* 7.

30. David Rittenhouse, *An Oration, Delivered . . . Before the American Philosophical Society* (Philadelphia, 1775), 20. On the cyclical imperatives of the organic model, see Stow Persons, "The Cyclical Theory of History in Eighteenth-Century America," *American Quarterly,* 6 (1954), 147–63; and Drew McCoy, *The Elusive Republic: Political Economy in Jeffersonian America* (Chapel Hill, N.C., 1980).

31. Madison, "Vices of the Political System of the United States," in Gaillard Hunt, ed., *The Writings of James Madison,* 9 vols. (New York, 1900–10), II, 366–69; Alexander Hamilton, James Madison, and John Jay, *The Federalist,* Benjamin F. Wright, ed. (Cambridge, Mass., 1961), 129–36, 355–59; *National Gazette,* January 23, 1792, in Hunt, ed., *Writings of Madison,* VI, 86; Madison to Jefferson, October 24, 1787, ibid., V, 27–32. The best short treatment of the Madisonian synthesis is Douglass Adair, "That Politics May Be Reduced to a Science: David Hume, James Madison, and the Tenth Federalist," *Huntington Library Quarterly,* XX (1957), 343–60.

32. *National Gazette,* December 5, 1791, December 19, 1791, in Hunt, ed., *Writings of Madison,* VI, 67–69, 70.

33. *National Gazette*, December 5, 1791, February 6, 1792, in Hunt, ed., *Writings of Madison*, VI, 67, 91–93; Wright, ed., *Federalist*, 330, 356, 357–58.
34. John Adams to Zabdiel Adams, June 21, 1776, in Charles Francis Adams, ed., *The Works of John Adams*, 10 vols. (Boston, 1850–56), IX, 401; Adams to Rush, August 28, 1811, ibid., IX, 636; Adams, *Defence of the Constitutions*, ibid., VI, 219; IV, 521, 556–58; V, 29, 289–90; Adams to Jefferson, December 18, 1819, ibid., X, 386; Adams, *Discourses on Davila*, ibid., VI, 263; Adams to Henry Marchant, August 18, 1789, ibid., IX, 560.
35. Benjamin Hichborn, *An Oration, Delivered July 5th, 1784* (Boston, 1784), 8.
36. Montesquieu, *The Spirit of the Laws*, Franz Neumann, ed., Thomas Nugent, trans. (New York, 1949), book IV, 34; Rush, *Mode of Education Proper in a Republic*, 14–15.
37. [Rush], "To His Countrymen: On Patriotism," from the *Pennsylvania Journal*, 20 October 1773, in Butterfield, ed., *Letters of Rush*, I, 83; Jonathan Mason, "Oration Delivered at Boston, March 6, 1780," in Hezekiah Niles, ed., *Principles and Acts of the Revolution in America* (New York, 1876), 42; Samuel Wales, *The Dangers of Our National Prosperity; and the Way to Avoid Them* (Hartford, 1785), 19–20; William Wyche, *Party Spirit: An Oration to the Horanian Literary Society* (New York, 1794), 12.
38. John Locke, *Two Treatises of Government*, Peter Laslett, ed. (New York, 1963), 355; [Rush], "On Patriotism," 83.
39. Rush, *Mode of Education Proper in a Republic*, 9, 10; Webster, *On the Education of Youth in America* (Boston, 1790), in Rudolph, ed., *Essays on Education*, 45, 68.
40. Rush, *Mode of Education Proper in a Republic*, 11; Simeon Doggett, *A Discourse on Education, Delivered at the Dedication and Opening of Bristol Academy* (New Bedford, 1797), in Rudolph, ed., *Essays on Education*, 157–58.
41. McClure, *Oration on the Advantages of an Early Education*, 13; [Anon.], *An Essay on Education; Delivered at the Public Commencement, at Yale College* (New Haven, 1772), 3; "Speeches of Students of the College of William and Mary Delivered May 1, 1699," *William and Mary Quarterly*, 2nd ser., X (1930), 324–25; Jeremy Belknap, *An Election Sermon, Preached Before the General Court of New-Hampshire* (Portsmouth, 1785), 22; Philanthropedia [pseud.], "An Essay on Education," *Columbian Magazine*, May 1789, 296–97.
42. Washington to the Commissioners of the Federal District, January 28, 1795, in Edgar W. Knight, ed., *A Documentary History of Education in the South Before 1860*, 5 vols. (Chapel Hill, N.C., 1949–53), II, 17; Extract from Washington's will, ibid., 25; Washington to Gov. Brooke of Virginia, 6 March 1795, quoted in Edgar W. Knight, "Early Opposition to the Education of American Children Abroad," *The Educational Forum*, XI (1947), 203.
43. Webster, *Education of Youth in America*, 73, 72, 76.
44. "Y.Z.," *Columbian Magazine*, September 1786, 12; Rush, "The Bible As a School Book," in Dagobert D. Runes, ed., *The Selected Writings of Benjamin Rush* (New York, 1947), 118; Mason, "Oration Delivered at Boston," 42; Rush, "On Patriotism," 83.
45. James Sullivan, *Observations upon the Government of the United States of America* (Boston, 1791), 52.
46. "Constitution or Form of Government for the Commonwealth of Massachusetts" (1780), chap. V, section II, in Robert J. Taylor, ed., *Massachusetts, Colony to Commonwealth: Documents on the Formation of Its Constitution, 1775–1780* (Chapel Hill, N.C., 1961), 142–43; Samuel Harrison Smith, *Remarks on Education: Illustrating the Close Connection*

Between Virtue and Wisdom (Philadelphia, 1798), in Rudolph, ed., *Essays on Education*, 210, 190; Coram, *Political Inquiries*, 113; [Anon.], "Concerning Education in Public Schools," ms., American Philosophical Society Library.

47. Rush, *Mode of Education Proper in a Republic*, 14, 13, 22, 21; Smith, *Remarks on Education*, 192–93; Rush, "The Amusements and Punishments Which Are Proper for Schools," in Runes, ed., *Writings of Rush*, 114.

48. Webster, *Education of Youth in America*, 69, 68, 71; Rush, *Thoughts upon Female Education*, in Rudolph, ed., *Essays on Education*, 28, 33–34; Rush, *Mode of Education Proper in a Republic*, 21; Smith, *Remarks on Education*, 192–93. Female education in the early republic is discussed in Mary Beth Norton, *Liberty's Daughters: The Revolutionary Experience of American Women, 1750–1800* (Boston, 1980), 256–94; and Linda K. Kerber, *Women of the Republic: Intellect and Ideology in Revolutionary America* (Chapel Hill, N.C., 1980), 189–231.

49. Smith, *Remarks on Education*, 208, 209, 206, 207–08.

50. John Demos, *A Little Commonwealth: Family Life in Plymouth Colony* (New York, 1970), 180–90; and "The American Family in Past Time," *The American Scholar*, 43 (1974), 422–46, summarizes the argument concerning the diminution of the social space occupied by the family.

CHAPTER 17

Creating a Usable Future: The Revolutionary Historians and the National Past

Lester H. Cohen

Thirteen years after the American colonies declared their independence from the mother country, Noah Webster declared their independence from the mother tongue. The English language, like England's politics, had become corrupt, no longer capable of articulating the experience of a free people. Thus in 1789 Webster set out to reform the "abuses" of the language, and "introduce order and regularity" into the "AMERICAN TONGUE." Webster's concern was not solely linguistic—it was ideological. He characterized his project as the quest for a national language, for "a *national language* is a band of *national union*. Every engine should be employed to render the people of this country *national;* to call their attachments home to their own country; and to inspire them with the pride of national character."[1]

Not only national pride was at issue in creating a distinctively American language and literature. At risk was the future of American historical and political consciousness. The language of the people was a central concern, because in the long run public values and attitudes were the chief bulwark against encroachments on liberty and republican principles, and language was the fundamental force shaping consciousness. Thus as early as 1789, Webster encouraged the government of New York "to reform the abuses and corruptions" of American speech, so that the nation could be "rendered as independent and illustrious in letters as she is already in arms and civil policy."[2] For Webster, as for other cultural nationalists, those who influenced language molded the assumptions, principles, values, and aspirations of the people. And these could never be taken for granted in a republic.

Webster was the most articulate American exponent of the theory that there was a dialectic between culture and politics, so that a corruption in language or literature was not only symptomatic of political decline but might actually cause it. "I assume it as a fact, conceded by all philosophers and historians," he wrote, "that there has been, in every civilized nation, a particular period of time, peculiarly favorable to literary researches; and that in this period, language and taste arrive to purity; the best authors flourish, and genius is exerted to benefit mankind." The obvious corollary of this theory was that there comes a point at which improvement ends and corruption begins. "This has been the case in all nations, and is now true of England," he asserted. Whereas Britain had attained its cultural zenith in the century preceding the reign of George II, "the candid" of that nation now lamented the decline. "Very few valuable writings appear in the present age: plays, novels, farces, and compilations fill the catalogue of new publications; and the library of a man of fashion consists of Chesterfield's Letters, Tristram Shandy, and a few comedies."[3]

It was clear that this decline in literary merit paralleled Britain's political degeneration. Indeed, the very notion that "taste" and "fashion" governed English discourse was itself a sign of corruption, when measured against the rigorous, almost ascetic standard of American republicanism. The problem, however, was that Americans still spoke and wrote "English"—still, that is, looked to Britain as a cultural model. The Americans may boast of the freedom of their government and their political independence from Great Britain, Webster argued, "yet their *opinions* are not sufficiently independent." Instead of emancipating themselves from the influences of English culture, "an astonishing respect for the arts and literature of their parent country, and a blind imitation of its manners, are still prevalent among the Americans." Such "habitual respect" for British culture, though once deserved and laudable, had become an impediment to the creation of an autonomous American character.[4]

The decline in England's cultural fortunes was nowhere better evidenced than in its historical writings, and Edward Gibbon's recently published *Decline and Fall of the Roman Empire* was a perfect target for Webster's vitriol. Gibbon's "general fault," said Webster, was that he was more concerned with style and form than with content. "[H]e takes more pains to form his sentences, than to collect, arrange and express the facts in an easy and perspicuous manner. In consequence of attending to ornament, he seems to forget that he is writing for the *information* of his reader, and when he ought to *instruct* the mind, he is only *pleasing* the ear." Gibbon's self-conscious focus on style rendered historical narrative suspiciously like fiction. Hence, his chronicle should not properly be called "a '*History* of the decline and fall of the Roman Empire.' " Instead, it should be entitled, "a 'Poetico Historical decription of certain persons and events, embellished with suitable imagery and episodes, designed to show the author's talent in selecting words, as well as delight the ears of his readers.' " In short, Webster chided, this monument of English historiography ought to be called: "A display of words."[5]

Although Webster focused on what appeared to be a purely literary matter, the relationship between content and form had real political consequences as well. Indeed, Webster and other American commentators excoriated Gibbon principally (though not explicitly) because he had so insightfully laid bare the reasons for the decline of Rome—particularly its internal corruption—yet failed to see the eighteenth-century British empire prefigured in the Roman. Gibbon and Samuel Johnson deserved to be condemned for writing in a style that was obscure, overly Latinate, and multisyllabic—a style designed for the erudite elite, and one that revealed their intent to make the lessons of history and society inaccessible to "unlearned readers." As critics pointed out, American historians had no such contempt for the masses. To the contrary, they premised their histories on an audience of republican citizens. Thus, George Richards Minot "rendered his work entertaining to *every class* of readers." And David Ramsay's style was so "simple and elegant," "the leading events are so ably traced to their causes; and the manner in which those causes produced their effects, are stated in so masterly a manner, that the whole form . . . a well connected history, calculated to inform the judgment, and, at the same time, to captivate the attention of the reader."[6]

Webster's encouragement of an American historical language derived in great measure from his concern that the new nation was insufficiently prepared to attain cultural autonomy. He was hardly alone. David Ramsay, whose own work was praised because its "Dress is altogether American," lauded Jeremy Belknap's *History of New Hampshire* (1784–92) because it was beautifully designed to overcome the local and regional prejudices that still tended to divide Americans. This was, for Ramsay, a remarkable achievement, for Belknap's history was national in spirit, even though its topic was ostensibly a single state. Ramsay, like Webster, worried about the divisions in America that resulted from parochial attachments. "We are too widely disseminated over an extensive country & too much diversified by different customs & forms of government to feel as one people [,] which we are," he confided to John Eliot. But through such histories as Belknap's, "we might become better acquainted with each other in that intimate familiar manner which would wear away prejudice—rub off asperities & mould us into a homogeneous people."[7]

Webster's theories lead in a variety of interesting directions. I am principally concerned here with focusing them on two points: that language and literature are intertwined with politics, a theme to which I will return; and that Americans needed to generate a distinctively national history, one that would be accessible to the masses in both content and form, that centered in the struggle between liberty and arbitrary power, and that was designed to promote sentiments favorable to virtue and republican principles.

For the Revolutionary generation, historical writing could be a means of fostering nationhood, an instrument for promoting the sort of national character or "homogeneity" that Webster and Ramsay craved. And, in fact, in the two dozen or so histories published between 1785 and 1805, the historians of the Revolution achieved an impressive single-mindedness about the historical unity of the American people.[8] Yet Webster, Ramsay, and the other historians—experienced in politics, knowledgeable about world affairs, and armed with records and documents they thought to be the most complete any society had ever collected—knew perfectly well that America's past, like its present, had been filled with social, economic, and political conflicts and tensions that from time to time had erupted into hostilities. The Revolutionary era alone, the period from 1763 to 1776, presented a model of unity—*if* the historians deemphasized the significance of the Tories, and *if* they assumed that Revolutionary unity had not been founded on the presence of a common enemy, in which case unity had been, at best, negative, if not purely illusory.[9] Thus, when the historians wrote of a unified colonial past they purposefully diminished the importance of internal tensions and conflicts, and invented the colonists in the image of the revolutionaries—an image of consensus, unity, and an unfaltering commitment to republican principles.

I will suggest here that the historians' creation of a consensual, national past was a self-conscious ideological and literary effort, one fueled by the conviction that historical writing was valuable chiefly as an incitement to ethical and political action, rather than as a means of edification. This conviction, in turn, reveals the historians' assumption that historical narrative could define the categories and vocabulary in terms of which the historical consciousness of future generations could properly be articulated. The first item on their unfinished agenda, that is, was the struggle for the power of language, much as Webster had outlined it, for that was the battle for control over the attitudes and values of unborn millions. Motivating both the ethical and ideological ideas was the historians' anxiety about the present and apprehension over the future. Before turning to their portrayal of colonial history and the ways in which they invented the past, it is important to consider their perceptions of the world in which they lived. For the historians' version of a usable past was both rooted in and designed to serve their vision of what a usable *future* ought to look like.

In the 1780s and 1790s, when their histories were taking shape, the historians saw all about them signs of disintegration. Writing in what should have been the warm afterglow of the successful republican revolution, harmony, unity, and homogeneity appeared to be little more than fond wishes. In their correspondence as early as the 1770s, and later in their histories, they pointed to precisely the kinds of problems that had destroyed all earlier republics: a debilitating partisanship that threatened to undermine the revolutionary unity of the states and people; financial insolvency that placed in doubt the continued existence of state and confederal governments; unprecedented social rivalries—unleashed, ironically, by the very democratic spirit that sustained the struggle against Britain—that mocked the very notion of one people; and, above all, moral and political degeneration that already spread its virulent germ through the body politic. It would be difficult to overstate the importance of their perception of decline, for it energized their commitment to history and governed their understanding of the past.

As participants in the struggle against Britain, years before they wrote their histories, the historians were already concerned about partisanship, fraud, deceit, and corruption in the decade following the Declaration of Independence. " 'Tis mortifying to think that such a horrid corruption hath spread itself so rapidly thro' the American states; and that in the first year of our existence we should have adopted so many of the Old England vices," William Gordon wrote to John Adams in 1777. Money appeared to be the central problem, for there was too much of it in circulation, yet too little for the war effort. "As to abuses, they are enormous and almost without number," Gordon observed. "Instead of having our affairs conducted with economy, the Continent hath been plundered, and business carried on at the most expensive rate, that Jack, Tom and Harry might make a fortune & live like gentlemen . . . ." Heedless of the relationship between private ambition and public calamity, the people blithely ignored the symptoms of decline. But the historian saw them, and he argued that "The fraud, the peculation, and the profusion that have been practised among us, have done us more injury than the whole of our foreign enemies." In short, Gordon wrote to George Washington, "Selfishness has so far prevailed over that patriotic spirit which at first wrought wonder through the Continent, that I have little dependance on the virtue of the people." "Honest, upright patriots are thinly scattered through the Continent: Here and there one."[10]

Gordon was a minister whose sermons also dwelled upon the political consequences of private and public corruption. His letters mourning the decline of patriotism and virtue and the rise of speculation were consistent with his mission. Indeed, he confessed to Washington in 1777 that "I have begun to preach up the danger we are in. . . . It can do no hurt, and may have a good effect by tending to awaken the stupid, for we still abound with lethargic souls."[11] Yet David Ramsay, a South Carolina physician, was equally appalled, and he expressed himself in the same language. "A spirit of money-making has eaten up our patriotism," he wrote to William Henry Drayton. To Benjamin Rush he added: "I most devoutly wish for peace. Our morals are more depreciated than our currency, & that is bad enough." By the mid-1780s the theme of corruption became more insistent. "I feel with you the declension of our public virtue. Liberty which ought to produce every generous principle has not in our republics been attended with its usual concommitants. Pride [,] Luxury [,] dissipation & a long train of unsuitable vices have overwhelmed our coun[try]." Ramsay was increasingly driven to the grim thought that "We have neither honesty nor knowledge enough for republican governments." And though his hopes revived in contemplation of a strong government that might cement the union, he suspected that the damage could be irreparable. "During the war we thought the termination of that would end our troubles. It is now ended three years & our public situation is as bad as ever."[12]

One would suppose, correctly on one level, that these expressions of

American corruption were a function of politics. Ramsay and Gordon, like Noah Webster, were nationalists who supported the Constitution and attributed many of the ills of the new nation to the weakness of the Confederation. For them to identify social, moral, and political corruption was to win points for a stronger government. They also might have been more inclined to invent a national past, in contrast to a splintered present, where others might have seen a variety of forces operating in history. In fact, Ramsay even delayed the publication of his *History of the American Revolution* until the fate of the Constitution was decided, for "The revolution cannot be said to be compleated till that or something equivalent is established."[13]

Yet nationalism in the cultural terms I have been outlining was not political in any narrow sense. It was broad enough to comprehend the views of Mercy Otis Warren, the most vehement Anti-Federalist among the historians. Warren published a scathing indictment of the Constitution in 1788, and her letters of the late 1780s and 1790s excoriated the Federalists for what she perceived as their repudiation of republican principles. And Warren was, if anything, quicker than the others to identify corruption during the decade after independence was declared, more fulsome in her denunciations, and more insightful about corruption's systemic consequences.[14]

As early as 1774 Warren was concerned about the "many instances of a sordid selfish spirit prompting men to act diametrically opposite to the welfare of society . . . ." She attributed much of the corruption to the influence of the war, for war is "always unfavourable to virtue." But not even armed hostilities and the presence of foreign troops could account for "such a total change of manners in so short a period [which] I believe was never known in the history of man. Rapacity and profusion, pride and servility, and almost every vice is contrasted in the same breast." By the 1780s, she, like Ramsay, feared that "we are already too far advanced in every species of luxury to recede . . . ." Despite all the suffering and hard work, with the fruits of the Revolution ready to be harvested, "But alas! if we have any national character, what a heterogenous mixture." America, it appeared, was going to realize all the worst tendencies of constitutional history: "we have a republican form of gover[n]ment with the principles of monarchy, the freedom of democracy with the servility of despotism, the extravagance of nobility with the poverty of peasantry."[15]

The historians wrote about human nature in general and the post-Declaration period in particular with more optimism in their histories than in their letters, for one of the principal purposes of the histories was to exhort the rising generation to match the exertions of the Revolutionaries. Nevertheless, the historians pulled few punches even in their histories. John Lendrum and David Ramsay seized on the period of the late 1770s, when depreciation of the currency had transformed paper money into what Mercy Warren called "immense heaps of paper trash." It was a time, Lendrum contended, that "the morals of the people were corrupted beyond any thing that could have been believed prior to the event." Even as "the paper currency in Philadelphia was daily sinking . . . yet an assembly, a concert, a dinner, or supper, which cost two or three hundred pounds, did not only take men off from acting, but even from thinking of what ought to have been nearest their hearts."[16]

Ramsay was saddened and frustrated that the virtuous suffered most during those years of licentiousness. With the reversal of "the commonly received maxims of prudence and economy," virtuous people, concerned with their neighbors' welfare, refused to pay their debts in depreciated currency; instead, they preferred to risk their reputations as well as their fortunes against a day when they would repay them in dearer money. Meanwhile, however, "many bold adventurers made fortunes in a short time by running in debt beyond their abilities. Prudence ceased to be a virtue, and rashness usurped its place. The warm friends of America, who never despaired of their country, and who cheerfully risked their fortunes in its support, lost their property, while the timid, who looked forward to the re-establishment of British government, not only saved their former possessions, but often increased them." In a grisly echo of the popular song "The World Turned Upside Down," Ramsay observed: "In the American revolution for the first time the friends of the successful party were the losers." Such financial problems were also ethical problems, for the evils produced by currency fluctuations struck at the principle of virtue, diminished the people's commitment to honor and justice, and turned their attentions "from the sober paths of industry to extravagant adventures and romantick projects."[17]

Motivating these statements about American decline was the zeal of the revolutionary-as-historian who sees the present reneging upon its promise to the future. Something had to be done to avert disaster. David Ramsay called upon the press, the pulpit, and "all the powers of Eloquence . . . to counter-act that ruinous propensity we have for foreign superfluities & to excite us to the long neglected virtues of Industry & frugality."[18] Historical writing was just such an instrument of eloquence, one the historians believed they could use to shape political and ethical consciousness. And it was precisely in this context of imminent American decline that Mercy Warren identified the obligation of the historian. If America should ever exhibit the signs of public corruption and degeneracy, she wrote, "let some unborn historian, in a far distant day" point up "the contrast between a simple, virtuous and free people, and a degenerate, servile race of beings, corrupted by wealth, effeminated by luxury, impoverished by licentiousness, and become the *automotons* of intoxicated ambition."[19]

That "far distant day" obviously had arrived, for the generations that had settled the wilderness, suffered British oppression, declared independence, mobilized for war, and created republican constitutions were being superseded by a younger generation that was blindly sacrificing the legacy of the past on the altar of private ambition. To this rising generation the historians addressed—and in many cases dedicated—their histories, at once condemning them for their avarice and corruption and exhorting them to return to the example of the forebears. The histories were thus radically contemporary documents, less concerned with the past for its own sake than with its bearing on the present and future.

To create a consensual, national past, inhabited by industrious, virtuous republicans, was to place in sharp relief "the contrast" to which Warren had pointed. While the passions of the present led to a kind of amnesia in the rising generation—who "cease to look back with due gratitude and respect on the fortitude and virtue of their ancestors"—a national history might restore their memories.[20] But even if this dialogue with the future failed to convert the younger generation, it would at least serve to establish the fundamental terms in which historical, and therefore political and ethical, discourse could properly be undertaken.

The historians' principal strategy in presenting the colonial past was to create a republican genealogy, a succession of generations that, from the beginning of new world settlement, manifested the spirit of Revolutionary republicanism. While the historians sometimes referred to internal tensions among the colonies, they focused on the intellectual, even spiritual, consensus of the people in order to drive home the contrast between the several generations that developed and preserved the principles of the Revolution, and the younger generation, which seemed willing to sacrifice it all in the pursuit of private interest.

At the heart of the historians' presentation was the image of the colonists as strenuous republicans. The past was consensual primarily because the colonists were universally committed to a coherent set of principles and values upon which they were willing to act. The historians gave focus to this complex of interdependent values by emphasizing three central themes: the colonists were politically dedicated to ordered liberty within the context of law and balanced, representative government; they were ethically committed to the rational obligations of conscience and public virtue, so that social life was simple and felicitous and individual conduct was marked by industry and prudence; and they were convinced philosophically that people were free and efficacious beings who were responsible for their actions and for the consequences their actions brought about. What sharper contrast could the historians have presented in their quarrel with the rising generation, who appeared willing to give up the principles and practices of republican politics, to abandon the ethical commitment to the public good, and to ignore the relationship between their licentious behavior and the disastrous consequences that were almost certain to ensue from them?

It is to this constellation of values that the historians pointed when they referred to the "opinions" of the colonists and to the "character" of the people. The historians insisted that these principles were not new to the Revolutionary era. The conflicts of the 1760s and 1770s merely called forth the character that had energized the colonists from the beginning of settlement. "The unexampled unanimity of sentiment against the stamp act," for example, "which instantaneously appeared among two or three millions of people . . . was not the work of a day or a year," wrote Timothy Pitkin. To the contrary, the ideas manifested then "were the opinions of their fathers, which they brought into this country . . . and handed down to their posterity." These were the ideas of Ludlow and Sidney, Milton and Harrington, and of "the learned, enlightened, and renowned Locke," agreed Mercy Warren. And even earlier, "These were the rights of men, the privileges of Englishmen, and the claim of Americans: these were the principles of the Saxon ancestry of the British empire, and of all the free nations of Europe"; they were the principles the colonists' forebears brought with them "to the dark wilds of America."[21]

This intellectual consensus was apparent from the beginning of settlement, and successive generations, including immigrants, took "their colouring . . . from the peculiar manners of the first settlers." But the antiquity of these ideas was not important per se to the historians. That they were ancient and universal was significant only because they had had time to become deeply ingrained in colonial experience. The settlers, wrote David Ramsay, "not only conceived themselves to inherit the privileges of Englishmen," but *actually possessed them*" in practice. The colonies were "nurseries of freemen," said John M'Culloch, because the people "grew up" knowing their rights and the principles of government. Such experience became habitual. Just as New England's enmity to the ecclesiastical policies of the Church of England fostered antipathy to monarchy, which "gradually matured into an habitual and systematized opposition" to all arbitrary government, wrote Noah Webster, so "the endless contentions between the governors and the assemblies . . . formed the principles of opposition into a habit." Americans' rights, echoed Jedidiah Morse, had not merely been "stipulated and confirmed by royal charter"; more important, they had been "enjoyed by the colonists for more than a century." Indeed, these were "natural rights" precisely because they had become ingrained in the everyday conduct of the people. Rights and principles were little more than abstract propositions unless they were "improved in society and strengthened by civil compacts," wrote Mercy Warren; added Ramsay, colonial society favored just such a "spirit of liberty and independence."[22]

By demonstrating that the principles and practices of republican politics and ethics were deeply ingrained in the people, the historians were able to vivify the image of a Revolutionary past and to indicate how far the generation of 1800 had declined from the political and ethical standards of their forebears. "The circumstances under which New-England was planted, would a few centuries ago have entitled them, from their first settlement, to the privileges of independence," wrote David Ramsay. Having been denied their political and spiritual rights at home, the colonists set out, at their own expense, with no prospects other than hard work in an unknown world, to build homes and civilize the wilderness. They purchased their lands from "the native proprietors," and, like proper Lockeans, exerted themselves through their labor to reap the bounties of nature. It became clear to the colonists that the only obligations they owed Britain were those that "resulted from their voluntary assent" as revealed in "express or implied compact." Imbued from the beginning with ideas of English liberty, the colonists established republican governments and jealously guarded their rights. They knew that government rested upon contracts freely entered; that taxation and representation were inextricably intertwined; that they held and alienated their property by voluntary consent; that the end of government was the happiness of the people; that the people were free to assemble and petition the government for redress of grievances; and that, all proximate means failing, the people had the right to rebel against tyrannical rule.[23] This "independent condition of the colonists," observed Timothy Pitkin, combined with equality and the general diffusion of knowledge, "naturally produced a love of liberty, an independence of character, and a jealousy of power" which ultimately led to the American Revolution.[24]

The colonists were not only republicans in politics, they were also dedicated to those personal and social practices that conduced to the public good. They were "a plain, frugal, industrious people, strict observers of moral and religious duties," who "enjoyed that happy state of mediocrity, which is especially favourable to strength of body and vigour of mind." The settlers were "all of one rank," and disposed to democratic forms of government. This was a "liberal minded" people, "sober, industrious, and persevering"; "an intrepid race" who loved liberty enough to hazard their fortunes against the wilderness, and who, "with a degree of fortitude and patience that would have done honour to the annals of Sparta and of Rome," cultivated government and society as well as the earth in order to secure the future to their posterity.[25]

An American, wrote John Lendrum, "is unaccustomed to the idea of distinction of ranks, and hereditary titles, which the feudal system has established in Europe." Thus, unlike the Europeans, whose society was based upon "slaves attached to the soil," the "sons of America" shared a natural equality. The colonists, wrote Mercy Warren, "lived many years perhaps as near to the point of felicity as the condition of human nature will admit." Even the colonists' readings, though few in number, "generally favoured the cause of liberty," said David Ramsay. "Cato's letters, the Independent Whig, and such productions" were favored in some places, while "histories of the Puritans kept alive the remembrance of the sufferings of their forefathers, and inspired warm attachments, both to the civil and religious rights of human nature." New England, wrote John Marshall succinctly, was "originally settled by republicans."[26]

Given the colonists' ingrained intellectual commitment to such principles, and their practice of industry, fortitude, and simplicity, it was obvious to the historians that the Revolution was "not the sudden effect of a tremendous opposition to a particular act of parliament," as Noah Webster put it. Resistance and revolution were the inevitable and justifiable responses of a people long habituated to such values. Indeed, "what might not have been expected from such a people, in such a country, and in such a situation, when their liberties were attacked?" asked John Lendrum. It was unimaginable that "an united body of three millions of people would tamely surrender up their natural and chartered rights." Only "the height of infatuation" could have led one to believe that the colonists would submit.[27] Here was the final element in the historians' message to the younger generation and the most glaring feature in the contrast between the past and the future: in the face of danger the colonists, unlike their unworthy descendants, were prepared to act on their principles and take responsibility for their destiny.

Everything the historians learned from the study of the past demonstrated that life was precarious and contingent; that people's expectations, even their best calculations, were frequently dashed by unforeseen events; that their hopes were often trampled under the boot of the avaricious and corrupt; and that, therefore, only a vigilant attention to their rights and a constant regard for stable, republican government could prove security against a chaotic future.[28] The colonial past exemplified these lessons only too well, and the historians portrayed the colonists as heroic patriots prepared to fight against encroachments from without.

The Revolution provided the most obvious examples. From 1763 to 1776, confronted by a British conspiracy to deprive them of their rights and privileges, "the watchful guardians of American freedom never lost sight of the intrigues of their enemies, or the mischievous designs of such as were under the influence of the crown on either side [of] the Atlantic." Apprehensive early on, they were certain by the mid-1770s that "Great Britain, instead of redressing American grievances, was determined to dragoon the colonists into submission."[29] Obviously, the Revolutionaries manifested the spirit to resist.

But American fortitude and resistance did not begin in 1763; it had characterized the colonists since the seventeenth century. And the historians lost no opportunity to demonstrate to the generation of 1800 that the colonists had been the true ancestors of the revolutionaries. "The colonial history, indeed, exhibits a constant struggle for prerogative and power on the one hand, and freedom and the privilege of self-government on the other," wrote Timothy Pitkin. Disputes over charter rights "commenced as early as 1635, nor did they end, till the American Revolution." Indeed, added John Lendrum, "from the year 1629 to 1639, [the Virginians] were ruled rather as the vassals of an eastern despot, than as subjects entitled to English liberties." Even so, the message was clear: "But it is to their credit that they opposed with a firm spirit, during the reign of Charles [I], all attempts against their liberties."[30]

Noah Webster argued that "during the reign of Charles the First, the colonies were frequently alarmed with the report of some act of the English government, to abridge their freedom." When the colonists resisted such encroachments on their rights, "their enemies represented the people as aiming at an entire independence, and a plan was devised and nearly matured, to deprive the colonies of their charters, and place over them a general governor." Later the plan did mature, and there arrived in Massachusetts the despotic Edmund Andros as agent for the tyrant James II. As expected, Andros "overacted his part; and his tyrannical proceedings only served to alienate the people's affections from the parent state, and prepare the way for that independence which the king dreaded." Resisting Andros's unconstitutional actions, the people of Ipswich, led by their minister John Wise, rebelled and were brought to trial before "star chamber judges . . . and a packed jury." But Wise and the others refused to submit, and, wrote Timothy Pitkin, they "may justly claim a distinguished rank among the patriots of America."[31]

Through a variety of seventeenth-century episodes—from attacks on colonial charters to efforts to establish military governors, from the dissolution of the Virginia Company to the Navigation Acts, from Bacon's Rebellion to the overthrow of the Dominion of New England—the historians lost no opportunity to prefigure the conduct of the Revolutionaries in the actions of the colonists. They made abundantly clear that the colonists had manifested the sort of courage and patriotism only rarely witnessed in history. The lesson was obvious: independence was not "a gift" that the Americans asked for: "the boon was their own; obtained by their own prowess and magnanimity." The colonists had emancipated *themselves*, "by the uncommon vigor, valor, fortitude, and patriotism of her soldiers and statesmen."[32] The historians thus demonstrated an unbroken succession—a genealogy of republicanism—from the earliest settlement to the Revolutionaries, a blood-line that was in danger of running out with the post-Revolutionary generation.

The dominant image of the colonists in the Revolutionary histories is one of a virtuous, simple, vigorous, industrious folk who paid unfaltering allegiance to republican politics, ethics, and philosophy. Out of this set of values and practices, the historians forged a consensual past. What unites the historians in their portrayal of the past is two powerful urges: their profound discomfort over their perception that imminent decline was possible, even likely, if Americans' growing penchant for luxury, power, and self-aggrandizement were portents of a trend toward corruption; and their commitment to the view that historical narrative could serve as an instrument of ideological redemption, by fixing the language appropriate to discuss history and politics, and therefore serve to shape public consciousness.

The historians saw all about them—or said that they did—the signs of corruption that had signalled the demise of all earlier republics: a spirit of money-making, fraud, deceit, factionalization, a quest for power—in short, a greater regard for self and immediate material reward rather than for the stability and patient improvement of the civic order were pervasive in the rising generation. The signs were ominous. The new nation ran the risk of stillbirth before it had a fair chance to survive. Republicanism appeared to have too few heirs for the lineage to remain productive. What this grim picture suggests is the defeat of the historians' expectations as proponents of the republican revolution.

Yet the picture is manifestly unbalanced for the modern reader; it is painted in blacks and whites and in bold strokes. Indeed, it is more a caricature than a portrait—a distorted feature here, an exaggerated trait there—and there is reason to believe that it was intentionally so. The historians played out their anxiety over the future—almost literally *staged* it as a tragedy—in terms of the contrast between the past and the future; specifically, in terms of a moral and political declension from the colonists and the revolutionaries to the rising generation. Presented starkly, the contrast is almost comical. While the past was inhabited by those dedicated, virtuous, liberty-loving, public-spirited patriots, who jealously guarded their rights and manifested the valor to resist oppression, the post-Revolutionary generation was characterized by avarice and corruption, a preference for wealth, titles, and position, and a yearning for artificial distinctions—traits that better fitted them to be subjects of a monarch or slaves of a tyrant than citizens of a republic.

But why invent the colonists in the most cherished image of the Revolutionaries, and why caricature the younger generation? For two reasons, both of which indicate that the historians' creation of a usable past served their vision of a usable future. First, because it was possible to employ history as a mode of exhortation and thus to prompt a reawakening of sensitivity to first principles. And second, because, failing such redemption, historical writing might still be capable of rescuing the very language that people could properly use to understand history and politics; it still had the potential to establish linguistic and therefore intellectual hegemony over the future.

"History is philosophy teaching by examples," wrote the celebrated Bolingbroke; it trains people "in private and public virtue" by inculcating images of virtue and vice. Consistent with the ethical aim of historical writing, David Ramsay insisted that "I write not for a party, but for posterity," because the recording of past events "for the instruction of man, ought to be the object of history." Ramsay thought that John Eliot's *Biographical Dictionary* (1809) admirably served this exemplary purpose, for "it rendered an essential service to the living by holding up so many excellent models for their imitation from the illustrious dead." The historian, William Gordon concurred, "should oblige all, who have performed any distinguished part on the theatre of the world, to appear before us in their proper character; and to render an account at the tribunal of posterity, as models which ought to be followed, or as examples to be censured or avoided."[33] Each time they addressed the purpose of historical writing the historians invoked "posterity," "the living," the "youth" of America, "future generations," even "unborn millions."

These are the ideas of which hortatory history is made, and the narratives are filled with passages, obviously addressed to the nineteenth century, that reveal the style and terms of the secular jeremiad.[34] Equally important, the exemplary theory of history led the historians to privilege *ethical* terms, though it is clear that ethics, politics, and philosophy were so profoundly interrelated that even as the historians wrote of "virtue," "prudence," "simplicity" or "fortitude," they simultaneously invoked "freedom," "balance," "rationality," "enlightenment"—and, of course, their opposites.

To a significant degree, the historians' use of this vocabulary was mandated—even coerced—by the authority of what modern historians have called the republican synthesis. Thus a constellation of political, ethical, and philosophical categories, pervasively used throughout the culture and articulated in and through a vocabulary that was charged with a range of appropriate meanings and values, established constraints on what it was possible for the historians to think and say about history. In this way all systematically employed languages define at least the limits within which discourse is ordinarily possible.[35] And yet it was precisely this insight—that language had the capacity to shape consciousness, indeed *must* shape it— that lay beneath the historians' gestures toward "posterity" as the motive for writing history. It was also this insight that made it possible and desirable for the historians self-consciously to invent the colonists in their own image and to create caricatures of the rising generation.

Mercy Warren came closest to articulating this assumption when she wrote of her obligation "to cultivate the sentiments of public and private virtue" in everything she authored. She saw it as her special obligation "to *form* the minds, to *fix* the principles [and] to *correct* the errors [of] the young members of society" through her poetry, plays, and history.[36] Although Warren was the most precise in her formulation, several of the other historians recognized the crucial intersection of ethics, aesthetics, and politics in historical writing, and the capacity of narrative to shape thought. David Ramsay, for example, drew an analogy between writing history and writing fiction: "Novelists take fiction & make it a vehicle of their opinions on a variety of subjects," he observed. "I take truth & the facts of history for the same purpose."[37]

William Gordon's views are even more illuminating. Gordon nagged George Washington for several years to have access to Washington's war- time papers. He did so, he said, because "truth and impartiality are what I aim at; and therefore am for having a recourse to original papers in the possession of those who have borne a distinguished and active part in the transactions of the day." Washington's papers were invaluable, Gordon wrote, "for I am in search of genuine truth and not a fairy tale." At the same time, Gordon knew that the writing of history required careful liter- ary construction, that language and style were the vehicles through which history became comprehensible. Thus, though he followed Noah Webster in acknowledging that too much adornment made history suspect, he nevertheless argued that the artful historian—the historian concerned with truth—"proportioned" and "wrought" its lines in order to make history attractive. Hence the style and language of a narrative were crucial, and Gordon thought he could clothe the truth "in a colour that shall suit [its] complexion—in a taste that shall please present and future generations— and in a dress that shall *improve* instead of concealing [its] beauties."[38]

Gordon knew, moreover, that when he spoke of language, style, and narrative, he also imported ideological interests into the discussion. He remarked, for example, that if England reformed its politics, "an Historian may use the impartial pen there with less danger than here." He believed that too many Americans had so high a stake in the kind of history that was written, that America "will be most horribly affected by an *impartial* history." In England, on the other hand, he could write "not only the *truth* but the truth *truly* represented, for you may tell the truth so as to make a lie of it in the apprehension of him who reads or hears the tale."[39] If one could distinguish between "the truth" and "the truth truly represented," then clearly the modes in which the truth was presented were crucial to a narrative's veracity.

The point is that "truth" and "veracity" in the Revolutionary histories mean something different from the commonsense notion that what is true or veracious is a quality that inheres in a thing or idea independent of anyone speaking, writing, or acting upon it. Instead, truth and veracity in historical writing were created by the particular images and impressions that the narrator wished to convey in and through the language and style with which he structured his narrative. In short, for the Revolutionary historians the "facts" of the past were brute and unmeaning until given voice and shape by historians. And historians could, through narrative presentation, "improve" the truth, or make of history a grotesque deceit. Given these possibilities for truth and deceit, it mattered enormously *whose* categories and vocabulary of historical presentation would prevail, for to the victor in the struggle for language went the power to establish intellectual hegemony over the future. However the struggle was resolved, historical writing was in some sense—a sense the historians did not or could not elaborate any further—a process of inventing or fictionalizing.

The historians knew they were using "art" and ideology in the service of history. Moreover, they followed contemporary English commentators, who discussed the understanding of history in terms of Lockean epistemology. Because "the human understanding is a blank, which may be filled up with various kinds of matter," John Bigland argued, historical writings could operate environmentally or sensationally to stimulate impressions of virtue and vice.[40] The Revolutionary historians made a similar assumption. Indeed, only an assumption that drew the connection between mind and literature—so that what one read generated impressions upon which the mind operated—can account for the passion with which the historians addressed the younger generation. It was this connection that made history *useful.*[41]

The historians feared that the Revolution would be too *successful*—that the generations of giants had wrought so well that a generation of moral and political pygmies could take over the reins of government and society, appear to perpetuate traditional principles, yet not really understand them. They feared that future generations would come to take the creation of the republic so much for granted that they would become oblivious to the effort it took to establish it. And they feared, above all, that the very conception of the Revolutionary republic would gradually fade into obscurity, because a new language of history and politics was insensibly replacing the language of republicanism, and that the new language could be used to justify and rationalize values that were, finally, antithetical to those of the Revolution.

What governed the historians' portrayal of the past, finally, was their sense that historical writing possessed practical utility. Deeply imbued with the notion that, as revolutionaries themselves, they were responsible for a share in the "made culture" their generation was creating, they felt obliged to *make* a history that would perpetuate the principles, values, and language of the Revolution. It was useful—vital, as they saw it—to depict the colonists as revolutionary republicans, because in doing so they could point to a persisting tradition that shaped generations of historical and political discourse as well as institutions. This created, in effect, an instantaneous tradition for a revolutionary people. And it was useful to stage the tragedy of decline and potential disaster, played out in the personae of the colonists and the rising generation, precisely because the historians could show by their very performance how powerfully evocative and explanatory the language of republicanism remained.

NOTES

1. Noah Webster, *Dissertations on the English Language* (Boston, 1789), 397.
2. "Memorial to the New York Legislature," in Harry R. Warfel, ed., *Letters of Noah Webster* (New York, 1953), 5–6.
3. Webster, *A Collection of Essays and Fugitive Writings on Moral, Historical, Political and Literary Subjects* (Boston, 1790), 94.
4. Webster, *Dissertations*, 397–98. See Mercy Otis Warren to Catharine Macaulay, August 2, 1787, in "The Letter-Book of Mercy Otis Warren," mss. in the Massachusetts Historical Society, 22.
5. *Massachusetts Magazine* (July 1789), 441–42. See Warren to Winslow Warren, March

1785, and to George Warren, July 1795, "Letter-Book," 309–10, 419–20; *American Magazine* (June 1788), 467, (July 1788), 536–37; "On the Literature, Wit and Taste of the European Nations," *Columbian Magazine* (July 1788), 384–88, (August 1788), 424–26.

6. *Universal Asylum and Columbian Magazine*, 6 (April 1791), 237; *Massachusetts Magazine*, 1 (August 1789), 475; *American Magazine*, 1 (September 1788), 740 (emphasis added); *Columbian Magazine*, 4 (June 1790), 374. See, in general, Lester H. Cohen, *The Revolutionary Histories: Contemporary Narratives of the American Revolution* (Ithaca, 1980), chap. 6.

7. Rev. James Madison lauded Ramsay's *History of the Revolution of South-Carolina* (1785) in a letter to Thomas Jefferson, March 26, 1786, in Robert L. Brunhouse, ed., *David Ramsay, 1749–1815: Selections from his Writings*, American Philosophical Society, *Transactions*, n.s., 55, pt. 4 (1965), 226; Ramsay to John Eliot, August 11, 1792 (ibid., 133). "To write, to speak, or even to think of a separation of the states is political blasphemy," Ramsay wrote to Jedidiah Morse. " 'One Indivisible' is my motto." (May 5, 1813, ibid., 174).

8. See Arthur H. Shaffer, *The Politics of History: Writing the History of the American Revolution, 1783–1815* (Chicago, 1975).

9. Jeremy Belknap, for example, mused: "if an union could not be formed until we were driven to it by external oppression and tyranny, is it likely that such an union will hold when that pressure is removed?" To Ebenezer Hazard, March 3, 1784, in MHS, *Collections*, 5th ser., II, 310.

10. Gordon to John Adams, June 5, 1777; to *The Independent Chronicle*, February 26, 1778; to George Washington, June 12, 1780; to Horatio Gates, May 25, 1781, in *The Letters of William Gordon*, MHS, *Proceedings*, 62 (October 1929–June 1930), 340, 381, 434, 455.

11. Gordon to Washington, July 17, 1777, in Gordon, *Letters*, 347. See, for example, Gordon, "A Discourse Preached December 15, 1774," in John Wingate Thornton, ed., *The Pulpit of the American Revolution* (Boston, 1860), 187–226. Also see Nathan O. Hatch, *The Sacred Cause of Liberty: Republican Thought and the Millennium in Revolutionary New England* (New Haven, 1977).

12. Ramsay to Drayton, September 1, 1779; to Rush, July 18, 1779; to John Eliot, August 6, 1785; to Rush, August 6, 1786, in Brunhouse, ed., *Writings of Ramsay*, 64, 62, 90, 105.

13. Ramsay to Benjamin Rush, February 17, 1788, ibid., 119.

14. See Lester H. Cohen, "Mercy Otis Warren: The Politics of Language and the Aesthetics of Self," *American Quarterly*, 35 (Winter 1983), 481–98. Warren's pamphlet, erroneously attributed until recently to her friend Elbridge Gerry, is reprinted in Herbert J. Storing, ed., *The Complete Anti-Federalist*, 7 vols. (Chicago, 1981), IV, 270–87. In a letter to Catharine Macaulay, December 18, 1787, Warren appears to acknowledge her authorship of the pamphlet. See "Letter-Book," 26.

15. Warren to Hannah Winthrop, 1774; to John Adams, October 15, 1778 and April 27, 1785; to Elbridge Gerry, June 6, 1783, in "Letter-Book," 70, 167, 189, 469. See Warren to John Adams, December 1786; to Catharine Macaulay, August 2, 1787 and December 18, 1787, in "Letter-Book," 195, 22, 25–26. Also see Lester H. Cohen, "Explaining the Revolution: Ideology and Ethics in Mercy Otis Warren's Historical Theory," *William and Mary Quarterly*, 3rd ser., 37 (April 1980), 200–18.

16. Lendrum, *A Concise and Impartial History of the American Revolution*, 2 vols. (Boston, 1795; reprinted Trenton, 1811), II, 170, 90.

17. Ramsay, *History of the Revolution of South-Carolina, From a British Province to an Independent State*, 2 vols. (Trenton, 1785), II, 83–85, 93.

18. Ramsay to John Eliot, August 6, 1785, in Brunhouse, ed., *Writings of Ramsay*, 90–91.

19. Warren, *History of the Rise, Progress and Termination of the American Revolution*, 3 vols. (Boston, 1805), III, 336–37.

20. Warren, *American Revolution*, I, 4.

21. Timothy Pitkin, *A Political and Civil History of the United States of America*, 2 vols. (New Haven, 1828), I, 3–4; Warren, *American Revolution*, III, 304–07.

22. Ramsay, *American Revolution*, I, 27; McCulloch, *A Concise History of the United States, from the Discovery of America, til 1813*, 4th ed. (Philadelphia, 1813), 230–31; Webster, *Letters to a Young Gentleman Commencing his Education; To Which is Subjoined a Brief History of the United States* (New Haven, 1823), 275–76; Morse, *Annals of the American Revolution* (Hartford, 1824), 99; Warren, *American Revolution*, I, 31.

23. Ramsay, *American Revolution*, I, 332–35, 27–33.

24. Pitkin, *Political and Civil History*, I, 154.

25. Lendrum, *American Revolution*, I, 132, 201; Ramsay, *American Revolution*, I, 31; Warren, *American Revolution*, III, 302; McCulloch, *Concise History*, 32; Warren to Catharine Macaulay, June 9, 1773, in "Letter-Book," 1–2.

26. Lendrum, *American Revolution*, I, 204–05; Warren, *American Revolution*, I, 20; Ramsay, *American Revolution*, I, 30; Marshall, *Life of Washington*, II, 74.

27. Webster, *Letters to a Young Gentleman*, 275; Lendrum, *American Revolution*, I, 232–33.

28. See Cohen, *The Revolutionary Histories*, chaps. 2–4.

29. Warren, *American Revolution*, I, 37; Ramsay, *Revolution of South-Carolina*, I, 28. See Cohen, *Revolutionary Histories*, 146–60; Gordon S. Wood, "Conspiracy and the Paranoid Style: Causality and Deceit in the Eighteenth Century," *William and Mary Quarterly*, 3rd ser., 39 (1982), 401–41.

30. Pitkin, *Political and Civil History*, I, 137; Lendrum, *American Revolution*, I, 113.

31. Webster, *Letters to a Young Gentleman*, 271, 273; Pitkin, *Political and Civil History*, I, 116–19.

32. Warren, *American Revolution*, III, 201, 327–28 (emphasis added).

33. Isaac Kramnick, ed., *Lord Bolingbroke: Historical Writings*, (Chicago, 1972), xvi; Ramsay to Jedidiah Morse, August 12, 1807, in Brunhouse, ed., *Writings of Ramsay*, 160; Ramsay, *Revolution of South-Carolina*, I, vi; Ramsay to John Eliot, April 7, 1810, in Brunhouse, ed., *Writings of Ramsay*, 166; Gordon, *The History of the Rise, Progress, and Establishment of the Independence of the United States*, 4 vols. (London, 1788), I, i.

34. See Cohen, *The Revolutionary Histories*, chap. 7.

35. See J.G.A. Pocock, "Languages and Their Implications," in *Politics, Language and Time: Essays on Political Thought and History* (New York, 1971), 3–41; Cohen, "Mercy Otis Warren."

36. Warren to Winslow Warren, September 1785 and November 20, 1780, in "Letter-Book," 314–15, 256–57 (emphasis added).

37. Ramsay to John Coakley Lettsom, October 29, 1808, in Brunhouse, ed., *Writings of Ramsay*, 163.

38. Gordon to Washington, August 30, 1781 and June 18, 1783, in *Gordon Letters*, 457–58, 493; Gordon to Horatio Gates, March 16, 1778, August 31, 1784, ibid., 393, 506.

39. Gordon to Gates, October 16, 1782, ibid., 475.

40. Bigland, *Letters on the Study and Use of Ancient and Modern History* (Philadelphia, 1806), 27 ff. See Joseph Priestley, *Lectures on History and General Policy*, 2 vols. (Philadelphia, 1803); David Fordyce, *Dialogues Concerning Education* (London, 1745–48); John Turnbull, *Observations upon Liberal Education* (London, 1742).

41. In a 1771 letter to Robert Skipwith, who had asked Thomas Jefferson to list books that

would further the young man's education, Jefferson played on the relationship between mind and literature in a revealing way. Jefferson argued for the merits of fiction in education, because "the entertainments of fiction are *useful* as well as pleasant." "[E]*very thing* is useful which contributes to fix us in the principles and practice of virtue." Although history was perhaps a better educator than fiction, "we never reflect whether the story we read be truth or fiction. If the painting be lively, and a tolerable picture of nature, we are thrown into a reverie, from which if we awaken it is the fault of the writer." Thus the fictitious murder of Duncan by Macbeth in Shakespeare excites in the reader "as great [a] horror of villainy" as the real murder of Henry IV by Ravaillac. Jefferson concluded that one took one's moral lessons where one could find them: from history, when history was sufficiently lively and instructive; from fiction, when history was deficient. "Considering history as a moral exercise, her lessons would be too unfrequent if confined to real life. . . . We are therefore wisely framed to be as warmly interested for a fictitious as for a real personage. The spacious field of imagination is thus laid open to our use, and lessons may be formed to illustrate and carry home to the mind every moral rule of life." Jefferson to Skipwith, August 3, 1771, in Merrill D. Peterson, ed., *The Portable Thomas Jefferson*, (New York, 1975), 349–351 (emphasis added).

CHAPTER 18

Familial Politics, Seduction, and the Novel: The Anxious Agenda of an American Literary Culture

Jay Fliegelman

The visions of America as a promised New World Utopia whose "superior advantages for happiness over all the rest of mankind, whether considered in a physical, moral or political point of view" that are presented in literary epics like Timothy Dwight's *The Conquest of Canaan* (1785), David Humphreys's *Poem, On the Happiness of America* (1786) and Joel Barlow's *The Vision of Columbus* (1787) are anxiously overstrained.[1] Beneath their republican optimism is a vast fearfulness of mobocracy, of the fragility of the republic, and of the dangers of the entire Revolutionary enterprise. Such sentiments would become explicit in another set of epics, such as Barlow's, Humphreys's, and John Trumbull's co-authored *Anarchiad*, written in 1786 in response to the uprisings in western Massachusetts, Dwight's *Triumph of Infidelity* (1788), and Hugh Henry Brackenridge's satire on democracy, *Modern Chivalry*, begun in the late 1780s.

There is, however, another ambivalence that characterizes the literary works of this period that is perhaps even more telling. All these works are self-consciously written as evidence of America's literary nationalism, yet stylistically and thematically they are consciously derivative. They assert both their own and America's novelty at the same time that they insist on

Rather than building on or departing from my book, *Prodigals and Pilgrims: The American Revolution Against Patriarchal Authority, 1750–1800*, this chapter reprints, with only slight emendations and a new introduction, several disparate sections of that work, sections that have been reorganized to form a coherent whole.

the necessity of preserving the authority of European literary traditions. They adopt the form of the classical epic, but simultaneously reject the authority of Homer and Virgil, who are seen as militaristic and monarchical.[2] It is precisely in what might be called their subversive reverence, by which an earlier work is invoked only then to be taken liberties with, that these texts may be seen as fascinating reenactments of the late eighteenth-century debate over the proper balance of authority and liberty, tradition and innovation, that characterizes virtually all aspects of late eighteenth-century Anglo-American culture.[3]

Let me offer a couple of other examples of textual liberty, taken with the most authoritative text of all: the Bible. Benjamin Franklin rewrites the Lord's Prayer so as to read "Keep us from temptation" rather than "Lead us not into temptation," objecting, at the same time that he praises it, that the original verse makes God the author of temptation.[4] Though in his primer's catechism Noah Webster substitutes "A is for apple pie served by the cook" for the *New England Primer*'s earlier Calvinistic versification of *A*, "In Adam's fall, we sinned all," he is still giving us a cooked version of eating the apple.[5] Suppressing the verse "we must be as little children in our understanding to enter heaven," Thomas Jefferson the deist scissor-edits the Gospels to make Christ over in the image of a scientific rationalist.[6] The anxious intertextual relationships of Brackenridge's *Modern Chivalry* with its antecedent, *Don Quixote*, or Freneau's poem "The American Village" with Oliver Goldsmith's great English poem "The Deserted Village," or *The Anarchiad* with Pope's *Dunciad* show Brackenridge, Dwight, and Freneau, no less than Jefferson, mixing aggressive revisionism with pious appreciation, literary independence with an act of literary conservation.

In this chapter I examine the origins, ambivalent politics, and early American transformation of an enormously popular late eighteenth-century literary genre, the sentimental novel of seduction. In their treatment of the theme of the fallen woman, the early national examples of this genre subversively reconceive rather than reject their English models. In so doing, they radically recast the Biblical story of the Fall in order, ironically, to call into question the very doctrine of original sin, the essential assumption of the story, as well as, in a broader context, the false understanding of parental authority that the rhetoric of the Revolution had insisted characterized England's political treatment of its colonies. In its reconceptualization of the relations of parents and children, this literature draws extensively on the political themes of the Revolution and articulates powerfully the fundamental cultural values and anxieties of the early republic. To appreciate the familial politics and rhetoric of the early American novel requires some foregrounding.

GENEALOGY

Writing a year after the Treaty of Paris, which ended the American Revolution, Immanuel Kant defined the term that would later be used to describe his age: "Enlightenment is man's emergence from his self-imposed nonage. Nonage is the inability to use one's own understanding without another's guidance . . . 'Have the courage to use your own understanding' is therefore the motto of the enlightenment." Though laziness and cowardice are two reasons "why such a large part of mankind gladly remain minors all their lives, long after nature has freed them from external guidance," another reason is that one generation is all too willing to violate the laws of nature and impose a protracted adolescence on another generation. Such an imposition of "perpetual guardianship" was, according to Kant, the ultimate tyranny.[7] Each generation must be allowed the full growth of its mind by being given an education that encourages an independence of mind; as Kant concludes, "Man can only become man by education."[8]

Such a call for filial autonomy and the unimpeded emergence from adolescence into rational and self-sufficient independence echoes throughout the rhetoric of the American Revolution. It is its quintessential motif and, as I shall suggest here, provided the themes that preoccupied American culture of the early national period. At every opportunity Revolutionary propagandists insisted that the new nation and its people had come of age, had achieved a collective maturity that necessitated them becoming in political fact an independent and self-governing nation.[9]

Jefferson's first draft of the preamble of the Declaration of Independence reads: "When in the course of human events it becomes necessary for a people to advance from that subordination . . . to assume the equal and independent station to which the laws of nature and of nature's God entitle them . . . ." The language of the draft makes clear the generational argument that underlies the necessity identified in the final draft: "that political bands be dissolved."[10] Like the revolution of the spheres or the changing of the seasons, "the course of human events" must also obey the laws of nature that required, in the language of Blackstone's *Commentaries on the Law*, that "the empire of the father . . . gives place to the empire of reason."[11] For

Britain to deny its child colonies "that equal and independent station" was to confess itself, in the popular phrase of the period, "an unnatural and tyrannical parent." "If in a private family," asked the *New York Packet* in February 1776 with reference to Britain's treatment of the colonies, "the children instead of being so educated as to take upon them the function of good citizens, should be brought to years of maturity under the apparel, food, and discipline of infancy, what laws, natural or civil, would acquit the parent of the child of infamy and criminality?"[12] If history itself followed the developmental model of an individual's moral and biological growth, to impede a child's growth was to deliver a blow to the very process of history. It was to usher in an age of slavery—a term in Revolutionary rhetoric that suggested an unhistorical and unnatural fixed and static state.

In contrast, Tories responded by insisting on the dangers of children prematurely leaving the protective embrace of their parents. To take one of numerous examples, Francis Hopkinson likened the colonists to an all-too-seducible daughter (shifting the colonies' gender from male to female better served the Tory argument) making her way in a world of demagogues like Thomas Paine and Sam Adams: "Should the colonies with base ingratitude, attempt to throw off all dependence on the mother country, they would put themselves in the situation of a silly girl, who leaves the guidance and protection of a wise and affectionate parent and wandering away exposes herself to ruin by the artful insinuations of every wicked and designing stranger."[13]

The debate over the control parents should have over the lives of their children was a central preoccupation in late eighteenth-century culture for the simple reason that the problems of family government, of balancing a just authority against a circumscribed but real liberty, the claims of the past against the claims of the future, the necessity of a stable organic social order against the obligation to encourage individual growth and self-sufficiency, were the larger political problems of the age translated into the terms of daily life.[14] In this regard, the cultural texts of the period, so steeped in the reconsideration of the right relations of generations, are deeply political in the broadest sense of the word.

In addition, the cultural preoccupation with dramatizing the conflicting claims of parental authority and filial freedom for a child who has attained the age of reason addressed a great psychological problem: how to mediate between the psychological desire for self-assertion and the psychological desire for submission (what Jefferson as early as 1776 feared might be, reenacting the Restoration of 1660, the people's desire for the "reacknowledgement of the British king as our tyrant").[15] It also silently addressed an overarching philosophical problem of the period—how to render compatible the two great competing intellectual systems of the age: idealism that viewed the universe as other-directed, and materialism that saw matter as independent and self-moving.

The figure most responsible for popularizing the rethinking of family relations was John Locke, whose *Some Thoughts Concerning Education* (1693) influenced virtually all the best-selling books of the 1770s and 1780s. Locke insisted that the ultimate point of child-rearing was not to secure a child's obedience, but to prepare a child for his (and we are talking about male children for the most part) eventual emergence into the world, to develop a child's reason so that it would serve as an internal governor eventually replacing the parent. If arbitrary imperiousness alienates child from parent and thus secures only a fearful rather than heartfelt obedience, a parent's gradual granting of freedom and responsibility to a child would, in contrast, keep that child bound by the higher bonds of gratitude, esteem, and love. Parental authority must be earned by the exercise of active nurture; the accidental fact of physical paternity does not give a parent the right to dominate his son's life.

Indeed, the popular Scottish moralist Francis Hutcheson, extending Locke's argument in his *System of Moral Philosophy* (1755), would go so far as to insist that one's "father" was not a biological designation so much as a moral one. A true father is he who exercises the most influence over a child's mind and character and thus, he concludes, "Whoever voluntarily undertakes the necessary office of rearing and educating, obtains the parental power without generation."[16] In such a manner would George Washington after the Revolution be held up as "father of his country." Unlike George III, whom Paine called "wretch with the pretended name of FATHER OF HIS COUNTRY,"[17] Washington would not only be "first in war, first in peace," but also "first in the hearts of his countrymen."[18] The paternal mythologization of Washington drew extensively on the rhetoric of numerous late eighteenth-century popularizations of Lockean parenting, such as Lord Chesterfield's *Letters to his Son* (1774) and John Gregory's *A Father's Legacy to his Daughters* of the same year.

Locke's pedagogy followed closely on the implications of the theory of mind set forth in his *Essay Concerning Human Understanding* (1690). There he argued that there are no innate ideas brought into the world with the soul; rather, the human mind at birth is a tabula rasa or blank slate. As all reflection follows on sense experience or sensation, our knowledge of the world is a function of our experience of the world. The sum total of these sense experiences and the reflections on them constitute the self. The pedagogical implications of this thesis, as Locke made clear in *Education,* were enormous. Because the mind is not formed at birth, "the little and almost insensible Impressions on our tender infancies have very important and lasting consequences."[19] A parent's responsibility is to inform the mind, to imprint a character on the blank page of one's child, especially, as man is an imitative creature, by the force of his or her example. It is essential that the mind be formed and informed early, before it becomes permanently misguided and misinformed by the wrong set of influences, impressions, and experiences.

Because impressionable children are in Locke's view not corrupt but corruptible, it becomes essential not only to protect children in their early years from, but in their adolescence or early "age of reason" to prepare them for, a corrupt world of seducers and flatterers. In a fallen world of false appearances, where words no longer are actual but only virtual representations of things, a rational education is needed to create the independence of mind necessary to storm what Paine a century later would later call "the bastille of the word,"[20] to separate true representations from false ones.

The deeply anxious strain of Locke's preoccupation with the impressionability of the human mind was perhaps the greatest legacy of his pedagogy to the eighteenth century. The 1771 first edition of the *Encyclopedia Britannica,* the great document of the Scottish enlightenment, restated Locke's point in this way: "Unless both parents concur in this rightful task and continue their joint labours, till they have reared up and planted out their young colony, it must become prey to every rude invader, and the purpose of nature in the original union of the human pair be defeated."[21] Like a sovereign state, the individual is vulnerable to invasion, to having his mind misled and his heart enthralled.

Country party politics, so obsessed during the Revolution with the corrupting powers of flattering and conspiratorial ministers, had its philosophical origins in Lockean sensationalism's insistence on the impressionistic nature of the human mind, the power of positive and negative example, and the inherent predilection of man to surrender to subrational appeals. If education was to man as cultivation was to plants then flattery was the "poysonous and pernicious weed" that would destroy the carefully tended garden.[22] The analogy between child-rearing and gardening ubiquitous in eighteenth-century prose was a trope for the transformational power of nurture, which must direct and control the wild growth of nature.

The eighteenth-century figure who took Locke's moral understanding of parental responsibility to the limit was Jean-Jacques Rousseau, of whom Charles Willson Peale thought so highly he placed an engraving of the master entitled "the liberator of childhood" over the family hearth. In his novel *La Nouvelle Heloise* (1760), Rousseau adamantly declares in his introduction "The vices and misfortunes of children are owing chiefly to the father's unnatural despotism."[23] Such a sentiment was echoed in a variety of cultural contexts such that by the last third of the century the family, as one scholar has put it, had become "a context of explanation, a mitigation for the child's sin."[24] Implicitly denying original sin, the new pedagogy blamed not the fallen nature of the child, but the negligence of the parent.

If the end of education is the development of reason, Rousseau argued, pointing to a contradiction in Locke, one can not teach a child by addressing a reason that is not yet developed. A child must learn from carefully controlled experiences. What Rousseau calls a natural education is paradoxically controlled by the artifices of a tutor who arranges experiences such as to ensure that the child will be obliged, as he would in the carefully controlled Rousseauistic environment of Peale's Philadelphia museum, to come to certain necessary conclusions. Because it declared true authority to be incompatible with obnoxious shows of power and insisted that influence replace force, the antipatriarchal revolution taking place throughout the entire West obliged authority to go underground. Or as Rousseau put it in *Emile*, "There is no subjection that is so complete as that which preserves the appearance of freedom."[25] This fact introduced a new set of anxieties into Anglo-American culture about the manipulation of will, reason, motivation, and affections.

By the 1740s the issues raised by the new pedagogical tradition found their definitive popularization in the new literary form, the novel, a genre which had developed in large measure to articulate and debate the new character of family relations emerging in the eighteenth century. Samuel Richardson's novels, which were widely imitated by the first generation of

American novelists, especially addressed the key dilemmas raised by the rationalist pedagogy. In *Pamela or Virtue Rewarded* (1740), the first fully developed example of the genre in English and under Franklin's imprint (though no copy survives) the first novel published in America, Richardson details the history of a serving girl who eventually marries her master. In Part 2 of the novel, Richardson recounts the trials of Pamela's domestic life as wife and mother and devotes over a hundred pages to a discussion and eventual endorsement of Lockean pedagogy. Restating the Lockean credo in the vocabulary of the sentimentalized Puritanism of the mid-eighteenth century, Pamela concludes that to preserve both the poor and the wealthy from a servile state, self-sufficiency must be taught at the earliest age. "And to this end, as I humbly conceive, the novel doctrine of *independence* should be early instilled into both their minds, and upon all occasions inculcated and enforced."[26]

If *Pamela* began the novelistic popularization of Locke's doctrine of raising a child to a state of industrious independence, Richardson's next and even more influential work, *Clarissa or the History of a Young Lady* (1748) mounted an attack on the bourgeois patriarchal family to point two carefully balanced and complementary morals. Multiple evils will result from a parent putting wealth and social standing above the moral responsibility to his children as well as from a daughter's rashly disobeying her father. In this case Mr. Harlowe has insisted that his daughter Clarissa marry a man she hates in order to augment the family's fortunes and honor. Pridefully unwilling to submit to her father and seeking to escape his sway, Clarissa falls prey to the sweet promise of deliverance offered by Lovelace. He convinces her to leave her father, seduces her, drugs her, and rapes her. Later abandoned by Lovelace and rejected by her parents, Clarissa dies before a reconciliation can be achieved with her family. Though Clarissa must die for her disobedience to her father's will, because her disobedience was finally more unwitting than willful, she will be rewarded for her afflictions in heaven. Accepting passively the afflictions of providence, Clarissa dies with the words of David on her lips, "It was good for me that I was afflicted."[27] Thus does Richardson have it both ways. He attacks parental tyranny, but not to the point of fully sanctioning a principle of rebelliousness. Through Richardson's influence, the post-Lockean briefs against parental tyranny and filial pride would become controlling themes of American fiction of the 1780s and 1790s.

THE AMERICANIZATION

In the first surviving American edition of *Clarissa* (1791) (earlier editions of the 1780s were read to extinction), the text of the original is severely abridged and transformed. The title of the first English edition reads *Clarissa or the History of a Young Lady, Comprehending the Most Important concerns for Private Life and Particularly shewing, the Distresses that may attend the Misconduct Both of Parents and Children in Relation to Marriage.* The title of the four surviving American editions of the 1790s follows up to *Private Life* but then continues, *wherein the Arts of a Designing Villain and the Rigours of Parental Authority, conspired to Complete the Ruin of a Virtuous Daughter.* In the American editions "the misconduct of children" is deleted. Clarissa is presented purely as a victim caught between two tyrannies; her rebellious spirit is not censured.

The same interpolated first paragraph—in one or another state—opens all the late eighteenth-century American editions. It limits the moral of the novel in a way Richardson certainly had not intended:

Miss Clarissa Harlowe, the subject of the following and the youngest daughter of James Harlowe, Esq. was adorned with great personal charms, and such perfections as rendered her the subject of a general admiration. Her father was a gentleman of a rigorous and inflexible temper and extremely tenacious of his authority as a husband and a parent. Her mother was a lady of mild and gentle disposition, but too much ruled by her demanding husband and imperious son, who left her little power of exerting the fine qualities she possessed.[28]

The Christian paradox of the original novel, the blessing of affliction, which had provided a spiritual context "justifying" Mr. Harlowe's severity, is wholly dismissed. Clarissa becomes less a prideful martyr to the glorious cause of filial obedience than a simple victim of unjustifiable parental severity. The title page of the earliest American edition also carries the announcement that the volume "has been familiarised and adapted to the capacities of youth." As Mr. Harlowe's sin is that he unreasonably demands perfection from his daughter and is unwilling to make any allowances for her "youthful capacities," the moral of the novel is reinforced in its abridged American edition by the form in which that novel appears. The very word "familiarised" carries with it the rejection of a too narrowly consanguineous understanding of family.

Two years before the Philadelphia edition of *Clarissa* appeared, the first

novel by an American to be published in the new republic, William Hill
Brown's *The Power of Sympathy* (1789), appeared from Isaiah Thomas's
press. Brown's novel follows closely the model of *Clarissa* and features a
heroine who is "caught between the ingratitude of her seducer and the
severity of her father's vengeance." Like Clarissa, she entreats her father "to
believe her misfortunes proceeded from credulity and not from an abandoned principle—that they arose more from situation than a depraved
heart; in asking to be restored to the favor and protection of a parent, she
protested she was not influenced by any other motive, than a wish to demonstrate the sincerity of her repentance and to establish the peace and harmony
of the family."[29] What Brown's heroine asks of her father is that he abandon
a Calvinistic understanding of moral accountability for a Lockean one that
demands nothing "beyond nature" and acknowledges that children are not
small adults but individuals whose reason is not fully formed. That the
misfortunes of children proceed "from credulity and not an abandoned
principle," that their "simplicity" does not condemn them but excuse them,
is the great filial insistence of the familial fiction of the period.

From the 1760s on, Arminian Calvinists in America such as William
Hart, Moses Hemmenway, and Jedidiah Mills challenged the New Divinity orthodoxy by insisting that man's inability, indeed his sinfulness, was a
matter of natural and not moral inability, of insufficient learning and not a
depraved character, and thus rectifiable not with a new gracious nature but
with a new nurture, a new habituation.[30] To an age radically calling into
question the doctrine of original sin and the orthodox understanding of
total accountability, the novel of seduction offered a refashioned account
of the myth of the Fall and therefore of the culpability of Eden's children.
In this version, Adam and Eve are less sinful prodigals who are deserving
of their punishment than they are victims more sinned against than sin-
ning. Jehovah is less the most gracious of parents than he is a parental
tyrant who demands perfect obedience from those who are guilty of nothing but natural inability. He is Calvin's God, whom liberal Christian rationalists will dethrone in a theological reenactment of the Revolution. Because her reason is not yet fully formed nor her education complete, the
fallen woman in this new myth is far less accountable. In its most radical
formulation, the daughter of Eden becomes an innocent martyr.

In the first volume of his *Decline and Fall of the Roman Empire* (1776–
88), Edward Gibbon argued that Christianity with its superstitious rituals
and supernatural mythos destroyed the critical philosophical spirit of classi-

cal and pagan thought and thus "secured the victory of infantile credulity over ancient philosohers." This superstitious spirit brought in by Christianity weakened the empire and was, finally, the remote cause of its fall. Like the fall of the sentimental heroine, so may the fall of nations and empires be attributed to a failure to form the rational faculty, a failure to make the credulous skeptical. Referring to the ease with which the popular mind may be misinformed by democratic demagogues, John Adams declared a generation after the war that in this regard "The people are Clarissa."[31]

Rational voluntarism in the marriage choice (a choice, the novelists insisted, that should be uncoerced by either parental pressure or irrational passion) was an issue with deep political resonances. In 1774, several months after arriving in Philadelphia from England where, because of irreconcilable differences with his wife, he had left behind an unhappy and childless marriage, Thomas Paine assumed the editorship of a journal entitled *The Philadelphia Magazine*. To it he contributed articles not only about politics but also about the true character of marriage and the necessity of liberalized divorce. One of these, "Reflections on Unhappy Marriage," appearing in June 1775, concluded with a critique of the institution of marriage as offered by "an American savage." In precise anticipation of the argument in *Common Sense* six months later, the Indian describes what Paine endorses as the ideal custom of his tribe: "But if any should be found so wretched among us as to hate where the only commerce ought to be to love, we instantly dissolve the bond."[32]

As the British government sought to prevent the American colonies not only from becoming independent but also from entering into a voluntary and inviolate union among themselves, British tyranny was, in its own way, nothing less than interference in the great article of marriage. The American cause was, in the broadest sense of a word so central to the political lexicon of America, the cause of union, of liberty not as a final autonomy but as the freedom to choose one's bond. Psychologically, it was vital to the colonists to believe that they were fighting not the cause of licentious freedom, but that of glorious voluntarism. Paine's insistence in *Common Sense* that "Independence is the only Bond that can tye and keep us together" made the point succinctly.[33]

A dozen years later in his play *The Contrast* (1787), Royall Tyler developed the standard dichotomies of his title—affectation and plainness, city and country, hypocrisy and sincerity—into a broad contrast between a patriarchal England and a virtuous and voluntaristic America. By making one suitor the product of an American education and the other of a British education, Tyler succeeded in unobtrusively having the conventions of the eighteenth-century stage serve a patriotic and antipatriarchal theme. Maria's American-bred suitor, Colonel Manly, proudly informs her that "in our country the affections are not sacrificed to riches or family aggrandizement." This emboldens her to confront her overbearing father: "I mean, Sir, that as marriage is a portion for life, and so intimately involves our happiness, we cannot be too considerate in the choice of our companions."[34]

Early in his minor epic *The Happiness of America* (1786), published the year before *The Contrast*, David Humphreys invokes a text often quoted in the period that was crucial to the literary reconsideration of familial politics: the "Wedding Hymn" of the fourth book of Milton's *Paradise Lost*. In it Milton holds that the fundamental relationship of all societies is not that of parent and child but that of man and wife, whose affections for one another are no less sacred than the affections held by blood to blood. From "wedded Love," "all the Charities/Of Father, Son and Brother first were known."[35] Accepting that radical inversion, Humphreys extolls a nation where "uncontroul'd foll'wing nature's voice,/The happy lovers make the unchanging choice while mutual passions in their bosoms glow."[36]

Whereas both Tyler and Humphreys insist that a parent ought not to force a child into a marriage repugnant to her, and that a child is justified in passively resisting such tyranny, both authors fudge, as do their predecessors, on the justifiability of *active* disobedience of the parent. However, two years before the American colonists chose to respond to English tyranny with a declaration of independence rather than a declaration of public fasting and humiliation, with its Old Testament assumption that tyranny was a divine affliction to be borne, a new kind of hero emerged in eighteenth-century fiction. Actively and violently seeking to free himself from a tyrannical fate, his story would deeply influence early national literature.

In 1774, Johann Wolfgang von Goethe revolutionized the Puritan/ sentimental tradition of the post-Richardsonian novel by publishing *The Sorrows of Young Werther*, in which his hero is hopelessly in love with a married woman. Werther refuses to accept passively the afflictions of Providence, denounces evangelical stoicism, and declares (I quote from one of the numerous American editions of the 1780s) that "human nature has certain limits . . . and beyond that degree is annihilated." Analogizing his act to that of "a people groaning under the yoke of a tyrant" who "at length throw off and break their chain," Werther commits suicide as an act of revolutionary defiance.[37] Denying the view of God as a dispenser of afflictions whose acceptance is necessary to one's salvation, Werther imagines God as an indulgent deity who will embrace his son "returning before the appointed time" and allow him to wait for his beloved to join him in a heaven that does not recognize the exclusive claims of marriage. Before 1774, the deaths of sentimental heroes and heroines are semivoluntaristic. Though almost always moralized against, after 1774 the suicide becomes a common figure in the sentimental novel. Thus passive resistance gives way to active (if self-destructive) resistance. Indeed, the hero of *The Power of Sympathy*, having taken his own life, is discovered in bed with an open copy of *Werther* beside his corpse. He, too, had chosen to escape tyranny and flee to another world.

The paradox of works of fiction whose subject is the dangers of reading works of fiction (a paradox at the heart of Cervantes's *Don Quixote*, an important text for this period) suggests not only an ambivalence in the early national period about the status of the imagination and the concept implied in the term "novel," but about the revolutionary novelty of America and the dangers of a historical optimism that encourages the imitation of that novelty. John Adams would put this question to Benjamin Rush a quarter century after the war: "Did not the American Revolution produce the French Revolution and did not the French Revolution produce all the calamity and Desolation for the human race?"[38] Novels like *The Power of Sympathy*, which was written during the debates over the ratification of the Constitution, insist in their subtitles that they are telling *A Tale of Truth*, that (as the Constitution would in a sense suggest about America) their realm is the actual rather than the possible. This, of course, ironically, intensifies their exemplariness and the degree of sympathetic identification by the reader, a sympathy that is precisely, once again, what the novel is written *against*. The title of Brown's novel refers to the dangers of a vulnerable heart overtaken by a sympathy or compassion that compromises the imperatives of self-interest and autonomy. Brown's heroine, drawn by the pull of an enormous sympathy, falls in love with a man who turns out to be her half-brother by her father's indiscretions. Sentimental identification leads to incest.

The political analogue to this is articulated in the isolationist character of Washington's Farewell Address (1796) to the citizens of America. Washington warns that too much compassion for other nations or an excessive sense of gratitude would involve America in dangerous "entangling alliances." Sentimentality leads to a delight in emotion for its own sake and an unwillingness to face harsh realities. For "one nation to look for disinterested favors from another," Washington warned, sounding like any number of parents addressing their children in the sentimental fiction of the time, ensures that it will "pay with a portion of its independence for whatever it may accept under that character."[39] The Farewell Address powerfully made clear the ultimate legacy of Lockean rationalism for the cis-Atlantic world: an intensified fear of the power of sympathy, of noncontractual or affectional relations—relations based on trust and involuntary fellow feeling, rather than on declared and calculated common interest. Such relations, like a coerced or overly passionate marriage, led to a dependence that compromised rational autonomy.

The revolutionary events of the decade following the fall of the Bastille radically intensified the fear of corruption of mind and morals so much a part of the predominant Lockean (to use the the term as a convenient shorthand) world view and epistemology of the eighteenth century. The multiple editions of Franklin's *Autobiography* published in the 1790s and the calls at the end of the decade to imitate the great Washington were attempts to ensure that the national character would be formed before the course of violent events—to invoke Noah Webster's neologism describing the effects of the French Revolution on the impressionable mind—"demoralised" it forever. Before, that is, the contagious power of sympathy (the grateful obligation the "gratitudinarians" in Congress claimed was morally owed France for its earlier support of the American cause) implicated Americans in the French madness.

The Alien and Sedition Acts of 1798 attempted to do by law what Washington was to do by example: protect the American character from Jacobin seduction. Such seduction threatened not only the individual mind by misrepresenting the world to the informing senses, but also the collective national mind. In a republic that sought to implement the general will by relying on public opinion as the expression of that will, the republican experiment would be radically jeopardized if public opinion were manipulated rather than informed. Recognizing the connections between literary and political history, John Adams (in a letter alluded to earlier) identified his Jeffersonian opponents with Richardson's great villain and their Francophile idealism with the illusory dream of happiness and freedom from moral constraints Lovelace proffers: "The awful spirit of Democracy is in great progress. It is a young rake who thinks himself handsome and well-made, and who has little faith in virtue . . . Democracy is Lovelace and the people are Clarissa. The artful villain will pursue the innocent lovely girl to her ruin and her death."[40] Whereas Jefferson believed in the final triumph of educated reason, Adams feared that "human reason and human conscience are not a match for human passion, human imagination and human enthusiasm."[41] The fear that America would embrace Clarissa's fate underlies the radical changes that the American novel of seduction would undergo in the last years of the century.

THE FINAL TRANSFORMATION

In 1798, the year of the Alien and Sedition Acts, Charles Brockden Brown's *Wieland or the Transformation,* the first important American novel, took up the debate over the fragility and credulity of the human mind in a manner that would influence a great deal of subsequent American literature. Rather than merely implying the epistemological dilemmas implicit in the Richardsonian novel of seduction, Brown made those dilemmas his primary subject. Therein lies the crucial importance of the novel as a reflection of American culture in the wake of the French Revolution. The novel's primary assumption is vintage Locke, mediated by the skepticism of Hume and Berkeley: "The will is the tool of the understanding, which must fasten its conclusions on the notices of sense. If the senses be depraved, it is impossible to calculate the evils that may flow from the consequent deductions of the understanding." Thus Brown declares it is the didactic purpose of his novel to "inculcate the duty of avoiding deceit. It will exemplify the force of early impressions, and show the immeasurable evils that follow from an erroneous or imperfect discipline."[42]

The story takes place in Pennsylvania "between the conclusion of the French and the beginning of the Revolutionary war" and concerns Clara Wieland and her brother Theodore. Some years before, they had been left orphans when their father, a religious enthusiast, was killed in a fire of spontaneous origin. (Significantly, in this novel of the 1790s the father is absent; it is exclusively the seducer who now must be feared.) Wieland (as Theodore is called) marries a young woman named Catherine Pleyel, whose brother Henry comes to live with them and Clara.

After a period of peaceful fraternity, strange things begin to happen to this little community whose security hitherto "had never been molested."[43] Disembodied voices are heard—one warning Wieland of dangerous things to come and another, even more ominous, overheard in Clara's closet plotting her death. Shortly after these occurrences there appears at the Wielands' home an old acquaintance of Pleyel's by the name of Carwin, who ingratiates himself into their rural society. It is Carwin who is responsible for these voices. He has mastered the new eighteenth-century science of biloquism or ventriloquism, like mesmerism a profane embodiment of Locke's principle of the inner voice of the introjected governor and of Rousseau's concept of "*la main cachée.*"

Carwin's motives are never made fully clear. But the reader does learn that, having heard from Clara's maid admiring accounts of her mistress's courage and rationality, Carwin feels compelled to test that rationality. As part of his plan, Carwin arranges things such that Pleyel overhears from within Wieland's bedroom what he believes to be Clara's voice declaring her love for the strange visitor. Trusting all too absolutely the evidence of his senses, Pleyel (secretly in love with Clara, as, indeed, she is in love with him) reviles her for what he imagines to be her promiscuity and banishes her from his affections. Thus has Carwin, an updated Lovelace, succeeded in destroying Clara's reputation, not in fact but in appearance. He is seducer less of women than of opinion, that sacred entity to which the Declaration of Independence addressed itself with "a decent respect." As her virtue was unable to protect her from misrepresentation, so truth and "the consciousness of innocence" are not enough to vindicate her.[44] In this postsensationalistic world Clara lacks what has become most essential: demonstrable evidence. Her character is no longer evidence enough.

But it is not only Pleyel who is misled. Even more tragically, Wieland himself is convinced that he has heard a voice—the voice of God obliging him to prove his faith by murderously sacrificing his family. He unhesitatingly obeys what he imagines is "an unambiguous token of God's presence:"[45] he slays his wife and children. Because it is never clear whether the voice is Carwin's or is of Wieland's own enthusiastic imagining, Carwin seems to confess in the very act of denying responsibility. The novel ends with the mystery of agency unresolved and the question of moral accountability intractably problematic. Brown's novel of authority misrepresented and authority imagined is a terrifying post-French Revolutionary account of the fallibility of the human mind and, by extension, of democracy itself. Ventriloquism and religious enthusiasm, its central dramatic devices, seem with a sardonic literalness to call into question all possible faith not only in the republican formula vox populi, vox Dei but in the confidence, as Jefferson put it, that our senses do indeed "evidence realities . . . without plunging into the fathomless abyss of dreams and phantasms."[46] In the year of the Alien and Sedition Acts here were embodied the larger fears that informed the Jacobin anxiety.

Wieland is, in fact, the dark side of Franklin's *Autobiography*, that other great text first published in the 1790s. The importance of the *Autobiography* (the first part of which was written in 1771) lies in the fact that in it the terrifying implication of Lockean epistemology, that things are not as they seem, turns out to provide opportunities for the successful manipulation of appearances. As easily as we may be victims of language, so may we be its masters when we have succeeded in learning—here Franklin quotes Alexander Pope with Rousseauistic approval—that "Men should be taught as if you taught them not."[47]

In *Wieland*, however, the same postsensationalist world is invoked, but in all its terror rather than its freedom and glorious opportunity. A generation after the first part of the *Autobiography*, the story is told from the point of view of the victim, rather than that of the self-satisfied and winning opportunist. Gone is the Franklinian optimism (and Crèvecoeur's fantasy of controlling the influences that will form America's "new man"); in its stead are epistemological terror and moral confusion. The book's subtitle, *The Transformation*, refers not only to the transformation of Wieland but to a broad historical transformation, the shift from a world that assumed stable forms and fixed relations between appearance and reality and between man and society to a world sensitive to shifting values, deceptive appearances, mixed motives, and most significantly, the tyranny of language over things, rhetoric over logic and moral feeling. A secure world has been made insecure and that, Brown announces, is the price of its having become "free."

In this transformed world both freedom of rational inquiry and the enthusiast's belief in religious determinism lead to fatal consequences. The insistence of Rousseau's *Emile* (with its echoes of Jonathan Edwards's discussion of the will a decade earlier) that the manipulation of human motivation was not a violation of human freedom, that the "willing" slave was, in fact, free, no longer seems tenable. In this transformed, though presumably enlightened, world in which Carwin declares himself "a friend, one come, not to injure, but to save you"[48] liberators cannot be distinguished from seducers, the pseudoaristocracy of charm from the natural aristocracy of virtue, and those that promise you the world cheat you of it.

The Power of Sympathy opens with the Lovelace figure announcing his scheme of seduction in these terms: "I will shew you my benevolent scheme: it is to take this beautiful sprig and transplant it to a more favourable soil, where it shall flourish and bloom under my own auspices."[49] Here "the benevolent scheme" of nurture and cultivation, the great enterprise of the Enlightenment, is mocked and perverted. Crève-coeur's environmentalist faith that as "men are like plants," transplanted Europeans would find in America "that everything tended to regenerate them"[50] is no less punctured and deflated. Significantly, that perversion serves as the point of departure for American literature, which for the next hundred years will be concerned in its greatest works with both the character and the betrayal of the American promise of liberty.

The necessary fall of man from familial security into a deceptive and competitive social world—the great story and history of the eighteenth century—created a new species of man: "the man of the world" who superimposes onto his original familial identity a new, self-made identity based on his relationship to society. In *Emile*, Rousseau described that new man and the transformation of his appearance: "The man of the world is entirely covered with a mask; he is so accustomed to disguise, that if, at any time he is obliged for a moment to assume his natural character his uneasiness and constraint are palpably obvious . . . reality is no part of his concern, he aims at nothing more than appearance."[51] Like Franklin, he preferred his persona. No longer are those who venture out into the world young men who wish to embrace a universal fraternity, who seek the liberty to exercise their social nature. They are instead opportunists like Montraville, Charlotte Temple's seducer, whose name, like that of his French collaborator, Madame La Rue, suggests the dangers of being "shown the city."

If seventeenth-century children's literature preached the Fifth Commandment by threatening death and damnation to the disobedient, its eighteenth-century counterpart made the scriptural injunction all the more terrifyingly immediate by dramatizing the vulnerability of the parental heart. In violation of its own rationalist emphasis, the new pedagogy encouraged the manipulation of heart and mind and will. Thus did it, especially in its Rousseauistic modification, suggest the terms of a new emotional or affectional authoritarianism by which the old-style family might be reconstituted. One finds this characteristic sentiment in *The Happy Family . . . Intended to Shew the Delightful Effects of Filial Obedience*, published in Philadelphia in the 1790s: "I would rather do anything than offend my papa and mama for they do look so unhappy when we are naughty, so cheerful when we are good, that I cannot bear to disobey them."[52]

Though the new sensibility conferred upon children "the power to make your parents and yourself happy or sad,"[53] it impressed upon them the terrifying responsibility attendant on that power. No longer might filial disobedience result only in the damnation of a child, but now, too, in the death of a parent. Such was the guilt-inducing message of the multitude of eighteenth-century deathbed paintings.[54] Filial disobedience becomes a species of parricide, a heartbreaking betrayal of love. When confronted with her suitor's demand that she flee her parents' house with him, Charlotte Temple, the heroine of that most popular eighteenth-century novel, declares (echoing the influential verse of Genesis 42:38): "But I can not break my mother's heart, Montraville; I must not bring the grey hairs of my doting grandfather with sorrow to the grave."[55]

A later incarnation of the seduced and abandoned heroine is forgiven her credulity by benevolent parents, but is either so terrified of grieving the guardians of her infancy or so reproached by a parent's kindness that she either dies of shame or chooses, as does Eliza, the heroine of Hannah Foster's *Coquette* (1797), to end her own life. "Oh Madam!" she asks, "Can you forgive a wretch, who has forfeited your love, your kindness and your compassion?" When her mother answers that "however great your transgression, be assured of my forgiveness, my compassion and my continued love," Eliza declares: "This unmerited goodness is more than I can bear . . . Your Eliza . . . flies from you . . . to escape the heartrending sight of a parent's grief occasioned by the crimes of a guilty child." It is a parent's grief, not anger, authority, or indifference, that is feared in the postpatriarchal family. Eliza kills both herself and the child she is carrying, "the monument of her sin."[56] She embraces God not because she has no one else to call by "the tender name of parent," but because she *has*. It is the sensitive parent, not the unfeeling one of the Revolution, that one now must flee.

Ultimately, however, both varieties of martyrs—Richardson's Clarissa and Foster's Eliza—are victims of a new, possessive parental solicitude which, in part, was the ironic consequence of the rationalist pedagogy's redefinition of the parental role. That sentimental code elevated children to such a sacred position as to make their honor identifiable with the honor of their family. Thus they became victims of what Phillipe Ariès has described as the tyrannical character of the "new" family relations of the eighteenth century which, by an obsessive parental love that sought to protect the family, "deprived the child of the freedom he had hitherto enjoyed among adults." The eighteenth-century family organized "itself around the child and raised the wall of private life between the family and society." It thus "satisfied a desire for privacy and also a craving for identity: the members of the family were united by feeling, habits and their way of life. They shrank from the promiscuity imposed by the old sociability."[57]

Whereas earlier the child was oppressively enclosed within the patriarchal family that the rhetoric of the Revolution had so violently called into question, now the nuclear family is, itself, walled off from the world. Indeed, it has become a world unto itself. The power of sympathy against which both Locke and Washington warned as a threat to independence is no less than the forbidden impulse to embrace once again "the old sociability." In picaresque texts like *Robinson Crusoe* or Franklin's *Autobiography* (both structured as revisionist retellings of the parable of the prodigal son), as well as in the post-Richardsonian novels of seduction, the loss of the family had been the price of choosing the world. Now, however, the price of choosing the family has become the loss of the world, a sense of anxious separateness from it.

As late eighteenth-century American culture extolled the closed garden of the family, it also longed for the sense of a larger community, of whose loss it was deeply aware. The preoccupation with sentimentality, benevolence, self-love, extended stewardship, republican fraternity, the Scottish insistence on sociable instincts of the soul, and, in the world of music, the "philoharmonium" or symphony orchestra with its utopian harmonization of disparate instrumental voices, all attested to this profound sense of loss. Embittered at the acquisitive machinations of her family, Clarissa spoke the silent sentiment of her age, the larger motive for her flight from her father's garden: "And yet, in my opinion the world is but one great family. Originally it was so. What then is this narrow selfishness that reigns in us, but relationship remembered against relationship forgot?"[58]

As the dream of a universal family must be surrendered to achieve the safer, more practical goal of perfecting the nuclear family, so an internationalist piety must give way to moralism in religion, and universalism, with its enlightenment ideal of "the citizen of the world," to nationalism in politics, with its fearfulness, in James Madison's dying words, of "the serpent creeping with its deadly wiles into paradise."[59] The sacred national union isolated from the world recapitulated the sentimental nuclear family isolated from society. Sealed off by its independence from the temptations of sociability, the new American nation (such is the suggestion of its earliest literature) would have to pay an enormous price for its independence: the failure to learn what Rousseau in *Emile* described as the "one art absolutely necessary to a civilized man, the art of living among his fellow men."[60]

NOTES

1. David Humphreys, cited in Kenneth Silverman, *Cultural History of the American Revolution* (New York, 1976), 517. On the epic poets in general see Leon Howard's still useful *The Connecticut Wits*.

2. On this point see Barlow's statement in "The Vision" in William K. Bottoroff and Arthur L. Ford, eds., *The Works of Joel Barlow* (Gainesville, 1970), I, 389.

3. The studies that in very different fashions chronicle this debate are Silverman, *A Cultural History;* Emory Elliott, *Revolutionary Writers: Literature and Authority in the New Republic* (New York, 1982); Michael Kammen, *People of Paradox* (New York, 1973); Henry F. May, *The Enlightenment in America* (New York, 1976); Joseph Ellis, *After the Revolution: Profiles in Early American Culture* (New York, 1979); Robert Ferguson, *Law and Letters in American Culture* (Cambridge, Mass., 1984); and my *Prodigals and Pilgrims: The American Revolution Against Patriarchal Authority, 1750–1800* (New York, 1982).

4. Chester E. Jorgenson and Frank Luther Mott, eds., *Benjamin Franklin, Representative Selections* (New York, 1962), 414.

5. Noah Webster, *The New England Primer Amended* (New York, 1789), 13.

6. See O. I. A. Roche, ed., *The Jefferson Bible with the Annotations and Commentaries on Religion by Thomas Jefferson* (New York, 1964). See also Susan Bryan "Authorizing the Text: Jefferson's Scissor Edit of the Gospels," *Early American Literature* (Spring, 1987).

7. Immanuel Kant, "What is Enlightenment" in Peter Gay, ed., *The Enlightenment: A Comprehensive Anthology* (New York, 1973), 383.

8. Immanuel Kant, *Education* (Ann Arbor, 1971), 6.

9. In their seminal study "The American Revolution: The Ideology and Psychology of National Liberation," *Perspectives in American History*, 6 (1972), Edwin G. Burrows and Michael Wallace cite over two hundred examples of familial language drawn mostly from the critical year 1775.

10. See Saul K. Padover, ed., *The Complete Jefferson* (New York, 1943), 29, for a facsimile of the revised manuscript page.

11. William Blackstone, *Commentaries on the Laws of England*, 4 vols. (1765; reprint ed., Chicago, 1979), I, 441. On the other side of the question, however, Blackstone would

insist "the tie of nature [and consequent obligation] is not dissolved by any misbehavior of the parent." (I, 442).

12. "Letter from a Member of the Virginia Convention," in Frank Moore, ed., *Diary of the American Revolution* (1860; reprint ed., New York, 1968), 98.

13. Quoted in Burrows and Wallace, "Ideology and Psychology," 195–96.

14. In the eighteenth century the powerful desire for social and political order is associated with a faith in a fixed "natural" order and a number of related taxonomies for which, to take the most obvious example, a Chippendale highboy stands as a good iconographic representative: everything has a drawer and everything in that drawer.

15. Jefferson in Gordon S. Wood, *The Creation of the American Republic, 1776–1789* (Chapel Hill, N.C., 1969), 123.

16. Francis Hutcheson, *A System of Moral Philosophy* (London, 1755), II, 192.

17. Philip S. Foner, ed., *The Complete Writings of Thomas Paine*, 2 vols. (New York, 1945), I, 25.

18. The phrase seems to have first appeared in Richard Henry Lee, *Funeral Oration* (Boston, 1800), 3.

19. James Axtell, ed., *The Educational Writings of John Locke* (Cambridge, 1968), 111. All future references are cited in the text.

20. Harry Hayden Clark, ed., *Thomas Paine: Key Writings* (New York, 1961), 101.

21. "Moral Philosophy" (unsigned) in *Encyclopedia Britannica or a Dictionary of Arts and Sciences*, 3 vols. by a Society of Gentlemen in Scotland (Edinburgh, 1771), 11, 270. Whereas Locke's individualistic assumptions led him to assert the importance of nurture, the communitarian assumptions of the Scots led them, by another route, to the same conclusion. In their view human sociability, the essential component of moral life, is finally no more than nature's divinely designed response to that initial parental nurture. The article above stresses this point repeatedly. Without such nurture society suffers no less than does the individual soul of the child.

    Both the Lockean and Scottish traditions addressed the problem of man's relationship to society through a reconsideration of the obligation parents and children owed one another. Both insisted on a noncoercive model of the family. Both, perceiving man as corruptible rather than corrupt, posited the necessity of an internal guide, be it reason or the moral sense, to enable one to lead a virtuous life in a corrupt world.

22. John Trenchard and Thomas Gordon, *Cato's Letters*, 4 vols. in 2 (New York, 1969), II, 3.

23. On Peale and Rousseau see Charles Coleman Sellers, *Mr. Peale's Museum* (New York, 1980), 22.

24. Ronald Paulson, "A Chapter from Tobias Smollett," in G. G. Rousseau, ed., *Tobias Smollett: Bicentennial Essays Presented to Lewis M. Knapp* (New York, 1971), 78.

25. *Emilius and Sophia, or a New System of Education*, 4 vols. (London, 1762–63), I, 204. All citations from this edition and translation.

26. Samuel Richardson, *Pamela or Virtue Rewarded*, 2 vols. (London, 1962), II, 399.

27. *The Novels of Samuel Richardson*, 19 vols. (New York, 1902), VIII, 102.

28. Samuel Richardson, *Clarissa* (Boston, 1795), 1. For the popularity and early American reception of *Clarissa* see especially R. E. Watters, "The Vogue and Influence of Samuel Richardson in America: A Study of Cultural Conventions 1742–1825" (Ph.D. diss., University of Wisconsin, 1941). For a different presentation of Richardson's literary influence see the opening chapters of Leslie Fiedler, *Love and Death in the American Novel* (New York, 1960). My account of editions follows the entries in Clifford K. Shipton and James E. Mooney, eds., *National Index of American Imprints through 1800:*

The Short-Title Evans, 2 vols. (American Antiquarian Society, 1969). No *English* edition with the revised title I discuss appears in the National Union Catalogue. (The British Museum Catalogue gives short titles only.) My point here is not to deny that comparable British redactions exist—most American abridgments presumably had British sources. My point is that *only* such abridgments are published in eighteenth-century America and that the American interest in this and other great works coincides, most noticeably, with the phenomenon of editions "adapted for youth."

29. William Hill Brown, *The Power of Sympathy* (Boston, 1961), 38.

30. For an overview of the Arminian challenge see Joseph Haroutunian, *Piety versus Moralism: The Passing of the New England Theology* (New York, 1932). For a representative primary text see Hemmenway's *A Vindication of the Power, Obligation and Encouragement of the Unregenerate* (Boston, 1772), 24.

31. The letter is dated March 15, 1804. In *The Correspondence between the Hon. John Adams and the late William Cunningham, Esq.* (Boston, 1823), 19.

32. *The Pennsylvania Magazine*, 1 (April, 1775), 152.

33. Clark, ed., *Paine: Key Writings*, 1, 19.

34. Arthur Hobson Quinn, ed., *Representative American Plays* (New York, 1927), 76.

35. John Milton, *Paradise Lost*, IV, 157–59. On Milton's influence see George Sensabaugh, *Milton in Early America* (Princeton, 1964).

36. David Humphreys, *Miscellaneous Works* (New York, 1804), 37.

37. *The Sorrows of Werther*, 2 vols. (Litchfield, 1789), I, 60, 72.

38. Quoted in Alfred J. Beveridge, *The Life of John Marshall*, 4 vols. (Boston, 1916–19), III, 2.

39. John C. Fitzpatrick, ed., *The Writings of Washington*, 39 vols. (Washington, D.C., 1940), vol. XXXV, 235–36.

40. *The Correspondence between the Hon. John Adams and the late William Cunningham, Esq.*, 19.

41. Lewis Cappon, ed., *Adams–Jefferson Letters: The Complete Correspondence between Thomas Jefferson and Abigail and John Adams*, 2 vols. in 1 (New York, 1971), 461.

42. *The Novels and Related Works of Charles Brockden Brown* (Kent, Ohio, 1977), I, 35.

43. *Novels of Charles Brockden Brown*, I, 56.

44. Ibid., 113.

45. Ibid., 167.

46. Cappon, ed., *Adams–Jefferson Letters*, 461.

47. Leonard W. Labaree, et al., eds., *The Autobiography of Benjamin Franklin* (New Haven, 1964), 66.

48. *Novels of Charles Brockden Brown*, I, 63.

49. W. H. Brown, *Power of Sympathy*, 4.

50. Hector St. John de Crèvecoeur, *Letters from an American Farmer* (1782; reprint ed., New York, 1957), 35.

51. Rousseau, *Emilius and Sophia*, II, 183.

52. Anon., *The Happy Family or Memoirs of Mr. and Mrs. Norton* (Philadelphia, 1799), 28.

53. Ibid., iv.

54. For an account of this popular genre of painting see Robert Rosenblum, *Transformations in Late Eighteenth-Century Art* (Princeton, 1967), 114ff.

55. Clara M. and Rudolph Kirk, eds., Susanna Rowson, *Charlotte Temple* (New Haven, 1964), 77.

56. Hannah Foster, *The Coquette* (Boston, 1797), 248.

57. Philippe Ariès, *Centuries of Childhood: A Social History of the Family*, trans. Robert

Baldick (New York, 1962), 411–13. Noting the similarity of findings in three recent books on the American family, Lawrence Stone offers a succinct confirmation of the Ariès overview of the eighteenth century: "It therefore seems an established fact that there was a fundamental psychological and social change in family life in this gentry sector of the Anglo-Saxon world in the mid-eighteenth-century." In *New York Review of Books*, XXVI, 1 (February 5, 1981), 35.

58. Richardson, *Clarissa*, 1, 41.
59. Marvin Meyers, ed., *The Mind of the Founder: Sources of the Political Thought of James Madison* (Hanover, 1981), 443.
60. Rousseau, *Emilius and Sophia*, IV, 204.

CHAPTER 19

Illusions and Disillusions in the American Revolution

Gordon S. Wood

These three exciting chapters by Melvin Yazawa, Lester H. Cohen, and Jay Fliegelman represent a new kind of cultural history. Such history doesn't deal with formal ideas as such, ideas abstracted from their social situations, but instead it moves along the borderland between society and ideas, where ideas become ideologies, attitudes, or mentalities and constitute the very consciousness of the society. This sort of cultural history is less interested in what a few great minds conceived and is more interested in the ways a past society tried to make reality meaningful. In such cultural history ideas become sets of symbolic meanings that shape and give cohesion to the society. It involves, as Joyce Appleby has put it, the collapsing of morals and ideas into values and relating these values to social behavior.

Such cultural history presupposes our modernist self-consciousness; it assumes the constructed nature of reality. In fact, the originality and success of each of these chapters lie in their authors' understanding that it was the American Revolutionaries themselves who initially grappled with the beginnings of this modernist assumption that now threatens to engulf us: that culture is manmade, and since this culture gives meaning to our social reality and thus creates it, reality itself is fabricated.

The Revolutionaries hardly saw the implications of what would become our modernist crisis, but perhaps for the first time in American history enlightened Americans sensed that they alone were responsible for their culture, for what they thought and what they believed; and it was this sense that gave their Revolution such a problematical quality. The Revolutionaries were certainly excited and optimistic at the outset, and they took up their responsibility with a sense of urgency and nervous expectancy. People were not born to be what they would become. Lockean sensationalism told the Revolutionaries that human personalities were unformed, impressionable things that could be molded and manipulated by controlling people's sensations. Suddenly anything seemed possible, and the Revolutionary leaders were faced with the awesome task of creating their own culture.

All three of these historians have a special interior appreciation, an inner feel, for this awesome task that more traditional, more exterior accounts of the Revolution have lacked, and this inner feel for what was going on in Revolutionary culture is the source of the significance of their chapters. For each of these historians the Revolution was all about education, but education of a special sort.

Education is defined broadly by Professor Yazawa as "the dynamics of socialization," and that is a definition that the other two historians seem to share. Such education involves far more than formal schooling; it comprises all the Americans' efforts to cultivate new attitudes and beliefs and to remake their culture. Such a conception of education not only includes Professor Cohen's Revolutionary histories and Professor Fliegelman's advice manuals and sentimental novels, but it also embraces a variety of other Revolutionary icons that we have not paid much attention to: from Thomas Jefferson's Virginia capitol to John Trumbull's paintings and the Great Seal. Although the American Revolutionaries' educational efforts may pale beside the efforts of Jacques-Louis David and the French Revolutionaries, by colonial standards they were impressive enough. These chapters not only suggest the extent and depth of these efforts, but they also convey the sense of anxiety that often underlay them.

Cohen's historians wrote histories that the twentieth century has usually found strange and disturbing. The Revolutionary historians made little attempt to represent reality impartially or objectively. Their accounts were not as much a reproduction of the past as they were, in Cohen's terms, "an incitement to ethical and political action." Their histories were rhetorical efforts in which the criterion of truth lay in the moral effect of the work on its readers. Such a criterion of truth, common to all neoclassical art, justified the historians' avoidance of a sometimes sordid reality and their omission of unpleasant facts about the Revolutionary heroes. For these eighteenth-century historians the possibility of the future was far more important than the reality of the past. The kind of history they wrote was not fiction, but it was not quite (in William Gordon's words) "the truth *truly* represented" either. Only in the last decades of the twentieth century, with our own criterion of truth becoming soft and mushy from the seepage of modernism into the discipline of history, have present historians like Cohen been able to give these eighteenth-century works the serious attention they deserve.

Like Cohen, Yazawa and Fliegelman are concerned with education in the Revolution, and they too suggest the sense of anxious urgency that lay behind the Revolutionaries' educational efforts. Both historians, however, range well beyond describing any particular means by which the Revolutionaries sought to educate the rising generation. Indeed, both of them attempt to grapple with nothing less than the major cultural issue of the Revolution if not of the eighteenth century itself: How do individuals relate to one another? How does society hold itself together? Both Yazawa and Fliegelman are concerned with the erosion of traditional patriarchal ties and their replacement by new sorts of attachments or adhesive forces. Both rightly see this transformation in the way individuals related to one another as the essence of the Revolution.

Yet ultimately Yazawa and Fliegelman differ fundamentally over exactly what relationships were transformed in the Revolutionary era. Yazawa argues that the old monarchical society was characterized by familial ties and by the affection presumably characteristic of such face-to-face familial relationships. The Revolution, he says, destroyed these personal and natural bonds of feeling and created more artificial and impersonal ones in their place. This change constituted the move from monarchy to republicanism. "The new republican character," he writes, "was no longer bound by the prescriptions of affection so central to the familial order. . . . The commitment to republicanism undermined the social significance of the bonds of affection."

Fliegelman sees the process of change in all these eighteenth-century relationships differently. For him, the attitudes of loving affection that Yazawa identifies exclusively with the old monarchical order were in fact new and were not inherently monarchical. If anything, such ideas of feeling and affection belonged to the emerging republican and anti-authoritarian world of the late eighteenth century. These new enlightened attitudes about filial affection, which Fliegelman traces back to John Locke's *Some Thoughts Concerning Education* (1693), gradually eroded the older patriarchal and authoritarian bonds between parents and children, indeed between all superiors and subordinates in the society, and eventually created something of a crisis of authority in the Atlantic world in the last third of the eighteenth century. In this new enlightened era the burden of authority's proof shifted: if children or other subordinates misbehaved, then it now became the parents' or the superiors' fault. To be enlightened was to believe that authority now had to earn its respect and obedience—largely by cultivating love and affection. That's what republicanism really came to mean.

It is true, as Yazawa says, that republicanism rejected relations of dependency among white male adults. But republicanism did not reject affection as well. In fact, the Americans' republican revolution was a political expression of the antipatriarchal attitudes that Fliegelman describes. It was an attempt to do away with fear, force, blood, or patronage as the basic forces holding people together and to substitute in their place love, affection, sympathy, or compassion. This secularized version of Christian love was central to the Enlightenment and to republicanism. In fact, these enlightened eighteenth-century hopes formed the foundation for all subsequent liberal thought. We still yearn for a world in which everyone will love one another.

By the time of the Revolution these antipatriarchal hopes—the emphasis on affection and affability in personal and social relations—had profoundly reshaped the character of classical republicanism and the republican adhesive of virtue. By the late eighteenth century, republican thinking about virtue in the English-speaking world had already shed a good deal of its ancient or civic humanist severity. Commerce and the increasing complexity of society had attenuated and domesticated the stark ascetic virtue of antiquity and had made it more Addisonian than Spartan. Virtue had become less the harsh self-sacrifice of civic humanism and more the willingness to get along with others for the sake of both peace and prosperity.

Classical virtue, as expressed for example in David's *Oath of the Horatii*, had always been a supremely masculine attribute. But this new identification of virtue with love and sociability eventually made it much more of a feminine characteristic (and thus especially capable of being taught by women). Only such a shift in the meaning of virtue allowed the eighteenth century to reconcile classical virtue with the progress of civilization. Without some such shift, as David Hume and others noted, virtue would have remained a primitive trait associated with barbarism and opposed to commerce, luxury, and civilization. Affection and fellow feeling were thus not contrary to republican virtue but at the heart of it. Still, the question always remained: Could Americans be educated to obey authority, and to relate to one another out of sheer affection and sociability? Doubts about the answer to this question lay behind their pervasive anxiety.

The Revolutionaries' obsession with education rested on their belief in Lockean sensationalism. But they were not such out-and-out Lockeans that they counted on men and women being able all by themselves to control the environment's chaotic bombardment of the senses. Something else was needed. As Thomas Jefferson said, "the Creator would indeed have been a bungling artist, had he intended man for a social animal, without planting in him social dispositions." Americans thus modified their stark Lockean environmentalism by positing some sort of moral sense or sympathetic instinct existing in every human being. Such a moral gyroscope—identified with Scottish moral or common-sense thinking and resembling Kant's categories—was essential to counteract the worst implications of Lockean sensationalism and to keep individuals level and sociable in a confused and chaotic world. But this moral instinct was just a germ in each person, and it needed to be cultivated and developed. So education, as all these chapters make clear, remained central to the Americans' experiment in republicanism.

What is most striking about the Revolutionaries' educational hopes is how hollow they eventually came to seem. All the leaders' educational efforts to make Americans into good, virtuous republicans seemed to go awry. Their valiant attempts to inculcate benevolence and to control the scramble for moneymaking were simply overwhelmed by the new commercial forces let loose in post-Revolutionary society. Demagoguery and vulgarity seemed almost everywhere to supplant affection and civility. Few people read the historians that Cohen writes about. Instead, they read the likes of Parson Weems, whose messages of virtue were very different from those of Mercy Otis Warren. Although the leaders' dream of a republican education for all was not lost, little was done in the decades immediately following the Revolution, largely because ordinary people did not want to spend their money on taxes for public schools. The first six presidents called for the establishment of a national university, but none was created. Even in Virginia, Jefferson to his astonishment had to fight like the devil to create his university in the face of evangelical opposition. Everywhere the secular humanism of the Revolutionary leaders was beset by real moral majorities.

We today usually like to think of elites as "exploiters" or "social controllers" and the "people" as their hapless victims. But, in the immediate aftermath of the Revolution at least, the process worked the other way round: it was the gentry elites who were victimized by the people, their grand plans, and dreams undone by a powerful, mobile, moneymaking, democratic society. Everywhere in the decades following the Revolution the high hopes of the leadership were dissipated or destroyed. A pervasive pessimism, a fear of failure, runs through the later writings of the Founding Fathers. Of the Revolutionary leaders only Benjamin Franklin seems to have died happy, and that was because he died in 1790, before the full force of the future became apparent.

Yazawa has focused on Benjamin Rush, and appropriately so, because no Revolutionary figure, including Jefferson, so personified the Enlightenment, and none believed so zealously in education. "Mr. Great Heart," Jeremy Belknap called him after the character in Bunyan's *Pilgrim's Progress* who attacked all the giants and hobgoblins that stood in the way of getting to the Celestial City. Because Rush expected so much from the Revolution, his disillusionment was especially profound. By the early nineteenth century his letters were filled with bitterness and despair. He looked back "with deep regret" at all his public efforts on behalf of the Revolution. Only by considering the people of Pennsylvania "*deranged* upon the subject of their political and physical happiness" could he contain the anger and contempt he felt. He wanted to burn all his "dreams," he said, and like Charles Thomson he eventually threw all the notes and documents for his history of the Revolution in the fire. Americans, he wrote, had no national character and little likelihood of ever getting one. The Revolutionary experiment on behalf of liberty, he concluded, "will certainly fail. It has already disappointed the expectations of its most sanguine and ardent friends." Like John Jay, Elias Boudinot, Noah Webster, and others, Rush ended by becoming a Christian enthusiast. The republican hope of educating people was over: "nothing but the gospel of Jesus Christ will effect the mighty work of making nations happy." This return to the mysteries of Christianity was a measure of just how badly the Revolution and the Enlightenment had turned out.

Rush exaggerated the despair, but nearly all the Revolutionary leaders felt it to one degree or another. All of them spent their final years wondering anxiously what they had wrought. Everyone sensed that the Revolution might eventually be a failure—everyone, that is, but the people. Most Americans had no fear of failure. Most ordinary people were ebulliently confident of the success of the Revolution and the promise of America. It was in fact precisely this expansive confidence and the excited pursuits of profits and happiness by the masses of ordinary Americans that lay behind the Revolutionary leaders' disillusionment. They simply had not known the explosive force of what they were dealing with.

CHAPTER 20

Whither the Sons (and Daughters)?
Republican Nature and the Quest for the Ideal

Catherine L. Albanese

In July of 1776, not long after the signing of the Declaration of Independence, Royall Tyler was graduated from Harvard College. Several months later Yale accorded him an honorary baccalaureate, and by the end of the year he had joined the patriot army. He did not see much active service, though, and was already reading law during the Revolution. With a master of arts degree conferred by Harvard in 1779 and admittance to the Massachusetts bar in 1780, the young man began what seemed an unexceptional career as a lawyer, punctuated most notably by a short-lived romance with Abigail ("Nabby") Adams, daughter of John and Abigail. Then, in March 1787, on a political mission to New York for Massachusetts Governor James Bowdoin, Tyler spurned New England rule and attended the theater. In little more than a month, his own play *The Contrast* was being staged at the John Street Theatre in New York City.[1]

The Contrast was the earliest American comedy to be presented by a group of professional actors. And, although after 1787 Tyler continued to join letters to his legal calling, his first effort became his best-known work. Produced, significantly, in the month before the beginning of the Constitutional Convention, *The Contrast* at once expressed and encouraged a new national pride. It was the first American play staged more than once, and in New York alone, it drew audiences five times in 1787, with a return engagement at the time of George Washington's inauguration two years later. Before the close of the century *The Contrast* had played probably fifteen times outside New York City, including performances in Baltimore, Philadelphia, Boston (where it was called a "Moral Lecture"), and

Charleston. One contemporary reviewer called the work the "effusions of an honest patriotic heart," while, in our own century, Allan Gates Halline hailed it as "a spiritual Declaration of Independence."[2]

What was it that this young man—a Harvard graduate in the shadow of the Declaration—had done to stir the enthusiasm of his compatriots and even later audiences? Why, while other American plays had been produced only once, did this one appear again and again? When one reads *The Contrast* today, it seems decidedly wooden, a stilted eighteenth-century farce, which, we learn, relied at least in part on a British model.[3] But closer scrutiny shows that Tyler turned his model upside down, imitating it to say something Americans found new. More than that, the newness Tyler spoke on their behalf was an ideology of republican nature in the wake of the Revolution.

Through the characters and action of his play, Tyler gave his citizen audiences nature as a roughhewn quality of Revolutionary innocence and simplicity, a sacred estate to be cherished and favorably contrasted to the artifice of England. In the person of Colonel Henry Manly, the patriot soldier who emerged as postwar protagonist, the old Puritan motif of wilderness trial was evoked and expanded to the limits of a changed society. Striding across the stage of nature's nation in his plain, unfashionable regimental coat, Manly preached in word and deed that American nationhood was a moral category demanding personal commitment. "Luxury" was "surely the bane of the nation," he said, and it was obvious that he thought natural simplicity its highest blessing.[4] In such a context, Manly's symbolic use of natural themes to express his political faith signaled the oblique appropriation of a religious heritage, even as it was rapidly achieving new form.

The "contrast" of the play was clear in the names and demeanors of male and female characters. Foppish Dimple, who was engaged to the virtuous and quietly heroic Maria Van Rough, in every respect countered the Manly creed. He was, as he bragged, "a gentleman who has read Chesterfield and received the polish of Europe"; he demonstrated how well he had learned his lessons by simultaneously maintaining his engagement to Maria and courting Charlotte Manly (sister of the colonel) and her friend Letitia. Meanwhile, Charlotte's embrace of European etiquette seemed complete, as she boasted to her visiting brother of the "faces of the beaux," which were "of such a lily-white hue! None of that horrid robustness of constitution, that vulgar cornfed glow of health."

Maria, on the other hand, sat home and endured her engagement to Dimple, dutifully obeying her father's wishes. While Dimple was away in England, she had schooled herself on the ideal of the Christian gentleman by reading Samuel Richardson's *Sir Charles Grandison*. More tellingly, one day disconsolate in her room she sang the death song of the Indian, the son of Alknomook, praising "the manly virtue of courage" it bespoke for her:[5]

> Remember the wood where in ambush we lay,
> And the scalps which we bore from your nation away:
> Now the flame rises fast, you exult in my pain;
> But the son of Alknomook can never complain.[6]

Maria lamented that she must "marry a depraved wretch, whose only virtue is a polished exterior," but in the end she was spared the sacrifice. A chance meeting with Colonel Manly meant love at first sight for both. Then, in the farcical denouement of the plot, Dimple's machinations were uncovered, and the senior Van Rough, restored to his republican senses, blessed a Manly–Van Rough connection. The shamed Dimple departed abruptly, presumably taking his dapper servant Jessamy, who once had told his master that Colonel Manly looked "the most unpolished animal your honour ever disgraced your eyes by looking upon." No doubt, too, the innocent young natural Jonathan, who had pointedly told Jessamy he was no servant to Colonel Manly but his waiter, accompanied the happy couple.[7]

In the midst of the laughter, Tyler's politicized use of nature was revealing. If *The Contrast* expressed the civil religion of the Revolution, it read the faith in decidedly New World ways. Gone was Jehovah God of battles and gone the city on the hill that lit the world's path to Israel redivivus.[8] Here, instead, was the plain country virtue of those who dwelled in the free air of nature. And here, in Alknomook's son, was the haunting dark of the forest that nourished with its wilderness energies. Indeed, the initial success of Tyler's play, at the end of the Revolutionary era, signaled the prestige of nature during at least the previous two decades. All unawares, the comic drama fostered a species of nature religion, mirroring the values of a culture which found political will in the strength that nature provided.

Yet, for all its achievements, *The Contrast* was only one sign, and it expressed only one public form of the symbol. It was but one instance of the power of the media—and of the patriot leaders who simultaneously shaped and were shaped by public evocation. Indeed, and to be sure, for many nature never did attain symbolic stature, and its capacity for nonsacral ordinariness should not be overlooked. To be sure, too, the explicit fear of wild country expressed by seventeenth-century Puritans continued and by the Revolutionary age was shared by recent immigrants such as, in the most well-known example, J. Hector St. John Crèvecoeur. The Frenchman thought that living in proximity to woods and forests brought an echoing wildness to humans, with "lawless profligacy" and an "eating of wild meat" that tended "to alter their temper." He argued that the chase rendered hunters "ferocious, gloomy, and unsociable," reducing life to a state of degeneration.[9]

Here, however, we need to direct our gaze elsewhere—to the identifiable collective symbolism that was linking nature to the life and destiny of the republic. For all the fear of wilderness, there was also patriotic fascination and even veneration for it, as the song of the son of Alknomook suggests. And for all the "secular" response to nature by those who struggled with and against it in order to survive, there was also exaltation of it in the public ideology that was the legacy of the Revolution. Thus, it is instructive to search for the religious appropriation of nature within the republican venture.

When we do so we find that, in the main, nature functioned in republican religion in three related ways. First, as in Tyler's *Contrast,* nature meant New World innocence and vigor, the purity and wholesomeness of clean country living on the edge of an empowering wilderness. Second, in an American appropriation of Enlightenment religion, nature meant the transcendent reality of heavenly bodies, which moved according to unfailing law, and—corresponding to it—the universal law that grounded human rights and duties within the body politic. Third, fusing with an aesthetic tradition of landscape veneration, nature meant the quality of the sublime as it was discovered in the glory of republican terrain.

Each evocation of nature built on the other, together adding to the enormous weight accorded to the symbol and, so, to its accretion of spiritual power. Unlike signs, which are distinguished by their straightforwardness, symbols are multivalent and multidimensional. What they point toward can never categorically be articulated in rational language, and their very mysteriousness leads to an amassing of energy that translates as Otherness. Hence, the symbol of nature acquired a life of its own as it commanded the imaginations of the patriots. Collective passion was displaced onto the symbol, and nature became what historians of religions call a sacrament. The emblem of more-than-human power, it also *was* that power in real and inarguable terms. Nature, as Other, had become religious center and sacred force.[10]

We do not have to look far to find instances, during the Revolution and thereafter, of the first meaning of nature—that of the politicized rhetoric of nature that permeated Royall Tyler's play. If we want to underline the side of the rhetoric that proclaimed natural wholesomeness, we can turn to the ritual wearing of homespun before and during the war. It was true, certainly, that the intertwining of politics and economy overtly prompted the move. Why should protesting Americans, angered by the Townshend Acts of 1767, support the British economy by their purchase and use of imported manufactures? The nonimportation movement tightened the screws on Britain with an economic boycott that was widely successful in 1768 and 1769, and its effectiveness could be measured by the repeal, in 1770, of all the Townshend duties except the one on tea.

Yet, signficantly, the constitutional protest that gave voice to colonial objections to the Townshend Acts came from the pen of the Philadelphia lawyer John Dickinson, who published his installments in the *Pennsylvania Chronicle* as "Letters from a *Farmer* in Pennsylvania to Inhabitants of the British Colonies." And, as the sanction movement spread, the negative act of economic refusal assumed positive form and function. "There began a vogue for spinning bees, wearing clothes of home-woven cloth, and brewing raspberry-leaf or Labrador tea," wrote Samuel Eliot Morison. "A freshman in the College of New Jersey who later became the fourth President of the United States, wrote to his father that every one of the 115 Princeton students was wearing homespun. The Harvard Corporation voted to let commencers wear homespun gray or brown instead of imported black broadcloth."[11] When the Continental Congress mandated nonimportation in 1774, the stage was set for a wearing of homespun that would join the symbolic counters of patriotism, rural wholeness, and uncorrupted virtue. That the ethos lived on long after the war is suggested by Colonel Manly's regimental coat, evoking in its plainness and simplicity its American homespun virtue.

If, on the other hand, we want to underline the side of the politicized rhetoric of nature that stressed its wilderness edge, we can point to the Liberty Tree and its meaning in pre-Revolutionary America. The Tree rose, first, at the boundary of the citied world of Boston. Protesting against the Stamp Act of 1765, "a few gentlemen hung out, early in the morning on the limb of a large tree, *towards the entrance of Boston,* two effigies, one designed for the stamp master, the other for a jack boot, with a head and horns peeping out at the top. Great numbers both from town and country came to see them. A spirit of enthusiasm was diffused among the spectators. In the evening the whole [of the effigies] was cut down, and carried in procession by the populace, shouting 'liberty and property forever, no stamps.' "[12]

As use of the Liberty Tree spread, demonstrating its practicality as a place from which to regard symbols of American estrangement from British power, the choice of the Tree told more. It spoke of patriot involvement in a process of religious symbolmaking that was at once universal and distinctively American. The Tree expressed themes of centering, evoking ancient myths of trees that were the axis of the world. It made implicit statements about fertility and the continuance of life—recalling the maypoles of European and, especially, English country life—now joined to the quest for liberty. And it disclosed intuitions of the requirement of blood and violence for abundant life (in the effigy deaths on the Tree)—as in sacred myths of origin from many cultures.[13]

But, in the end more important here, the Tree marked the place where the negotiated life of the *polis,* the city, touched the wilderness spontaneity of natural power. In the ceremonial performances of the Sons of Liberty under the huge elm tree in Boston or under other trees in other parts of the colonies, strength was communicated through the medium of the land itself. In the background lay the language of the dissolution of government into a "state of nature," a philosophical metaphor that distinctly captured the universal mythic sense of chaos and formlessness as the source of new societal form.[14] In the foreground was the understanding that, in America, nature already modeled its forms, providing a blueprint for the kind of society that was truest and best. When, later, frontiersmen in the patriot army adopted hunting shirts as their uniform, they not only succeeded in frightening the British and accommodating the shortfall in the congressional treasury. They also proclaimed a warrior mentality that only made sense in the shadow of the Liberty Tree.

The warrior mentality was reflected in Tyler's Colonel Manly, fallen in love with the maiden who approvingly sang the song of the son of Alknomook and the wood of his ambush. Yet, curiously, this graphic figure took his power from a second understanding of nature that moved the symbol from native ground to starry sky. In the Enlightenment language that shaped the Revolutionary generation's public, political grasp of nature, concreteness evaporated in a quest for the universal. Impressed by the machinery of the heavens and their ceaseless motion according to canons of universal law, the sons and daughters of the Revolution learned to speak a lofty, abstract dialect. If, as Marjorie Hope Nicolson has argued, "what men see in Nature is a result of what they have been taught," then the patriots, as heirs to European intellectual life, saw what their mentors pointed toward and spoke their seeing in absolute terms.[15]

Beginning in the seventeeenth century, English writers had conceived of space as the infinite realm of divinity. Likewise, in a parallel intellectual move, a doctrine of absolute time was articulated, finding eventual fruition in the work, among others, of Isaac Newton.[16] With the order and regularity of the Newtonian universe, the harmony of the spheres moved from ancient Greek philosophy to modern scientific law. Meanwhile, the absoluteness of nature set a new standard for estimating the significance of any human endeavor. When Colonel Manly praised American virtue, his compliment corroborated an absolute law that—following the classical dictum, "As above, so below"—moved from heaven to earth and back again in concepts of reason and the reasonable life. Universal law existed in the motion of the sun and the other stars, and it existed in the human species with its natural perception of the requirements of morality. Among the heirs of the Revolution lay the possibility for the reasoned gathering of humans in society and the reasoned life through moral law.

Before and through the years of their Revolution, educated upper- and middle-class patriots had been exposed to the natural religion of British worthies whose books appeared in New World libraries. Some had learned with Joseph Butler to contemplate "the conduct of Nature with respect to intelligent creatures," comparing "the known constitution and course of things . . . with what [the Christian] religion teaches us to believe and expect." Or they had understood with William Wollaston that the religion of nature was equivalent to morality, with its great law "*that every intelligent, active, and free being should so behave himself, as by no act to contradict truth.*" Or, if they had read Samuel Clarke, the close friend of Isaac Newton, they had been taught that originally the natural consequence of eternal rule was happiness. Subjecting their appetites and passions to reason, they would find the most direct way "to preserve the *Health and Strength of the Body,"* while intemperance naturally brought *"Weakness, Pains, and Sicknesses* into the *Body."*[17]

The clear bow to pragmatic gain in Clarke's reference to health and disease was implicit in the philosophic language of universal natural law. If nature meant revelation through the regular working of natural law, and natural law equaled natural morality and, so, religion, the presence of all three would guarantee the right working of society. Nature religion implied abundance and plenty. The pursuit of life, liberty, and property could flourish under the benediction of universal nature, and the grasp of metaphysical principle could prove, in the republic, a very tangible business.

Familiarized with Enlightenment ideas of nature, the American patriots learned their lesson well. When, during the debates of the Continental Congress in 1774, they sought a rationale for their resistance to the British government, they decided to pursue their claims by taking their cue from Richard Henry Lee of Virginia. Lee wondered out loud "why we should not lay our rights upon the broadest bottom, the ground of nature. Our ancestors found here no government." Others argued for the British constitution and their rights as Englishmen, but in the end the universalist sentiments of Lee prevailed.[18] He had conveniently transposed the abstract law of the starry heavens to an earthy bottom; and, in doing so, he had inadvertently revealed the uses of idealism to further specific class and ethnic aims in the American republic.

Still, ethnic idealism needed sociological embodiment in a community and ceremonial expression in public settings. So the lawful revolution sent its leaders to Freemasonic institutions, where the symbol of Enlightenment nature could be appropriately expressed. Freemasonry mediated the scientific culture of the Newtonian world, and, with it, a religion of nature that in America provided a model for the new democratic impulse within the body politic. Linked together in a fraternal web, the American Masonic brothers formed an intercolonial network that facilitated the flow of news and the shaping of opinion. Like the Great Awakening, which had spread a sense of unity of purpose and ideal in the colonies, the Masonic brotherhoods worked, in their own way, to achieve that end. One student of the phenomenon, Bernard Faÿ, argued that the Sons of Liberty (to whom we owe the Liberty Tree) as well as the Revolutionary committees of correspondence were Freemasonic "puppet" groups. Another Masonic scholar has stated that with the exception of Benedict Arnold, all of the American generals during the war were Masons. Certainly, the majority of members of the Continental Congress were, and so, too, were perhaps fifty-two of the fifty-six men who signed the Declaration of Independence. And after the war, we know that Masonic membership swelled, with war heroes and prominent public figures known to be Masons attracting the membership of other Americans.[19]

One need not lose sight of the obvious social reasons men joined the lodges to inquire what they were learning and what they were doing within these bastions of religious secrecy. How was Masonry shaping its initiates, and what kinds of ritual performances expressed and reinforced their affirmations? When, in 1783, Captain George Smith's *Use and Abuse of Freemasonry* appeared in London, it explained proudly that the Craft "supereminently excels all other arts, by the bright rays of truth which it sheds on the minds of its faithful votaries, illuminating their understandings with the beams of a more resplendent light than is to be derived from the assemblage of all other arts whatsoever."[20] Smith had offered a classic sun-reason-truth analogy and, in the process, had pointed toward that chief star in the heavens on which Masonic ceremony turned. If Enlightenment nature, on the Newtonian model, eschewed particularity of place and landscape, Enlightenment ritual in Freemasonry appropriately moved beyond the provincial to the universal sun.

Smith, and Thomas Paine who followed him, asserted Masonry's derivation from the religion of the ancient Druids, who were priests of the sun. But we need not accept their historiography to take their cue regarding symbolism within the eighteenth-century lodges. "When the lodge is revealed to an entering mason," wrote Smith, "it discovers to him a representation of the world, in which, from the wonders of nature, we are led to contemplate her great original, and worship him from his mighty works." Smith meant by the "great original" God, the great Architect and Creator; but in the ambiguity that was characteristic of Freemasonry, it was the sun, that "emblem of God's power, his goodness, omnipresence, and eternity," that figured prominently in the lodge.[21] One gazed at the sun in order to understand the deity—and in the sacramental life of symbols, we know, the emblem in some sense *became* what lay behind it, invested with a power that moved beyond the representation.

Paine noted that the orientation of the lodges, along an east-west axis, conformed to the sun's apparent motion through the heavens. "The master's place," he added significantly, "is always in the East." In a formal ritual that stressed the symbolic geography of sacred space, Entered Apprentices (first-degree initiates) were questioned by the master regarding the lodge's orientation. Meanwhile, apprentices wore leather aprons, white in color and, so, filled with Christian meanings related to baptismal purity, but also, for Smith and Paine, reminiscent of the garb of Druids and of Egyptian and Grecian priests. The floor of the lodge seen by the apprentices told the story of creation, while overhead the roof displayed the great sign of the sun. Finally, with space, officiant, and objects proclaiming the solar cult, Masonic time, too, promoted the religion of the sun. For in the Christian feasts of the two Johns—Saint John the Baptist on June 24 and Saint John the Evangelist on December 27—Masons discovered a convenient pretext for celebrating the summer and winter solstices.[22]

In fact, the prestige of the sun in the lodge was shared with the architectural symbols of the great Temple of Solomon in Jerusalem, and there was a visible evocation of Biblical themes in Masonic rites. One could, of course, go further and point to the gnostic and metaphysical readings of Biblical lore that were favored in certain Masonic texts. However, it is clear that the nature religion of the sun was intertwined with other themes in the lodges. Indeed, with its symbols of the Square and Compass—the emblems of the operative mason's craft—and with the use of these and related objects to construct a mythic model for moral development, the quest for the ideal disclosed its ethnic edge.[23]

To be sure, the Masonic ethic symbolized in the stylized construction tools spoke a language as universal as the Enlightenment could make it. With Captain Smith, Masons understood their work, or "art," as "coeval with creation; when the sovereign Architect raised, on masonic principles, the beauteous globe, and commanded that master science, geometry, to lay the planetary world, and to regulate by its laws the whole stupendous system in just, unerring proportion rolling round the central sun." However, the triumphalism of the universal was also hardly subtle. If God had been English for early colonists, he was Mason for a key segment of their Revolutionary descendants. With Smith, they contemplated their "virtuous deeds," assuming "the figures of the sun and moon, as emblematical of the great light and truth discovered to the first man; and thereby implying that, as true masons, we stand redeemed from darkness, and are become the sons of light."[24]

This Easter glory of the brotherhood at once exalted and masked the content of the moral life required of initiates. Counseled by their speculative and metaphysical Masonry, they fostered regard for active virtue—

fairness and honesty in dealing with one's fellows (being "square" and "on the square"); charity and concern for brother Masons and their families; equality in community among members of the lodge; respect for secrecy and strength in maintaining silence and the bond it brought; love of country and willingness to sacrifice, and even die, for it. In short, American Masons were encouraged to the full panoply of Anglo-Saxon virtue, to the proverbial Protestant ethic that was linked, as Max Weber had it, to capitalism and to the thriving mercantile classes.[25]

If the list seems unremarkable enough, we need to notice at least part of what was *not* there, what was not, evidently, written into the universal, natural law. In the paradox that was central to Freemasonry, universal virtue was predicated on elitist organization. Women, by definition, were excluded from a male society, but—as privileged men of their times— neither did the Masons accord equality in the brotherhood to blacks, or to the poor, or to other groups who did not "belong." Masonic virtue, in fine, was clubby, and so was the religion of nature it preached. The law of the starry skies and its human equivalent in the moral life were the concomitants of a recently nationalizing and ethnic class consciousness.

That consciousness, as we have already seen, was regularly drawn from heaven to its earthy foundation. Hence, nature held a third meaning for the Revolutionary generation. This third meaning lay in the landscape they had begun to glimpse in North America. Once again, Europe had given its gift to its New World relatives by shaping and cultivating patriot sensibility, so that Americans would know what to see as they looked at nature. By the late eighteenth century, what some of them saw was the sublimity of a wilderness terrain. Taught to recognize the quality of the sublime, they lifted mind and emotion to higher realities, infusing landscape with mingled awe and admiration and even with astonishment that verged on terror. Still more, in a peculiarly republican aesthetic that separated them from Old World vision, these Americans learned to understand the sublimity of what they saw as a sign of the stature and destiny of the new nation. Even nature had smiled her beneficence on the grand political experiment the patriots had begun. She had prepared the choicest portions of the planet—indeed, the most mammoth and stupendous—as the space for republican government.

Like other Englishmen, the patriots had been schooled to recognize the sublime by a generation of "sublime" writers, but probably most clearly by

Edmund Burke. In his *Philosophical Enquiry into the Origin of Our Ideas of the Sublime and Beautiful* (1757), Burke had distinguished between the two. He discovered the source of the sublime in whatever operated "in a manner analogous to terror" and linked the sublime to "the strongest emotion which the mind is capable of feeling." Burke explained to readers that the great and sublime in nature caused astonishment, "that state of the soul, in which all its motions are suspended, with some degree of horror," and he went on to tell them of the "inferior effects" of the sublime in "admiration, reverence and respect." There was "nothing sublime" that was not "some modification of power," said Burke; and, likewise, he connected the sublime to qualities such as vastness, infinity, and magnificence.[26]

It would be almost two centuries before another European, Rudolf Otto, would dissect the experience of the Holy to find in it elements of awe, overpoweringness, and urgency, as well as a perception of total Otherness and a mysterious fascination.[27] Yet it is not far from the mark to read into Burke's description of the emotion of the sublime much of what Otto was trying to chart in his book *Das Heilige*. The patriots would behold the American landscape, at certain privileged moments, with a quality akin to universal religious awe. At the same time, they would never forget that, in the idealism of their vision, it was the *American* landscape they were seeing and that, with America as a moral category, the land itself shared in political virtue.

When Jedidiah Morse published his *American Geography* in 1789, his admiring description of the natural features of the new United States, in fact, could not qualify as sublime. But the book loudly proclaimed the virtue of American republicanism, as Morse followed his geographic account with a discussion of the patriot government, a reprinting of the recently adopted Constitution, a series of convention resolutions, and—after consideration of economic and military matters—a history focusing on events beginning with the Revolution. Still, some of the patriots did look to the sublimity of wild land to feast their republican sentiments. "In at least one respect Americans sensed that their country was different," wrote Roderick Nash. "Wilderness had no counterpart in the Old World." "In the early nineteenth century," he noted, "American nationalists began to understand that it was in the *wildness* of its nature that their country was unmatched."[28] The wilderness was nature in its most unsullied form; and, for deists, it was the place par excellence where God could manifest himself.

Even in the city of Philadelphia in 1786, there were adumbrations of the meaning of wild country in Charles Willson Peale's natural history museum. By the 1790s, Peale's welcoming sign at the museum's front door announced "the great school of nature" within. At the south entrance, another sign invited citizens, "the book of Nature open," to "explore the wond'rous world./A solemn Institute of laws eternal." Peale aimed to retain natural form, attitude, and—if practicable—a sense of habitat in the exhibits, and so he kept a live menagerie attached to his museum. When creatures died, they were preserved and mounted; and the specimen collection grew to include an assortment of animals, birds, and even insects from throughout the world. Meanwhile, scriptural quotations inscribed in oval frames on the walls pointedly told of the Creator's power. In its heyday in the early nineteenth century, with the bones of at least one American mastodon and a stuffed buffalo part of the collection, the museum's visitors could contemplate in imagination the grandeur of the continent that had become their domain.[29] They could travel in mind to the wilderness boundary from which not only law, but also a profusion of life forms, hinted of the spiritual power that nature gave Americans.

Not merely in mind, one native Philadelphian, William Bartram, had traveled personally through the South, partly while the Revolution was being fought. From 1773 to 1777, the naturalist absorbed messages from the wilderness more than early rumors and later reports of war. He thought the magnolia groves along the Alátamáha river, "on whose fruitful banks the generous and true sons of liberty securely dwell," rose "sublimely" to greet his view. Elsewhere in his journey he owned that he found some of his "chief happiness" "in tracing and admiring the infinite power, majesty and perfection of the great Almighty Creator." On the top of Occonne mountain, Bartram called the view "inexpressibly magnificent and comprehensive," the landscape "infinitely varied, and without bound"; at the summit of Jore mountain, he "beheld with rapture and astonishment, a sublimely awful scene of power and magnificence, a world of mountains piled upon mountains." With instincts that George Smith and Thomas Paine would no doubt have endorsed, Bartram watched the sun rise near a Seminole camp. "Behold how gracious and beneficent smiles the roseate morn! now the sun arises and fills the plains with light, his glories appear on the forests, encompassing the meadows, and gild the top of the terebinthine Pine and exalted Palms, now gently rustling by the pressure of the waking breezes. . . . All nature awakes to life and activity."[30]

The Quaker naturalist had learned his love of nature from his botanist father, who, according to a friend—the "American farmer" Crèvecoeur—had placed an inscription over his greenhouse door: "Slave to no sect, who takes no private road,/But looks through nature, up to nature's God!"[31] If so, the son had transformed the Enlightenment republican version of nature supported by his father to a more romantic sublime that celebrated the grandeur of American landscape.

Meanwhile, the younger Bartram's contemporary, the more self-consciously republican Philip Freneau, mused in the words of his "Philosopher of the Forest" on the divinity once present in the American "woods and solitudes." There, he said, "the mind still finds itself in the best humour to contemplate, in silent admiration, the great and inexhaustible source of all things." Poet that he was, Freneau in patriotic vein could contemplate the Hudson river "On whose tall banks tremendous rocks I spy,/Dread nature in primaeval majesty." Or he could recall the awe he felt on the hills of "Neversink":

> These heights, for solitude design'd,
> This rude, resounding shore—
> These vales impervious to the wind,
> Tall oaks, that to the tempest bend,
> Half Druid, I adore.[32]

Freneau had joined to his sense of the American sublime a developed understanding of the first and second meanings of nature from the Revolutionary era. Not only did he speak through his journalistic Philosopher of the Forest, but he also found an Indian voice through the papers of the fictionalized Creek Tomo Cheeki. Using the pages of the *Jersey Chronicle* and, later, *The Time Piece, and Literary Companion,* Tomo Cheeki spoke of the wilderness vigor that would infuse American virtue. Likewise, Freneau's poems echoed the language of the Enlightenment with idealist references to nature's God who was the guarantor of the liberty of the American republic.[33]

The poet Freneau was joined in his merging of the various meanings of nature by other patriots such as Timothy Dwight and Joel Barlow. No deist, Dwight—most notably in "Greenfield Hill"—waxed eloquent on the wholesome rural virtue of American country life, which was not also without its grandeur and, more, its millennial promise: "Profusely scattered o'er these regions, lo!/What scenes of grandeur, and of beauty, glow."

Barlow, more comfortable with the Enlightenment God of Freneau, in a series of ambitious poems culminating in "The Columbiad" (1825) but already in "The Vision of Columbus" (1787), had pulled all stops, celebrating nature in a millennial vision of the republican future. "For here great nature, more exalted show'd/The last ascending footsteps of her God."

> What lonely walks, what wonderous wilds are these?
> What branching vales run smiling to their seas?
> The peaceful seats, reserved by Heaven to grace,
> The virtuous toils of some illustrious race.[34]

Roderick Nash has noted some of these connections, linking concepts of the sublime and the picturesque to deism in order to explain developing American attitudes toward the wilderness.[35] Here, however, we need to remember that republican nature meant more than wilderness, and we need to immerse ourselves fully in the ambiguity of the symbol. Wholesome country virtue and wilderness vigor, stars in planetary motion according to unchanging law, reason's rule and its expression in human moral life, American landscape sublimity, all were evoked in the nuanced life of nature among the patriots. Still more, all of the meanings, whether they were aligned along a horizontal (earthbound) or a vertical (heavenly) axis, perceived in nature the conceptual expression of a spiritual ideal. And yet—and this was the rub and the distinctively American paradox—all used the ideal as a means to feather material nests and, at the same time, to refuse to see what others might have termed the real state of affairs. For nature provided the theological frame on which to hang a civil religion of the American republic, and it also provided a grand principle of obfuscation to confute the patriots in the decades, even centuries, that followed.

None of the meanings of nature came to grips with what we might call a "secular" version of the events of the Revolutionary era, with the quite ordinary struggle of a prosperous group of colonists to free themselves from an empire they no longer required. Liberated from the older power, the former colonists could begin to fashion an empire of their own, glorying in the self-determination that would enable them to conquer a continent. They could be universal when they chose (and avoid the particulars of blacks, Indians, immigrants, and even their female counterparts). Or they could be particular when expansionist stirrings so dictated, amassing vast reaches of territory for the civilizing mission of the virtuous republic.

In short, the patriots, with nature as their banner, could have things any way at all and, mostly, any way they chose.

Yet this reading of the symbol of republican nature should not deny the bright and hopeful dreams it mediated. Idealism still was idealism, and as nature religion fused with civil religion in the person of the patriot leaders we catch a glimpse of the grandly seductive vision they beheld. We can look at Thomas Jefferson as one representative man among them, for in his words and deeds he clearly articulated the conceptually and morally ambiguous meanings of nature that helped form the emerging republican mentality.

Chosen to the subcommittee to draft the Declaration of Independence, Jefferson had quite literally stumbled into formal authorship. A brusque John Adams decided that the younger man should do the actual writing, and so it was that the Virginian composed the political statement which became a national creed. Jefferson's document gave classical utterance to the Enlightenment view of nature and also, in its lofty universalism, justified a specific revolution. Predicated on a contract theory of government, the Declaration assumed that a people had the power and right "to dissolve the political bands which have connected them with another." It announced forthrightly that "the laws of nature and of nature's god" entitled them to a "separate and equal station" "among the powers of the earth" and went on to list their endowments from a Creator God. In the list of grievances against the British monarch that followed, Jefferson, in his original draft, attacked the king for his role in the slave trade, accusing him of waging "cruel war against human nature itself, violating it's most sacred rights of life & liberty in the persons of a distant people." His earlier, more general statement had already proclaimed "life, liberty, and the pursuit of happiness" among the inherent rights of humanity and had understood government as security for these rights.[36]

Jefferson's Declaration, in effect, offered a brief for nature as an ideal and metaphysical principle. Far removed from the flora and fauna of a Virginia landscape, nature had become a fixed source of right and order in the world. Like the inactive deities of many small, noncitied societies who created but then withdrew from preoccupation with the world, nature could explain without involvement and legitimate without interference. The claims of the past had been nullified, and the new order of ages could emerge unparented out of universal nature.[37]

At the same time, the Freemason Jefferson was no abstract philosopher, and his empiricism as firmly brought nature back to earth. Natural rights were "inherent" rights; they could be found, not floating in ideal realms, but constituent in human beings. They were akin to the voice of nature speaking through the moral sense that informed each individual life. Writing over a decade later to his nephew Peter Carr, Jefferson told him that "the moral sense, or conscience, is as much a part of man as his leg or arm." This sense of right and wrong was "as much a part of his [man's] nature as the sense of hearing, seeing, feeling."[38]

Conscience was, in fact, the individual version of universal moral law, and Jefferson could tie it to Christianity in the person of Jesus of Nazareth, whose teachings embodied the law of nature. In the two compilations of New Testament extracts that Jefferson carefully constructed, he excised miraculous and divinizing materials to present Jesus as the quintessential natural man of the Enlightenment. What Jesus taught was universal ethical doctrine; and Jefferson's view of moral law, as Charles Sanford has suggested, seemed "similar to the law of gravity." Even so, Jefferson had taken great pains to historicize the universal teaching by discovering it in the words of the founder of Christianity: his ideology of nature was in the end pragmatic and concrete.[39]

Indeed, Jefferson's materialism was thoroughgoing. He had learned from Joseph Priestley, buttressing his own convictions that spirit was matter with the Englishman's arguments. Writing late in life to John Adams, Jefferson succinctly stated his position, explaining to Adams that he considered thought "an action of a particular organisation of matter, formed for that purpose by it's [sic] creator." Still more, after drawing an analogy between the power of thinking in matter and, tellingly, the power of attraction in the "Sun . . . which reins the planets," he launched into full confession. "To talk of *immaterial* existences is to talk of *nothings*. To say that the human soul, angels, god, are immaterial, is to say they are *nothings*, or that there is no god, no angels, no soul."[40]

Jefferson's brief for the material spirit was radical doctrine among the patriots, but he had only uttered explicitly what they were already absorbing in more intuitive terms. The ideal of nature became real in the public, political life of the republic: functionally, spirit had no existence apart from matter and more—if the whole truth would be told—matter on the American continent. In the nineteenth century, there would be other Americans who would push the implications of such materialism further still. In fact, it could be said that if any genuinely *new* religion arose in New World America, it was a nature religion of radical empiricism, in which the aim of religion was to conflate spirit with matter and, in the process, turn human beings into gods.

In Jefferson's case, as Daniel Boorstin reminds us, "his materialism was no appendage to the rest of his thought, but an assumption—or rather a predisposition—which colored all his ideas." And if the materialism was no appendage, it might properly be said to have sprung from the Virginia soil. Whatever else they may be, religions are human constructions, expressions of human labor to effect definite ends and goals. Jefferson's first understanding of work was the farmer's, and Adrienne Koch was surely right in saying that "he never quite lost the farmer's sense that the products of the orchard, the garden, and the fields are born of arduous labor."[41] Hence, we are brought squarely to Jefferson's involvement in agrarian life and, within it, his appropriation of a second understanding of nature, that rural country wholesomeness that strode across the New York stage in the person of Colonel Manly.

Before Colonel Manly ever graced the John Street Theatre, however, Jefferson was writing from Paris to John Banister, Jr., warning of the dangers of a European education. Away from home, one acquired "a fondness for European luxury and dissipation and a contempt for the simplicity of his own country." Jefferson found the consequences "alarming," for in Europe an American lost "in his knowledge, in his morals, in his health, in his habits, and in his happiness." By contrast, as his *Notes on the State of Virginia* explained, "corruption of morals in the mass of cultivators is a phenomenon of which no age nor nation has furnished an example." As for the individual, so for the body politic. "The proportion which the aggregate of the other classes of citizens bears in any State to that of its husbandmen, is the proportion of its unsound to its healthy parts, and is a good enough barometer whereby to measure its degree of corruption."[42]

Yet beyond his fears of corruption, whether from European immorality or, as in *Notes*, from excessive manufactures, Jefferson held a positive religious vision of life in tune with the land. "Those who labor in the earth are the chosen people of God, if ever He had a chosen people, whose breasts He has made His peculiar deposit for substantial and genuine virtue. It is the focus in which he keeps alive that sacred fire, which otherwise might escape from the face of the earth."[43] Jefferson's language recalled Puritan notions of special destiny in a New World garden, linking to them the high moral ground that had inspired the old Puritan ethic of righteousness. Still, the evocation of the past should not obscure that Jefferson had advanced that particular "deposit" for another day. The idyllic nature religion of the soil was, if examined from a different perspective, a charter for expansion. Manufactures required concentration of resources into smaller, more efficient units. They fostered geographical compression and citied living. Agriculture, on the other hand, demanded wide, open spaces; and so it demanded the acquisition of territory—and, implicitly, an encounter with wilderness—to support the multiplying American generations.

When, in 1802 as president, Jefferson learned that Spain had ceded the Louisiana territory to France, a concatenation of American anxieties and European events led to the huge sale of French real estate, annexing perhaps 828,000 square miles to the national domain. The new Constitution had been silent about the acquisition of territory, but by the end of 1803 the United States Senate had confirmed the Jefferson purchase. The sage of Monticello could dream of the agrarian future he had negotiated for the nation. For whatever the immediate circumstances of the great land transfer, the Louisiana Purchase was, as Boorstin wrote, "an authentic expression of the Jeffersonian spirit." Now Americans could flourish, as Jefferson had proclaimed in his First Inaugural Address, "kindly separated by nature and a wide ocean from the exterminating havoc of one quarter of the globe; too high-minded to endure the degradations of the others; possessing a chosen country, with room enough for our descendants to the hundredth and thousandth generation."[44]

Surely, there was an irony in the Manly wholesomeness that Jefferson likewise embraced. As Boorstin incisively remarked, the Jeffersonian's "professed belief, deeply rooted in his cosmology, that no piece of the universe was more important than another, that man's task everywhere had to emerge from his local condition, was overshadowed by the magnificence of the American destiny." And, indeed, "expansiveness and boundlessness seemed themselves a kind of destiny and definition."[45] Jefferson himself dreamed on, thinking of Canada and Cuba as part of the American empire. Thus, it is in light of the dream of empire that we need to view his appropriation of the third understanding of nature, when Jefferson beheld the national landscape as American sublime.

Writing to Maria Cosway, for whom he had formed a romantic attachment, Jefferson in Paris painted the scene that Cosway, a landscape artist, might paint at Monticello:

Where has nature spread so rich a mantle under the eye? mountains, forests, rocks, rivers. With what majesty do we there ride above the storms! How sublime to look down into the workhouse of nature, to see her clouds, hail, snow, rain, thunder, all fabricated at our feet! And the glorious Sun, when rising as if out of a distant water, just gilding the tops of the mountains, and giving life to all nature![46]

If the expanse was awesome, it was also clear that Jefferson was in the high place looking down. Expansion and expansiveness gilded the sight he saw: it was the aesthetic and religious equivalent of his republican dream. "The Falling spring, the Cascade of Niagara, the Passage of the Potowmac thro the Blue mountains, the Natural bridge," Jefferson told Cosway. "It is worth a voiage across the Atlantic to see these objects."[47]

Nor did he save these sentiments only for private communication. "This scene is worth a voyage across the Atlantic," he wrote in *Notes on the State of Virginia* after he had described for readers the passage of the Potomac river through the Blue Ridge mountains. It was, "perhaps, one of the most stupendous scenes in nature."

You stand on a very high point of land. On your right comes up the Shenandoah, having ranged along the foot of the mountain an hundred miles to seek a vent. On your left approaches the Potomac, in quest of a passage also. In the moment of their junction, they rush together against the mountain, rend it asunder, and pass off to the sea.[48]

Jefferson went on, in a Burkean move, to write of the "distant finishing" of the picture, of its "true contrast to the foreground . . . as placid and delightful as that is wild and tremendous."[49] However, if the sublime yielded to the beautiful for the distant gaze, we need to notice that, in the foreground, the sublime equaled wilderness equaled power. The equation had been shaped in Europe, but it was being reshaped in America under the aegis of forces that stressed magnitude as a way of being, a necessary landscape for the virtuous republic.

It was at Natural Bridge, though, that Jefferson found "the most sublime of nature's works." Although few had walked to the "parapet of fixed rocks" to look out over the "abyss," he had done so. "You involuntarily fall on your hands and feet, creep to the parapet, and peep over it," he wrote. "Looking down from this height about a minute, gave me a violent head-ache." The view from the bridge had been "painful and intolerable," but that from below was "delightful in an equal extreme." Jefferson was enthusiastic: "It is impossible for the emotions arising from the sublime to be felt beyond what they are here," he affirmed. "So beautiful an arch, so elevated, so light, and springing as it were up to heaven! the rapture of the spectator is really indescribable!"[50]

Yet if Jefferson had conformed his memory to Burkean categories, he had also confused them, finding sublimity in the view from below that gave him delight as well as in the (painful) view from above. Moreover, as Garry Wills has shown for Jefferson's delight, he had altered his evidence. Immediately following his account of the spectator's rapturous pleasure below, Jefferson described the scene as the mountains were cleft by the fissure. Significantly, he told of what could only be viewed from the high place. "The fissure continuing narrow, deep, and straight, for a considerable distance above and below the bridge, opens a short but very pleasing view of the North mountain on one side and the Blue Ridge on the other, at the distance each of them of about five miles."[51] Jefferson had been caught in the act, so to speak. It was an *American* sublime that he had experienced; and in American sublime, rather than being terrified, one liked and enjoyed being on top. That Jefferson was the legal owner of Natural Bridge as real estate only underlined the connection: American sublime hinted of empire and dominion.

But beyond that, the Americanness of American sublime mediated a certain danger. What was stupendous bore the risk of becoming merely stupefying in dimension, as if magnitude in size could serve as equivalent for moral magnitude. Already, in his *Notes*, Jefferson was expressing the American mentality that would flourish into the nineteenth century and beyond. He boasted of the "tusks, grinders, and skeletons of unparalleled magnitude" found in large numbers on the Ohio river and elsewhere. And he waxed, for the benefit of the French naturalist the Count de Buffon and others, on the putative mammoth whose remains had been recently discovered on American soil. Its skeleton told of "an animal of five or six times the cubic volume of the elephant," and it was certain the mammoth was "the largest of all terrestrial beings." With one animal, even such as this, not sufficient, Jefferson painstakingly assembled and elaborated on a chart that compared the body weights of the "Quadrupeds of Europe and of

America." He would establish to his and his countrymen's satisfaction the superiority of American specimens.[52]

The patriotism of Jefferson's polemic was evident. But what is important here is how patriotism, for Jefferson and his countrymen, was—for all the starry skies of Enlightenment law—mingled inextricably with an "earthy bottom." The land and its products must correspond in their stature to the perceived stature of the young republic. Nature must stand beside liberty; and if true liberty broke down Old World bonds and limits, nature, too, must defy Old World categories in its expanse. Surrounded by the unending space of the continent, the American translation for value was becoming size and magnitude. Nature religion meant communion with forces that enlarged the public life of the nation. And with Jefferson and other American patriots always on top, it meant conquest to insure that nature's forces would flow as the lifeblood of the body politic.

The logic and energy of the symbol were real: it contained power and mediated power, acting as mythic broker for an evolving American mentality. Meaning piled on meaning even for the Revolutionary generation. And as decades passed, the lens of the Revolution, turned by new times, would lend surprising and even contrary line and form to republican intuitions. The religion of nature would become the theological ground for dominance over the land and, simultaneously, for escape and illusion. As the quest for the ideal would fuse with the pragmatism of expansionist aims, the embrace of matter—man on top—would continue. But the embrace of matter would also cloak the avoidance of matter. It would celebrate a grandeur that glanced off the reality of the continent and its peoples in fulfillment of the urge to empire. The Enlightenment would bend its rationalism to the mythic mentality it reprobated. Dream would come to shape destiny, as nature, turned to new American purposes, presided over the unfoldment—and terror—of history.[53]

NOTES

1. For material regarding Royall Tyler and the early history of his play *The Contrast*, I have relied on Ada Lou Carson and Herbert L. Carson, *Royall Tyler* (Boston, 1979), 15–43.
2. Quoted ibid., 29, 31.
3. On a British model for *The Contrast* (Richard Brinsley Sheridan's *The School for Scandal* [1777]), see Carson and Carson, *Royall Tyler*, 31, 34, 35, and Arthur Hobson Quinn, *A*

History of the American Drama: From the Beginning to the Civil War, 2d ed. (New York, 1951), 69–70.

4. See Royall Tyler, *The Contrast: A Comedy in Five Acts*, introduction by James Benjamin Wilbur (1920; reprint ed., New York, 1970), 50, 79. I owe the phrase "nature's nation" to the title of Perry Miller's posthumously published collection of essays (Cambridge, Mass., 1967), although I use the phrase here in a context different from Miller's work.

5. See Tyler, *Contrast*, 112, 48, 26, 32. "Chesterfield" was Philip Dormer Stanhope, the fourth earl of Chesterfield, whose letters to his son on well-bred etiquette and worldly wisdom were published after his death in 1773. So popular did the letters become that they were printed in a fifth edition within a year. For a relatively recent edition, see the Fourth Earl of Chesterfield, Philip Dormer Stanhope, *Letters to His Son and Others*, Everyman's Library, no. 823 (London, 1973). Samuel Richardson's seven-volume novel *The History of Sir Charles Grandison* was published in 1753–54. For a useful study of the themes reflected here, see Richard L. Bushman, "American High-Style and Vernacular Cultures," in Jack P. Greene and J.R. Pole, eds., *Colonial British America: Essays in the New History of the Early Modern Era* (Baltimore, 1984), 345–83.

6. Tyler, *Contrast*, 32. I have quoted the third stanza of the four-stanza song.

7. Ibid., 38–39, 66, 54.

8. For a discussion of these themes, see Catherine L. Albanese, *Sons of the Fathers: The Civil Religion of the American Revolution* (Philadelphia, 1976), esp. 81–111, 19–27.

9. J. Hector St. John Crèvecoeur, *Letters from an American Farmer* (1782; Gloucester, Mass., 1968), 57–59. I should note here that my chapter has ranged widely over a period from the 1760s, to what I call the end of the Revolutionary "age" with the new federal Constitution in 1789, and to the early nineteenth century through, roughly, 1825.

10. For the classic account of the sacred as the wholly Other, see Rudolf Otto, *The Idea of the Holy: An Inquiry into the Non-Rational Factor in the Idea of the Divine and Its Relation to the Rational (Das Heilige)*, trans. John W. Harvey (New York, 1958), esp. 25–30.

11. Samuel Eliot Morison, *The Oxford History of the American People* (New York, 1965), 198. See also Morison's discussion of John Dickinson's "Farmer's Letters," ibid., 191. The Dickinson letters appeared in the *Pennsylvania Chronicle* from November 1767 to January 1768. Emphasis on "farmer" in the text is added.

12. David Ramsay, *The History of the American Revolution* (1789; Lexington, Ky., 1815), I, 83–84 (emphasis added). For a fuller discussion of the Liberty Tree in a religious context, see Albanese, *Sons of the Fathers*, 58–68.

13. See the discussion in Albanese, *Sons of the Fathers*, 58–60. For a fuller account, on which my own work draws, see Mircea Eliade, *Patterns in Comparative Religion*, trans. Rosemary Sheed (Cleveland, 1963), 265–78, 309–18; and, for the classic account of maypoles, see Sir James Frazer, *The Golden Bough: A Study in Magic and Religion*, abr. ed. (New York, 1963), 139–56.

14. For a discussion of the "state of nature" with reference to the American colonists, see Albanese, *Sons of the Fathers*, 48–55.

15. Marjorie Hope Nicolson, *Mountain Gloom and Mountain Glory: The Development of the Aesthetics of the Infinite* (1959; reprint ed., New York, 1963), 3.

16. See the discussion, ibid., esp. 134–43, 157–59.

17. Joseph Butler, *The Analogy of Religion, Natural and Revealed, to the Constitution and Course of Nature*, Everyman's Library, no. 90 (1736; London, 1906), xxx; William Wollaston, *The Religion of Nature Delineated* (London, 1726), 26 (emphasis in text original); Samuel Clarke, "A Discourse concerning the Unchangeable Obligations of Natural Religion, and the Truth and Certainty of the Christian Revelation" (1705), in

The Works of Samuel Clarke, D.D. (1738; reprint ed., New York, 1978), 643–44 (emphasis in text original). The definitive study of the American Enlightenment is the nuanced and illuminating work by Henry F. May, *The Enlightenment in America* (New York, 1976).

18. John Adams, *The Works of John Adams, the Second President of the United States,* ed. Charles F. Adams (Boston, 1850–56), II, 370–71. Reportedly, the debate occurred on September 8, 1774.

19. Bernard Faÿ, *Revolution and Freemasonry, 1680–1800* (Boston, 1935), 315; C.W. Moore, according to Robert Frike Gould, *Gould's History of Freemasonry throughout the World,* ed. Dudley Wright, et al. (New York, 1936), IV, 277; Faÿ, *Revolution and Freemasonry,* 241–42; Philip Davidson, *Propaganda and the American Revolution, 1763–1783* (Chapel Hill, N.C., 1941), 101; Herbert M. Morais, *Deism in Eighteenth-Century America* (1934; reprint ed., New York, 1960), 148.

20. Captain George Smith, *The Use and Abuse of Freemasonry; A Work of the Greatest Utility to the Brethren of the Society, to Mankind in General, and to the Ladies in Particular* (1783; New York, 1914), 134. The sun-reason-truth analogy here is strikingly consonant with Mircea Eliade's assessment of connecting themes in sun symbolism and sun religion. See Eliade, *Patterns in Comparative Religion,* 124–51, esp. 125–26, 150–51.

21. Smith, *Use and Abuse of Freemasonry,* 16–17; Thomas Paine, "Origin of Freemasonry" (1805), in Philip S. Foner, ed., *The Complete Writings of Thomas Paine* (New York, 1945), II, 832–33; Smith, *Use and Abuse of Freemasonry,* 147 (and see Smith's quotation from Hermes Trismegistes, ibid., 150).

22. Paine, "Origin of Freemasonry," 835–36; Smith, *Use and Abuse of Freemasonry,* 156–58; Paine, "Origin of Freemasonry," 840, 834, 836–37. On the floor and roof of lodges, see also Smith, *Use and Abuse of Freemasonry,* 148, 72–73; and for another pointed comment on the Johannine festivals, see Gould, *Gould's History of Freemasonry,* II, 38.

23. For further discussion of the Freemasonic mythic model for moral development, see Albanese, *Sons of the Fathers,* 133–36.

24. Smith, *Use and Abuse of Freemasonry,* 11, 147–48.

25. Max Weber, *The Protestant Ethic and the Spirit of Capitalism* (1904–05), trans. Talcott Parsons, 2d ed. (New York, 1958).

26. Edmund Burke, *A Philosophical Enquiry into the Origin of Our Ideas of the Sublime and Beautiful,* ed. J.T. Boulton (London, 1958), 39, 57, 64, 72–73, 77–79. (Boulton's text is that of the second edition in 1759.)

27. Otto, *Idea of the Holy (Das Heilige),* esp. 12–40.

28. Jedidiah Morse, *The American Geography; Or, A View of the Present Situation of the United States of America* (1789; reprint ed., New York, 1970), esp. 34–126; Roderick Nash, *Wilderness and the American Mind* (New Haven, 1967), 67, 69, 46.

29. Charles Coleman Sellers, *Charles Willson Peale,* vol. 2, *Later Life, 1790–1827* (Philadelphia, 1947), 229; Edgar P. Richardson, "Charles Willson Peale and His World," in Richardson, et al., *Charles Willson Peale and His World* (New York, 1983), 87; Sellers, *Charles Willson Peale,* 224, 228, 235, passim; Hans Huth, *Nature and the American: Three Centuries of Changing Attitudes* (Berkeley, 1957), 17.

30. William Bartram, *The Travels of William Bartram,* ed. Francis Harper, naturalist's ed. (New Haven, 1958), 31, 48, 212, 229, 154–55.

31. Crèvecoeur, *Letters from an American Farmer,* 192.

32. Philip Freneau, "The Philosopher of the Forest," *Freeman's Journal* no. 1, (November 1781), in Philip M. Marsh, ed., *The Prose of Philip Freneau* (New Brunswick, N.J., 1955), 198; Philip Freneau, "The American Village" (1772), in Fred Lewis Pattee, ed.,

The Poems of Philip Freneau: Poet of the American Revolution (New York, 1963), III, 386, and Philip Freneau, "Neversink" (1791), ibid., 3. ("The American Village" was Freneau's first distinct published poem.)

33. See the Tomo Cheeki papers from the *Jersey Chronicle* (1795) and *The Time Piece, and Literary Companion* (1797), in Marsh, ed., *Prose of Philip Freneau*, 331–53, 357–62. (Freneau's philosophical Tomo Cheeki took his name and a tenuous identity from the Creek chief Tomo-Chi-Chi who, in 1734, traveled with his wife to England.) For nature's God in Freneau's poetry, see, e.g., "The Pictures of Columbus, the Genoese" (1788), in Paltee, ed., *Poems of Philip Freneau*, I,117; "On a Book Called Unitarian Theology" (1786), ibid., II, 307–09; and "Ode to Liberty" (1793), ibid., III, 95. For Freneau's late poems, cf. "On the Universality and Other Attributes of the God of Nature" (1815) and "On the Uniformity and Perfection of Nature" (1815), in Harry Hayden Clark, ed., *Poems of Freneau*, Hafner Library of Classics, no. 19 (1929; reprint ed., New York, [1960]), 422–24. For a useful introduction to Freneau's thought, pointing to its complexity, see Nelson F. Adkins, *Philip Freneau and the Cosmic Enigma: The Religious and Philosophical Speculations of an American Poet* (1949; reprint ed., New York, 1971).

34. Timothy Dwight, "Greenfield Hill (1794)," in William J. Mc Taggart and William K. Bottorff, eds., *The Major Poems of Timothy Dwight* (Gainesville, Fla., 1969), 510; Joel Barlow, "The Vision of Columbus" (1787), in William K. Bottorff and Arthur L. Ford, eds., *The Works of Joel Barlow* (Gainesville, Fla., 1970), 135, 142.

35. Nash, *Wilderness and the American Mind*, 44.

36. [Thomas Jefferson], "The Declaration of Independence" (draft form), in J.R. Pole, ed., *The Revolution in America, 1754–1788: Documentaries and Commentaries* (Stanford, 1970), 30, 33, 31, passim. For a recent and succinct summary of the Adams anecdote, see Charles B. Sanford, *The Religious Life of Thomas Jefferson* (Charlottesville, Va., 1984), 17.

37. By "inactive deities," I intend reference to the kind of high god known to historians of religions as the *deus otiosus*. See Mircea Eliade, *The Sacred and the Profane: The Nature of Religion*, trans. Willard R. Trask (New York, 1959), 121–25. For alienation from the past, see Daniel J. Boorstin, *The Lost World of Thomas Jefferson* (1948; Boston, 1960), 169.

38. Thomas Jefferson to Peter Carr, August 10, 1787, in Merrill D. Peterson, ed., *The Portable Thomas Jefferson* (New York, 1975), 424–25, 424.

39. Sanford, *Religious Life of Thomas Jefferson*, 47. For the concreteness of the Jeffersonian cosmology, cf. Boorstin, *Lost World of Thomas Jefferson*, 43–44. For Jefferson's two New Testament compilations—"The Philosophy of Jesus" (1804) and "The Life and Morals of Jesus" (1819–1820?)—see Dickinson W. Adams, et al., eds., *Jefferson's Extracts from the Gospels: "The Philosophy of Jesus" and "The Life and Morals of Jesus,"* vol. 1 of Charles T. Cullen, ed., *The Papers of Thomas Jefferson, Second Series* (Princeton, 1983); for an insightful discussion of these extracts in the context of Jefferson's religion as a whole, see the introduction, by Eugene R. Sheridan, to the volume (3–42). See also the useful discussion of the so-called "Jefferson Bible," in Sanford, *Religious Life of Thomas Jefferson*, 102–40.

40. Thomas Jefferson to John Adams, August 15, 1820, in Lester J. Cappon, ed., *The Adams-Jefferson Letters: The Complete Correspondence between Thomas Jefferson and Abigail and John Adams* (Chapel Hill, N.C., 1959), II, 567, 568. See also Thomas Jefferson to John Adams, March 14, 1820, ibid., 562; Thomas Jefferson to John Adams, January 8, 1825, ibid., 606. For a short and helpful discussion of Jefferson's materialism, see Sanford, *Religious Life of Thomas Jefferson*, 147–52.

41. Boorstin, *Lost World of Thomas Jefferson*, 118; Adrienne Koch, *The Philosophy of Thomas Jefferson* (1943; reprint ed., Gloucester, Mass., 1957), 190. For a series of masterful interpretations of religion as an expression of human labor, see the essays in Jonathan Z. Smith, *Imagining Religion: From Babylon to Jonestown*, Chicago Studies in the History of Judaism (Chicago, 1982), esp. 43–44, 89, 100–01.

42. Thomas Jefferson to John Banister, Jr., October 15, 1785, in *Portable Thomas Jefferson*, 393–94; Thomas Jefferson, *Notes on the State of Virginia* ([1784] 1861; reprint ed., New York, 1964), 157.

43. Ibid.

44. Boorstin, *Lost World of Thomas Jefferson*, 231; Thomas Jefferson, "First Inaugural Address (March 4, 1801)," in *Portable Thomas Jefferson*, 292.

45. Boorstin, *Lost World of Thomas Jefferson*, 232, 233.

46. Thomas Jefferson to Maria Cosway, October 12, 1786, in *Portable Thomas Jefferson*, 404. (These are the words of the "heart" in Jefferson's literary dialogue "between my Head and my Heart" [ibid., 400] for Cosway's benefit.)

47. Ibid.

48. Jefferson, *Notes on the State of Virginia*, 16.

49. Ibid., 17.

50. Ibid., 21.

51. Garry Wills, *Inventing America: Jefferson's Declaration of Independence* (Garden City, N.Y., 1978), 264; Jefferson, *Notes on the State of Virginia*, 21.

52. Jefferson, *Notes on the State of Virginia*, 38, 39, 41, 45–55. In his essay "De la Dégénération des Animaux," in volume 14 of his great *Histoire Naturelle, Générale et Particulière* (1749–1804), Georges-Louis Leclerc, the Count de Buffon, pointing to the effects of climate and of food, had argued for the "degeneration" of animals in the New World.

53. For history and its "terror," see Mircea Eliade, *Cosmos and History: The Myth of the Eternal Return*, trans. Willard R. Trask (New York, 1959), esp. 141–62.

CHAPTER 21

In Pursuit of Religious Freedom:
Church, State, and People in
the New Republic

Nathan O. Hatch

In the *Herald of Gospel Liberty* for Thursday, December 8, 1808, the
religious firebrand Elias Smith, writing from Portsmouth, New Hampshire, unveiled what he described as a portrait of liberty: "The picture, is
this: two companies standing in sight of each other, one large, the other
small. The large containing every profession useful to society, the other
small, wearing marks of distinction, appearing as they did no labour, yet in
rich attire, glittering with gold and silver, while their plump and ruddy
countenances, prove them persons of leisure and riches."

The hypothetical dialogue Smith relates is a savage lampoon upon the
distinction between gentlemen and commoners—and as such an attack
upon the very fabric of traditional society. "Why do you stand thus a part
from us?—Are not ye of our number?" the people ask. "No (replied the
other), ye are *the people;* but we are quite a different order; we are a
dignified and *privileged class;* we have separate *laws, customs, & rights* peculiar to ourselves." "And what species of labour is it, that yet have a share in
performing in this society of ours?" the people query. "None," answer the
Privileged Class, "we are not made to labour . . . to mix and place ourselves on a level with the *common people,* would be beyond all measure
degrading and villifying."

After civil and military rulers are unsuccessful in enjoining the people to
submit, the gentlemen bring on the clergy to "*awe* and *intimidate* them
with the names of *God* and *religion*": "Ye cannot do without *mediators* to

intercede and act in your behalf," the clergy contend. "Your services are too expensive"; the people answer, "henceforth we mean to take the management of our affairs into our own hands . . . When the people declare themselves free, such *privileged classes* will be as useless as candles at noon day."[1]

In the wake of the democratic revolutions, there is little surprising either in this portrait of society as horizontally polarized or in the democratic agenda undergirding it. What is remarkable is that this radical critique was penned by an evangelical minister who spent most of his days as an itinerant revivalist in the Whitefieldian style.[2] On behalf of the experiential religion, Smith happily appropriated a language of liberty and equality which in England and France were being used as a battering ram against the church.

The experience of persons such as Elias Smith suggests that the quest for religious liberty animating the American republic in its infancy may be understood better at the higher reaches of society than at the lower. Studies have assessed carefully the dynamics surrounding the formal separation of church and state, particularly as they were played out in Virginia in the 1780s and in New England into the nineteenth century. A comprehensive understanding now exists as to the interactions among stalwarts of Enlightenment conviction, such as Thomas Jefferson and James Madison, traditionalists within Episcopalian, Presbyterian, and Congregationalist camps, and evangelical spokesmen such as John Leland and Isaac Backus.[3] And we are aware of the extent that pragmatism colored actions concerning church and state at the federal level, as framers of the Constitution and of the First Amendment sought to forestall yet another occasion for divisive debate.[4]

Yet the study of legislative debates and political maneuvering about the exact nature of disestablishment do little to convey the extent to which the quest for religious freedom became a genuinely popular movement. For those outside the normal boundaries of power, the Revolutionary events of the last quarter of the eighteenth century raised a host of pressing questions and made the issue of religious liberty an unfinished agenda far broader than the mere separation of church and state. In fact, if the quest for religious liberty had been principally a struggle to remove the meddlesome hand of the state in matters religious, it would have had little reason to gain momentum outside pockets of New England; and most certainly would have stalled as settlers poured into the unfettered environs of New

England's hill country, of western New York and Pennsylvania, and of Kentucky. On the contrary, at the exact moment that government in the republic was slipping away as a mediating agency, popular religious leaders continued to champion the cause of religious freedom. By the time of Jefferson's election in 1800, a sign for many that the age of religious establishments was crumbling, the real drama concerning religious liberty had shifted to new ground. With the authority of government increasingly "at a distance and out of sight,"[5] the issue of religious authority revolved increasingly around who would come to rule the church at home.

On that score Americans for the next generation were free to experiment with abandon. A long heritage, including the clergy's role in the American Revolution, had made the spirit of liberty and of religion "one undivided current" in America, to use Alexis de Tocqueville's phrase.[6] During the era of the Napoleonic wars, what is equally clear is that American churches did not face the kind of external social and political pressures that in Great Britain forced Christianity and liberty often to march in opposite directions. In particular, American churches were insulated from two wrenching issues that bedeviled religious dissent in Great Britain in the years 1790–1820, a period of vast ecclesiastical and political turbulence.

In the first place, Americans were exempt from the threat of government intervention against dissent. Continuing, if unspecified, threats by the British government against radical dissent forced Methodists into a conservative posture during these years. Convinced that their preaching privileges depended upon continued loyalty and good order, Methodist leaders were prepared to stand with the forces of order even if that meant an increasing gap between mainstream Methodism and working-class Englishmen. They were all too aware that they enjoyed religious liberty still at the hands of civil government.[7]

In the early years of the nineteenth century, furthermore, social upheaval and industrial strife in America were muted and restrained. Few Americans had to make the difficult choice of being radical or loyal to their church, as English Methodists did when faced with Luddite discontent. Nor did they watch great social divisions emerge within the church with the poor and the radical on the one side, and the preacher in alliance with "the leading friends" on the other.[8] The Rochester of Charles Finney's revivals saw hundreds of wage-earners join middle-class churches; and in Fall River, Massachusetts, Baptist, Christian, Methodist, and Universalist clergymen were active, if restrained, supporters of the labor movement.[9] In Manchester at roughly the same time a tough Methodist superintendent expelled four hundred from the rolls for radical activity and aimed to give "the sound part of this society a decided ascendancy." The result, in David Hempton's estimation, was that Wesleyan Methodism ceased to operate as a force in working-class culture and politics.[10]

Such polarization also meant that British radicals and libertarians, finding little solace within the church, turned far more readily to intellectual moorings beyond its walls. Virulent attacks against Christianity in the name of reason and democracy, such as those of Thomas Paine or William Cobbett, tainted any quest for the rights of man and turned the devout away from radical libertarians.[11] The continuation of monarchy and aristocratic privilege, on the one hand, and of reform impulses that railed against Christianity, on the other, meant that common folk found it difficult to align the cause of God with the pursuit of freedom.

In America, on the other hand, many who had not known formal education and high social standing—such as Elias Smith—began taking literally dreams of individual freedom, volitional allegiance, and self-reliance that had been the fare of the respectable during the Revolution. The result was a rude democratization of the Enlightenment as notions of religious liberty evolved in many unexpected directions. Pushed to its limit, liberty came to imply absolute freedom from ecclesiastical and confessional restraint, the privilege of the untutored to expound upon sacred matters, the radical subjection of leadership to popular will, and confidence that an age of freedom would supplant superstition and ecclesiastical tyranny. The right to think for oneself became, quite simply, the hallmark of popular Christianity.[12]

This ransacking of the vocabulary of liberty on behalf of Christianity is an interesting, and perhaps the most profound, interrelationship of church and state in the early republic. The study of legislative debates about the exact nature of disestablishment do little to convey the extent to which the quest for religious freedom came to be a popular movement and raised a whole range of pressing questions for those outside the normal boundaries of power. The last quarter of the eighteenth century witnessed a breakdown of confidence between the people-at-large and established churches.

The early republic is a time when a coterie of religious upstarts— Methodists, Free-Will Baptists, Disciples, Christians, Universalists, Adventists, and Mormons—challenged the cultural hegemony of the respectable triumvirate that had held sway in colonial America—Anglicans, Presbyterians, and Congregationalists. In Gordon S. Wood's recent assessment, these years represent "the time of greatest religious chaos and originality in American history."[13]

The result is difficulty in conceptualizing what is happening to American popular religion in the generation after Isaac Backus. How does one come to terms, for instance, with the family of Joseph Smith? According to Richard Bushman, they had for two generations been religious without being church people, had little relationship to mainstream Protestantism, and had been affected more by Enlightenment skepticism than by Calvinist evangelism.[14] In a similar vein, the Presbyterian minister David Rice despaired of the religious climate that he found in Kentucky in 1805—not because men were irreligious but because "religious practices" were "revolutionizing with so much rapidity." In a climate of what he described as unrestrained freedom, Rice admitted that the force of arguments against Calvinism seemed "irresistable."[15]

This chapter attempts to assess the popular rhetoric of religious liberty in the early republic. From many sources and locations, a language emerged that represents a profound revolt against the institutional religion of the time. Sources for this popular rhetoric are manifold, given the rising conviction at the turn of the century that common people had the right, even the responsibility, to break into print. Elias Smith expressed the credo which fueled an explosion of popular religious print: "As truth is no *private man's opinion,* and all *Christians* have a right to propagate it, I do declare, that every *Christian* has a right to publish and vindicate what he believes."[16]

This chapter suggests that this revolt was part of a crisis of authority within popular culture, a process that discredited institutional forms of Christianity, at the same time it renewed the wellsprings of popular religion, and sent them cascading in countless directions. Such popular ferment altered the center of gravity of American religious structures, ensuring that staid university graduates, who had defined the meaning of America so eloquently for a century and a half, would have trouble competing with upstart prophets whose appeals resonated in accents of America's people.

When and how did explicitly democratic values come to assume high religious priority? Evangelical dissent throughout the eighteenth century pushed at the boundaries of the social order, but by no means undercut its legitimacy. The legacy of revivalism included a revived Calvinism, a greater emphasis on discipline and purity within the church, and a clear reverence for the past.[17] Isaac Backus's definition of true liberty was premised much more on human depravity than on rationality or inalienable rights, and reflected John Winthrop's sermon on Christian Liberty and Jonathan Edwards's definition of true virtue: "The true liberty of man is to know, obey and enjoy his Creator and to do all the good unto and enjoy all the happiness with and in his fellow creatures that he is capable of. . . . Hence it is so far from being necessary for any man to give up any part of his real liberty in order to submit to government, that all nations have found it necessary to submit to some government in order to enjoy any liberty and security at all."[18] Similarly, Rhys Isaac has suggested that the central impulse of the Baptists in Virginia was toward a tighter, more effective system of values.[19]

The strength and energy created by the American Revolution and the fierce debates surrounding the advent of republican government profoundly influenced the nature of religious commitment, pressing ideals of liberty closer to the core of religious values and raising unsettling questions about authority structures that were not volitional.[20] The dissident Presbyterian Jacob Green, for instance, criticized the Synod of New York and Philadelphia in 1781 for failing to adapt its structures to the self-evident verities of freedom:

This is a time in which civil and religious liberty is attended to, is contended for, and we trust, is about to take place, if not to be established. It is a time in which a spirit of liberty prevails, a time in which the externals of religion may properly be new modelled, if needful, and fixed upon a gospel plan. . . . The plan of church government which we have chosen, and we think derived from Scripture, is a plan for liberty; the land we live in is a land of liberty; the time we live in is, especially a time of liberty; and we cannot but desire, and even expect, that many others, within the bonds of the synod, and elsewhere also, will revise their ecclesiastical principles, and see if they do not want something to make them more fully consistent with christian liberty.[21]

Among humbler folk, the pursuit of religious liberty became a root and branch assault upon the established order, a revolt that came to be expressed in at least three ways: in a rejection of the wisdom of tradition, in strident anticlericalism, and in a denial of the very ground for ecclesiastical authority. "Liberty is a great cant word with them," Walter Harris, the

Congregational minister at Dunbarton, New Hampshire, said of local sectarians in 1811:

> They promise their hearers to set them at liberty. And to effect this, they advise them to give all their old prejudices and traditions which they have received from their fathers and their ministers; who they say, are hirelings, keeping your souls in bondage, and under oppression. Hence to use their own language, they say, 'Break all these yokes and trammels from off you, and come out of prison; and dare to think, and speak, and act for yourselves.'[22]

Despite the luxuriant variety of Christian idioms that flowered in the early republic, most seemed to spring from a common conception of history: a pervasive sense that Christian tradition since the time of the Apostles was a tale of sordid corruption in which kingcraft and priestcraft wielded orthodoxy in order to enslave the minds of the people. This severing of ties with both Catholic and Protestant traditions was coupled with a heady sense of anticipation that a new restoration of the primitive church was at hand. Men like Benjamin Randel, founder of the Free-Will Baptists, called for a new dispensation of gospel liberty, radically discontinuous with the past.[23]

What gave credence to the idea that they were standing on the brink of a new age? Such attitudes rested on the conviction that people were witnessing in the American and French Revolutions the most momentous historical events in two millennia—a *novus ordo seclorum*. Not since the English Civil War had such swift and unpredictable currents shaken the traditions of Western society. What fired apocalyptic imaginations far more than the mere fact that battles had been won and constitutions written was the realization that the very structures of society were undergoing a drastic democratic winnowing. The opening line of the *Herald of Gospel Liberty* proclaimed that "the age in which we live may certainly be distinguished from others in the history of Man," and Smith was quick to point out that it was the struggle for liberty and the rights of man that set it apart. Alexander Campbell, the founder of the Disciples of Christ, argued that the War for Independence unveiled a new epoch that would deliver men from "the melancholy thraldom of relentless systems." America's "political regeneration" gave her the responsibility to lead a comparable "ecclesiastical renovation."[24]

William Miller, Elias Smith, Alexander Campbell, Barton Stone, and Joseph Smith all believed that, since the age of the Apostles, a great falling away had severed the relationship of God and man, leaving the visible church during the "Dark Ages" controlled by the "Whore of Babylon." They agreed also that, whatever good the Protestant Reformation had done, it had not reopened the heavens nor restored authentic Christianity. Each was also convinced that they were part of a process by which God was restoring the purity of the primitive gospel—"the ancient order of things."[25]

Such a decisive expatriation from the past has few parallels among eighteenth-century evangelicals, either British or American. It is much closer to Thomas Jefferson's thoughts on breaking the grip of custom and precedent. Similarly, it paralleled Paine's Revolutionary rejection of the sovereignty of one generation over the next. In *The Rights of Man* (1791), Paine defined the new era that had dawned: "All men are born equal, and with equal and natural rights, and in the same manner as if posterity had been conceived by creation instead of generation. . . . The world is as new to him as it was to the first man that existed, and his natural right in it is of the same kind. Each generation must be free to act for itself . . . as the age and generations which preceded it."[26]

The most common expression of this revolt against history turned out to be an appeal to the idea, "No creed but the Bible." "I have endeavored to read the scriptures as though no one had read them before me," claimed Alexander Campbell, "and I am as much on my guard against reading them to-day, through the medium of my own views yesterday, or a week ago, as I am against being influenced by any foreign name, authority, or system whatever."[27] By mid-century, John W. Nevin claimed, after reading the statements of faith of fifty-three American denominations, that the distinctive feature of American religion was this attempt to disentangle the pure teachings of scripture from the corruptions of any human mediation.[28] This impulse clearly had popular origins as people drew upon a wide range of sources—many of them radical critiques of Christianity itself—to gain leverage against what dissenters called the "grave clothes of tradition," or "the strong chains of tradition."[29]

Elias Smith's definition of religious liberty itself revolves around extricating oneself from the clutches of tradition: "Religious liberty does not consist in an opportunity to believe and practice what our fathers did . . . but in being wholly free to examine for ourselves, what is truth, without being bound to catachism, creed, confession of faith, discipline, or any rule excepting the scriptures."[30]

A zeal to dismantle mediating elites within the church was the second standard raised by people working out the implications of religious liberty. The stridency of this anticlericalism is surprising, given that it was a ferment among professing Christians. Its force was less to single out clergymen for their deficiencies in theology or preaching and more to call into question the fundamental norms defining the clerical office itself.[31] What rankled dissenters most at the turn of the century were the elite positional codes that symbolized clerical social position and authority—a cultural style that Harriet Beecher Stowe depicted superbly in "The Old-Meeting House":

Nor were our Sunday services, though simple, devoid of their solemn forms. The mixed and motley congregation came in with due decorum during the ringing of the first bell, and waited in their seats the advent of the minister. The tolling of the bell was the signal for him that his audience were ready to receive him, and he started from his house. The clerical dress of the day, the black silk gown, the spotless bands, the wig and three-cornered hat and black gloves, were items of professional fitness which, in our minister's case, never failed of a due attention. When, with his wife leaning on his arm, he entered at the door of the meeting-house, the whole congregation rose and remained standing until he had taken his seat in the pulpit. The same reverential decorum was maintained after service was over, when all remained standing and uncovered while the minister and his family passed down the broad aisle and left the house. Our fathers were no man-worshippers, but they regarded the minister as an ambassador from the Great Sovereign of the universe, and paid reverence to Him whose word he bore in their treatment of him.[32]

As a young Baptist minister in Massachusetts, Elias Smith was acutely sensitive about the significance of clerical dress. He recalls that after accepting a church in Woburn, certain Boston ministers criticized his plain dress. "I was soon dressed in fashionable black, a large three cornered hat, and black silk gloves, to wear in the meeting house." Smith felt terribly uncomfortable with these trappings and later recounted his experience of rejecting them:

While setting and conversing together, Doctor [Hezekiah] Smith said to me, 'I advise you to wear a band on Lord's day.' I asked the Doctor what the band meant? He replied, 'That as I lived near the metropolis, it would make me appear respectable; and besides, said he, it will show that you are an ordained minister.' I then asked him how ministers came to wear bands? He said, 'He supposed it was taken from the *high priest's breast plate.*' My reply was, if that is the way bands came, I will never wear one again; for my *high priest* has his on in glory; and for me to wear a band, would be taking that to myself which belongs only to him. From that day to this I have held as abominable, the *band, surplice,* and the other part of the clerical, anti-christian attire of the mother of harlots, and abomination of the earth.[33]

The clergy appeared to be such an evil force because they denied people the right to think and act for themselves. In this sense, the anticlericalism of the early republic is an integral part of the broader attack upon the professions—lawyers and physicians as well as men of the cloth.[34] According to Elias Smith, "ignorant, corrupt and wicked hirelings," have attempted "to draw men into a *slavish dependence* on them; that by representing the Scriptures as a *dark book,* they have *hood winked* the followers of Christ, and others, that they might render them *implicit believers* in their arbitrary *decrees,* and make them, without control, subservient to the views of their *ambition, avarice, pride* and *luxury.*" Elsewhere, Smith argued that thousands in America remained "under *mental bondage*" of the clergy despite "the contest for LIBERTY and the Rights of man, which are obtained by the constitution of the general government, and that of each state."[35]

Alexander Campbell used the same logic to attack the "kingdom of the clergy." By their scheme "people have been shrewdly taught to put out their own eyes, to fetter their own feet, and to bind the yoke upon their own necks." According to Campbell, both Protestants and Catholics had attempted to exercise "sovereign dominion over the bible," claiming "an exclusive right, an official right, to affix the proper interpretation to the scriptures; to expound them in public assemblies; insomuch, that it would be presumptuous in a layman to attempt to exercise any of those functions which they have assumed." After denying any inherent authority either in the process of ordination or the clergyman's sense of divine "calling," Campbell demanded that the traditional distinction between laity and clergy be abolished: "To suppose the contrary is to constitute different order of men, or to divide the church into the common classes of clergy and laity, the two principal sources of clerical authority. . . . Nothing is more essentially opposite to the genius and spirit of christianity." Campbell's intent "in exposing them and their kingdom" was "to emancipate those whom they have enslaved; to free the people from their unrighteous dominions and unmerciful spoilation."[36]

The egalitarian force of this kind of anticlericalism was reinforced by its use of powerful forms of rhetoric that had come to the fore in the Revolutionary era and by new strategies of communication. The most common rhetoric was that of civil and religious liberty, which the respectable clergy had made popular in mobilizing people during the Revolution. Sectarians exploited the potent themes of tyranny, slavery, and antichrist to topple those who had so ingeniously made the cause of liberty sacred. Simply put, antichrist now worked his evil machinations through elites of all kind, particularly the clergy. In a splendid example of the multivalency of language, rhetoric that had seemed benign when used by respectable clergymen during the Revolution came to have radical connotations when abstracted from a restricted context and transferred to people who had reason to lash out at vested interests.[37]

This kind of dissent also capitalized on the new forms of popular print that were emerging at the end of the eighteenth century—particularly among radical Jeffersonians. The explosion of religious print in the early republic included an array of pamphlet and newspaper copy which in form and content conspired against social distinction. The coarse language, biting sarcasm, earthy humor, and common-sense reasoning appealed to the uneducated and left the professional clergy with little effective defense. In a pamphlet written in 1817 to combat the influence of Elias Smith, the Congregationalist Thomas Andros recognized the new tactics:

Ridicule, sneer, malignant sarcasm and repreach, are the armor in which he goes forth. On this ground, and not on sober argumentation, he knows the success of his cause depends. . . . If he knows the doctrine of original sin is not true, let him sit down and write a manly and candid answer to President Edward's great work on that subject. . . . Were he a dignified, candid, and intelligent controversialist, there would be enough to answer him, but who would wish to attack a windmill? Who can refute a sneer?[38]

The pursuit of freedom in popular religious culture was also worked out in a third way: skepticism about the authority of the church as an institution to bind the free will of the individual. Three incidents from the hill country of New England are deeply revealing of the way in which deeply religious people come to express religious liberty in terms of overt individualism. Born in 1772 of Baptist parents, plain farmers from Royalston, Massachusetts, Abner Jones grew up in Woodstock, Vermont. By his son's testimony, Jones had but six weeks schooling in his life, but developed a great love of books, and, at about the age of twenty, a definite call to become a preacher. "If I must preach," he later recounted, "*what* shall I preach?" Not being satisfied with any church he could find, he "took the bible, and that alone, and without consulting any individual, or receiving sympathy from any living being, commenced a prayerful and careful examination of the sacred pages." As Jones studied, his religious views underwent a drastic alteration—what he called a "*disintegration.*" The one thing that seemed clear was that "the whole system of theology in which he had been educated was erroneous." Still, he sought ordination to preach and was invited to join the fledgling Free-Will Baptists, themselves champions of radical freedom in matters religious. Jones told them that he would like their ordination but not at the expense of submitting to any of their constraints: "I will never be subject to one of your rules; but if you will give me the right hand as a brother, and let me remain a *free* man, just as I am, I should be glad. On these grounds the right of fellowship was cheerfully given. A number of months after this, they voluntarily appointed an ecclesiastical council, and ordained me a free man."[39]

Jones's refusal to allow any human mediation of his conscience was very similar to the experience of Lucy Smith, the mother of Joseph Smith, Jr. At a similar time and place, Lucy also despaired of the validity of any institutional religion and turned to the Bible alone as her guide. She sealed this individualization of conscience by finding a minister who would agree to baptize her as a solitary Christian—without attachment to any congregation.[40]

In one nine-month stretch in 1802 and 1803, William Smythe Babcock estimated he traveled 1,500 miles and preached 297 sermons as an itinerant minister in the hill country of New Hampshire and Vermont. History would have swallowed the memory of this folk preacher had he not kept an extensive journal between 1801 and 1809. Babcock founded a Free-Will Baptist Church in Springfield, Vermont, in 1801 and from there proclaimed a gospel that revolved around the issue of bondage and liberty.

The Free-Will Baptist Connection exercised no real authority over Babcock, yet he repeatedly expressed the fear of relying too much on other men or of being coerced by them. By 1809 even the slight contact he did have became unbearable. He unilaterally severed all ties with the monthly meeting of the Free-Will Baptists. "I told them that I now stood alone, unconnected to or with any one." The members of Babcock's congregation followed his lead and agreed to renounce all denominations and set up a church "independent in itself, free from control or of domination of any other churches whatsoever." They agreed to defer to only one authority, the rule and guide of the Scriptures. Pressing the notion of Christian freedom to its logical conclusion, Babcock could not abide anyone having the right to suggest to him the parameters of Biblical teaching.[41]

The two most articulate spokesmen denying the very basis of ecclesiastical authority were Barton W. Stone, who founded the Churches of Christ in Kentucky and Indiana, and James O'Kelly, a Methodist dissident in the South. In rejecting the authority of Presbyterian polity, Stone wrote *The Last Will and Testament of the Springfield Presbytery*, which argued that any power of making laws for governing the church or executing them should forever cease.[42] "All juridical authority which any society has over an individual, is in consequence of a voluntary compact tacitly or explicitly made, by which he is connected with that society, and under its laws. When such compact is dissolved, which may be done at any time, by the voluntary act of the individual, the authority ceases." "Should we attempt to impose any form of government upon the church," he suggested elsewhere, "we should justly be abandoned by every child of gospel liberty." Stone argued at length that no minister could speak in the name of God and by his authority:

To speak in the name of God, is to speak as God. . . . If God has given this authority to uninspired men, who has it? Is it the Pope, or Luther, or Calvin, or Arminius? To what one sect of the many is it given? Is it given to one or all of them? If to one only, it is important to know that one; for that one sect speaking truly in the name of God, and acting by his authority, must be infallible. . . . The Pope of Rome this presumes, and therefore consistently, pretends to infallibility. Shall every sectarian make the same pretension? If not, let him never presume to say that he speaks in the name of God, and by his authority, without sufficient proof of his assertion.[43]

With similar argument, James O'Kelly bolted from the Methodist Episcopal Church in 1794 to undo its "ecclesiastical monarchy." O'Kelly could not abide the bishopric of Francis Asbury and withdrew with over thirty ministers to form a connection which had as many as twenty thousand members when it merged with the forces of Elias Smith in 1809 under the name Christian. "Episcopacy makes a bad appearance in our republican world,"

O'Kelly argued in 1798. "Frances [Asbury] was born and nurtured in the land of Bishops and Kings and what is bred in the bone, is hard to get out of the flesh." When the Methodists attacked O'Kelly for scoffing at the scriptural text Hebrews 13:17, "Obey them that have rule over you," he responded by denying any human claim to mediate divine authority:

Observe, Sir, the Roman Clergy claim obedience from this text. The Protestant Clergy claim obedience from this text. Bishop Asbury, the Dissenter, claims obedience from this text. The Protestants refuse to obey the Roman Clergy. The Methodist Clergy refuse to obey the Protestant Bishops. And we refuse to obey Bishop Asbury. Who is guilty? But who is judge? When a person claims obedience from me, I demand his authority, whether it be from God, or civil government. If it be from God, he must be a Prophet or Apostle.[44]

The real significance of this religious hostility to orthodox authority was that it combined the logic of an Ethan Allen, Tom Paine, or Elihu Palmer with radical strains of evangelical piety. The result was a powerful discrediting of the old order that nourished religious experience at the same time it allowed people to see themselves carrying out the finest traditions of the American Revolution and exalting the American republic as the means to deliver the people from what Alexander Campbell called the "melancholy thraldom of relentless systems."[45] In this climate, the lengths to which dissenters allowed political idioms to color their thinking are sometimes difficult to comprehend. Similarly, it may seem odd that people so committed to the separation of church and state held up a given political structure as a model for the church. To a man, they endowed the American republic with the same divine authority as did the defenders of the standing order such as Timothy Dwight or Noah Webster, but for opposite reasons. The republic became a new city on the hill not because it kept faith with Puritan tradition, but because it sounded the death knell for corporate and hierarchic conceptions of the social order. In short, a government so enlightened as to tell the churches to go their own way must have also had prophetic power to tell them which way to go.

The sense that the old order was collapsing created a paradoxical mood of quest, a confidence that a new age was at hand coupled to a deep insecurity about how it was to be achieved. In fact, the more confident dissenters became in their attack upon the traditional order, the more they helped to create a world of confusing and fluid expectations that offered few set boundaries and specific definitions. The resulting popular culture pulsated with the claims of heterodox religious groups, with people veering from one sect to another, and with the unbridled wrangling of competitors in a "war of words."[46] The staid Presbyterian David Rice described the volatile religious climate that he experienced in Kentucky where people had thrown off the yoke of religious authority: "They were then prepared to imbibe every new notion, advanced by a popular preacher, which he said was agreeable to scripture. They were like a parcel of boys suddenly tumbled out of a boat, which had been unaccustomed to swim, and knew not the way to the shore. Some fixed upon one error, and some upon another."[47] The dissenter Abel Sargent captured superbly in 1807 the acute crisis of authority that he and others faced:

The very reason that religion at this time is so universally cramped and yet the religious world so universally agitated, is, because its votaries, in all denominations, have carried it as far as they possibly can, and yet they find there is something wanting;—after this "*something*" they are all reaching (especially the most faithful among them) like men groping in the dark for something they cannot find; and although they are not able to describe what this "something" is, they feel conscious and are convinced there is a certain "*something*" for them that is yet wanting, and for want of which they feel in a starving situation. This fills them with anxiety and agitation; some suppose it to be *this*, some *that*, and some the other thing; which occasions the poor creatures to reach, grasp, grapple, run and catch, different ways, and to suffice their hungry and longing souls, they are induced to seize almost any thing that bears resemblance of good.[48]

The pursuit of religious liberty in the early republic was a profoundly popular movement that shifted the ground rules for the way Americans would relate to churches and church leaders. For one thing, dissent in America became universalized, as sociologist David Martin argues in his comparative study of secularization.[49] The democratic winnowing of the church produced not just pluralism, but striking diversity. The flexibility and innovation involved in American religious organizations meant that, within certain broad limits, an American could find an amenable group no matter what his or her preference. Churches ranged from the most egalitarian to the most autocratic and included all degrees of organizational complexity. The relative success of the Shakers, Mormons, and the Oneida Perfectionists, Lawrence Foster suggests, was their development of an authoritative church structure to overcome the religious and social disorder that their members had found so unacceptable.[50] Such "boundlessness" also characterized American law and medicine in the early republic. But long after lawyers and physicians reasserted their professional prerogatives, religious leaders in America have continued to be subject to popular whim. America's common people not only are the most religious of any Western democracy; they also have continued to defer principally to leaders of their own choosing, heeding the dictum of Elias Smith that "liberty is nowhere safe in any hands excepting those of the people themselves."[51]

NOTES

1. *Herald of Gospel Liberty*, December 8, 1808, 29–30. On the career of Elias Smith, see "Elias Smith and the Rise of Religious Journalism in the Early Republic," in William L. Joyce, et al., *Printing and Society in Early America* (Worcester, Mass., 1983), 250–77.
2. On the tradition of radical New Lights in the era of the American Revolution, see Stephen A. Marini, *Radical Sects of Revolutionary New England* (Cambridge, Mass., 1982) and G.A. Rawlyk, *Ravished by the Spirit: Religious Revivals, Baptists, and Henry Alline* (Kingston and Montreal, 1984).
3. Thomas E. Buckley, *Church and State in Revolutionary Virginia, 1776–1787* (Charlottesville, Va., 1977) and William G. McLoughlin, *New England Dissent, 1630–1833: The Baptists and the Separation of Church and State*, 2 vols. (Cambridge, Mass., 1971).
4. On the pragmatism of the Constitutional Convention, see Jack N. Rakove, *The Beginnings of National Politics: An Interpretive History of the Continental Congress* (New York, 1979).
5. The phrase is that of Alexander Hamilton in *The Federalist*, no. 27. For the weakness of government institutions in the new republic, see James Sterling Young, *The Washington Community, 1800–1828* (New York, 1966).
6. Alexis de Tocqueville, *Democracy in America*, trans. Henry Reeve (New York, 1945), I, 313, 317.
7. David Hempton, *Methodism and Politics in British Society, 1750–1850* (Stanford, 1984), 85–115.
8. W.R. Ward, *Religion and Society in England, 1790–1850* (New York, 1973), 90.
9. Paul E. Johnson, *A Shopkeeper's Millennium: Society and Revivals in Rochester, New York, 1815–1837* (New York, 1978), 141. Jama Lazerow, "A Good Time Coming: Religion and the Emergence of Labor Activism in Antebellum New England" (Ph.D. diss., Brandeis University, 1983).
10. Hempton, *Methodism and Politics*, 105.
11. This is the persuasive argument of James K. Hopkins, "Joanna Southcott—A Study of Popular Religion and Radical Politics, 1789–1814" (Ph.D. diss., University of Texas, 1972). "After the publication of Paine's *Age of Reason* in 1794, the words Deist and Democrat became virtually synonymous and popular millennialists and radical libertarians in England were rent asunder" (402). See also Albert Goodwin, *The Friends of Liberty: The English Democratic Movement in the Age of the French Revolution* (Cambridge, Mass., 1979).
12. On the profound cultural change in this period, see David Hackett Fischer, *Growing Old in America* (New York, 1977); Richard E. Ellis, *The Jeffersonian Crisis: Courts and Politics in the Young Republic* (New York, 1971); and Gordon S. Wood, "The Democrati-

zation of Mind in the American Revolution," in *Leadership in the American Revolution* (Washington, D.C., 1974), 63–89.

13. Gordon S. Wood, "Evangelical America and Early Mormonism," *New York History*, 61 (1980). See also Nathan O. Hatch, "The Christian Movement and the Demand for a Theology of the People," *Journal of American History*, 67 (1980), 545–67.

14. Richard L. Bushman, *Joseph Smith and the Beginnings of Mormonism* (Urbana, Ill., 1984), 3–42.

15. David Rice, *An Epistle to the Citizens of Kentucky, Professing Christianity* (Lexington, Ky., 1805), 191–92.

16. Elias Smith, *The Life, Conversion, Preaching, Travels and Sufferings of Elias Smith* (Portsmouth, N.H., 1816), 353. For the fascinating attempt of one unlettered farmer to publish his democratic convictions, see Samuel Eliot Morison, "William Manning's *The Key of Libberty,*" *William and Mary Quarterly*, 3rd ser., 13 (1956), 202–56. I discuss Manning and Smith in "Elias Smith and the Rise of Religious Journalism in the Early Republic," in William L. Joyce, et. al., *Printing and Society in Early America* (Worcester, Mass., 1983), 250–77.

17. See James B. Walch, "The Conservative Nature of Connecticut Separatism," *Connecticut Historical Society Bulletin*, 34 (1969), 9–17; John W. Jeffries, "The Separation in the Canterbury Congregational Church: Religion, Family, and Politics in a Connnecticut Town," *New England Quarterly*, 52 (1979), 522–49; and Richard D. Brown, "Spreading the Word: Rural Clergymen and the Communication Network of 18th-Century New England," *Proceedings of the Massachusetts Historical Society*, 94 (1982), 1–14.

18. William G. McLoughlin, ed., *Isaac Backus on Church, State, and Calvinism: Pamphlets, 1754–1789* (Cambridge, Mass., 1968), 42.

19. Rhys Isaac, *The Transformation of Virginia, 1740–1790* (Chapel Hill, N.C., 1982), 168–70.

20. For the importance of the idea of volitional allegiance in this period, see James H. Kettner, *The Development of American Citizenship, 1608–1870* (Chapel Hill, N.C., 1978), 173–209.

21. [Jacob Greene], *A View of a Christian Church, and Church Government* (Chatham, N.J., 1781), 55.

22. Walter Harris, *Characteristics of False Teachers* (Concord, N.H., 1811), 19.

23. On Randel, see John Buzzell, *The Life of Elder Benjamin Randal* (Limerick, Me., 1827); and G.A. Rawlyk, *Ravished by the Spirit*, 48–64.

24. *Herald of Gospel Liberty*, September 1, 1808, 1. *Christian Baptist*, February 6, 1826, 213.

25. Alexander Campbell put it this way in one place: "Catholic and Protestant Popery are plodding and plotting for supremacy" (*Christian Baptist*, 1828, 541) and in another: "If the mother sect was a tyrant, the daughter will ape her temper; and when of mature age and reason, she will imitate her practice" (*Millennial Harbinger*, 1833, 469–470).

   Most strident in this conviction were the Mormons, who claimed that the corrupt, diseased old order tottered on the brink of destruction: for the first time in eighteen hundred years, the brazen heavens were to reopen. See Klaus J. Hansen, *Mormonism and the American Experience* (Chicago, 1981), 28.

26. On Jefferson, see Edmund S. Morgan, *The Meaning of Independence: John Adams, George Washington, Thomas Jefferson* (Charlottesville, Va., 1976), 71–79; and Daniel J. Boorstin, *The Lost World of Thomas Jefferson* (Boston, 1948). On Paine, see Jay Fliegelman, *Prodigals and Pilgrims: The American Revolution Against Patriarchal Authority, 1750–1800* (Cambridge, 1982), 169.

27. *Christian Baptist*, April 3, 1826, 229.

28. John Williamson Nevin, "Antichrist and the Sect," in James Hastings Nichols, ed., *The Mercersburg Theology* (New York, 1966), 93–119. I discuss this theme extensively in *"Sola Scriptura* and *Novus Ordo Seclorum,"* in Nathan O. Hatch and Mark A. Noll, eds., *The Bible in America: Essays in Cultural History* (New York, 1982).

29. The phrases are from the William Smythe Babcock papers, American Antiquarian Society, September 6, 1801; and from Henry Alline, quoted in G.A. Rawlyk, *Ravished by the Spirit,* 19.

30. *Herald of Gospel Liberty,* July 4, 1809, 26.

31. For an excellent portrait of the traditional role of the clergy, see Donald M. Scott, *From Office to Profession: The New England Ministry, 1750–1850* (Philadelphia, 1978).

32. Harriet Beecher Stowe, "The Old-Meeting House," in Henry F. May, ed., *Old Town Folks* (Cambridge, 1966), 101–02.

33. Elias Smith, *Life,* 243–46.

34. For the attack upon lawyers, see Richard E. Ellis, *The Jeffersonian Crisis: Courts and Politics in the Young Republic* (New York, 1971); and G.S. Rowe, "Jesse Higgins and the Failure of Legal Reform in Delaware, 1800–1810," *Journal of the Early Republic,* 3 (1983), 17–43. The rise of sectarian medicine is treated in Joseph F. Kett, *The Formation of the American Medical Profession: The Role of Institutions, 1780–1860* (New Haven, 1968); and Ronald L. Numbers, "Do-It-Yourself the Sectarian Way," in *Medicine Without Doctors: Home Health Care in American History* (New York, 1977), 49–72.

35. Elias Smith, *The Age of Enquiry* (Exeter, N. H., 1807), 352; *Herald of Gospel Liberty,* September 15, 1808, 5.

36. *The Christian Baptist,* October 6, 1823; Robert Richardson, *Memoirs of Alexander Campbell* (Cincinnati, 1913), I, 63–64.

37. On the multivalency of language, see J.G.A. Pocock, *Politics, Language and Time: Essays on Political Thought and History* (New York, 1971), 3–41; and Harry S. Stout, "Religion, Communications, and the Ideological Origins of the American Revolution," *William and Mary Quarterly,* 3rd ser., 34 (1977), 538.

38. Thomas Andros, *The Scriptures Liable to Be Wrested to Men's Own Destruction* (Taunton, Mass., 1817), 18–21. On developments in the popular press in this period, see Donald H. Stewart, *The Opposition Press of the Federalist Period* (Albany, N. Y., 1969); David Hackett Fischer, *The Revolution of American Conservatism: The Federalist Party in the Era of Jeffersonian Democracy* (New York, 1965); and Alan V. Briceland, "The Philadelphia Aurora, the New England Illuminati, and the Election of 1800," *The Pennsylvania Magazine of History and Biography,* 100 (1976), 3–36.

39. Abner Jones, *Memoir of Elder Abner Jones* (Boston, 1842), 24, 50–51.

40. Lucy Smith, *Biographical Sketches of Joseph Smith, the Prophet* (Liverpool, 1853; reprint ed., New York, 1969), 37, 46–49.

41. Miscellaneous Papers, William Smythe Babcock Papers; Journal of Preaching, December 1809, William Smythe Babcock Papers.

42. "The Last Will and Testament of Springfield Presbytery," in John Rogers, *The Biography of Elder B. Warren Stone* (New York, 1972), 51–53.

43. *The Christian Messenger,* 1827, 9, 51, 149. [Robert McNemar,] *Observations on Church Government, by the Presbytery of Springfield* (Cincinnati, 1807), 9.

44. James O'Kelly, *The Author's Apology for Protesting against the Methodist Episcopal Government* (Richmond, 1798), 21, 49. See also Charles Franklin Kilgore, *The James O'Kelly Schism in the Methodist Episcopal Church* (Mexico City, 1963).

45. Alexander Campbell, "An Oration in Honor of the Fourth of July, 1830," *Popular Lectures and Addresses* (Philadelphia, 1863), 374.

46. The phrase is that of Joseph Smith, who reacted strongly to the sectarian competition he knew as a young man. Joseph Smith, *The Pearl of Great Price* (Salt Lake City, 1891), 56–70. See also Mario S. De Pillis, "The Quest for Religious Authority and the Rise of Mormonism," *Dialogue: A Journal of Mormon Thought*, I (1966), 64–88.

47. David Rice, *An Epistle to the Citizens of Kentucky, Professing Christianity* (Lexington, Ky., 1805), 200–201.

48. *The Halcyon Itinery and True Millennium Messenger*, November, 1807, 127.

49. David Martin, *A General Theory of Secularization* (New York, 1978).

50. Lawrence Foster, *Religion and Sexuality: Three American Communal Experiments in the Nineteenth Century* (New York, 1981), 18.

51. *Herald of Gospel Liberty*, September 15, 1808.

CHAPTER 22

Religion in the Aftermath of the American Revolution

Patricia U. Bonomi

The Revolutionary War had a baneful effect on American religious life. Many churches were damaged as the fighting churned around them, and some were burned to the ground. In the larger towns and cities, houses of worship were commandeered as barracks or converted into hospitals, leaving their congregations without a place to meet. Congregations were further disrupted when male parishioners departed for military duty or ministers left their flocks to serve as chaplains. The Church of England experienced the sharpest setback of any denomination, losing first its establishment status and then a large part of its Northern clergy to Loyalism. The Loyalist taint spread also to the Quakers and other quietist sects, which never recovered their earlier standing or numbers. Some Americans, moreover, did not welcome the postwar movement for separation of church from state—as embodied in such instruments as the Virginia Statute for Religious Freedom and the religion clause of the First Amendment—fearing that the loss of official sanction would weaken the churches' ability to instill morality and republican virtue at the time when it was most needed. Perhaps the severest problem of all was the shortage of ministers, as the war not only reaped a melancholy harvest of death and disease among the chaplaincy but also disrupted the training of the next generation of clergymen. When the war finally ended, church leaders looking out upon this scene of devastation and institutional dislocation knew that a monumental task of reconstruction lay ahead.

The chapters by Catherine L. Albanese and Nathan O. Hatch trace two of the paths by which Americans expressed their religious sensibilities and remodeled religious institutions between the Revolution and the Age of Jackson, paths that serve to define that process by delineating its outer boundaries. Professor Albanese, on the one side, explores how Enlightened rationalists sanctified nature and appropriated its symbols to express their own sublime, even providential, vision of republican grandeur. She focuses on the orderly, more hierarchical face of nature, rather than on its untamed or chaotic aspect. Thus the nature she portrays tends to be elitist, a product of the genteel culture of that time. Professor Hatch, on the other side, describes how radical evangelicals employed Revolutionary rhetoric to denigrate ecclesiastical hierarchies and "dismantle mediating elites" in a quest for total religious freedom. His actors are those religious zealots—known to every age from at least Luther onward—who justified their schismatic activities on the grounds that they were saving a remnant of the church from corruption. These two chapters, then, reveal what was happening at either end of the early national religious spectrum. To fill out the picture, we also want to examine what was taking place in the great middle range of religious activity and denominational life that lay between these two extremes.

It is almost a commonplace of recent historical writing that the early nineteenth century saw the triumph of evangelical Protestantism in American life. Before the Revolution, the Congregational, Presbyterian, and Anglican churches were by far the largest denominations. By about 1805, however, membership in the evangelical Baptist and Methodist churches exceeded that of all other denominations, and it has been estimated that by mid-century some 70 percent of American Protestants were affiliated with those churches. Two factors were especially important to this development. One was the advent of religious voluntarism in America as church was separated from state. With all denominations now on an equal footing, those that had opposed the official colonial churches could turn from fighting establishments toward the promotion of their own beliefs. Such a redirection of energies fostered, to give but one example, the tremendous expansion of the Baptist churches in late eighteenth-century Virginia.

A second equally crucial factor was that Baptists and Methodists valued preachers more for their religious convictions and hortatory skills than for their educational attainments. Unlike the Congregationalists, Presbyterians, and now Episcopalians, who required several years of higher education of their candidates for ordination, the Baptists and Methodists could draw from the laity a steady supply of preachers for their rapidly multiplying congregations. The Presbyterian minister Jacob Green, shaken by his own denomination's failure to meet the demand for clergymen, urged that educational standards be lowered—to no avail. Yet Green's assumption that the denominations which could best supply preachers to an expanding and westward-moving population would gain the largest membership was fully borne out in the years ahead.

Still, numbers do not tell the whole story, and the conventional notion that American culture as well as American religion succumbed to evangelical influences in the post-Revolutionary decades is subject to a number of modifications. For one, the 70 percent figure for evangelical church membership does not mean that evangelicals exercised a comparable ratio of influence in other aspects of the nation's life, especially its political and commercial life. After all, the evangelicals' kingdom was not of this world. Thus political and economic leadership continued to rest disproportionately in the hands of individuals whose religious affiliations were with the churchly or rationalist denominations. Indeed, no candidate of evangelical allegiance was elected to the Presidency (and few to other high offices) throughout this period, and commercial leadership continued to be centered in communities where the old colonial churches were dominant. Similarly intellectual leaders, as well as those men and women at the forefront of various reform movements, were far more likely to be drawn from the ranks of Eastern Congregationalists, Presbyterians, and Episcopalians than from the evangelical denominations.

Though nonevangelicals comprised a minority of American Protestants by the early nineteenth century, their concentration along the seaboard and in cities tended to give them a disproportionate voice in the religious press and on the public platform, and thus over the direction of church life. True, the seaboard–frontier division should not be overstated. Baptists and Methodists had a significant presence in the East as well, forming numerous congregations, supporting Bible and mission societies, participating actively in the Sunday School Union, and in the case of the Baptists joining the American Tract Society. Nevertheless, it was in the West that the evangelical denominations made their greatest gains. The Methodists set up orderly circuits by which preachers kept in touch with scattered congregations, whereas Baptist leaders encouraged preachers to accompany each westward-moving group from that denomination. As Robert Baird wrote about this time, more than "10,000 neighbourhoods" were indebted to such men for their good order and piety. To be sure, the more traditional churches also sent ministers to the frontier when they could. But the difficulty they faced is captured in the lament of one Presbyterian itinerant; wherever he went "the Methodist missionary had been there before me."

Attempts to measure the relative influence of evangelical and churchly denominations in the early nation are further complicated by the problem of differentiating between them. The issue of ecclesiastical structure and clerical hierarchy offers a case in point. A strong governing apparatus is usually viewed as an attribute of churchly traditionalism. Yet no denomination was more autocratically organized than the Methodist, with its bishops, presiding elders, and highly regulated circuits and camp meetings. Nor did the Baptists fail to erect ecclesiastical structures as their success in attracting adherents led inevitably to the bureaucratization and professionalization of church government. In both denominations, of course, such growth and rising professionalism led to schisms and a series of disputes about the degree of autonomy that should be accorded to individual congregations, resulting in the shearing-off of some radical factions from their parent bodies. Meanwhile, the Presbyterian and Congregational churches were themselves dividing over matters of doctrine into more or less orthodox and evangelical wings. New England Congregationalists, for example, actually founded three separate seminaries between 1808 and 1834 in order to educate future generations of ministers in the variant versions of their theology.

Indeed, these schisms—which occurred in every major and minor denomination—are so characteristic of American Protestantism in the fifty years or so after the Revolution, and their outcomes are so resistant to neat classification as evangelical, traditional, or rationalist, as almost to confound the historian's effort to depict religious life in the early nation. Volatile and disorderly it certainly was. Vigorous and expanding it was too, as reflected in rising membership rolls and the enormous popularity of a galaxy of preachers in both city and countryside. And if the largest proportion of churchgoers adhered to denominations of evangelical tendency, yet the influence of the cosmopolitan, nonevangelical churches over both the religious and the public culture was great. In the years ahead, moreover, all of the major denominations would come to look more alike as they stabilized and erected networks of regional associations, conferences, synods, Sunday schools, and mission societies.

That the era of the American Revolution, marked as it was by upheaval in religious life and an accelerated separation of church from state, should have been followed by a period of disarray and church schisms is perhaps not surprising. That no single denomination or theological point of view would triumph over all the others may have been as inevitable as it was American. Such an outcome was foreseen by James Madison in *Federalist* No. 51, where he observed that the "multiplicity of sects" in the new United States would be the best guarantee of the religious rights of every sect. Spread over a large territory, and divided over issues of theology, education, governance, and soon slavery, the churches of the young nation would continue to form, break apart, and form again throughout the years ahead. But despite it all—or, perhaps, because of it all—Alexis de Tocqueville could write from the midst of this turbulent scene that "there is no country in the world where the Christian religion retains a greater influence over the souls of men than in America."

Index